Peculiar People

S. Wilbur

This book is a work of fiction. Names, characters, places and incidents are products of the author's imagination or are used fictitiously and are not to be construed as real. Any resemblance to actual events, locales, organizations, or persons, living or dead, is entirely coincidental.

Peculiar People Copyright © 2021 by S. Wilbur
Cover Artwork Copyright © 2021 by S. Wilbur

All rights reserved

No part of this book may be used or reproduced or transmitted in any form or any means, electronic or mechanical, including photocopying, recording, or by any information storage and retrieved system or in any manner whatsoever without written permission of the publisher, except in the case of brief quotations embodied in critical articles and reviews.

Paperback ISBN: 978-0-9971423-6-5
Hardcover ISBN: 978-0-9971423-7-2

Published by S & P Enterprises

ACKNOWLEDGMENTS

Through the process of writing this book, beyond the myriad of rewrites, the nightmare of a corrupt file and issues my mind and memory have graciously allowed me to forget, I am now and will be eternally grateful to my editor, B. J. Harris. She helped me to hone a body of work I am truly proud of.

In addition, she revealed another ray of light from within her prism of talents with her cover art work which festoons the cover of this book.

Excellent production my friend — thank you.

CHAPTER ONE

Once upon a time not so long ago, there was a man. There are some individuals who would prefer to refer to this man as a "shrink," a "head doctor" and even a "charlatan," when referencing his chosen profession. The man referenced, you see, was a prominent doctor of psychiatry.

The doctor was married to a woman who was of equal prominence and was also a doctor of psychiatry. They both thought of themselves as part of the upper crust of society. Between the two of them (borrowing a quote from someone remaining anonymous), "they had more money than God" and were — pardon the vulgarity — hell bent on obtaining even more.

In accordance to a statistic at the time, this professional couple checked off all the boxes when it came to fitting within the perimeters and social standards reserved for the better educated and financially well-to-do including, but not limited to, having achieved the appropriate and most acceptable — perfect family size. In order for them to meet the criteria of the "perfect family size," they had to have two- and one-third children. A child of each gender was considered good form and preferred but was not an absolute requirement. The doctors came in right under that number with having only two.

Their first born was a boy and had the suffix, "Jr.," aptly appointed to the end of his name. Conveniently, their second child was a baby girl thus allowing them to check off two of the final boxes making their perfect little family fit within the appropriate social standard of the time.

There was not a third — or better — a one-third child. And with that, we may all breathe a sigh of relief, as that would clearly conjure up thoughts of a rather unpleasant and morbid nature.

*****

The man's name was Dr. Phillip William Marksdale, Sr. He was "Phillip" to friends and family. The woman, his wife of twelve young years in length, was Dr. Estelle Cummings Marksdale. To those she felt a closeness to, she preferred the nickname "Stelle." Their childrens' names were "Phillip William Marksdale, Jr." and "Lara Cummings Marksdale" respectively.

The Marksdales' lavish waterfront mansion was nestled comfortably on Lake Washington in the city of Medina in Washington State. Sharing their zip code with the likes of Bill Gates made a clear statement the Marksdales should not want for much of anything, except in their particular case — they wanted more of everything.

In this story, the doctor shares the spotlight with a group of five patients who were referred to him. Specifically, they were referred to him by an old college pal and colleague of the same profession.

The colleague's chosen path, from which he practiced his own psychiatric profession, took him into the arena of "more of the ordinary citizen" when weighing in on an economic scale than that of Dr. Phillip Marksdale. Compared to the average patients Dr. Marksdale treated from his high-rise office in the notable high-rent district of downtown Bellevue (east of Seattle), the colleague's patients paled by their affluent light.

Dr. Marksdale's well-to-do patients made it possible for him to afford a high-rise office with luxurious picture windows — windows which revealed expansive views of Lake Washington, the Seattle skyline, Puget Sound and the rising Olympic mountains beyond. The view was no less than spectacular any time of day or night.

His old college pal and professional colleague chose to work with patients Dr. Marksdale would have considered to be less fortunate. These patients were generally referrals from the county's court referral system.

The working environment of Dr. Marksdale's old college pal was a long-shot from being lavish. Indeed, practicing his profession from the large, sterile-looking county building, he was provided a view quite a bit less than remarkable. This is where some would say Dr. Marksdale's old college pal whose real name was Dr. Elan Glenn garnered the name "good doer."

Early on in his professional career, Dr. Elan Glenn made another, in his opinion, important decision. Simply, he would drop the "Dr." prefix before his name when treating his patients. He would offer them the option of calling him "El" — something he felt would create a more comfortable environment for both himself and his patients.

The term "to treat" a patient, or conversely a patient receiving "treatment" from a doctor, left Dr. Elan Glenn uneasy. This less-than-traditional approach was well received by his patients resulting in most of them choosing to address him as El.

On the other hand, Dr. Elan Glenn's approach in dealing with patients was not received as well by his colleagues of the same profession. One, in particular, was Dr. Phillip Marksdale, and when Dr. Marksdale heard his old pal's professional name had been reduced to "El" in addition to his nickname, "good doer," it was nearly intolerable for him. Unfortunately, in the professional circles Dr. Marksdale chose to spin in, he heard both of these names more than he cared to.

Upon hearing his old pal's name(s) — something which took place far too often from his prospective — Dr. Marksdale managed to hide his growing displeasure with the accolades that followed. However, when the mere thought of his old pal crossed his own mind — it was clearly visible — his left eyebrow would rise ever so slightly, while his right eyelid would twitch closed. His face would then contort in such a way, it gave the appearance he may be experiencing a twinge of nausea.

Due to a longtime debt (with Dr. Marksdale being the said "debtor") originating from an as yet unspoken incident — and putting aside the possibility the "as yet unspoken incident" may have been somewhat diabolical in nature — Dr. Marksdale mustered up the energy to lean towards a good and honorable action. He would never settle for anything short of his being diligent in keeping his reputation respectable. And, to do this, he generously agreed to take on the five patients; however, it was still too early to discern if the transaction was offered disingenuously by his old college pal. After all, settling a long-time debt was the honorable thing to do.

El believed, due to all outward appearances, his old pal Phillip, the good doctor, was well-to-do in all professional and personal aspects of his life. Due to that belief, El felt his old pal Phillip was more than capable of handling that which was handed to him. At least, that was the impression he gave. One would not expect the notable Dr. Elan Glenn, the doctor known as the "good-doer," to have any untoward intentions or underlying malice in mind — no — certainly not.

As Dr. Elan Glenn presented his offer to Dr. Marksdale, he alluded to having a true connection with each patient he was referring and expressed his belief his old colleague, and more importantly his professional equal, would be able to genuinely assist in their treatment.

Dr. Marksdale was not one to shy away from acknowledging his own skillset and would never find himself disagreeing with someone else's observation of his extensive talents. Humbly, he agreed to take on the five patients his old pal was willing to settle his old debt with. Quietly, he mused, "what a piece of cake this will be."

As one may assume, each of these individuals brought with them a blend of their own personal life's circumstances. One could go so far as to say each member of this group brought with them their own unique peculiarities. It would not be long before Dr. Marksdale, the good doctor, would discover just how unique and peculiar his new group really was.

*****

Dr. Marksdale and his old pal and colleague, El, agreed to meet with one of the five patients early on — prior to the entire group meeting. During that first meeting, Dr. Marksdale met a man appearing to be in his early sixties. The doctor noticed how stylishly dressed the man was. He wore a well-tailored, light gray, three-piece suit and expensive and extremely well-kept loafers — charcoal in color. Dr Marksdale observed the man's hair was perfectly coiffed and yet, he thought, not pretentious. It was gray with silver highlights complimenting his good looks. Dr. Marksdale could not help but reflect it made him somewhat uncomfortable when he viewed another man as good looking.

The doctor kept these thoughts to himself, as he did so many others. He attributed most of his discomfort in areas such as this to his tendency to over analyze every action of everyone, including his own. Being a psychiatrist had its pitfalls.

This first patient's name, seeming to fit perfectly with his English accent, was Dillard — Dillard Bigley. He introduced himself as "Dill."

"There has been on occasion" — Dill announced to the good doctor — "When I am first being introduced, my name is mispronounced and sounds more like Dell." This was a most unacceptable event, by all appearances, for the fastidiously formal and quite properly mannered Dillard Bigley. It was at this point when he informed the good doctor, he would correct whoever had mispronounced his name by saying in the most articulate and polite manner, of course, "My name is pronounced, Dill, like the pickle — thank you."

"That shouldn't be a problem, Dill," the good doctor clearly and correctly pronounced as he jotted something in his notebook — a notebook most of the general population would expect a conscientious psychiatrist to have on hand. He also made note of Dill's demeanor and general attitude. This was a practice which had become like second nature to the doctor and included all of his patients, whether new or established. He was used to this practice and saw no reason to change the behavior. After a session, he would be sure to log into his files notes and voice recordings of any particular point(s) he felt were worthy.

In short order, Dr. Marksdale became familiarized with all five individuals who made up his new group, and it was then the good doctor's note taking waned in frequency and volume — at least, during their sessions. What had come to the good doctor's attention was his maintaining of his usual practices and processes of treatment — or trying to keep within the boundaries of that which was status-quo — would not pan out with those making up this new group.

As it turned out, the good doctor discovered his initial estimation of making no adjustments to his normal protocol — or possibly only minor ones — fell pitifully shy of the actual adjustments required. When it came to the treatment of these five patients, in particular, the good doctor became keenly aware adjustments were not only necessary but, more often than not, those adjustments would need to be a good deal more major — than minor.

CHAPTER TWO

Dillard Bigley, the fine British gentleman whose preference was to be referred to as "Dill," had at an earlier time been appointed the "group's" spokesperson. El, the group's original treating psychiatrist had briefly explained this to his old college pal, the good Dr. Marksdale. El had left out most everything else about the group the good doctor was about to inherit, including the how and the why of its formation.

As this was an old debt Dr. Marksdale was fulfilling, he let the many questions he had brewing in his mind fall by the wayside. The good doctor felt he would have time to read the patient files prior to his meeting them. The files, he believed, would provide him all he needed to make any necessary, preliminary assessment of this group of future patients. Those files still had not arrived by the time the group showed up at the good doctor's office for their first session on that particular cloudy and windy Wednesday.

Twenty minutes before 9:00 a.m., Mrs. Marlene Fins, Dr. Marksdale's loyal and dutiful receptionist, rang into the good doctor's office with a noticeable, awkward and nervous tone in her voice.

"Dr. Marksdale, your patients have arrived." Then, lowering her voice — "There are several of them, doctor." Attempting to maintain a discreet presence, she continued, "Their appointment isn't until ten o'clock. What shall I do with them?"

Although a bit thrown off by his new group's early arrival as well, Dr. Marksdale found her tone somewhat peculiar and her question, questionable.

"Well, Mrs. Fins, send them in please."

"Now?"

"Yes, Mrs. Fins. Now will be fine."

This was all highly unusual for Mrs. Fins. Being late was more the norm than patients being on time. Arriving this much earlier than a scheduled appointment, well, that was unheard of. For patients to arrive so early and, more notably, for Dr. Marksdale to oblige such behavior was unsettling for Mrs. Fins. However, having been a receptionist for almost twenty-five years and Dr. Marskdale's receptionist for nine of those years, Mrs. Fins was quite capable of handling her duties, even when under duress.

Holding her posture in a perfect pose, including holding her slender chin high, her body displayed an elegant steadiness, which indicated she had attended the finest of finishing schools. Mrs. Fins remained expressionless as she got up from behind her desk and gestured to the group for them to follow her.

Mrs. Fins was neither model tall nor was she model thin. She was not a heavy-set woman either. She appeared to be somewhere in her late-fifties and could be described as somewhat petite in stature, standing less than 5-feet 5-inches tall. Her size, however, was of no importance or consequence when it came to one individual in the group of patients awaiting their session with Dr. Marksdale.

That which stood out to this individual was notably her fastidious and controlled manner, and as he observed her passing by and then walking in front of him, Mrs. Fins' movements did not go unnoticed by Dillard Bigley. He observed Mrs. Fins in the most tactful and gentlemanly manner, while he thought quite discreetly to himself — "how exquisite."

Following Mrs. Fins, Dillard Bigley led the rest of the group down a short hall until they arrived at a tall, highly polished teak-wood door. She knocked so lightly, it could barely be heard. Mrs. Fins opened the door very slowly and addressed Dr. Marksdale — "Your patients, doctor."

She then turned to the five individuals awaiting her instruction and moved off to the side of them, her arm gently sweeping across her body towards the open door while declaring, "The doctor will see you now." Quietly, she closed the door behind them as the last one entered the good doctor's office.

Upon entering Dr. Marksdale's office, the group's first sight was not of the back of the chocolate brown, Corinthian leather, swivel office chair the doctor was sitting in, nor was it of the spacious and tastefully designed room. Instead, the group of five were in awe of the breath-taking vision unfurling before them through the enormous windows. It was best their attention was enrapt with the view; because, once the good doctor looked up and saw all five of his new patients for the first time, his eyes bulged and his jaw dropped leaving his mouth agape. This uncontrolled reaction by Dr. Marksdale was a reaction better left unseen.

"Holy crap! That's a hell of a view!" A tall slender man with slicked back, pitch-black hair belted out. Everyone in the group walked around the good doctor's desk and towards the windows.

"We're way uptown now." This same man said in a tone which sounded almost like an insult. He was wearing very near-to-skin-tight chartreuse slacks with a shirt donning a checkered pattern displaying a variety of greens, blues and white squares. His shoes were stark white and so shiny, they looked like they had just been highly polished. The gold colored three-inch square buckles on each side of his shoes which faced away from his body matched his belt buckle in every way — except, the belt buckle was twice their size.

As he sauntered towards the windows, he reached into his shirt pocket and removed a pack of gum and pulled two pieces out of the pack. He did this with his right hand, where on his ring finger, he wore a wide-banded gold ring which was heavily encrusted with shiny stones. As it would be presumptuous to say at the most, and too early to say at the least, they may have been — but most likely were not — real diamonds. He pushed both pieces of gum into his mouth as he continued to speak while beginning to chew.

"We're in the high-rent district now, groupies. Who wants ta bet what the doc has ta fork out for this shack?"

Between his loud voice and his almost horse-like chewing (both in mannerism and sound), he took in a good deep sniff with his flared left nostril while slightly twisting his face. He then chuckled, seemingly quite pleased with himself as he lightly rocked on his shiny white shoes — his head going from left to right — while he perused the expansive view.

Appearing to be in his mid-forties, the tall and slender man turned back to face the doctor and said in a husky and rough tone, "I'm James — James Elliot Jeffries. Don't go by that, though." The gum he had just started chewing made a high-pitched snapping sound as he continued with, "I go by Bud. That's it. Won't answer to nothin' else." Bud, then turned to face the window with the view exclaiming a good deal louder, "If you don't call me 'Bud,' you might as well blow cold air up your own *blank!*"

The good doctor had already begun hurriedly taking notes prior to this juncture which now notably included the fact that "Bud" chose to censor some of his own colorful language. For a brief moment, the good doctor thought, "interesting." There was not enough time between that brief moment and the next, when an even louder voice — a woman's voice — came audibly crashing onto the scene.

"Oh Jesus, buddy boy, you're such a wipe! There's nobody breaking down walls to talk to you!"

The good doctor's writing hand was moving erratically, and the notes he continued to take were quickly taking on the appearance of a child's scribbles. Under normal circumstances, the good doctor would have been entirely aware of his own behaviors, for he was extremely confidant in his own abilities as an astute observer priding himself on being keenly self-aware. These were not normal circumstances, however. Thus, he had not observed his handwriting going astray, nor was he aware there were beads of perspiration beginning to form on his brow which were, by now, clearly visible.

An occurrence such as this, if it were to happen anywhere in the arena of the norm, would be more than the good doctor could tolerate. His pride would not allow anything less than *everything* about his persona being exactly how he wanted it to appear — *perfect* — not unlike the Armani suits he wore or the crispness of his perfectly tailored dress shirts and his Gucci, Donnee Brit loafers. Everything about the good doctor had to be *just so*. In addition to and perhaps more to the point, the good doctor possessed the need to be in complete control. At the least, he needed to appear that way.

If ever the grandiose view from his high-rent office were to be compared to the "expansiveness" of the good doctor's ego, the view would fall tremendously short of a win.

"Look, you rat-faced shrew, don't you have a garbage can to rummage through?" Bud's voice was harsh as he faced off with the woman standing next to him.

Although she was a good eight inches shorter, barely making it to 5-feet 3-inches tall and maybe 115 pounds, the woman fearlessly stood toe-to-toe with Bud.

"I left 'em all for you to lick out, slug ass!"

With a firm and authoritative voice, Dillard Bigley interjected, "*Please! Let us display some semblance of decorum.* May we at least get through our self-introductions?"

"We are here to seek this good man's assistance which, it can be clearly noted, we need." Dillard's stern tone seemed to calm the less than cordial narrative down — at least, for the moment.

"Dr. Marksdale, may I introduce you to the group?" Dillard Bigley took a stance between the four other members of the group and the good doctor's desk.

"First," gesturing to his immediate left, he gracefully held out his left hand pointing in the direction of the woman who had just had a brief verbal scrap with Bud.

"This is Ms. Gillian Perciple."

The woman reached out to shake the doctor's outstretched hand, because by this time, he had set down his notebook and made his way around to the front of his desk.

"It is a pleasure to meet you, Ms. Perciple." The good doctor's voice came out sounding high-pitched and off key. He had not realized until he started to speak that he needed to clear his throat.

"Excuse me, Ms. Perciple, it seems I lost my voice for a moment."

Ms. Perciple politely said, "No problem, Dr. Marksdale," sounding nothing like she had moments earlier. "I have that happen to me all the time."

In that instant, Bud's voice — though lower than it had been before — could barely be heard, he said it so quietly. "Yeah, it comes from licking all that hair off your rat face — must be a fur ball caught in there somewhere." He followed this with a snicker which ended with a sneer.

"That will be quite enough, Mr. Jeffries!" Dillard Bigley's voice was stern and unwavering.

"Oh, shove it up your fat, *blank!* You're nothing more than a lousy imitation of a man!" Bud's face was turning red and Dillard Bigley's jaw was visibly, firmly set.

Just then, the office door suddenly swung open, and Mrs. Fins entered with a concerned expression on her face.

"Doctor, is everything alright in here?" A slight (but noticeable) quiver could be heard in her voice.

"Yes, Mrs. Fins, thank you. Everything will be fine. Mr. Jeffries, would you and everyone else please take a seat?"

The good doctor looked in the direction of all the chairs neatly placed around the room as well as two very comfortable appearing couches available to the group.

"Bud."

"Excuse me?" The good doctor asked.

"My name is Bud, and if you want me to respond to you, use it."

Mrs. Fins — noticeably upset having heard the raised voices from outside the doctor's office and now witnessing first-hand the tensions within the room — stood perfectly still.

Whether from fear or from a sincere, protective nature for the good doctor (who was clearly younger than herself), Mrs. Fins held her stance, and by all appearances, she was not going anywhere, anytime soon.

Three members of the group started to head towards separate chairs, and the remaining two went to one of the couches. Once all were seated, the good doctor, still standing in the middle of the room, cleared his throat once again and began with, "Now, let's start over, shall we?"

Mrs. Fins was still standing in the exact same place, as everyone made what sounded like positive, though muffled, responses to the doctor's request. The doctor noticed she did not appear to feel comfortable or, perhaps, capable yet of leaving and gently addressed her.

"Mrs. Fins, everything will be fine, you may go back to your office now."

"Of course, doctor, if you are sure."

"Yes, Mrs. Fins, I'm quite sure. Thank you." Mrs. Fins nodded her affirmation to the good doctor which was immediately followed by graceful pivoting on her heel, as she turned and headed for the door.

Observing every movement and moment of her presence, Dillard Bigley felt a brief racing of his heart, a slight chill and a mild body quake. This was something no one else in the room noticed, as he maintained a perfect upright posture while remaining perfectly still in his chair.

Dr. Marksdale knew he had to gain control over the five individuals staring at him from their chosen seated positions. He knew, too, it was quite out of the ordinary for him not to have been in control of the situation from the beginning.

You see, Dr. Marksdale was not known to take fondly to the thought of not being in control of anything — let alone a group of his patients — no matter how odd they may appear to be. He always took pride in his ability to be a confident leader — at least, he had, up until this particular Wednesday.

"Let me clarify, I am a stickler for order." The good doctor started. "Order is the best tool we have to do the job we are here to do." Everyone in the room continued to stare at him without saying a word.

"We will start from the left side of the room and go around the room, until everyone has introduced themselves to me." The doctor took a quick survey of the five sets of eyes that were fixated on him before continuing. "Interrupting is not an appropriate behavior. Everyone will get their turn." The good doctor then turned to the first person seated on his left, a woman in her early- to mid-20s.

Seemingly tall — though hard to tell while she was seated — she was dressed in a brightly colored, zip-up windbreaker which was cinched at her waist. The colors ranged from pastel to deep hues of every color in the rainbow.

Her pants were white leggings and she had on six-inch heels, metallic blue in color, with seriously pointed toes. Her hair was dyed and broken into sections of blue, white and pink. It was apparent, a fair amount of hair balm was required to hold the multi-colored spikes — going in every which way — in place.

She had several earrings, varying in size and sparkle, going around from the top to the bottom of her right ear. Her make-up, the doctor thought, was a bit too generous, but he could not help but notice it was applied with a great deal of artistry, especially her eyeliner. Detailed to perfection, the lines gave the impression her eyes were shaped like a cat's. And her eye color, as the doctor noticed immediately, was nowhere close to natural.

Once the doctor realized her left eye was a different color than the right eye, he assumed she wore colored contacts. The left eye had a slight brownish and orange hue, while the right eye was almost emerald green.

"Let's start with you." The good doctor directed.

The young woman sat up straight while crossing her ankles and introduced herself, "I'm Anna Leigh Kirby. You can call me 'Ally.'" She then relaxed back into her chair with a slight grin.

"Nice to meet you, Ally. It is 'Ally,' right?" The doctor pursued.

"Yep, Ally."

Seated next to Ally was Ms. Gillian Perciple, of whom the good doctor had already had a brief introduction — of sorts. Nothing about her appearance stood out as remarkable to him. Although the doctor's first impression of her was "average looking," she was still attractive and looked like she was in her early-40s. She had blonde, shoulder-length wavy hair, and due to her overall height and weight, she was what would be considered petite. The doctor's second impression of her was that his first was a bit off. He realized she was really quite stunning the more he observed her.

"And you, Ms. Gillian Perciple, do you have a preference as to how you wish to be addressed?"

"Glad ya asked. Yes, please refer to me as 'Percy.'"

"Certainly, Percy. It is a pleasure to meet you as well."

The next patient seated was Dillard Bigley, whose earlier meeting with the good doctor had already instilled his preferred name of Dill in the doctor's mind. So, after a couple of brief pleasantries batted back and forth between them, the good doctor moved his attention to the couch where the notable James Elliot Jefferies sat, snapping and blowing bubbles with his gum.

"And, Mr. Jefferies," the doctor began — immediately catching himself and making the correction before the self-censurer could pop his bubble to make any comment — "I apologize, Bud. It is also a pleasure to meet you."

Bud nodded his head in acceptance, and he gave the doctor a thumbs-up. What had been a sneer on Bud's face now gradually morphed into something more resembling a smile.

Sitting next to Bud on the opposite side of the couch was the last of the five new patients. She was quite attractive and somewhere in her mid- to late-60s, and the doctor was surprised he had not noticed her earlier. She was neither non-descript nor flashy or outlandish.

Now, as the doctor saw her for the first time, he felt a strong sense there was something about her — something different. Whatever it was — this "something" which alluded the good doctor, and which he was unable to pinpoint — it gave him the sense she was the only other person in the room.

Dr. Marksdale was all too aware his thinking this was out of character for him. Yet, he felt a sense of comfort contemplating such thoughts. Taking into consideration all which had just transpired during the initial meeting of his inherited group, his thinking something strange was now somehow comforting and did not seem to be odd at all.

"Hello Dr. Marksdale." The woman stood and reached out to shake the doctor's hand.

"My name is Emma Griffin."

The good doctor, while shaking her hand, asked, "And Emma Griffin, what name would you prefer to go by?"

This last patient to be introduced took a brief look around the room at all of the other patients. She then returned her gaze directly into the good doctor's eyes, and with a soft smile and in a gentle tone, she answered, "Emma, you may call me Emma."

"Fine, Emma — it is." Dr. Marksdale made his way back to his desk, picked up his notebook and sat down in his high-back, leather swivel chair.

"Now that the introductions are behind us, let's get better acquainted." The doctor, turning to a new page in his notebook, looked up at the group and stopped when his eyes met Dill Bigley's.

"I'm as acquainted with this batch of freaks as I ever want to be!" Bud's voice was cold, and he wore an expression of disdain as he looked around the room at the other patients.

"Now," the doctor began as he looked away from Dill and re-directed his attention towards Bud — in a calm and controlled tone, he continued — "Negative commentary is not conducive to our shared goal, Bud."

In the dark recesses of Dr. Marksdale's mind, there existed a tremendous urge to smack the back of Bud's head — oily hair or not. He envisioned himself smacking this loud and obnoxious new patient's head until the gum he continued to pop went shooting out of his mouth. And while the doctor enjoyed this brief respite and fantasy, his resentment towards El, the good-doer doctor, grew exponentially.

Originally, El had approached the good doctor under the premise of asking for a favor. Both doctors knew, at the time, the truth of the matter was that he had come to collect on a long-time debt — a debt the good doctor felt he could not readily refuse to pay.

Normally, far from being a glutton for punishment, the good doctor recognized now he had more on his plate than he had prepared for himself to be served.

"*Damn him.*" In the quiet of his own mind, the good doctor cursed his old pal. As of yet, there had been no explanation as to why these five patients had to be treated together. Clearly, the good doctor's old pal's promise he would provide the good doctor all the information he would need, as well as any patient files which may have helped in giving the doctor a heads up on each patient, had not been kept. The good doctor began to think it was a deliberate act on the part of his so-called pal. For sure, though, he knew El had reiterated in no uncertain terms that — it being a direct order from the court — all five of the group were to be treated together.

"Hey, I got an idea Doc!" A woman's voice interrupted the doctor's thoughts. "How's 'bout you just kick ol' Bud's ass to the curb?"

"Why don't he kick your lard *blank* to the curb?" Bud's irritating and now recognizable, unpleasant voice piped up in response to Percy's suggestion.

"Wait, that won't work. He'd break his foot trying to get that thing to move anywheres, let alone to a curb!" Bud laughed at his own rude comment.

"I wish you both would just stop. Can't you put your differences aside for once?" Ally's question rang with a tone resembling sincerity.

"Why don't you just shut-up and mind your own business." Percy loudly snapped.

"You shut-up, rat face. Don't you talk that way to her!" Bud's face was red and puffed out as he started to stand up. He looked as if he was going to head in the direction of where Percy was sitting.

"Why don't you all shut up? I've had quite enough of this behavior from every one of you." Dill Bigley spoke with firm assuredness as he, too, rose from his chair with his body language clearly stating he was at the ready to intercept any physical aggression Bud may have been contemplating.

The doctor attempted to shake clear the image of Dill, the proper British gentleman, and Bud, the crass grease ball (a mental slot the doctor had already given to this rude and unpleasant patient), getting into any kind of physical altercation. That image was a bit more than the already uneasy doctor felt able to cope with. Anything close to such a physical altercation transpiring made the good doctor more than ill at ease. To his dismay, it was then the good doctor envisioned his perfectly designed office space with its exquisite antique Persian carpet (a fine find acquired at a Sotheby's auction by his lovely wife Stelle) being damaged. This would be more than the good doctor could endure.

"That will be quite enough from all of you!" The good doctor's raised voice resonated throughout the room, and it was louder than even he had expected it to be. He stood up and made his way to the middle of where everyone was seated. Somehow, he looked taller than earlier, and there was no question his body stance was noticeably formidable.

He continued in a stern and non-wavering voice. "I've not seen your files, so I must admit, I am at a bit of a disadvantage as to each of your situations." He looked from his right to left making eye contact with each patient before continuing — "We will or we will not begin treatment as ordered by the court." He immediately noticed everyone's body language flinched slightly at the mention of the word "court."

"It is all up to you. Make your decisions — here and now." With that, he turned and walked back to his chair. Once seated, he panned the faces in the room and, in an obvious and deliberate gesture, he closed his notebook.

The air in the room felt heavy, and a pregnant pause followed which seemed to linger for a few, very uncomfortable moments. Then, neither a loud nor intrusive (yet unfamiliar) voice to the doctor's ears interrupted the heavy silence.

"Aside from all of our differences, I think we are willing to cooperatively proceed, Dr. Marksdale."

Emma Griffin slowly looked at each one of the other four patients. Her eyes had a gentle questioning expression in them.

"We all have something at stake here. Can we at least start by agreeing to that?" As she looked around the group, each of the other patients nodded their affirmation silently indicating their willingness to comply.

Emma's voice was calm and steady. "Doctor, I believe our group is finally in agreement. If it is okay with you, I'd like to start."

"Wait, hold on there! I will start. I can tell it all a hell of a lot faster than any of you, *blanks!*" Bud's voice had elevated to an even higher nerve grating pitch. "I just want to get all this *blank* over with."

"Mr. Jeffries, I've had just about enough from you. If you wouldn't mind — oh hell, even if you do" — the agitation in Dill's voice was apparent, "Let Emma fill the doctor in with the gory details."

The good doctor readily empathized with Dill Bigley's frustration. He too *so* wanted all the delays to cease so this first session could get underway.

Without having any real footing as to who all these players were or the *why* behind all of them being ordered by the court into a group therapy environment, Dr. Marksdale was left feeling measurably dissatisfied.

Privately, the good doctor felt good ol' Buddy Boy was nothing more than a royal pain in the ass — an irritating, agitating gum-popping *idiot* — who needed to just shut the hell up!

CHAPTER THREE

Time is an invisible dimension, where within it, mighty and powerful dynamics exist. Throughout history, civilizations have developed any number of methods to keep track of it. Countless efforts have been extended in the attempt to cordon it off into blocks and spaces comprehensible to the human brain — including going to any number of extremes of trying to control it — the latter, to no avail. Time ultimately wins and does so on its own terms.

Case in point: Nine months had passed between that windy Wednesday when Dr. Marksdale first met the group, and this particular morning the doctor was nervously preparing for his first court appearance as the group's attending therapist. He was scheduled to appear before the court the following week. From the doctor's perspective due to the court generously having extended the original date for this hearing twice before — and having done so on the shaky, "unforeseen circumstances" of an excuse the doctor used — he was well aware he could no longer buy time.

Taking into consideration all of which had transpired since that first meeting with the group, including all of the preparations for the upcoming hearing, the doctor wrestled with his feelings of, *if it was even possible* given the fact three-quarters of a year had passed.

On one hand, it seemed too much had happened to fit within the time constraints of a nine-month period. The old saying, "on the other hand," came to his mind. This is where the good doctor found himself facing an internal struggle. He struggled with knowing the time which had passed seemed to stretch out longer than any other nine-month period of time he could recall. Yet, having reached this point in his relationship with the group and readying himself to address the court, he felt the same nine-month time span had gone by far too fast and fell short of the time he needed.

True, the calendar reflected nine months had passed; but, as the good doctor surmised, if he had to describe all of which had occurred involving his five inherited patients during those nine months, it would have taken him *at least* thirteen months to do it.

In the final analysis, he could not deny almost three full seasons had passed since that first meeting with the group; that is, when the good doctor finally succumbed to the facts as they were. In a low whisper he said aloud to himself, "Suck it up, Phillip!" He immediately followed this with — volume elevated and distinct agitation in his voice — "Just great. Now, *I'm talking to myself!*"

The doctor continued to review and prepare his notes (stacks of pages which reached well into the hundreds) for his group's first court appearance and momentarily reflected, "No matter what you do, time really does fly by." This left him at a loss for words — a pleasant though brief upside for a nervous psychiatrist worried about his developing the habit of talking to himself.

He ran his fingers through his thinning hair — regrettably having to acknowledge since he began his sessions with the "group," he had experienced a fair share of loss of that too.

Yes — time ultimately wins.

Although Dr. Marksdale knew he would never be able to share all of the individual experiences he had been exposed to during that nine-month span, he highly doubted he would want to try. He felt assured most would think he would have been spinning fairy tales when, really, he would be revealing bizarre truths. Even so, the good doctor found himself in the middle of preparing for his big day in court where he was keenly aware — he would have more than a little storytelling to do when he went before the judge.

In that first session nine-months earlier, the doctor had been made aware of the reason he was treating all five members together instead of each one individually. This discovery did not come from the files he had been promised. Those files never arrived.

Dr. Marksdale did receive a hand-written note with a brief synopsis of each patient's situation in regards to the court's orders from his old pal El, a.k.a. the good-doer. However, that note would not arrive until well into the seventh month following the beginning of Dr. Marksdale's treatment of the group. This was a fact the good doctor kept at the forefront of his growing animosity for his old pal, El.

Over the course of the seven-month period prior to the hand-written note finally arriving, no less than a hundred messages were left for the good-doer by both the good doctor and Mrs. Fins. The agitation this evoked within the good doctor festered. He was nothing, if not a highly structured and organized individual. For him, no response was a far worse affront to his sensibilities than a response which would prove to be useless.

On rare occasions, in the privacy of his own mind, Dr. Marksdale briefly allowed himself a playful, even whimsical, thought. One of those thoughts was maybe the good-doer had not been in contact because he had tripped and subsequently fallen off the edge of the earth. Generally, a man of science, the good doctor knew that thought was too far-fetched. Still, it put a smile on his face. It was then he reluctantly, but within the boundaries he was used to setting for himself, came back to a relative plateau of reality.

Not wanting to end his temporary respite from the norm, the good doctor visited one more fleeting fantasy. He entertained the thought of how greatly it would please him if the good-doer would indeed lose his footing and consequently fall helplessly away from the safety of the planet's gravitational pull. Indulging himself with such a thought allowed the good doctor a brief, but joyful, moment of bliss. Bliss — at least, as the good doctor knew it — was known to be a brief interlude. This time was no different as the moment was followed by a damnable plague of self-deprecation.

The good doctor had always strived to reach what seemed to be a never attainable level of perfection. Due to his own self-sabotaging nature, the hope to attain such a level seemed to remain inevitably just out of reach. And so begrudgingly, the good doctor concluded — if the good-doer were to experience such a fall, no doubt, a serendipitous event would prevail.

This event presented itself in the good doctor's mind as a blessed one — one in which a group of angels would expeditiously come to the wildly falling, and out of control, good-doer's rescue. They would gently float, as the doctor imagined angels would do, and swoop the good-doer up in a loving, protective embrace. Then, ever so gently, they would place him back down on the safety of terra firma. With this thought, the good doctor huffed and his face twisted into a rather unpleasant expression while he cursed aloud: "*Damn angels.*"

When Dr. Elan Glenn's hand-written note did arrive — seven-months into Dr. Marksdale's treatment — it proved to be of no value. By that time, the good doctor had already learned more than enough about each member in his group. He did find himself having a difficult time believing some of what he had come to know — but there was no doubt — by that time, he knew it.

The doctor's recorded notes would be tremendously helpful when addressing the court with each individual patient's progress. Those same notes were integral to his presentation. Everything had to be in order, as there was a great deal riding on this hearing — not only for all members of the group but for himself as well. Now that he was the noted attending psychiatrist, everything which would transpire before the court would directly reflect on his professional reputation.

Dr. Marksdale felt his heart rate beginning to speed up. Then he thought the one thought that, so far that morning, he had been able to keep at bay. The dreaded thought he had safely submerged in the dark recesses of his mind now came swimming frantically to the surface. How would each of his patients present themselves during this hearing?

There were only a couple of people in the group the good doctor felt would behave in an appropriate manner. But the others — "Oh God," he said aloud, "what if?" This thought made the doctor's blood run cold; hence, he had a hard time swallowing, as his heart rate had accelerated into a full gallop.

★★★★★

While reflecting on that first meeting with the group — the same meeting when the good doctor learned the reason all five of the group were to be treated together — he saw the challenge before him. He knew time was of the essence, and it was imperative he use it wisely.

"They have come so far," the good doctor uttered in almost a whisper, "from that first meeting." The good doctor rubbed the palm of his hand over his lips and down his chin — "amazingly far."

Now, time was drawing close to when all of them, the five members of the group and the good doctor himself, were to appear before the court.

The judge referenced, The Honorable Judge Eleanor Glib, had found all five of these clearly odd individuals (the clarity of their oddness was not lost on the good doctor) to be in contempt of that court, and Judge Eleanor Glib concluded each member of the group had committed a myriad of improprieties during the aforementioned hearing. Although none of the group had any affiliation with each other prior to that day in court when things went terribly wrong, Judge Glib believed each of the five, in one way or another, were contributors to her court being disrupted. And, thus, the group of five were sentenced together — as one.

In addition, it was the judge's order each of these five individuals were to be evaluated by a licensed therapist or psychiatrist. Each of the five were to receive weekly therapy sessions over no less than a nine-month period, and no more than a twelve-month period of time.

An additional order of the court established that at the sixth-month point, the attending therapist's resultant cumulative evaluations were to be presented to the court. This same order concluded: All five members of the group were required to be present when those evaluations were presented.

Then, and only then, with the help of the attending therapist, would The Honorable Judge Eleanor Glib deem what, if any, further sentencing or treatment would be appropriate. The group and the good doctor were three months past the court's order for their six-month due date of appearance. This explained why now, as the hour crept ever faster into the early evening, the good doctor's heart raced, and his three-fingered shot of Scotch went down so easily.

Shaking off the shudder caused by the 95-percent-proof libation, the good doctor thought more recently — and more often than not — he found himself in quite a pickle. It did not evade the good doctor either, since beginning treatment of the group, his indulgence into the world of liquid spirits had increased exponentially. He cautioned himself that his association with the group could lead him into more pickles. Yet, indeed, his newly found, fast friendship with "the drink" caused him to be uncomfortably aware: He may very well end up *becoming the pickle himself!*

"I don't know if the details are all that gory, doctor, but I will start." The last shot of scotch was beginning to affect the good doctor's senses when, in his memory, he heard the sound of Emma Griffin's calm voice. This, in turn, interrupted Dr. Marksdale's train of thought — a train which for the past nine months inched closer to going off the tracks.

The good doctor's mind and body began to relax. It was then the memories of that first meeting on that very windy day, nine-months earlier, began to forge their way into his consciousness.

"I was with my daughter, Monica. I was there to watch my granddaughter, Lizzie, while her mother attended a hearing."

"May I ask what the hearing was for?" The doctor remembered having asked Emma.

"The hearing was for a slight auto mishap she'd been involved with."

"Now, here we go — slight auto mishap? C'mon Emm's, your daughter is a disaster behind the wheel!" Surprising to the good doctor, it was not Bud's voice interrupting with the somewhat blistering observation of Emma's daughter. Instead, it was Anna Leigh Kirby's voice, a.k.a. "Ally."

Unsure of which eye to look into — the emerald green one on the right, or the left one with its brownish orange hues — the good doctor just went back and forth between them. This took intense concentration and effort on his part, as he did not wish to give attention to Ally's spiked, pink-white-and-blue hair either. Most likely, his being distracted by her appearance was lost on Ally, as Emma was already responding to her comment.

"Monica is not a disaster behind the wheel, Ally. She is actually a very good driver."

"What a joke, Emma!" Bud blurted out. "Monica — no, *Moronica* — is more than a disaster behind the wheel! She's just a plain disaster."

"No name calling, Mr. Jeffries." Dill Bigley interjected, clearly agitated.

"Get a grip *English*! If it weren't for that moron, Moronica, none of us would even be here!"

"To be fair," Ms. Perciple (Percy) interjected. "We all played a role in our ending up in this fix." Squinting her eyes, she turned to look at Bud. His head was wobbling slightly as he continued to noisily pop his gum.

"Hey, you! Happy cheeks! It was *you*, more than *anyone else*, that helped in getting us here!"

"Hold on, rodent breath!" Bud swung his body around towards Percy's direction and began to stand as his voice elevated: "I'm only here because Emma's stupid daughter started this whole mess. *Moron* — stupid moron — that's what *Moronica* is!"

Dr. Marksdale remembered how surprised he was to witness Bud sitting right back down after this outburst; then, swiftly crossing one leg over the other, Bud picked up where he had left off — incessantly chomping on and popping his gum. Dr. Marksdale, though relieved by Bud's choosing not to offend further with any kind of altercation, verbal or other, still found himself adequately puzzled.

"To be fair, we all played a part in our having to be here." Emma's voice sounded thoughtful, not forced. "I, for one, behaved in a fashion very much out of character for me — foreign to my perception of myself, really." The good doctor noticed Emma's expression alter from being seemingly thoughtful to one indicating slight embarrassment.

"Emma, you stated your daughter, Monica" — Dr. Marksdale quickly looked around the room at all of the other patients before proceeding — "had been in a car accident. I assume you were in traffic court, is that correct?"

"More like a circus of freaks!" The doctor chose not to turn to look at Bud. Instead, with a professional calm, he queried, "Was everyone there for some kind of traffic violation?"

"Yes, doctor. As best I recall, all five of us had dealings with the court in relationship to our having visited upon ourselves prior driving infractions," Dill said quietly.

The doctor looked around the room for any sign of disagreement with Dill's comment. When he saw none, he looked directly at Emma and asked, "What then, may I ask, happened?"

"As I started to say," taking a breath, Emma continued. "My daughter needed me to watch Lizzie, while she went before the judge." Shifting slightly in her chair, Emma took a quick glance at Ally and then Bud as if to see if either was going to interrupt her again.

"My intention was to stay outside the courtroom, but Monica —"

"Moronica, you mean — get it right!"

Without having to look in his direction, Dr. Marksdale would have sworn, though highly improbable, he could hear Bud's sneer.

"Monica," Emma repeated (her tone never changing), "asked me to come inside the courtroom. She thought it would be a good civic lesson for Lizzie."

"Good lesson? Ha! If you wanted to show the kid how stupid her mother was, yeah, that woulda done it."

Dr. Marksdale, whose normal outward demeanor was of a calm and controlled nature, remembered how, at that time, he felt his hands began to shake. He was fraught with visions of an uncommon and violent aggression. This was an emotion quite foreign to him. He remembered, too, how he fought to suppress the ever growing desire to place his hands firmly around Bud's neck, after which he would begin to squeeze tighter and tighter. He envisioned Bud's face — his bulging, empty black eyes staring straight ahead — with his mouth agape and exposing his wad of gum trapped at the back of his throat. The visions continued with Dr. Marksdale keeping a steady grip around Bud's neck until no sounds escaped his still, and finally, silent body.

The good doctor took in a full hearty breath, methodically exhaled, and nodded in Emma's direction indicating his desire she continue.

Emma did so by relaying the events of the first day the five members of the group had met. The main gist of her story, as best as the doctor could remember, was that then, as now, everyone seemed to talk over the others.

All of this caused havoc in Judge Eleanor Glib's courtroom. This was something which was quite unacceptable to Judge Glib. How bad could it have been, the good doctor asked himself, to cause Judge Glib to order all five of these individuals to receive therapy for their mental state — and together, no less. What could have transpired in court that day, the doctor's mind wondered, which would initiate an extreme measure such as the one Judge Glib took when ordering the group to meet such requirements?

The answer to this question was soon to come. Before Emma had finished her rendition of the events which led up to the group being ordered into the hands of a therapist — and ultimately into the hands of Dr. Marksdale — she had relinquished the floor to Ally who, by that time, expressed a need to share her own view of that day's events.

"So, it was Monica who was the first one to go before the judge. She said she was innocent of all charges." Ally, who seemed determined to get her two cents' worth in, was absent mindedly looking at her long, sparkly manicured nails as she continued: "I was going to do the same, when this loud crashing sound happened in back of me."

Immediately, the doctor thought it had to be something Bud had done. It seemed to be a fair assumption; and, as it turned out, he was mostly correct.

"Turns out, the sound was Mr. Bigley falling over the chair in front of the one he was sitting on."

"Let us be clear, young lady. I did not *fall* over it. I was *hurled over it* by this — this oily haired, hunched back Troglodyte!" Dill's voice cracked as he pointed in Bud's direction.

"If I'd a hurled you, you miserable joke of a man, you'd a ended up head first stuck in the *blanking* wall!" The doctor could see Bud's hands were now clenched into fists.

Not more than two seconds passed, before Bud was out of his chair and on top of Dill. Fists were flying every which way, when Percy jumped on top of both men in what appeared to be an attempt to get between them. She made several screaming sounds. Some were audible enough to decipher the words, "*Knock it off!*" Her orders were muffled by a variety of other sounds which mostly resembled grunts, groans and flesh smacking flesh.

Now there were six arms madly flailing, while the three of them — Bud, Dill Bigley and Percy — were all rolling back and forth on the floor. Ally jumped up while taking off one of her blue, metallic-colored high heels and started smacking anyone's body parts she could make contact with. The sounds emitting from the punches being thrown, the slapping sounds of flesh on flesh along with the thuds Ally's shoes made when making contact with one's head and other bones were most unpleasant.

Dr. Marksdale found himself in a near state of shock at what he was witnessing. His mouth dropped open and remained that way while indescribable sounds came out of it. Then he too jumped up, but instead of intervening, he ran to move the antique coffee table out of the path of the writhing mass who made up the mad ball of human fury. By this time, Emma, the controlled and somewhat calm one, was rolling on the floor with the other four patients screaming to everyone, "*Stop this insanity!*"

Suddenly, there were gasps and choking sounds, as all five of the group found themselves drenched with stagnant smelling water. While untangling themselves from the others, each of them found stems, blossoms and fern leaves from an array of cut flowers which had, only moments prior, made up a beautiful gargantuan arrangement in Dr. Marksdale's waiting room.

Now, Mrs. Marlene Fins, with her petite frame, stood firmly above the group. In her hands, she held the now vacant, large and elegant glass vessel in which the flowers had been housed.

Dill Bigley began to get his bearings. He wiped water from his eyes — one of which was already bruised and swelling shut.

Emma, as politely as a woman can spit, spit out a small white pedal. She believed it may have come from a Chrysanthemum blossom.

While attempting to restructure her soaking wet hair spikes, Ally noticed the pointed tip of her lovely, shiny blue, shoe heel had several hairs stuck to it — none were the colors of any of the hair on her own head. This is when she also became aware the hairy heel was dangling so precariously, it was barely being held onto her shoe's sole.

Percy, finally in a sitting position, was tilting her head to the left in an attempt to drain water from her ear. It was then when she noticed the odor of less than fresh smelling water had permeated her clothes.

Bud, who had already rolled himself away from the others, was standing and straightening his clothes. Swiftly, he started smoothing his oily and wet hair back with his hands, when he noticed a long string of gum stuck to the front of his shirt and an even larger mass of the sticky substance stuck to his belt buckle. Grabbing both and rolling them back together before anyone else could see, he plunged the unsightly wad back into his mouth.

Dill's vision was slightly compromised from the water which had splashed in his eyes as well as the effects he was experiencing due to his eyelid continuing to swell shut. Nonetheless, when he looked up, he could easily see Mrs. Fins. She stood in place, firmly holding a flower vase near half her height, while glaring down at the four of them.

"Oh my . . ." he thought as he gasped for breath. "Oh, Mrs. Fins, you are as exquisite from this angle as any other." And for that moment, Dill Bigley felt no pain — just the racing of his heart.

*****

"Everything is clear to me now," Dr. Marksdale remembered saying aloud to himself that first day upon his meeting the group. Then quietly in his mind, "Yes, indeed. I know exactly why Judge Glib's court order for mental observation was in place. *These people are NUTS!!!*"

But why, he still wondered, did the judge insist they all be treated together? Having not been present on that day when Judge Glib's court had to have been so terribly disrupted by this group, he could only surmise the judge must really have it in for people of his chosen profession.

After his witnessing the complete lack of control and utter hysteria which had just taken place, the good doctor dreaded what he dared not imagine was ahead of him. Briefly, he pondered the reasoning behind his old pal choosing this time to settle an old debt, and could only conclude it was a deliberate and cruel maneuver.

"Yes indeed," the good doctor thought to himself. "You son-of-a-bitch!" But that was all he could do or say about his old pal, Dr. Elan Glenn. Taking into consideration the debt he owed, the good doctor thought, "Yes, we will finally be even, when this is done."

The good doctor observed the group had come a long way since that first windy day. Bothersome as it was, the question kept creeping up into his slowly numbing brain, "Was he or the group ready to stand before the bench of Judge Eleanor Glib?"

The thought of the answer being a "negative" almost paralyzed Dr. Marksdale. And so, he thought, "I'll have just one more shot of scotch."

CHAPTER FOUR

"Phillip — Phillip —" A voice, a woman's voice, was coming from somewhere which sounded like it was quite a distance away. The voice kept getting closer and louder, too. It continued to call Dr. Marksdale by his first name.

"Phillip — Phillip —"

For a moment the good doctor thought the voice sounded familiar. He recognized it — it sounded like his mother's voice. The doctor wasn't expecting to see her today, and this left him confused.

If it was her, where was she? Why not just come into the office? He was sure he had left the door open.

The voice continued calling his name.

"Phillip — Phillip — where are you?"

The doctor turned his head and saw a house. It looked like the house he had grown up in but, somehow, different. The porch wrapped around the entire front and sides of the house, just the way he remembered it.

There was a mature, overgrown Lilac bush. Its fully blossomed and heavily laden branches were hanging over the sharp-pitched roof just above the porch. He could smell the pleasant and familiar fragrance the blossoms emitted — "so sweet," he thought, "almost delicious."

And then, it happened again. The same woman's voice, still sounding as if a distance away, but now there was more eagerness to it. He felt the sensation of being shaken.

"Phillip — Phillip, wake up!"

Opening his eyes took an enormous effort — once opened, they were as dry as his mouth. It took his brain more than a few moments to focus, both visually and mentally.

As he attempted to sit up from the crumpled slump he lay in, he found the sleeve to his fine Desmond Merrion suit jacket (a suit which was only a mere $47,000 investment) wet from his drool. He also realized he was more than a little off balance and ended up sitting back down when the room began spinning around him.

"You scared me to death when you didn't come home." Stelle stood above her husband. "You leave me a message that says you don't think *you* can take anymore?" She started to pace back and forth, her voice high and sounding exasperated, "*You can't take anymore*? You should be in *my shoes!*"

Stelle bent down to pick up the wrappers from what was left of the take-out food the doctor had apparently partially eaten the night before.

"And this drinking," Stelle held up the almost empty bottle of scotch which was precariously leaning against a pile of file folders which lay in disarray on the doctor's desk.

"I can't take *this* anymore. We've got a family, and once upon a time, *we had a life!*" She slammed the bottle down on the desk which made Dr. Marksdale grimace.

He attempted to stand once more but was too overcome by vertigo. Instead, he hurriedly leaned forward just in time to get the waste basket in front of his face. It was then, the good doctor proceeded to repeatedly — wretch.

*****

Poor, proper — Mrs. Fins. Upon opening the door to his office and seeing him evacuating his bodily fluids — or what was left of them — into a wastepaper basket, Mrs. Fins rushed to the aid of Dr. Marksdale.

"Oh dear! Oh — my goodness — oh —" She sounded a tad more than a little panicked.

"*I'll be sooo — kay.*" The good doctor looked up at Mrs. Fins — her face clearly contorted with grave concern. He wiped his flushed and sweaty face with the only dry sleeve left of what he liked to think was his greatly coveted (but to most people, absurdly over-priced) Desmond Merrion suit jacket.

"*Why din — why din I wear Armani, yes — yes — terday?*" Though his voice was soft, both Mrs. Fins and Stelle could hear he was slurring his words.

"Oh my — my — Dr. Marksdale — please let me help you to the bathroom."

"If you wouldn't mind, Marlene, you could help me get him in there."

Mrs. Fins jumped when she heard a woman's voice. Only then, did she notice Stelle was standing by the window on the other side of the office.

"Dear heavens!" Mrs. Fins gasped. "Mrs. Marksdale! I mean, Dr. Marksdale." The fact Mrs. Fins was completely taken by surprise by Stelle's presence evaded no one. "I had no idea — I — I —" Mrs. Fins' stuttering continued. "I — I — Dr. Marksdale you gave me *such a start*!"

Mrs. Fin's facial expression was now a mix of concern, helplessness and confusion.

"I'm so sorry Marlene," Stelle headed towards her husband, "about all of this. Please, call me Stelle, and help me get the doctor into the bathroom."

"Of course, Mrs. Marksdale."

With that, Mrs. Fins immediately took one of Dr. Marksdale's wet-sleeved arms, while Stelle took the other. Between the two women, they managed to get the good doctor up on his wobbly feet and proceeded to maneuver his unsteady, staggering body through the doorway and around the corner into the private bathroom. This particular bathroom was meant to be used only by the Marksdales and Mrs. Fins.

Bud had made a fair observation during the group's first session with Dr. Marksdale. It was on that occasion, his observation led him to state, "Groupies, we're in the high-rent district now."

Dr. Marksdale's private bathroom was almost the size of Mrs. Fin's entire living and dining room areas, combined, in her mid-century home — a beautiful home she loved and had lived in for several decades. Located in a well-to-do neighborhood of Seattle, it was not all that far away from where she worked with Dr. Marksdale.

Besides the marbled, double-headed shower, this private bathroom contained a comfortable sauna with two additional areas. One area had wall-to-wall mirrors with two rectangular sinks. The other area had two beautifully upholstered chaise lounges for which, one may assume, were for lounging.

Though the bathroom had always been available for her use, Mrs. Fins chose to use the smaller of the two.

Measuring close to a 12- by 14-foot room, the smaller bathroom did not include a walk-in shower nor a comfortable sized sauna. It was specifically meant for the good doctor's patients. Mrs. Fins found this smaller bathroom large compared to most bathrooms she had seen and quite adequate to suit her needs.

Mrs. Fins, even with her fastidiousness and well-groomed mannerisms, was nothing close to being pretentious. In fact, she presented herself to be quite modest in all noticeable aspects.

Both women carefully sat Dr. Marksdale down on a high-backed, overstuffed chair directly in front of one of the two vanity sinks. Stelle then asked Mrs. Fins, "Would you please get me a washcloth and a couple of towels?"

"Certainly," Mrs. Fins responded, "Would you like me to get the doctor a change of clothing as well?"

"Yes, please." Stelle — busy pulling on the last sleeve of the doctor's jacket enabling her to remove it — looked up at Mrs. Fins offering her a quick and partial smile. "Thank you, you can find everything over there." Stelle pointed to the corner where a large and elegant, solid walnut French armoire stood.

Mrs. Fins had almost made her way to the armoire before Stelle had finished her comment. Being quite familiar with what the beautiful piece of furniture held — as Mrs. Fins had retrieved any number of clothing items for the good doctor on many occasions before — she knew where everything she felt the doctor may need would be found.

While putting together a complete outfit (being ever so careful to make sure every piece was properly coordinated with every other piece), Mrs. Fins thought of how she had done this for the good doctor on so many occasions in the past. Whether it was for an event at which he had to speak before an audience of other professionals or Mrs. Fins' favorite — when the married doctors were going somewhere together — she was always astute when addressing the doctors' special needs. Those needs mainly consisted of being sure his appearance was nothing shy of being perfect.

For a moment, Mrs. Fins felt a pang of sadness. She had not seen the doctor in this current light and had never had to help him previously in regards to, or under, such extraordinary circumstances.

Gathering all which she felt the doctor would require, Mrs. Fins returned to Stelle, her arms filled. She placed the linens and undergarments where she felt they would be easiest to reach and hung the doctor's change of clothing on a bar in the vanity area meant for that purpose.

"You should be able to find any toiletries you may need under the cabinet below the sink." Stelle's eyes followed Mrs. Fins' hand gesture towards the right-hand side of the large vanity area.

"I will lock the office and tend to cancelling any appointments set for today," Mrs. Fins said quietly. "If you should need me further, please use the intercom." She then excused herself and returned to the main office where, as she had stated, she would see to the clean-up in the doctor's office as well. Before Stelle could respond, Mrs. Fins was gone.

"Okay, Phillip, you've got to get into the shower — preferably, without breaking your neck." Under her breath and in a serious tone, Stelle continued, "Save that pleasure for me."

Stelle, a lovely and statuesque woman, now looked drained and tired. She took the doctor's hand in hers and helped him to his feet.

"Can you finish undressing yourself?" The doctor, becoming a little steadier on his feet, took in a deep breath and nodded in the affirmative.

"Okay, I'll get the water going." Holding onto her husband's arm, Stelle looked closely at the doctor to see if he looked as if she could leave him to stand on his own. When she felt he could, she very slowly let go of his arm.

Without looking at his wife, the good doctor said quietly, "I'm better." His words were a little clearer than those which tumbled through his lips just a few minutes earlier.

Although his thoughts were still cloudy, Dr. Marksdale was keenly aware of being horribly embarrassed. It was bad enough Mrs. Fins had found him in this most unfortunate state. Adding to that experience, Stelle being a witness to his current condition felt to him like being stabbed in the gut. That was really saying something, for at that moment, his body was so numb when he managed to kick off his shoe and smack his toes into the edge of the chair leg in front of him, all he could muster was, "How'd that get there?"

Holding on to the edge of the vanity with one hand, the doctor clumsily turned on the water and bent down to rinse off his face. Water splashed on the vanity, the mirror in front of him and down the front of his shirt. Though his vision was partially impaired, he knew Stelle saw it all. Her facial expression in the mirror reflected a mixture of waning anger and saddened disappointment — an expression the good doctor hoped never to see on his wife's face — at least, not in direct relationship to himself.

While keeping her husband within her view, Stelle went towards the shower room. Only after she felt her husband was able to be alone for a few moments did she turn away from him to turn on and adjust the water temperature.

Both of the Marksdales knew in their own way, this incident was not the end of the world. It was, however, the absolute breaking point for both of them.

Stelle knew she could no longer ignore the good doctor's most recent erratic behavior. As for the good doctor, he knew he had to come clean to his wife with what was going on in his professional life — that is, if he wanted to keep that which he treasured to continue in his personal life. This revelation was precisely wherein the good doctor's biggest fears had lain, and there they festered, ever since his old pal Dr. Elan Glenn had rested an old unpaid debt upon him. Once the good doctor divulged what had gotten him into the predicament he was in, would Stelle stay with him? It was this realization in itself he had come to the night before.

The unnerving question — would Stelle ever be able to forgive him? — was most frightening to the good doctor. Would she stay with him after revealing to her what he felt he had no way to avoid revealing to her? It was a short duration between his facing these most pressing questions and his polishing off more than half a bottle of scotch.

Stelle helped her husband into the shower and then gathered all of his dirty clothes together. She found a linen garment bag she knew was used by the dry cleaner, and she stuffed the doctor's dirty clothes inside of it. There was no way she was going to let anyone else know, other than Mrs. Fins and herself, the condition of her husband's clothes. These clothes were going home with her. The odors of souring meat grease, catsup, mustard and old mayonnaise (marked by a large stain on the jacket's lapel and a pant leg) mixed with body odor and vomit turned her stomach. If left up to her, these clothes would never be seen or smelled again.

As he showered, the good doctor suffered through a convulsive bout of dry heaves which at first made him hot and then so cold his body shivered, even as the hot water washed over him. It was then, while in the shower, he had to accept coming clean would mean revealing everything. That was something, up until the night before, he felt he could avoid. Now, as he held onto the shower wall naked and shivering, he knew there was no way he could hold back on anything. That meant his explaining the truth about the group and the myriad of their personalities and peculiarities which, in his opinion, had driven him to this fragile and tremulous edge. It was at that exact moment, the good doctor felt relief. A feeling he had not experienced for a very long nine months.

Meanwhile in the doctor's office, Mrs. Fin's intestinal tract was not doing much better than Dr. Marksdale's or, for that matter, Stelle's. In the smaller of two bathrooms while disposing of the waste basket's curdling inhabitant, some of its contents spilled out and onto her modest, but tasteful, dress pumps. She managed to wash it off and flush it away before succumbing to her own gag reflexes' sudden urge for acrobatics. Mrs. Fins, in all aspects, was nothing short of an efficient and dedicated employee.

When she exited the bathroom with a clean waste basket in hand, Mrs. Fins saw out of the corner of her eye the door to Dr. Marksdale's office was slowly opening. Quickly turning her attention towards the door, she saw the back of a man's head peering around the corner of the partially opened door. When the man's head turned in her direction, the expression his face wore was one of a pensive and cautious nature. Even so, Mrs. Fins could clearly see it was the familiar face of Mr. Dillard Bigley.

"Good gracious! Mr. Bigley, you just startled me so."

"Please forgive me, Mrs. Fins."

Dill Bigley entered the office and quietly closed the door behind him.

"I'm pretty sure — no, I'm quite certain — you are not scheduled to see the doctor this early."

Mrs. Fins continued to walk to the side of the doctor's desk and set the wastebasket down.

"Your observation is correct, Mrs. Fins." Dill looked around the room as if he was expecting to see something or someone other than Mrs. Fins.

"Due to the fact I did not see you at your desk, I took the liberty of letting myself in." Seeming to be more than a little uncomfortable, Dill continued after clearing his throat. "Please excuse me." Clearing his throat once again with his nervousness becoming more obvious, "May I ask, do you know the doctor's whereabouts?"

"I must say, Mr. Bigley, this is quite unusual. Your appointment is several hours away. Is it not?" The inflection in Mrs. Fin's voice maintained a firm and unyielding tone.

"Why, yes — again, Mrs. Fins, you are correct." Although Dill stood in one place, the shifting of his weight from one foot to the other gave away how truly uncomfortable he was.

"You see." Nervously, Dill looked around the room trying to avoid eye contact with Mrs. Fins. "I was supposed to meet —" The long pauses between his words only contributed to Dill's discomfort, as he was normally very articulate when he spoke. Now his words and mannerisms bore witness to his growing anxiety, as his words fell out of his mouth much like that of someone with an uncontrollable stutter.

"The, the doc, doctor, that, is, is —" Taking a controlled breath in, Dill Bigley straightened his body as if at attention and blurted out, "Dr. Marksdale, I, I, was sa, sa, supposed to meet with," and while completely exhaling, "with, the, Dr. Marksdale."

Mrs. Fins made her way to Dill's side and wrapped her arm around his and began to lead both of them out of the doctor's office and into the waiting room.

"Now Mr. Bigley, I understand that you have an appointment." Mrs. Fins gently but purposefully squeezed Dill's arm with her arm. "You must realize, your arriving so early is really quite inappropriate."

Arm in arm they continued to head towards the door.

"I was preparing to make calls to cancel all of Dr. Marksdale's appointments for today and reschedule for another time."

As they made their way to the outer door, Mrs. Fins opened it and started to escort Dill through it, when Dill gently put his hand on her arm and stopped them both.

"I understand this is all highly unusual Mrs. Fins, but, you, you, see —"

Mrs. Fins took Dill's hand firmly in hers and walked them both out into the hall. With clear authoritativeness in her voice, her unwavering words — the words Dill Bigley would replay in his mind for some time to follow — were, "No, Mr. Bigley, *I do not see!*"

With that, she turned and before abruptly closing the door behind him, she stated distinctly, "I will call you shortly, Mr. Bigley, to reschedule. Now you must go."

Somewhat dazed, Dill Bigley stood alone in the hall with his mouth hanging open. Swallowing hard and feeling absolutely sure his heart beat could be heard through the door, Dill Bigley leaned against the wall for a few moments to catch his breath.

Looking down at his hand, the same hand which only a few moments before was tightly cupped in that of Mrs. Fins, he would have sworn he could still feel the presence and warmth which came from her soft — and as he had fantasized on many occasions before — delicate hand.

Although he would have very much preferred surrendering his nagging sense of responsibility to his greater, fanciful and romantic inclinations towards Mrs. Fins, Dill Bigley knew this was not the time nor was it the place to dally. Those ever so pleasing places where he held court with his daily dreams of Mrs. Fins, for now, would have to wait.

Just as he managed to put those thoughts aside, Dill Bigley straightened his body, lifted his chest and chin and turned to face the door Mrs. Fins had just abruptly, albeit tactfully, closed behind him.

"Dr. Marksdale needs to see me. I must get that across to Mrs. Fins." Dill Bigley quietly muttered to himself. "After all, that was exactly the good doctor's unexpectant request."

Rehashing the phone call which had come in the middle of the night — a call from Dr. Marksdale, wherein the doctor sounded confused and out of sorts — remained a great source of concern for Dill Bigley and was the driving reason behind his arriving at the good doctor's office so early that morning. And, it was this gnawing concern which assisted him in mustering the courage to begin knocking on the same door, he was only minutes before being escorted out through.

He lightly knocked three times, and then after a brief pause, harder — three more times. When there was no response to his knocking, he steadily, and not without trepidation, began to turn the doorknob. From behind him, and at the same time, he heard heavy breathing and the most unpleasant, but recognizable, sound of popping gum.

"Yo ho, English! What are you doing there, trying to break in?"

Bud's question was so typical of his general attitude — crudeness and overall rudeness.

Dill, startled by the sudden presence of anyone else in the hall, jumped slightly before turning to see a face bearing half a smile and half a sneer.

To an outsider it would not be apparent, but to some of those in the group, one of which was *not* Dill Bigley, there was a noticeable improvement in some of the more negative layers of Mr. James Elliot Jeffries' persona. It would seem some layers had slowly peeled away over the nine months the group had been receiving treatment.

Some members of the group may have gone so far as to say most of Bud's more negative qualities had waned, to a slight degree. Indeed, some may have said that but not Dill Bigley, not yet. He was still on the fence as to whether or not Bud had any other resemblances to a humanoid, other than the fact he stood upright.

"Of course, I'm not breaking in. What are you doing here so early, may I ask?"

With his hand releasing the doorknob, Dill turned to face his one-time sworn nemesis. Now, after nine months of treatment, he viewed him to be more of an unpleasant nuisance — something more along the line as resembling an irksome, recurring rash.

"The doc called me a few hours ago. Woke me right up. Said to meet him here this morning. What about you?"

Bud quickly turned his head — first to the left and then to the right. The audible result from his neck turning was a cracking sound followed by a louder than usual pop from the visibly large wad of gum his tongue masterfully switched from one side to the other in his opened mouth.

Generally, Dill Bigley would not categorize himself as being either small minded and petty or easily led to becoming upset over trivial matters. That was how he had viewed and would describe himself as recently as a year before the unfortunate circumstances which landed him in the mix with the other four members of the group — a group of people he could not imagine himself ever being a part of for any reason, none whatsoever — unless, of course, he was under a strict order from a court of law.

Now, standing toe-to-toe with the most unpleasant, loud and obnoxious member of that group, the oafish Mr. Jeffries, Dill Bigley found himself feeling a bit slighted by the fact he too had been called by the good doctor in the early morning hours.

The knowledge the good doctor's calling him personally was something quite out of the ordinary to start with. He felt the doctor's request he arrive at his office by 8:00 a.m. that morning left Dill with the impression it had to do with a matter of some importance. But now standing face to face with Bud, his least favorite member of the group, Dill Bigley found himself feeling a bit less important than he had up until that moment.

"Dr. Marksdale requested my presence early this morning as well."

"Well, how da ya like that, English? Maybe he thinks the two of us can get him outta a jam."

Bud's expression turned into a complete smile, something Dill could not remember ever having seen before.

Reflecting back to the early hours of that morning, Dill remembered he was in a deep sleep when the doctor's call came. Acknowledging to himself that even though he was quite groggy at the time, he too had sensed some urgency in the doctor's voice.

"His tone was a bit pensive when he rang me earlier."

"Wow, English, do you limeys ever stop being so stiff? Sounds like you gotta stick somewheres."

"I'll tell you where a stick should . . . ."

Dill's face was turning red as he started to continue, when to his surprise, Bud put his hand on his shoulder and said, "Ah ca' mon, I's just giving ya a hard time." Removing his hand from Dill's shoulder, Bud continued.

"Maybe the doc needs both of us."

Bud tilted his head slightly. The expression on his face gave Dill the impression Bud was trying to find words to express his thoughts. For Dill Bigley, that behavior was as odd as the whole morning had increasingly become.

"Don't know why, cuz he was so drunk, it was hard to figure out what he was talkin' 'bout."

Dill took a hard step back, his face beginning to pale.

"Intoxicated? You assume that Dr. Marksdale was intoxicated?"

The expression on Dill Bigley's face left no doubt he was sincerely surprised by Bud's comment.

"Hell yeah. More than a couple sheets to the wind."

"I beg your pardon?"

Dill's lack of understanding clearly amused Bud.

"Yeah, drunk as a skunk, I tell ya. You couldn't tell?"

"Certainly not. I thought, well, I thought he was tired — as tired as I was. It was the middle of the night you know."

The fact is — Dill was a little bit more than "groggy" when the good doctor's call had roused him from a deep sleep. That evening he and his date had watched a production of Richard Wagner's *Die Meistersinger von Nurnberg* playing on the local PBS station. It had long been a favorite of Dill's and, as he would argue, one of the most celebratory of operas.

There was no one for him with whom he could dispute this opinion, however, as his date had been the better portion of a bottle of his finest Port.

What a sad sack Dillard Bigley knew he had become. There was no possible way he would pursue who he most desired — no, not a gentleman of his character — certainly not — not ever. Even so, Dillard Bigley found himself longing to let his heart release what it had grown to feel over the past, long nine months.

The sad truth is that Dillard Bigley had to keep his heart's longing and desires imprisoned — those desires borne from within his true and unwavering love for the exquisite Mrs. Marlene Fins. He deeply felt the dread of never being able to express his love for her, or dare to think he may receive such a gift from her in return. The full scope and immensity of such emotions would remain reserved for the deeply envied and, in Dillard Bigley's mind, the forever blessed Mr. Fins.

"So, English, where'd ya go? Don't flake out on me now."

In that rare and unforeseen moment, Bud kept his thought, that Dill Bigley looked goofier than usual, quietly to himself.

The likelihood was nil, but the possibility did exist that nine months of rigorous therapy may have just begun to pay off.

"I beg your pardon? I was momentarily assessing the situation," Dill stated while straightening his posture.

"You see, Mrs. Fins ushered me out of the office only moments before your arrival."

"Why'd she do that? You try to get into her knickers there — English?"

Bud made his hips gyrate while he made a clicking sound with his tongue.

No matter which name he chose to go by — James Elliot Jeffries or the less attractive, thus, the more fitting name of *"Bud"* — Dill Bigley felt if there was anyone who could transcend from crude to base behavior in the blink of an eye, he was standing directly in front of him.

"Of course not." Dill frowned. "She felt my early arrival was untoward."

Looking directly at Bud, Dill wondered but felt relatively sure of whatever he may say to Bud, it would have little, if any, effect on him.

"However, nothing I would do could be construed as untoward as your last comment was."

"Ah, don't get a twig up your *blank*. I doubt you'd know what to do if you did get into her knickers anyways!"

"You *must* keep your voices down!" Mrs. Fins' face was taught, her eyes were squinting; and, what would have been her normally well-kempt appearance and controlled demeanor, now — to Dill and Bud — was noticeably disheveled.

Although both men were startled by Mrs. Fins' sudden appearance, only Dill's face blushed. He cringed at the thought of how long she may have been standing in the open doorway.

After both men made hurried glances at each other, they returned their gaze towards Mrs. Fins, as if waiting for her direction to their next move.

"I thought you understood, Mr. Bigley, this is *not* a good time to see the doctor. Why are you still here?"

Before Dill could answer her, she turned her attention — anger clearly growing in her voice — towards Bud's direction.

"And what on earth, Mr. Jeffries, are *you* doing here?"

"Well, I was — I was — gonna — gonna —"

It became apparent to Dill that Bud, too, became tongue-tied when reproached by Mrs. Fins.

"You were going to *what*, Mr. Jeffries!"

Mrs. Fins' voice left no doubt to anyone paying attention (something both Dill and Bud were doing without question), that she was in no mood to be trifled with.

Bud stammered some but successfully managed to get a few words out.

"I was only gonna see if the doc was here."

Mrs. Fins turned sharply in Dill's direction.

"Why did you not inform Mr. Jeffries of Dr. Marskdale's absence, Mr. Bigley?"

"I was just about to, when you opened the door, and I would have but —"

Dill closed his mouth realizing his body language could not hide the fact his nervousness had returned.

"Stop your fidgeting, Mr. Bigley. Do you hear me? Stop it!"

At that exact moment, out of the corner of her eye, Mrs. Fins saw that someone was opening a door which led into another office further down the hall. With both of her hands, she took a firm hold of each of Dill's and Bud's arms pulling them into Dr. Marksdale's office. When all three were safely out of sight from anyone in the outer hall — with her petite right foot — Mrs. Fins gave the door a good hard kick causing it to slam shut.

"Now, the both of you must understand —"

Mrs. Fins caught her breath and tried to push a few hairs that had fallen loose, and now laid over her right eye, back behind her ear.

"The doctor is not in. He can't meet with either of you today. I was going to call everyone in the group to . . . ."

Mrs. Fins' comment was interrupted when the door leading to the doctor's private lounge and bathroom opened.

Just as suddenly as Stelle had made it a few feet into the main office, she saw Mrs. Fins standing with two men she did not recognize. It was then she stopped and stood still.

Dill and Bud were also caught off-guard by the surprise presence of this unfamiliar woman; and, at first, both took a slight step backwards, as Stelle entered the room.

Within seconds of Bud seeing the lovely and statuesque Stelle come into the room, he felt as though he was witnessing a vision. Without hesitation, he made his way around Mrs. Fins and headed towards Stelle. With his right arm stretched out, Bud's heavily (and likely faux) gem-encrusted and sparkly ring revealed itself.

Stelle was caught off-guard by the garish garb this stranger walking towards her wore. She was used to the finest things. Both she and her husband never wore anything less expensive than most people's monthly home mortgage payment. She managed to retain a proper demeanor, though, and kept her thoughts hidden behind her expensive face while all the time thinking this stranger's clothing could be only knock-offs from some sort of thrift store — a place Stelle may have heard of but certainly had never shopped in. Nevertheless, she allowed herself to think it was appropriate to shake his hand too. After all, she assessed, that was the customary practice in a civilized society, and Estelle Cummings Marksdale was — above all — civilized.

As their hands connected, Bud cocked his head to the side. With his left eyebrow arched and a nostril flared, he said in a deeper voice neither Mrs. Fins nor Dill Bigley had ever heard come out of him before — "Hello, I'm James Jeffries. And who, may I ask, are you?"

Mrs. Fins' and Dill's heads turned sharply towards each other. No words needed to be shared between them, as their facial expressions said it all.

"What did he just say? He is who? Bud never refers to himself by that name! What just happened?"

"Hello — it is a pleasure to meet you, Mr. Jeffries."

Before Stelle could continue and while still holding onto her hand, his facial expression never changing, Bud said, "No, the pleasure is all mine. And your name is?"

"I'm Dr. Marksdale."

Suddenly, there was a noticeable, odd sound coming from Bud's throat.

Mrs. Fins and Dill, turning to look at each other, once again seemed to realize at the same moment, the sound they had heard coming from Bud — was that of his involuntarily swallowing his large wad of gum.

Bud took a jerked step back, his face turning red, his voice barely audible — "Damn doc! *Wha ja do?*"

Bud's eyes were bulging, and as fast as his face had turned red, now, the color had begun to drain from it.

"What would make you do somethin' like *this*? *Damn, doc!*"

Obviously, puzzled by this odd man's comments, Stelle looked at Bud and then in the direction of Mrs. Fins and Dill — her eyes clearly indicating she was seeking some assistance from either of them, so she may better understand what was happening.

"I apologize for my confusion," Stelle began, "I'm not sure I understand what . . . ."

Mrs. Fins and Dill turned towards each other, their eyes searching the other's for any kind of clarification in relationship to the most current events.

This was a moment of connection Dillard Bigley had long dreamed of. His cherished Mrs. Fins was looking right at him, right into his eyes. Her eyes were searching his for a non-verbal confirmation they were both experiencing the same thoughts. To his unrequited joy, Dill was sure they were. Bud's having said, "damn," made both Dill and Mrs. Fins aware Mr. James Elliot Jeffries was heading ever so near to the edge of his rail.

Dill felt a warm sensation overtaking him — it was as if Mrs. Fins was inside of his body. It was this sensation which made his toes twitch. He felt her presence, as he had never felt it before — not even in those most secret places he had held court for her. Now he could feel her so close inside of him, he was sure she could hear his thoughts. And so, when Dill thought Bud was nothing more than a greasy slime-ball dolt and was even stupider than Dill had ever believed he could be, in his mind, he graciously apologized to Mrs. Fins for her having to hear such thoughts.

Having reached the same conclusion, Mrs. Fins and Dill knew what Bud had initially thought when the doctor's wife introduced herself as Dr. Marksdale. Mrs. Fins looked at Mrs. Marksdale's and Bud's confused faces, and knew she must curtail the situation and get everyone to understand what had been so terribly misunderstood.

"Oh dear, Mrs. Marksdale. There has been an enormous misunderstanding."

Standing firmly in place, Dill realized he, too, had been set off balance by the events which had just unfolded and had momentarily felt as out of the loop as it appeared everyone else in the room was. That was until he and Mrs. Fins had shared a mental intimacy — an intimacy Dill thought may have possibly come close to that of a physical intimacy — possibly. Dill felt assured she would handle the situation quite adequately from that point forward, even though he would love to have called Bud out for the idiot he was.

Mrs. Fins kept her voice calm and controlled as it cut through the heavy atmosphere in the room.

"No, Mr. Jeffries, you are under the wrong impression. This is the *other* Dr. Marksdale — Dr. Marksdale's wife."

"Oh man — wow — you really had me going!"

Bud did not want to acknowledge how he had taken such a leap in his thought process.

"Yeah — sorry, really sorry. I thought the doc had gone, and . . . well, you know, changed some things around."

By now, Bud's face had returned to its normal color.

"Whew! Gotta say it." Bud, looking somewhat shyly at the doctor's wife — his eyes then diverting their direction to the safety of the window — "Gotta admit it, I thought he made a much better looking woman than a man!"

Dill shook his head while gritting his teeth and said to himself under his breath, "Good God, this man is an idiot!"

At that, Bud turned and walked to the nearest chair, which he promptly sat down on. A loud belch followed.

By all appearances, Mr. Jeffries' gum had begun to settle in.

CHAPTER FIVE

Whatever Stelle came into the waiting room for, she thought better of it after having met Mr. James Jeffries. Politely excusing herself, she returned to the private lounge. She was confident her leaving Mrs. Fins to handle the situation, whatever it may be, would be best. Her interest was to get to the bottom of what was going on with her husband — both in the present and in the prior several months. Her determination to reach a resolution to what was going on in his life to make him display such erratic and unusual behavior was her top priority.

Once seated, Bud began to play the recent events over in his head. He realized he had, without provocation and with only his boyish wishful thinking, presumed he was about to embark on an adventure of some adult nature with the lovely woman he saw enter the doctor's waiting room. Indeed, he was instantly smitten with her, but those thoughts had left as suddenly as they had arrived. His change of heart had nothing to do with the fact the woman turned out to be the doctor's wife, either. No, that was not the reason — not even near it.

Bud's change of heart came about because of his misguided conclusion, the good doctor had made himself up to look like a woman, or worse — had transitioned from a man into a woman. The most unnerving aspect of the entire fiasco to him was he had found himself immediately attracted to her — him — *whomever!* To say the least, this was quite unsettling. While deep in thought, Bud concluded it could not get worse — that is, until he reached into his shirt pocket. It was at that point, he realized it could get worse, much worse, when Bud found the pocket offered only one, lone, empty gum wrapper. He slumped back into the chair and let out a groan.

If anyone were paying attention, they would have thought he was suffering from some unpleasant intestinal aberration.

Simultaneously, and still in the dark as to knowing the full extent of Dr. Marksdale's reasoning for contacting him in the first place, Dill found himself in quite a quandary as well.

According to what Bud had said, the doctor seemed to be under some duress as well as having been under the influence when he called Bud in the middle of the night. This was a fact Dill found he could not collaborate; as he, himself, had been in a somewhat similar zone, when he received his call from the good doctor.

This was all so disconcerting for Dillard Bigley. These were the thoughts he entertained between hidden glances at Mrs. Fins; whereas, he could see the frustration on her face, as she appeared to struggle with getting a few remaining errant hairs back into place. He was keenly aware of the possibility if — when she returned her attention back to Bud and himself — she should insist they both leave. He felt it was imperative he formulate his words carefully. Somehow, he knew he had to get across to Mrs. Fins the doctor's need to see both himself and Bud per the good doctor's request.

With growing trepidation, Dill looked at Bud hoping to see a glimmer or indication he may be able to assist him when explaining to Mrs. Fins their shared need to be there. To his dismay when he looked at Bud, his hope was squelched. The empty eyes and blank expression on Bud's face left Dill with the certainty he had popped one too many bubbles. With all of his capacity for rationale, Dillard Bigley knew he was on his own. Bracing himself for whatever unpleasant response he anticipated would come from Mrs. Fins, he approached her, his knees shaking slightly.

"Excuse me, Mrs. Fins. I need to speak with you regarding —" Dill stopped speaking the moment Mrs. Fins looked in his direction. Appearing to have returned all of her loose hairs back to their proper place, she continued to fiddle with her hair albeit with just a few strands between her fingers.

"Regarding? Regarding what, Mr. Bigley."

"The purpose of my presence, Mrs. Fins — yes, regarding the purpose of my presence here this morning —"

Finally, free of hair, Mrs. Fins' hands formed the praying position, her fingertips touching underneath the tip of her chin, her lips somewhat pursed —

"Your presence, Mr. Bigley? Yes, I would be interested in knowing the purpose of your presence as you have stated." Tilting her head slightly to the side, the morning light accentuating her lovely profile, Dill watched as she lowered her hands from under her chin and then crossed her arms across her body.

"Well? Mr. Bigley?"

"You see, it was at the good doctor's request that I —" Dill glanced in Bud's direction, and saw he did not seem to be aware of the conversation he and Mrs. Fins were having. Knowing Bud may be able to shine more light on the situation than he could, due to his memory being a little foggy, Dill could not help but appreciate Bud in a somewhat catatonic state. Even so, he felt he should add, "Actually, it was the good doctor's request that both Mr. Jefferies and I come to the office early this morning to meet with him."

"I see." Mrs. Fins moved closer to Dill — a movement which made his heart skip a beat. "If you don't mind, Mr. Bigley, when did Dr. Marksdale make this request?"

Dill turned his face in Bud's direction, where he found Bud sitting perfectly still staring out the window, his face blanketed with an expression resembling someone in a state of comatose.

"To my best recollection, Mrs. Fins, the doctor's call came somewhere around three- or three-thirty this morning."

"Really?"

Dill found Mrs. Fins' tone to sound a bit skeptical, and still he was not as tongue-tied as he had found himself to be earlier. He did not have the time to analyze every nuance of their conversation. He was just happy they were having one, just the two of them. And, even though Bud was physically in the same room, he was in no way a part of the moment he and Mrs. Fins were sharing.

"Yes, Mrs. Fins. The doctor's call came as a surprise to me — and for that matter — a surprise to Mr. Jeffries as well."

"I'm sure that it did, Mr. Bigley. My question is this —" Mrs. Fins' eyes stared into Dill's without so much as a blink. "What was Dr. Marksdale's reason for such a questionable request?" Mrs. Fins' face did not alter expression as she held her body controlled and steady — something Dill Bigley had admired about her from the first time he set his eyes on her all those months before. "And," she queried, "at such a peculiar time?"

This answer was going to be a little more difficult to conjure up, as Dill had no clue as to what the doctor's reasoning was to call him in the first place.

Secretly, Dill wanted to keep this conversation going for as long as possible. Talking directly to Mrs. Fins and having her talk directly back to him left him with the sensation they were the only two people in the room — the only two people on the planet. Truth be known, in Dill's mind only one of them was on the planet, and it was not Dill — he was floating on an invisible cloud.

"Not wanting to sound an alarm, it was Mr. Jeffries who brought something of importance to my attention." Looking in Bud's direction once again and seeing there had been no change in his demeanor, Dill proceeded. "The doctor's sense of urgency in regards to meeting with us remains the cause for my insistence to wait for him."

Her overall protective nature towards Dr. Marksdale was at the foreground of most of her actions and upon hearing this, Mrs. Fins' face softened briefly. She entertained the notion Mr. Bigley did appear to be sincere in his commentary. And so, while being mindful of those rare occasions wherein she found herself intervening when he and Mr. Jeffries had engaged in one kind or another of a physical altercation, she found his concern for the doctor appeared to be credible. Most of the time (she quietly acknowledged), she viewed Mr. Dillard Bigley to be, in general, a gentleman.

"Urgency? There was a sense of urgency in his voice? And you have no idea as to what this 'urgency' was in regards to?"

"None whatsoever — I presumed his reasoning had to be extraordinary. My continued presence, now, is to find out that reason."

"Extraordinary."

For a split second in his dream-like mindset, Dill hoped Mrs. Fins was referring to him with her one-word comment. Thinking better of it, he again chose his words carefully.

"Yes, indeed, extraordinary. The reasoning for him to call both Mr. Jeffries and myself could be nothing less."

Dill's comment brought a soft smile to Mrs. Fins' lips which, in turn, sent a chill over Dill Bigley's entire body.

"He gave no reason for wanting you both to meet him, and he sounded as if it was of a serious nature?" Although Mrs. Fins was speaking out loud, it was more as if she was thinking out loud. "This is all quite unusual and on so many levels."

Suddenly, a loud crashing sound came from within the private lounge causing both Mrs. Fins and Dill to jump. The extremely loud sound resembled breaking glass and startled Bud so much, he jumped out of his chair and quickly made his way towards where the others stood. A few silent seconds passed before the door to the lounge flew open.

Simultaneously, as if deliberately orchestrated, the door to Dr. Marksdale's main office opened, too, and in walked Ally and Percy.

Dill's, Mrs. Fins' and Bud's heads turned in unison towards the door leading into the private lounge and, then again, in unison towards the main office door. Percy and Ally turned to look at each other and then back at everyone else in the room. It looked as if Ally was going to say, "hello," when Stelle came running out of the private lounge.

Mrs. Fins' loud gasp was followed by her involuntarily cupping her hand over her mouth. Bud's face reflected raw shock, and Dill took a few, sudden steps backwards while grabbing Mrs. Fins' arms and pulling her closer to him. He moved her to his side first, then he quickly stepped out in front of her.

Stelle's eyes were red, indicating she had been crying, and she headed towards the main door almost in a run.

Trying to get her bearings, Ally also gasped when she saw Stelle coming towards her with what looked like fresh blood on the knuckles of her right hand and splatters of what appeared to be blood on her blouse and cheek. Stelle ran past Ally and Percy and continued through the office door, disappearing down the hall.

Only seconds passed before everyone's attention turned to the open doorway to the lounge, where Dr. Marksdale was slumping against the door frame — his hair disheveled and still damp from his shower. His clean change of clothes hung on his body, as if they were made for a man two sizes larger; and, there was a noticeable trickle of blood running down the length of his face.

"Stelle! Stelle!" He cried out.

"Stelle come back!"

Mrs. Fins was out from in back of Dill and at Dr. Marksdale's side so fast, Dill did not know he had lost his protective grip on her arm.

Bud kept looking back and forth at the doctor and then the main door to the office, while Ally and Percy searched each other's faces for any kind of explanation the other may offer.

"Oh my, Dr. Marskdale. Let me help you back into the lounge. Mr. Bigley, would you please help me?"

"Would I?" Dill thought to himself. "Yes, I will help you do anything, anytime, anywhere."

Looking up at Dill while bracing herself between the door jam and the doctor's side — "Now, Mr. Bigley — Now, would be a good time!"

In the way only an Englishman can say it, Dill snapped back into reality and responded, "Yes — quite." Then he hurriedly made his way to her aid and maneuvered himself under the doctor's other arm. Between the two of them, they got Dr. Marksdale in a standing up position again.

Considerably louder than he had expected to sound, Bud asked, "Are you gonna be okay doc?"

As Dill Bigley and Mrs. Fins helped Dr. Marksdale back into the lounge, over his left shoulder, the doctor replied to Bud, "Yes, I will be fine."

"Are you sure?" While waiting for the doctor's response, Bud kept looking back over his shoulder towards the office's main door.

"I'll be okay. Thank you, Bud."

At that, Bud made his way past both Ally and Percy who, by this time, looked like two deer in headlights. Bud proceeded to run down the hall, until he too was out of sight. All the while, he was thinking Stelle could not have gone too far — there still may be time to catch up to her.

"Please sit down here, Dr. Marksdale." Mrs. Fins and Dill guided the good doctor to the closest chair in the lounge. They then both looked quickly at the room where there was shattered glass scattered around the floor which led into the vanity area. They looked at each other and then back at the doctor.

"Is there anything I can get for you, doctor?" Dill politely asked.

"I'm going to get a clean washcloth for your face, Dr. Marksdale." Mrs. Fins looked at Dill indicating she needed him to stay with the doctor while she was gone. Dill nodded in the affirmative towards Mrs. Fins and then said to the doctor, "Let me take a look at that nasty cut."

Mrs. Fins turned back around and gave Dill a look which let him know that was not an appropriate thing to say, and she interjected, "It doesn't look that bad doctor, head wounds often look worse than they are."

Her eyes expressed a gentle calm when looking at the doctor, and with a quick flash, those same eyes clearly indicated to Dill he had better follow her lead or not say anything at all.

"Isn't she the most beautiful creature?" Dill silently questioned. "Such a wonderful caretaker and a master at control."

Dill could not help but think this day, as strange as it had started and continued to be, was ever so much better with Mrs. Fins at the helm.

"But wait," he thought, "She must be extremely careful walking around and through all the broken glass." Upon closer observation, both Dill and Mrs. Fins could see the broken glass turned out to be shards of what was once one of the vanity wall mirrors.

"Mrs. Fins, please watch where you step. May I be of assistance?"

"No, Mr. Bigley, you've been quite helpful. I can handle this." Mrs. Fins made her way to one of the drawers in the armoire, her shoes making crunching sounds as she traversed the broken mirror pieces.

"I think you could be of better service elsewhere." Words really could cut like a knife, Dill concluded.

"In fact, if you wouldn't mind, it would be very helpful if you would find out why Ms. Perciple and Ms. Kirby are here."

Mrs. Fins was depending on Dill to help her with something else, and that evoked an emotion Dill found hard to put words to. At the same time, he could not help but feel the weight of the let down from her asking him to leave the room. Still, she was asking him for his help — something he could only have dreamed of a day ago.

"Yes," Dill thought to himself. "This day continues to surprise in strange and wonderful ways."

With puzzled looks on their faces, Percy and Ally were standing in the same place he had seen them last, when Dill re-entered the main office.

"Hello Ally." Dill nodded his head at her, and then looking at Percy, he began with, "This may not be the best time for —"

"What the hell is goin' on?" Percy's stance momentarily took Dill by surprise. He knew what these women had already seen was more than enough to create apprehension. In order to quash any investigation either woman may be ready to visit upon him and to abide by Mrs. Fins' request, he needed to convince both Percy and Ally to leave. This was a feat he must accomplish without creating more curiosity in regards to the situation they all found themselves in. What perplexed him most was how could he explain a situation he did not have an inkling to understanding himself? As these thoughts rushed through his head, he felt an uneasiness rising in his chest while he searched for words.

"I apologize ladies. There are some circumstances — some — a situation — I don't know if I can —"

"Cut the crap Dill! What the hell is going on? Who's the broad with blood splattered all over her?" After asking the question, Percy turned to look at Ally again who, by this time, looked to be in some kind of trance.

"Snap out of it, kid." Percy snapped her fingers directly in front of Ally's face making her mascara-laden eyelashes flutter up and down.

A one-word question, "What?" wistfully escaped from between Ally's perfectly shaped, lip-glossed covered lips.

Percy gave Ally a look of dismissiveness as she turned her attention back to Dill.

"What's happening? Should we call the cops? What's wrong with the doc? And why did Bud fly out a here?"

Dill's head turned so fast it looked like his neck would snap. His wide-opened eyes flashed from side to side, eagerly searching the room.

"Bud's not here? When did he leave? Where did he go?"

Percy let out a heavy sigh, "Look Dill, we're the ones with the questions." She turned to look at Ally again who, by this time, seemed to be back in control of her senses — at least, whatever senses Percy believed Ally was capable of possessing.

"What's been going on here? And don't make me ask again!"

"Wait a minute." Dill held his hand up to Percy. "How long ago did Bud leave?"

"He flew out a here just as you and Miss Prim were helping the doc."

"Where did he go? Why did you let him leave?" Dill did not attempt to control his shrill tone nor the urgency with which he asked the question.

"Do you think he went after Dr. Marskdale?" Now, in almost a full-blown panic, Dill's face was flushed as he ran to the main office door, whipping his head back and forth to see if he could see Bud anywhere in the hallway. When he did not see him, he ran back to the door leading into the room where the doctor met with his patients, his eyes frantically searching for any sign of Bud.

"I don't understand. Of course, he didn't go after Dr. Marksdale! What's wrong with you?" Percy's tone was stern and direct. "Only two minutes ago, you took the doc into that room." Percy thrust her right arm straight out and pointed at the private lounge door.

Then, her voice filled with growing agitation and raised to an unusual pitch — "What the hell is the matter with you? Bud went that way!" Percy turned in the opposite direction and pointed at the main office door.

"What is wrong with everybody today?" Percy slapped the palm of her hand against her forehead. "You're all acting like *crazy people!*"

Even in the state of panic Dill found himself in, he had to acknowledge the irony in Percy's well-founded observation.

"Percy, I must go after him. And I need to ask you both to leave and await a call from Mrs. Fins." Dill started back towards the main office door.

Percy held her hand straight out in front of her and belted out, "Hold it — right there! Where the hell do you think you're going?"

"I have to get to Mr. Jeffries — I mean, Bud."

"Not before you tell me what is going on." Percy moved her body between the door and Dill.

"You don't understand, Percy. I have to get to him right away."

Percy was aware that over the nine months the group had been meeting, all of the members had become much better acquainted. She would venture so far as to say the members had become intimate in their knowledge of the others' personalities. This would include the many twists and turns each individual had winding through the recesses of their disturbed and complicated minds. Even taking into account Dill and Bud had begun to behave in an almost civil manner towards each other over the ninth-month period, she found this — this urgency Dill was expressing to find Bud — to be quite out of character on any level.

"He went after the bloody broad, didn't he? Is that where Bud went? Did he go after her? Do you think he did?" Red blotches began to appear on Percy's face and started to make their way down her neck. "Well do ya think he did? Tell me! Do ya?"

"I think he may have. Now please move aside so I may pass." Dill looked at Percy who stood firmly in place.

"I'm goin' after him. Being a truck driver, I've been 'round my share of roughnecks." Looking sternly at Dill, she added, "Bud's not as tough as he acts. And the doc's crazy patient looks dangerous." Percy finished with, "I can handle myself."

Dill found Percy's comment interesting and somewhat revealing, if he was interpreting her motives correctly. He did not have the time nor the interest to indulge such thoughts at that point. He could have easily corrected Percy by letting her know the "bloody broad" was not the doctor's patient; instead, she was the doctor's wife. But that, too, was not a priority for him at that juncture.

His thoughts were now convoluted with needing to stay where he was, and with knowing he needed Bud to be his back-up (as to why he needed to remain at the doctor's office in the first place). And now, he had no idea where the gum-chomping idiot had gone!

After all the events which had transpired in the preceding few minutes, Dill Bigley secretly held hope Mrs. Fins may need him more than the doctor did. If that should turn out to be the case, Bud would be there to assist the doctor for whatever his needs were for both men to meet him so early that morning — that is, if he could find the bubble-popping fool.

"Is she nuts?"

"Pardon?" Dill queried.

"The bloody broad, I mean." Percy slowly started to move out of the doorway.

"I don't think so. No, she's not nuts. She's Dr. Marksdale — Dr. Marksdale — *Dr. Marksdale's wife.*"

Keeping the thought to herself Dill was beginning to develop a stutter, Percy proceeded.

"I'm going to find Bud. You should probably stay here in case Miss Prim needs you again."

Dill did not hear the name slight — Percy referred to Mrs. Fins as "Miss Prim." He only heard, "in case she needs you again." Kinder words, he mused, were never uttered.

And so, the decision was made. Dill would stay and wait with Mrs. Fins — just in case.

"Please send Bud back here when you find him." Dill saw Percy had left the doctor's office and was out of ears' reach, before he could finish his request. And so, his last words, "We still have to . . ." trailed off unobserved.

"I'm comin' with ya." Ally hurried to catch up with Percy who, by now, was already halfway down the long hallway.

"Hey, Percy, wait up." Ally was wearing what had become her trademark high heels. On this day, they were not metallic blue, they were bright orange with green stripes. When she left the carpeted hallway and onto the tile floor, they made a clickity clack sound.

"If you're coming with me, you better hurry up!" Percy did not slow down; in fact, she picked up her pace, practically flying down the hallway. Once at the elevator, she started to pound the "Down" button. She believed the harder and more frequently she pounded, the faster the elevator would arrive.

While the two women waited for the elevator doors to open, Ally stated simply, "It's Fins."

Percy turned to look at her and asked, "What?"

Just as the elevator doors opened, Ally added, "It's Fins — Mrs. Fins — not Miss Prim. Just thought you should know."

Together, the women entered the elevator, whereupon Percy turned to look at Ally who, by now, was looking for something in her green sequined purse. Turning her head so she could see the elevator buttons, Percy pushed the button which said "Lobby." While she waited for the elevator to descend, Percy looked first at the elevator's ceiling, then again at Ally. Subsequently, she shook her head, rolled her eyes and released another heavy sigh.

*****

Stelle struggled to find her car keys inside her (usually) orderly purse. Now, to her dismay, all of its inhabitants were in a state of disarray. In addition, her eyes were blurred by the tears which had welled up in them compounding her situation which did not help — nor did those same tears aid in discerning who the tall man was who was quickly running towards her.

Bud was breathing so heavily from trying to catch up to Stelle that when he reached her side, the only sounds he could manage were of a guttural nature. The words he had hoped to ask her — what he may do to be of assistance to her — instead came out as sounds resembling a pervert gasping for air.

Stelle, still rummaging for (and unsuccessful at finding) her car keys, located a small canister her hand easily recognized as her pepper spray. Through her tear-filled eyes, Stelle could barely make out the large form rapidly approaching her, but she was clearly aware it was a man — a man whose breathing was heavy and excessive. As Bud reached up to his face to push his hair off his sweaty forehead, his large shadow loomed over Stelle. And, as one can imagine — it was then — misfortune ensued.

To say the least, the screams and groans were loud and alarming. These sounds were something which would rarely, if ever, be heard in such a high-rent district too. And yet, there they were. So loud, they pierced the morning calm.

"Help me! What the — what the — what did you do? Are you crazy? Why did you do that? Oh, God, it hurts!"

Bud's hands were wiping his face, now revealing a scarlet complexion, as his nose began to run uncontrollably, and tears poured from his eyes.

"Oh, Mr. James, I'm so sorry. Why did you run towards me? You could have given me a heart attack! What's the matter with you?" Stelle started searching her purse again for a tissue to give to Bud.

Once they reached the street level, neither Percy nor Ally knew where to start looking for Bud. This proved to be a short-lived obstacle, as within seconds, loud screams and groans drew their attention towards the same direction where they saw Bud writhing in pain — his head in his hands. Percy started to run at full speed towards both Bud and Stelle, a few hundred feet away. Ally followed Percy, running as fast as she could while wearing six-inch heels — clickity-clack — clickity-clack.

Percy's face and body language resembled an angry bull beginning to stampede. When she got to him, Bud's body seemed to be convulsing.

"What did she do to you, Bud?" Percy grabbed hold of Bud's arm trying to get his erratic body movements under control.

"She sprayed me with something!"

"It's pepper spray, Bud, I can smell it." Percy took in a deep breath and immediately began to cough. Ally was already sniffling and wiping her eyes, as was Stelle.

"I didn't know it was Mr. James. I assure you, I would never have sprayed him if I knew it was him."

"*Who?*" Percy shot an angry glance at Stelle but was more interested in wiping Bud's face off with her cloth jacket (which she had just hurriedly removed) than delving into any further conversation with the woman she had earlier referred to as the "bloody broad." After removing her jacket, Percy was now exposed to the crisp morning air — something she did not feel as her adrenaline was pumping through her at an alarming speed.

"Mr. James," Stelle repeated, "I couldn't see very well, and he was running at me so fast, I just thought it was a strange man."

"Ally, get in my purse and get my bottled water out of it. Hurry!" Percy's voice was commanding.

Ally looked around to find it a few feet away from where Percy had dropped it to take off her jacket. She quickly retrieved the bottle of water and asked, "What now, what do you want me to do with it?"

Too exasperated to deal with long explanations, Percy screamed at Ally. "Just throw it on his face!"

The bottle (which was fortunately made of thin plastic) bounced off the side of Bud's head and hit the sidewalk, breaking open.

"Jesus! Why'd ya do that?" Bud's voice sounded like a cry from a wounded animal. Not only did his face and lungs feel like they were on fire, but now there was a bump on the side of his head which was swelling and beginning to throb.

"Not the bottle, you imbecile! The water!" Percy was clearly livid as she ran to retrieve the bottle which was now rolling away. The contents were rapidly spilling out of the cracks the collision with the side of Bud's head had created. Ally moved herself to a safe distance away from them, while Percy began to wipe what water was left in the broken bottle over Bud's eyes and face.

"I have some water in my car too, if I can find my damn keys!" Stelle started pouring the contents of her purse out on the hood of her car. She spread the pile around and grabbed her keys.

"Here we go! I think there were three bottles in there, actually."

A few more agonizing minutes passed, while both Stelle and Percy poured and wiped the water over Bud's face, as everyone continued to cough and sneeze — but none more than Bud himself.

"Mr. James, please forgive me, but you really shouldn't have approached me the way you did."

"Jeffries."

"Pardon?"

"My name is James Jeffries. Not Mr. James."

"It's what?" Stelle inquired once more.

"Mr. Jeffries, James Jeffries," Bud replied while continuing to clear his increasingly sore and raw throat.

"Oh, I apologize — Mr. Jeffries. I was under the wrong impression."

Remembering this was the strange woman who ran out of Dr. Marksdale's office and forgetting completely what Dill Bigley had told her prior to her leaving the doctor's office herself, Percy asked, *"Who the hell are you?"* Her angry glare was intimidating.

"I'm Dr. Marksdale — oh wait, it's just easier — I'm Mrs. Marksdale — Dr. Marksdale's wife."

Percy clenched her jaw. It was the only way she could keep her mouth shut. "Wow," she thought, "And I thought we were about as nutty as the doc had to deal with."

"It's really, Bud." Ally's voice broke into Percy's thoughts.

Everyone turned to look at Ally who was still standing a safe distance away from Percy.

For the first time, Stelle got a good look at Ally in all of her bright and unique attire. She could not help but wonder why such a pretty young woman would dress in such a way.

Ally, on the other hand, was thinking to herself, "And everyone thinks I'm the looney one. At least, I know everyone's *real name*."

Stelle and Percy helped Bud sit down on the sidewalk. Fortunately, her car was parked parallel to the sidewalk allowing all of them to lean against it — and not a moment too soon. Bud was very close to collapsing from fifteen minutes or more of uncontrollable coughing. His face, neck, ears and what was once the whites of his eyes were now bright red and his eyelids were still swelling.

From a safe distance, Ally continued to observe the other two women attend to Bud. She thought, between the swollen eyes and the knot on the side of his head (combined with the redness of any flesh from his neck up), Bud was beginning to resemble a big red, scary balloon. And when she finally felt safe enough, she meekly asked, "Is he going to be okay?"

"Yeah, he is! And it's no thanks to you, cotton brains!" Percy snapped.

"It's really all my fault." Stelle sat down next to Bud and let out a long sigh.

"If I could only have seen who was running up to me, but I was crying and my tears —" Stelle took in a deep breath, as tears began to well up in her eyes again.

"I guess anyone could have made that mistake." Bud's voice was shaky and uneven as he tried to make out Stelle's face through his swollen and burning eyes.

"Really Bud? Really?" Percy asked as she, too, sat down on the other side of Bud on the sidewalk.

"You really think it's okay to shoot pepper spray directly into the face of someone that is trying to help you?" Percy was incredulous.

"Help me? Why would you think I needed help?" Stelle turned to look at Bud but still could not make him out clearly. Her eyes were also burning some from the residual pepper spray which got into them. Though briefly, she thought, it seemed her own tears were helping to relieve some of that burning.

"You were crying and running out of the doc's office —" Bud started, when Percy interrupted him.

"First, you've got blood splatters all over you, and you're crying and running past all of us and out of the office!" Percy swiped her hand across the front of her body.

"Anyone who saw that would a thought ya needed help!" Shaking her head again, Percy pulled her knees up to her chest to rest her elbows on them.

"And then we got 'wild-arm Patty' over there," Percy pointed an aggressive finger in Ally's direction; at which point, Ally took a small step back and turned her head, as if something happening further down the street had caught her attention.

"The way I see it, you're lucky you got out of this alive, Bud." Percy did not attempt to hide her irritation. "It's a good thing I didn't ask ol' scrambled brains over there to get me a knife!"

"What a dumb thing to say," Ally thought quietly to herself. "You couldn't clean Bud's eyes with a knife!" In Ally's mind, Percy's most recent comment bordered on stupidity, and it was then, Ally rolled *her* eyes.

A few seconds passed before Percy with her eyes squinted looked in Ally's direction, where she could see that Ally was acting as if there was something of great importance she was thinking about. Percy believed — she knew better.

In Percy's opinion, the only thing Ally could have in her mind would be a head full of rainbows — similar to her hair. The only addition would be a few more colors. Actually, Ally *was* thinking of something of great importance — at least it was of great importance to her.

Dr. Marksdale had called both Ally and Percy in the middle of the night, just as he had called Dill and Bud. Neither of the women knew anything more regarding the reason the doctor requested a meeting with them than the two men knew. They just knew their showing up was of some importance to Dr. Marksdale, and as in the case of Dill and Bud, they made changes to their regular daily schedules to accommodate that meeting.

Bud worked alongside his brothers and his one sister in Bud's family's bakery and Italian Eatery. With very little more than a few recipes and a lot of hard work, their parents had started the business over fifty years earlier. Although all the kids worked hand-in-hand in operating the business now, they all worked under the auspicious guidance of Bud's mother, Camilla.

She was a first-generation American who immigrated from Italy with her parents as a young girl and earned her citizenship as a young woman.

Percy was an independent contractor who owned her own semi-truck and trailer. However, the main asset she possessed was her good business sense. This assisted her in building a reputation which drove business to her. She preferred to drive long hauls three to four days a week which allowed her to travel all over the country, something she loved to do.

Dill Bigley was a very successful financial advisor and operated his own private financial planning and accounting firm. He had made some very wise choices along the way which could afford him a lavish lifestyle. He preferred a more modest lifestyle and, more recently, had begun cutting down his clients' list. His goal was to keep somewhat busy but not tied down to a career, now that he was reaching retirement age.

Ally had only recently completed cosmetology school and was working at a trendy hair studio in Seattle. She became an instant celebrity and was quite sought after, as her artistic talents did not go unnoticed by the studio's clientele. Ranging from two to four nights a week, she was also a back-up singer for a struggling local grunge group which went by the name of "Shamed and Maimed."

While Dill Bigley remained in the doctor's high-rise office, three members of the group found themselves outside with the doctor's wife. Two of them, Bud and Percy, were sitting on the sidewalk sniffling and coughing along with the doctor's wife who was periodically wiping tears off her cheeks.

The third member outside was Ally who continued to remain several feet away from everyone else. She started to pace slowly back and forth in front of the others — her heels clickety-clacking — all the while, appearing to be deep in thought.

The only other member of the group not present or accounted for was Emma Griffin. Emma had retired early from her job as a high-school history teacher, and she was the one member of the group all the others had, in one way or another, trusted to be the most stable of the five of them.

The rest of the group found themselves comforted when leaving a lot of the final decision-making of any number of issues to her. They had, in a sense, turned the leadership of their group over to her, particularly when a situation seemed to be getting out of control and going haywire. Now Emma was the only member of their group not in attendance to what proved to be an increasingly odd morning.

"I guess we better go back in now," Bud offered as he started to get up — only to sit right back down when the planet started to noticeably spin.

"Yes, you probably should all go back in." Stelle sounded resigned.

"Wait, what about you? Are you going to be okay?" Bud sounded truly sincere.

"Yes, thank you, Mr. Jeffries. There is nothing anyone can do to help me."

When Ally heard Stelle's comment she stopped pacing and walked up to her. She proceeded to sit down in front of Stelle taking care not to poke herself with her spiked heels.

"What happened to you — to get blood all over yourself?" Ally asked.

For the first time, Stelle took notice of her blouse and the blood splatters on it. She sat quietly for a few moments before she spoke and, when she did, it was barely over a whisper.

"Oh God, I threw something at Phillip, but I missed."

"I'd hate to see what would happen if you had hit him!" Everyone except Stelle, looked at Percy. Her response to everyone looking at her was a sharp, *"What?"*

Stelle looked up at Ally and said, "I didn't want to hurt him. I was just so damn mad." Now Stelle's tears returned, and she buried her face into her hands as she began to sob.

"Great, now see what you've done!" Bud looked sharply at Percy.

"I didn't do nothing! Need I remind you, she's the one who has her husband's blood all over her!" Percy's sense of indignation had started to grow.

Ally's young and pretty face was all scrunched up when she looked at Percy, before she reached out and touched Stelle's leg.

"You want to talk about it? We're all pretty good listeners." Glancing at Percy again, she added, "That is, most of us are."

"Oh, I don't think so. I don't think anything can help, not now." Stelle wiped her tear-covered cheeks with the sleeve of her blouse transferring some of her eye makeup onto it. What remained of the eyeliner and mascara Stelle had put on earlier was now smears more than streaks down both of her cheeks.

"Ah com'on, it can't be that bad. You seem like a nice lady. It's probably something you two just gotta work out." Bud felt a warm feeling inside hearing Ally's natural sweetness come to the surface. Percy shoved down the urge to puke.

Stelle turned her face away from Ally and looked down the street. She let out a sigh and leaned back against her parked car.

"I don't understand. He said he was going to tell me everything — and then —" Stelle said softly, "We've always had a good marriage, and then something happened." Her head stayed turned away from Ally and the others.

Everyone remained quiet as she continued to speak. Stelle's voice was so soft she could easily have been talking to herself.

"He has never acted this way before. Now he says he can't tell me yet. I can't live like this." Tears started to roll down her cheeks again.

"I just wish I knew what's happening. I woke up one morning and my world had changed!"

While Stelle was sniffling, Ally interjected she knew the feeling Stelle described all too well and proceeded to recount the events of a break-up she had gone through with the drummer of the group she sang with.

Not attempting to hide her resentment, Ally listed more than a few reasons she and this unnamed drummer were no longer in rhythm. It was clear, too — when she snarled that her ex had stolen two pairs of her favorite shoes when, as she put it, "I kicked his butt to the curb" — she was still coming to terms, apparently, with their recent break-up.

"It's not like he was going to wear them or anything, at least, I don't think so. He stopped doing that a while back." Ally tilted her head as if thinking her ex may or may not have stolen her shoes for that purpose.

At that point, Percy dropped her head into her hands which were still resting on her knees. Even with her face in her hands, the animosity in her voice could be heard when she asked, "How many times do I have to be exposed to this story? Next thing, she'll start yapping about her damnable sparrows."

Stelle thought she heard Percy correctly but had to ask.

"Her sparrows?" Looking at Ally, Stelle repeated, "Sparrows? You have Sparrows? As in, pets?"

Ally's face lit up and she was just about to answer Stelle, when Bud interrupted — his voice still hoarse and shaky.

"She has been taking care of them — not like you would do, Percy." Bud turned to look at Percy with his bloodshot and watery eyes.

"They'd probably end up in your big yap. Their little feet dangling out between your choppers!"

"Really Bud? Why do you feel the need to hover over her like a big stupid bird!" Percy stretched her legs out on the sidewalk in front of her and crossed her arms over her chest.

"I just don't get it; you and I were getting along. Whenever miss bubble head comes around — "

"Don't call me a bubble head!" Bud's voice rose but cracked with every word.

"I didn't say you were a bubble head, Bud. I said — she —" Percy thrust out her arm in Ally's direction — her finger wickedly pointing at Ally. "I said *she* was a bubble head! *Jesus H. Christ!*"

Percy pulled up one leg to set her elbow on again and mumbled sarcastically, "One of the bubbles you like to blow must have plugged up the one lane oxygen uses to get into your brain."

Stelle was perplexed by the discourse she was witnessing which was taking place between the two individuals of whom she had only briefly met one — that being Bud. In an odd way, though, Stelle felt badly she had sprayed Bud directly in his face with pepper spray. She felt it had drawn the two of them a little closer together. At best, she felt closer to him than she did to either of the two women she found herself sitting on the sidewalk with. Sitting on the sidewalk with *anyone* would never have crossed Estelle Cummings Marksdale's mind as something she would ever find herself doing.

Under normal circumstances, Stelle would have thought the sidewalk was such a dirty place — a place where people walked making the bottoms of their shoes filthy and sometimes, it was a place (her mind regrettably led her to think) where people would spit. To find herself sitting there with these three strangers was as foreign to her as the makeup and blood-stained clothes she now wore.

Nothing seemed to fall within the realm of the ordinary for the doctor's wife at that juncture — which included her being the cause of her husband's bleeding and another man's writhing in extreme pain. And yet, there she was — the one person responsible for both the unfortunate aforementioned incidents. Now, the ever so proper and always impeccably dressed Estelle Cummings Marksdale found herself sitting on the dirty sidewalk — and only a few inches above the gutter.

"If you don't mind young lady, I would love to hear about these sparrows you have taken under your wing." Stelle realized what she said just as it came out of her mouth, and it was those words which brought a slight smile to her lips — something she had not done for a long time, a very long time.

With noticeable enthusiasm in her voice, Ally was quick to answer, "I found a nest that had fallen out of a tree, and inside it were three baby birds."

"Oh, I see. Were the parents around?" Stelle queried further.

"No, at least not that I could tell."

"That's odd. I would think that the parents would be in quite a panic."

"Sometimes, parents just don't care."

Ally's comment took Stelle by surprise and at the same time — being a psychiatrist — raised her therapist's antenna.

Playing the words over in her head, *"Sometimes parents just don't care,"* Stelle could not help herself from feeling it was such a sad thing to say. What stood out to her most, though, was the tone in which Ally said it. It was as flat — and as cold — as the sidewalk on which they all sat.

Ally continued to tell Stelle about how she learned from a veterinarian what to feed the baby birds and how best to care for them. It was clear to Stelle letting nature take its course was out of the question for Ally. She could see Ally was a natural caregiver, and Stelle listened intently to all Ally wanted to share with her. What was interesting to Stelle was she found herself listening more with pure interest in what Ally was telling her and observing less, as a psychiatrist. She could not help but think this pretty young woman had a unique way of expressing herself.

Looking down at her colorful long fingernails and twisting her already tightly twisted tri-colored hair, Ally skipped between one thought and another, surprisingly returning to the original subject. Stelle stopped seeing the colors and glitz and saw only a tender young woman, just past the age of a girl, who felt quite at ease expressing her deep fondness for the baby sparrows she was rearing.

When Ally explained to Stelle how one of the chicks had died and how that had made her feel, a few tears filled her two different colored eyes. The tears came and left quickly, and as soon as she wiped them away, she was back to telling Stelle about the progress the two surviving baby birds had shown — her eyes bright again.

Listening to Ally's story seemed to calm everyone down. Even Percy seemed to be more at ease. It was either that or she kept her seething quietly to herself.

As the time went by, Bud's eyes started to feel a little better, and his breathing became less painful and strained. His coughing had begun to subside, and by the time Ally had finished, Stelle's tears had all dried too.

"When do you plan to let them go? I mean, in nature they will be ready to leave the nest soon, I would think." Stelle continued cautiously, "You do want them to be free at some point, don't you?"

The sparkle in Ally's eyes quickly dimmed.

"She's never gonna let them go. She plans to keep 'em in their cage 'till they die." Percy sounded like she knew this to be a fact.

"I never said that — exactly," Ally responded. "I just want to be sure they'll be okay. You know they don't have their mother to teach them stuff."

"Yeah? Why do you act like that's what you are to them?" Percy asked with a matter-of-fact tone.

"Would you have left them to die, Percy?" Ally returned.

"No, I would a put the nest back up in the tree!"

Ally's surprised expression made it apparent that was the first time she had heard of, or considered such an idea.

"I — I — couldn't. Even the lowest branch was too high for me to reach."

"Hmmm," Stelle thought, "She almost sounds convincing."

"What difference does it make now, Percy? I've been taking care of them for weeks. I'm all they know."

"I thought you took their cage out every day to let them be outside. Did you stop doing that?" With his voice still quite shaky, Bud had re-entered the conversation.

"Doing that is probably good for 'em, I bet." He sounded thoughtful.

"You're probably right Bud. They seem to like to go outside —" Ally quickly glanced in Percy's direction before continuing. "They like being outside in their cage, it seems to make them happy."

"What would really make 'em happy is if they could fly. I'm not tryin' to be mean —" Percy's face looked almost kind, "Ally, I really think they would be happier flying than being held up in that cage."

Although she had only just been exposed to these three individuals, Stelle was beginning to see the dynamics of their relationships to one another.

Ally stood back up reaching her arms above her, stretching her back.

"I know that letting them go is the best thing to do. I just don't know when I should do that. How will I know they are ready?"

"Didn't the vet say they'd be ready shortly after fledging?" Percy persisted.

"Yeah, a little bit after, but being a fledging doesn't mean they are ready to fly." Ally was quick to put forth.

"Really?" Stelle's interest was piqued again. "I always thought that when a bird fledged, it meant it left the nest."

"No. I thought that too, until the vet told me that fledging only meant the chick had developed its flying feathers." Ally took a thoughtful breath before, "They don't leave the nest for another week or so, when they're ready."

"Well, there you go. I just learned something new." Stelle pulled her legs up to her chest and rested her arms on her knees and then her chin on her arms.

"Well this is all fine and grand, but those birds are way past the time to be set free." Impatience was returning to Percy's voice.

"This little PBS special has run its course. Now everyone looks like they will survive, I need to get back to the doctor. He asked me to meet him this morn —" Before Percy could finish, Stelle dropped her legs back down to the sidewalk while her arms shot out in front of her — her hands stretched wide open.

"What? He called you to meet him?" Stelle's voice cracked. "What in the hell could he have needed from you?"

"Hey, I don't know what you are implying but, yes, he did call me and it sounded pretty important." It was obvious Percy took offense to Stelle's words and the tone with which she had presented them.

"He called me too. I don't know why, but he said he wanted to meet with me this morning, early," Ally said just above a whisper.

Stelle turned sharply in Ally's direction and then back to where Bud was still recuperating next to her.

"Did he call you too?" Stelle's voice was beginning to quiver.

"Yeah — me and English. We both got calls in the middle of the night." Bud coughed again and wiped his nose on his sleeve.

"Who's English?" Stelle asked, but before Bud could answer, "Am I to assume he called all of you, giving no reason, only saying he wanted you all to come here this morning?"

Stelle's mind was spinning. She had only received a cryptic and frightening phone message from her husband. At the same time, it appeared he had personally invited these strangers to come see him — these strangers — all invited by the same husband who never managed to make his way home the night before!

Both Ally and Percy looked around nervously, while Bud leaned his head back against Stelle's car and let out a sigh.

"It would appear so." Percy's demeanor immediately took a more sheepish turn when she looked at Stelle. "He must ah called all of us."

"His name is Dillard Bigley, and none of us know why," Ally started.

"None of you know why his name is Dillard Bigley? *Who the hell is Dillard Bigley?*" Bud flinched at the pitch Stella's voice had reached, while her face suddenly took on the appearance; she had just swallowed something sour.

"English," Ally's voice was calm and soft. "Dillard Bigley's 'English.' And he's English, too."

Stelle's eyes filled with tears again, as she began to sob even harder than before.

Bud's head dropped down, while Percy, leaning her head all the way back — her face and the palms of her hands turned up to the morning sky — pleaded, "*What the hell do you want from me?*"

CHAPTER SIX

Observation is integral to the practice of psychiatry, and it would be fair to say both doctors, Dr. Marksdale and his wife, the other Dr. Marksdale who also addresses as Mrs. Marksdale — if they were to be rated — would rate above average in regards to their success at treating their patients. On that particular morning, however, they were both experiencing internal crises of their own. This simple fact left them to be more of the observed than the observers.

Dr. Marksdale, the husband, was being tended to by Mrs. Fins for a nasty cut just above his receding hairline — a wound initiated by his angry wife due to something he had said or, perhaps more to the point, due to something he had not said to her.

In conjunction, the other Dr. Marksdale, the wife, was sitting on a sidewalk being consoled by three of her husband's patients — one she had assaulted within that hour. And neither doctors' appearances bore their trademark — a fastidiousness they were both so keen to keep intact.

The husband was still sloppy drunk at nine o'clock in the morning. And she, the wife, sat on the sidewalk sobbing and looking like she had been up all night in some sort of street brawl. Neither bore a similarity to their usual respectable personas. It truly was a sad way to begin the day.

Dillard Bigley was getting anxious over the time it was taking Percy and Ally to return with Bud or for Bud to return on his own. He could hear the muffled voices of Mrs. Fins and Dr. Marksdale in the lounge. Becoming more anxious, he paced back and forth in the doctor's waiting room, as he wondered what they could be discussing for such a long period of time. Most of all, he hoped there would be some kind of assistance he may provide to Mrs. Fins, but the longer he waited, the more that hope diminished.

Always a gentleman first, the thought of leaning his ear against the lounge door, to hear what the conversation the doctor and Mrs. Fins were having was about, was too much of an impropriety for Dillard Bigley's comfort level.

Or was it?

Looking around the room which he found himself pacing alone in, Dill eased his way to the lounge door. While still keeping a safe distance between the door and himself, he strained only slightly before he could barely, but still, make out what Dr. Marksdale was saying.

"You said you had something similar happen to you?" Dr. Marksdale's voice was clearer than it had been earlier, but Dill could still detect a slight slur.

"Yes — only in that he was hiding the truth from me, and it created quite a rift between us." Dill had noticed early on Mrs. Fins spoke gently when she spoke to the doctor.

"I can understand that. He kept something very important from you."

"Yes, he did."

"If you don't mind my being so personal, Mrs. Fins, was it that which created the final wedge, you spoke of, between you?"

"There was so much more, doctor. I never really trusted him after that. And it would prove to be a wise decision on my part."

Dill leaned in closer to the door, being careful not to have his feet in front of it. He feared they or their shadow may be seen from the other side. He looked around the room to see if there was anything he could stand on which would support him while hiding his feet at the same time. He spotted Mrs. Fins' desk chair and quietly rolled it closer to the side of the door. It was not as stable as he would have preferred, but it did seem to accomplish what he needed it to.

Being sly was not Dillard Bigley's forte by any means, and so it was then he precariously balanced himself at an awkward angle on the chair waiting for Mrs. Fins to continue.

"Too many things happened between us to ever mend it. We were broken for a very long time."

"I'm sorry, Mrs. Fins, I didn't mean to stir up bad memories, I only —"

"It's alright, doctor. I've had many years to recover from the selfishness."

"Is that what you think it is when someone hides the truth? Selfishness?"

"I believe love can bear great weight, but even so, you must treat it with tender care. It is not easy to build it back to what it once was." Dill could hear Mrs. Fins clear her throat before she went on.

"We were very young and didn't know how to take care of what we shared." Mrs. Fins coughed lightly, and it sounded to Dill like she may have been crying. He wished he could be in the lounge with her to provide her the warm embrace he believed she needed.

"I didn't want to keep anything from Stelle. I was just so afraid of what she would do if she knew the truth." Dill could hear Dr. Marksdale's voice break when he said, "All I want is to keep our family together and be happy. Nothing else matters."

"Then tell her whatever this truth is, and do it soon. Do it before it is too late."

"I was going to do it this morning, but I — when I saw her, I knew I couldn't."

"Please forgive me doctor. You know I think the world of you, but —"

Dr. Marksdale interrupted, "You have no idea how bad this secret is Mrs. Fins, it will ruin us!"

"What do you think not telling her will do?"

"I can make something up, she never needs to know. I can't take the chance, I see that now."

Dill could not tell if the doctor had turned his head in another direction or if he had moved farther away from the door — only that he was harder to hear.

"God, I've made such a mess of things."

"Then don't add to it by being selfish too, please doctor . . . . She may surprise you, and then both of you can get past this."

After a few silent minutes, Dill heard Mrs. Fins softly begin again.

"Selfishness, doctor, was on both our parts. We were too young to pay attention to the details. Please don't make the same mistake."

"I still don't understand what you mean by 'selfishness.'"

"We keep truth from others to protect ourselves more than anything else. We do it from fear. Is that not a selfish act?"

"I see your point. But this — this, Mrs. Fins, it will change everything we are, everything we have. It will ruin our lives."

Dill could tell the doctor was indeed crying at that point.

"I've made so many bad decisions, but his one — God, this one — was the worst!"

"Your wife loves you, doctor. I think you should consider giving her the chance she deserves to decide for herself."

Dill, captivated by Mrs. Fins' gentle wisdom, tried quietly to shift his position as one of his legs was beginning to cramp.

"Whether or not she wants to stay after knowing whatever it is that you're hiding, should that not be her decision, and not yours?"

Another silent pause fell between the doctor and Mrs. Fins as well as between the door and Dill Bigley's ear.

The break in the silence came with the doctor asking Mrs. Fins how long ago it had been since she and whomever she was referring to had parted ways. Mrs. Fins' response was too hard for Dill to decipher. The doctor and Mrs. Fins seemed to have moved even further away from the door, so all they were saying no longer sounded like words, just muffled mumbling.

Dill waited patiently, listening carefully for anything which was being said, when suddenly he heard Mrs. Fins' voice sounding as if she was approaching the door.

"I don't need to know the details doctor, but was it — well was it — did it have —"

Mrs. Fins must have turned her head, as her voice sounded like it came from a little further away again.

"Did it have anything to do with Dr. Elan Glenn?"

"That bastard! That scourge. He is the bane of my existence! I wish I'd never met him!"

The anger the doctor expressed concerned Dill. He had heard the doctor get angry before, but he had never heard such deep animosity come from him — this was new to Dill and quite disconcerting.

Then again, the voices became more muffled and distant, as if both the doctor and Mrs. Fins had gone into another room entirely.

After a fair amount of time had passed — certainly longer than Dill was comfortable with and just about the time one of Dill's legs was beginning to cramp again and the other was going numb — he heard the doctor's voice.

"How long ago did this happen?"

"Oh doctor, so many years ago now. Let's see, twenty-five years ago, I believe."

"No!"

"Yes, doctor, twenty-five years going on twenty-six now."

"You mean that all these years we've worked together, you have not been married?"

"That is true, he hit me repeatedly about the head. He left me for dead and stole my car. After taking all the money in the bank, gratefully, I never saw him again."

Not absolutely sure of what he heard, but sure (he hoped) he had heard one thing correctly, Dill suddenly lost his footing and fell against the door. His head bounced once against the door itself, and while his body was in route to the floor, the bone above his right eye came harshly to terms with the hard-brass doorknob. His attempt to hide his involuntary and sudden moan from the sharp and relentless pain shooting through his head fell short of success. Mrs. Fins' office chair shot out from beneath his feet with such great force, it stopped only when it hit the wall across the room, where it spun several rotations before stopping completely.

"How dare that brutish slug. He's not even a man! My precious peach, Mrs. Fins . . . ." Dill thought to himself, as one last cruel assault was wielded upon his head when — with great force — his body slammed onto the hard floor.

And then it was dark.

*****

"Yes, that will work." Faint voices could be heard in the dark distance.

"Grab me some more ice too. Come on now. Come on, you must wake up."

A piercing pain started at the top of Dill's head and shot down to his toes.

"Should we call a doctor?" Now, a different voice had made its entrance onto the distant and dark stage.

"I am a doctor."

"I know, I meant to say — a real doctor — doctor."

"I am a real doctor for God's sake! Now lift his head so I can put this underneath it."

One of the distant voices sounded agitated.

There was a dim light entering the darkness. At first it fluttered slightly, and then it went out.

"Oh please, Mr. Bigley, please wake up." The voice was soft and urgent at the same time.

Dill's unconscious mind sensed a floating — almost flying sensation — and then excruciating pain surged through his entire body.

"Mr. Bigley, open your eyes." Mrs. Fins' voice was clear and getting closer, as Dill's eyelids involuntarily fluttered open.

The light was unbearable in those first few seconds, as it seemed to be penetrating straight through into Dill's brain. As for his body, the pain was no longer coming and going, it was prevalent and relentless.

"Oh my God — ohhhhh — bloody hell! What happened? I think I've broken all the bones in my body." Dill's voice was feeble and strained.

"I don't think so Dill, but you have taken a nasty fall and apparently hit your head in several places." Dr. Marksdale's voice broke through the agony which engulfed Dill. Then, the doctor turned off the flashlight he had been using to observe Dill's pupils, and when he let go of his eyelids, Dill's eyes rolled back into the safe darkness of his head.

Though Dill thought he could feel his body being lifted and set back down on something softer than the floor, it did not change the fact his pain was not subsiding. In fact, it was only settling into more specific areas of his head, chest, shoulders and legs.

"Whatever were you doing, Mr. Bigley, to take such a fall?" Even with Mrs. Fins' carrying herself with grace and elegant deportment, her face could not hide her deep concern as she looked down at Dill. When he looked up at her, whether induced by a possible concussion or not, he had no doubt — he was looking into the eyes of an angel.

"Mrs. Fins? Is that — is it really you?" That was the extent of Dill's utterance.

"Yes, Mr. Bigley. We heard such a ruckus and then — the most frightening groan and then —" Mrs. Fins gently moved the ice pack she had made just enough to cover another lump on Dill's cheek, just below his eye, before finishing.

"Nothing, no other sound at all — that's where we found you — sprawled out on the floor." Mrs. Fins pointed to the spot on the floor where she and the doctor had found him. Trying to show Dill the spot was to be of no avail, as his eyes never diverted away from her worried and beautiful face.

Dr. Marksdale was still taking Dill's pulse, while Mrs. Fins gently moved the ice pack once again. This time, though, it made Dill grimace.

"I'm sorry. Try to stay still, and let's keep this ice on. The swelling is quite pronounced over your right eye, in particular." Dill hoped it was not his imagination Mrs. Fins was being as gentle as she could be with him.

"Well now, Dill," Dr. Marksdale began in a tone Dill interpreted as somewhat fatherly — something Dill would normally find to be an interesting observation with his being a couple of decades older than the good doctor, but not so much now with the current condition he found himself in.

"It would appear that you were getting somewhat rowdy out there. What were you doing, mimicking your favorite soccer goalie?" The doctor chuckled as he gestured for Mrs. Fins to move from where she sat holding the ice pack on Dill's forehead. He wanted to take her place next to Dill on the chaise lounge in the doctor's private lounge where they had moved him to.

Until that moment, Dill had not noticed he had been moved a fair distance from the waiting room. His last memory was of his being in the waiting room pacing — yes pacing — pacing and waiting for Mrs. Fins to finish attending to the doctor's head wound.

Now, it was he who was in need of her help, and he lacked the memory of how he ended up in such a state.

"This day has certainly been filled with an unfair share of accidents." Mrs. Fins commented as she picked up where she left off: cleaning up what remained of the broken mirror glass from Stelle's and her husband's earlier encounter. "I would never have guessed this day would be as it is, that is for sure."

"Neither would I, Mrs. Fins. Thank you for all your help. You must think terribly of me now." The doctor's voice was apologetic.

"Oh, quite the contrary, doctor. I have a special place for both you and Dr. Marksdale. I only wish I could be of more help." The sound of broken glass hitting other broken glass being dropped into the wastebasket made Dill jump.

"Now, Dill. It's okay. You need to rest. You'll be fine. The best thing to do now is to lay still."

Dill had no intention of challenging the doctor's advice, even if he had wanted to. His energy had been completely sapped from his aching body.

The doctor got up and went to open a drawer in the lounge bathroom and withdrew a bottle, and from that, he poured out two pills. Returning to Dill's side, he bent down and handed both the pills and a glass of water to him.

"Here, Dill, take these and close your eyes. You will benefit from a short nap."

"Do I have a concussion? If I do, is it not unadvisable to sleep at all for some time?"

"Actually, Dill, it doesn't appear that you do have a concussion. But even if you did —" He took the glass back once Dill had finished drinking from it. "Which it appears you don't, your symptoms wouldn't suggest this method of treatment would be inappropriate."

Dill lay quietly while both the doctor and Mrs. Fins finished cleaning up the broken mirror glass. Then Mrs. Fins got a blanket out of the armoire and covered Dill. She could see his eyes were already closed: the right one by involuntary swelling; and the left eye, because he had fallen into a peaceful sleep. Due to that fact, he did not know Mrs. Fins had sat next to him again, where she remained for several minutes.

"Mrs. Fins," the doctor said barely above a whisper, "Here, please take this."

She turned her head and when she looked up, she saw the doctor handing her a fresh cup of hot tea. When she looked down into the cup, she saw it looked as though it was prepared just the way she would have done.

"How odd," she thought, "I would never have imagined the doctor would have noticed I added milk to my tea."

She got up from where she sat next to Dill and carried her tea into the waiting room, where the doctor was pouring himself a cup of freshly brewed coffee.

"Thank you, doctor. This tea is just the way I like it."

"Of course, Mrs. Fins, you are quite welcome." The doctor stirred some sugar into his coffee before continuing.

"My head has cleared a great deal from when you first came in this morning, and I feel the need to explain my actions."

Dr. Marksdale cleared his throat and headed into his office. Mrs. Fins followed closely behind.

"You need not explain anything to me doctor, but I am happy to lend an ear if you feel the need for one." Mrs. Fins spoke formally and sat stiffly on the couch across from the doctor's chair.

The doctor set his coffee cup down and sat in his luxurious Corinthian leather chair — this time, not thinking of how much it cost, but just grateful it was underneath him. He sat all the way back in it and looked up at the ceiling.

"Years ago, I made a decision — a decision that could ruin my life today. And though I've been paying for it —" The doctor looked like his senses were coming back to him, and with the serious inflection in his voice, Mrs. Fins found herself physically preparing herself for what she felt was about to come next.

"You see, Mrs. Fins, I committed a —" A long uncomfortable pause followed leaving them in total silence. Mrs. Fins was afraid the beating of her heart could be heard, as it pounded harder and harder keeping rhythm with the rate at which her anticipation grew.

"I couldn't tell Stelle, I just couldn't. That's when she threw the soap dish at me. A shard of the mirror glass got me." The doctor reached up to touch the bandage Mrs. Fins made for him, and when he touched it, the left side of his face flinched with pain.

"Do be careful, doctor. I know you didn't want stitches, though I do highly recommend at least a couple."

"Those butterfly strips should do the trick, Mrs. Fins; but, I must say, you are quite a competent nurse!"

The doctor got up from his chair, and with his coffee cup in hand, he walked to the massive window where he stood firmly in place — his back now facing Mrs. Fins. It was then Mrs. Fins moved from the couch to a chair, which she turned towards the window and the doctor's back.

"You see, Mrs. Fins, sometimes we do the wrong things thinking we're doing them for the right reasons. Do you understand?"

"I think I do, doctor"

"It's easy to justify our behavior under any number of circumstances, but then, there are laws too." The doctor took a few sips of his coffee before continuing.

"I'm not a stickler for laws, though I believe we need them in a civilized society, don't you, Mrs. Fins?"

"Yes, doctor, I do. They help to keep us from running amok."

The doctor turned momentarily to smile at Mrs. Fins whose face looked quite serious.

"Running amok, indeed, Mrs. Fins." Turning back to face the window, the doctor seemed strangely amused by her comment.

"I would have to say, I think I've done just that, Mrs. Fins — run amok, that is." Dr. Marksdale was solemn and quiet for a few, very long minutes.

He began again with, "I was a fair student when I was in college — fair enough, I'd say." The doctor looked back and forth across the city skyline. "Now Stelle — Stelle was remarkable. She worked very hard, harder than anyone else."

As he gazed out of the window, the expansive view of the skyline seemed to have a calming and relaxing effect on the doctor.

"You know, Mrs. Fins, I rarely do this — hardly ever, really. Just stop and look at the view."

"It is quite something, I would have to say, doctor. I enjoy it every time I enter this room."

"I've noticed, Mrs. Fins, you are always in a happy mood when I see you in the mornings. How do you do it?"

"Pardon, doctor?"

"How do you manage to be in such high spirits all the time?"

"I love my job and working with you, doctor. It is one of the most rewarding parts of my life."

Dr. Marksdale did not turn to look at her, but Mrs. Fins could see by his profile that he was smiling.

"Thank you, Mrs. Fins. I enjoy working with you as well. You're the most efficient receptionist I've ever had."

Knowing the doctor's age, Mrs. Fins could not help but think that that fact alone would have prohibited him from having too many receptionists before she came along. Taking into consideration, too, she had worked with him for the past nine years, and to the best of her knowledge, that was when he started his practice. The chance she had been his only receptionist did not overshadow nor did it dilute the strength of his compliment.

"Oh, Dr. Marksdale, you flatter me so." Mrs. Fins felt her face blush slightly.

"Doctor, if you don't mind my asking, how is it you feel you've run amok? That is a serious conclusion."

"I see you take the term 'running amok' for one of its darker, literal descriptions, Mrs. Fins."

The doctor using a deeper tone than usual added, "They proceeded forward in a murderous frenzy!" The doctor looked directly at Mrs. Fins when making the comment.

"Not quite as impactive or significant as that description, doctor, but yes, I did intend to lend the term a serious bent when I used it."

Mrs. Fins began to feel ill at ease. Speaking of a "murderous frenzy" had that kind of effect on her.

"Don't concern yourself, Mrs. Fins," the doctor sensed Mrs. Fins' growing discomfort. "I've done nothing like that, though, I have toyed with —" The doctor's eyes squinted slightly, "There have been those few occasions — more so — most recently when . . . ."

The doctor turned again to see Mrs. Fins' expression, revealing her concern, beginning to intensify.

"I apologize, Mrs. Fins, I see I have upset you. I've been such a fool as of late, the present being no exception." The doctor shook his head and hung it down before straightening back up and finishing his coffee in one final swig.

"No, doctor, you are not a fool. You have had so much to deal with — your patients, this particular group, deadlines to meet and the court."

"I'm so glad someone understands."

Mrs. Fins urged, "I am sure that Mrs. Marksdale will understand. You only need to muster the strength to tell her."

"I seriously doubt Stelle will ever understand any of it or ever be able to forgive me. I've ruined everything for us."

"Doctor, if you can't tell your wife, tell someone. Whatever this thing is, break its hold on you." Mrs. Fins' voice was soothing, and it made the doctor feel safe.

He wanted to get out from underneath the weight of this hidden truth and finally put words to the burden he carried. It had been a very long time he had held this inside, whatever his secret was.

The one truth which was not a secret was that the longer he kept this unspoken truth bottled up inside, the more it festered. That festering was getting closer to systematically bringing an end to the only life he knew and thus separating him from all the people he shared that life with.

Standing perfectly still, as if standing before a firing squad awaiting the final countdown, the doctor played his options over in his mind: What would happen once he revealed what he had been concealing for all of these years?

Like bullets once discharged from a gun's chambers, there would be no possible way of putting them back — the bullets, his words, all out and on a clear trajectory leading to his end.

The silence in the room was palpable. And then —

"Alright, Mrs. Fins, I will tell you all of it. I know it sounds childish, but would you please — not look at me?"

Her growing nervousness and apprehension began to cloud her thoughts. If she really wanted to be of help to the doctor, she would have to put those feelings aside. Whatever the doctor was about to tell her, Mrs. Fins felt it was better to overcome her fears and learn the truth. That would be far better than to have the doctor keep it to himself a moment longer. And with that thought, she committed herself to staying the course.

Early on in their professional relationship and subsequently as the years accumulated, the familiarity which grew between them left Mrs. Fins with a deep personal fondness for the doctor, and Mrs. Fins had long admired him. Moreover, she had developed a protective nature for the doctor and his family, much like the nurturing a mother would provide. She believed that whatever had been eating at the good doctor would surely destroy him, one way or another. At that moment, she knew she may be able to relieve him of, and possibly help him to alleviate, whatever ramifications may be borne from this burdensome truth yet to be revealed.

"Certainly, doctor, I will look away if that is what you would prefer." Mrs. Fins took one last sip of her lukewarm tea keeping her steady gaze down into her now empty tea cup.

"Years ago, I was involved in a rather, well, a rather unfortunate event. I don't speak of it often." The doctor cleared his throat.

"That's not entirely true. The fact is, I never speak of it." He took that moment of pause in his commentary to take in a deep, slow breath before continuing.

"My involvement in this event was limited, but I can't excuse my involvement in it — not any longer." The doctor stopped speaking entirely for what seemed to be, to Mrs. Fins, an extraordinary long period of time before he began again.

CHAPTER SEVEN

The words which came out of the doctor's mouth were easy enough for her to understand. It was the deeds those same words described which left Mrs. Fins feeling as if she were in a mental freefall. Presented with the difficult challenge of keeping herself from looking at the doctor, as she had agreed not to do, Mrs. Fins listened with a calm patience she was not even aware she had possessed.

Doing her best to keep pace with Dr. Marksdale as he briefly led her through his four-year college experience to acquire a bachelor's degree, Mrs. Fins found out the college degree was a prerequisite for him to be able to attend medical school. Dr. Marksdale enlightened Mrs. Fins further with the fact that, both he and Stelle had attended the same college and were both working towards their bachelor's degree in biology.

According to the doctor, Stelle came from a very wealthy family as did he. Both were able to get into college right after graduating from their respective private high schools. Once there, excellent grades were required of them, as the competition was, and is, keen to get into a medical school. In addition, the medical school both Stelle and the doctor wished to attend required them to take the Medical College Admission Test from the Association of American Medical Colleges. This was a feat that, the doctor made clear to Mrs. Fins, was not for the faint hearted.

The doctor prefaced the next bit of information with an emphasis on the weight of it. He indicated, before telling Mrs. Fins, the information would, at some point, have a meaningful consequence.

The bit of information he then imparted onto Mrs. Fins was simply that during his early college days, an old college pal, Dr. Elan Glenn, had introduced the good doctor to Stelle. Unbeknownst to the good doctor at the time, she and Elan Glenn had a brief relationship a year earlier. And, the good doctor had no idea at the time of his meeting her, she would turn out to be his future wife.

As the good doctor laid out a litany of strange events, none nearly stopped Mrs. Fins' racing heart more than that of his having broken into the Records Department of the college both he and Stelle had attended. Dr. Marksdale revealed to his dutiful and patient receptionist the purpose of the break-in was to change the test scores of a few pre-med students.

Once privy to that information, one may have cause to think, as Mrs. Fins did, changing the test scores would be to benefit the culprits committing the crime in some demented way. Yet, to her increased astonishment, while the good doctor admitted to his involvement in the break-in and raising the scores of a few lower scoring students too, the question of how anyone could possibly have benefited from those juxtaposing actions screamed into Mrs. Fins' brain.

In altering the high scores of those particular students, the good doctor had guaranteed those students would not get their bachelor's degree, subsequently disqualifying them from being able to attend medical school and denying them any number of opportunities presenting throughout their lives which would require such a degree.

The good doctor's actions were too hard for Mrs. Fins to wrap her head around. She could barely think. Still, she could hear the doctor say that, without passing the test, those students affected would not be able to get into a residency program. The residency program was a non-negotiable requirement for anyone working towards becoming a medical doctor or a psychiatrist.

Mrs. Fins' head felt as if it were spinning. The good doctor's actions not only altered test scores, but his actions forever and irreparably altered the lives of several innocent people.

Some would continue on to receive a degree they were not entitled to, and the others; well, the others had their hard-earned futures stolen from them. The question Mrs. Fins desperately needed an answer to was — why? Why would he have committed such an unconscionable act?

Mrs. Fins' forehead was damp with perspiration, and she began to feel physically ill. Looking down at her freshly washed dress pumps, she thought about what the odds would be if she had to clean vomit off of them twice on the same morning. Everything which had transpired so far that morning was completely out of her realm of comprehension. She wondered if she was still sleeping, as though she had not been awake through all which had taken place and was being held hostage by a dream.

"Yes, that's it," she thought. "I'm in a bad dream."

Sadly, she knew she could not indulge such silliness and would have to face reality. Now with what she was hearing the doctor reveal of his own raw truth, she had no alternative but to admit earlier that morning, as well as in that moment, she was wide awake.

What she had heard was more than she could have ever imagined — certainly more than she could have ever imagined her wonderful Dr. Marksdale would be capable of doing.

Mrs. Fins grappled with her connection to the man she had come to admire, even to love, and the man who stood with his back to her now. They seemed to her to be two totally different individuals, possessing nothing in common with the other. Now sitting behind him, Mrs. Fins had no idea what to do or what next may be coming at her.

As he continued, the flow of his words indicated the flood gates had opened, and for the first time, Mrs. Fins feared she would not be able to keep up with him. Even so, most of the details were not lost on Mrs. Fins as he bore open his involvement in the crime of breaking and entering and the resultant forged test scores of innocent people. Nor, did the doctor lose Mrs. Fins' rapt attention when he shifted his dialogue to an experience involving hazing at the beginning of his freshman year.

The hazing was meant for two potential new members as well as himself, and it all centered around a particular fraternity he wanted to get into. It was, as he rambled off, the best one at the college. If he could get in, he would be "in" for the remainder of his four years. But something went wrong, terribly wrong, and — at least, it sounded like — someone had died.

The doctor began to tremble. His back, still to Mrs. Fins, shook and his shoulders slumped forward as he began to sob, and he said something which sounded like, "Bastards — they knew he was sick, but they wouldn't help him out! They stepped on his fingers and jeered at him."

The doctor shook his head back and forth as if he could alter the ugly truth he spewed by shaking it faster.

"I didn't know what to do. I was naked, wet and freezing."

Mrs. Fins shook involuntarily as she tried to play over in her head what she thought she had just heard. Did the doctor really say someone had died, and they would not help that person out? Out of what — was it water? He had said he was all wet — where and why? "Oh yes," she remembered, "The doctor said something about hazing." His words were too hard to understand now as he cried even harder.

Mrs. Fins knew she had told him she would not look at him, but she did. When she saw his body shaking, she felt she could not stop herself from going to his aid.

"Doctor, please let me help you." Those were the only words she could come up with. Indeed, Mrs. Fins had no idea what to do at that point. She was at a loss as to how to help him, and feared there was no way she could. The only thing she knew for sure was she was not sure she could take hearing any more of what the doctor had to say.

"No, Mrs. Fins, you can't help me. I've kept these secrets in for too long. They're all coming out now."

Mrs. Fins could see the good doctor was trying to get control of himself. Still, even though he tried to regain composure, words kept pouring out like water escaping a burst pipe.

"That bastard! I told him everything, he may as well have been there. He knew I was innocent. The doctor's face was flushed and his hands had become clammy. "It wasn't until I broke into the Records Department that I did anything wrong."

Mrs. Fins remained seated, and the doctor remained with his back to her. She felt overwhelmed, confused and sick. The doctor did not seem to be faring any better than she was.

"The break-in was to even the score the best we knew how. Only the scores were changed for those people that —"

The doctor took in a deep breath.

"I figured I would raise the scores to help some I knew were going to fail. One was Stelle's. She'd worked so hard, but didn't cut it."

The doctor, visibly distraught, clenched his jaw before continuing.

"The others — they just had to pay, and that was the only way. But he has me over a barrel, and he's threatened to —"

The doctor went silent for longer than Mrs. Fins could manage.

"He's threatened to what, doctor? Please, doctor, let me help you. Threatened to do what? And, who is he?"

Mrs. Fins' voice sounded almost as panicked coming out as she felt inside.

"He's the lowest form of scum. He's always had it in for me — ever since —"

"Ever since what, doctor? Whoever this person is, what has he threatened you with?"

"He's the reason I have the group — the damned group that is driving me nuts!"

"Do you mean the group — the five patients that come together — group?"

"Yeah, he's blackmailing me, using the group."

"Blackmailing you? Oh doctor, that's horrible. What is he holding over your head, and what can he do with it?"

"He can tell Stelle! It's always been about Stelle. He threatened to tell Stelle!"

"Are you referring to the doctor we can never reach? That doctor, oh, what is his name?" Mrs. Fins shook her head as if that would make his name come to her mind.

"Are you referring to doctor — doctor — Glenn?"

"That bastard! He continues to threaten to tell Stelle."

"To tell Stelle what?"

The voice asking the question was sharp as it cut through the heavy air in the doctor's office, and it was neither the voice of the doctor nor of Mrs. Fins. They both turned around in unison and shock — to see Stelle standing in the doorway.

Mixed with stains from dried blood spatters, her dark eye makeup ran down the length of her cheeks, under her chin and proceeded down the front of her white silk blouse. Her red swollen eyelids strongly indicated she had cried for a fair amount of time since both the doctor and Mrs. Fins had last seen her. Momentarily, both the doctor and Mrs. Fins had difficulty recognizing her, but then — there was no doubt — it was she, the doctor's wife, they were seeing.

Standing firmly in the doorway, Stelle showed she had no intention of leaving her position. The length of time she had been standing there could have been of great consequence, the doctor thought to himself. But still, he could not bring himself to ask her. Mrs. Fins remained mute as well.

"Well, Phillip? Who is threatening you? And what is it they want to tell me? What is it?"

Mrs. Fins began to get up out of her chair when Stelle's harsh order forced her to sit back down.

"Don't you dare move a muscle, Marlene. Well, Phillip? Who is blackmailing you? And with what?"

Dr. Marksdale would have sworn he could feel Stelle's intentional stare burning straight into his eyes. Everything in the room began to spin and the good doctor had to grab hold of the chair closest to him.

"I — I will tell you — I just don't know where or how to — start." The doctor sounded sincere, regardless, Stelle was having none of it.

Through his studies, the doctor had learned how a woman may react when she feels her family may be in harm's way, or if she fears they are being threatened and in danger of some kind. Now, for the first time in his career or personal life, he was witnessing it firsthand.

"You've got three seconds to start. I'll help you. Start with your changing test scores."

Mrs. Fins and the doctor's eyes were fixed on Stelle who by now had come all the way into the room. She pulled one of the chairs closer to where her husband stood and sat down.

Although neither Dr. Marksdale nor Mrs. Fins dared to look at each other, the thought of how long Stelle had been standing in the doorway had to have crossed both their minds. And both must have assessed by then Stelle had been standing there for a fair amount of time. That would be the only way she was able to reference the test scores. But, in his having no way of knowing the time span for certain, the doctor was left in a precarious position. Even so, he was still trying to figure out a way he could tell her what she needed to know without really divulging too much. For some odd reason he honestly thought, even as bad as that moment was, he may be able to get himself out of it.

Deceit — secrets — and denial — all have a way of altering a person's perception of reality.

"Time's up, Phillip," Stelle said crossly as she began to get up.

Mrs. Fins braced herself fearing any movable object in the room may end up being hurled at the doctor at any moment. But actually, what she feared more was — getting up from her chair.

Stelle turned and faced Mrs. Fins and started to head towards her, a crazed look in her eyes, stopping right in front of Mrs. Fins' chair.

"Alright, Marlene, it's obvious my husband needs to grow a pair! What the hell is going on? You tell me everything that he told you."

Mrs. Fins had never felt what she was feeling at that moment before — a mixture of emotions encompassing shock, confusion and sympathy for both doctors — and an abject fear of Stelle's glare overwhelmed her.

"I think it best that Dr. Marksdale tell you what —" She barely got the words out when Dr. Marksdale put his hands on Stelle's shoulders and gently turned her to face him.

"No Stelle, I will tell you. I will tell you everything." He then proceeded to guide his wife to the couch and got her to sit down.

"Mrs. Fins, I think it best you go now. Thank you for everything. I don't know how to tell you what it means to —"

"Oh no you don't, Phillip." The good doctor may have been able to coerce his wife into sitting down, but clearly, she was still running the show.

"You're not going anywhere, Marlene. I want the truth, and I'm going to get it." Stelle's expression and the tenor of her voice were unyielding as she shot an angry glance at the doctor. "My husband told you first. Now you will tell me if what he tells me is the same."

Mrs. Fins looked at Dr. Marksdale seeking some sign from him as to what she should do. When he nodded his head succumbing to his wife's demand, Mrs. Fins folded her hands and set them in her lap, undoubtedly thinking she was to stay seated.

"Marlene, come sit next to me, here on the couch." Stelle patted the couch seat next to her, as Mrs. Fins nervously got up from her chair and made her way to her designated spot.

"Let's go, Phillip, you and I are running out of time." Stelle said this in such a way as to leave little, if any, doubt she was at the end of her patience; and for the first time, the doctor really understood — there was no turning back now, no matter where the truth would take them.

Everything the doctor told his wife, he had already shared with Mrs. Fins. This time around, though, the doctor left out some of the more minor details — details which Stelle would have already been privy to — but added some details which better clarified certain events for Mrs. Fins which the doctor had laid out earlier. He only omitted one thing. That "thing" being her test scores were among those he had changed.

"Why tell her that now?" He questioned himself. "There is far enough for my wife to absorb, there will be another time, a better time" — or, so he told himself.

The doctor stated he was unaware of just how wet behind the ears he had been when he entered college. He did not have a clue as to how his wealthy and privileged upbringing had spoiled him in such a way he not only exuded arrogance, he also acknowledged that, mixed with his immaturity and arrogance, he had possessed an air of entitlement too. The doctor was noticeably uncomfortable exposing his faults. Even under normal circumstances (which this situation was not), the good doctor abhorred any self-analysis of himself performed in front of anyone else.

Being all too well aware there were not versions of the truth — something was either true or it was not — the good doctor continued laying everything out in front of both women sitting in front of him. As difficult as it was and as hard as it was for the doctor to begin, he apparently came to terms with his predicament. Additionally, as the doctor began to unfold a series of stories which could shock some of the toughest longshoremen, neither of the women looked away from him nor did they barely blink an eye.

Interestingly enough, the good doctor enjoyed addressing subjects such as the human id. It was something he found to be a pleasant challenge when interacting with his patients. But there in his office and in front of his wife and receptionist addressing these very unpleasant matters — matters exposing his own private, long-coveted id — he struggled with having to acknowledge that for most of his life, he had, up until that moment, an unabashed sense of self.

While both Stelle and Mrs. Fins could see it was difficult for the doctor to be as transparent as he was being (and also being somewhat surprised by his candidness), they could not have been more surprised, however, than the good doctor himself.

*****

The college both the good doctor and Stelle attended was comprised of a very well-to-do student body. In fact, one could safely say without the concern of contradiction there was quite a bit more money on that campus than brains.

Upon his entering college, his parents, as well as his counselors, warned him there would be fraternities which would try to recruit new members by taking advantage of a freshman's unfamiliarity with campus living. He was repeatedly cautioned he should stay away from pledging to one — any one of them — at least, until his sophomore year.

Being so young and not at all skilled in the ways of the world, the doctor was easily targeted by the fraternity recruiters. The recruiters wanted to win him over — not because of him, personally, but because of his name and the deep pockets which came with it. A great accomplishment would be to get this newbie to pledge to their fraternity, thus, guaranteeing access to a sizable pot of gold. One particular recruiter with the help of his cohorts convinced the eager young Philip Marksdale he was just the sort of fellow they wanted in their fraternity. Being as egotistical and big headed as he was, he fell for it all — never thinking he was being duped into believing he was as big a deal to them as he had always been to himself. Everything about the college experience for the doctor at that time was about clout and show.

When the doctor spoke and heard those thoughts translated into words as he relayed them to his captive audience, it dawned on him, quite possibly for the first time, how much of a dolt he had spent the majority of his adult life being. That would be a shocking realization quickly dashed from his mind and not to be dwelled upon, for what then overcame him was unadulterated shame.

Shame, because he had been willing to continue to hide the truth at any cost — the truth surrounding another student's death — the truth about his involvement in changing the course of other students' futures all those years ago. Shame, because he had put such a high value on the value of things. Shame, because he had let his family down. And shame, not because he had to expose the truth, but because he was willing to keep it hidden and live his life as an arrogant elitist, thus pretending nothing had ever happened.

Both women sat and listened intently to all the doctor had to say. There were moments when Mrs. Fins had to control her strong urge to put her arms around the doctor — typical motherly reactions — and assure him everything would be alright. Stelle held back too. She experienced different emotions than those of Mrs. Fins. Her emotions ran the gamut. One moment she was having a strong desire to quietly hold her husband and cry with him. On the total opposite side of that emotion, she had to fight off a strong sense of wanting to kill him — a typical wife's reactions.

Neither of the women were prepared for what was to come next. A life was lost — the life of another student had pledged to the same fraternity the doctor had foolishly pledged to, too.

Death is a permanent condition. It leaves no option to pull away from its permanent grip, once it has taken the last and irretrievable breath that life requires from the one it has chosen.

This would prove no less true all those years earlier when a younger Phillip Marksdale, along with several other young men, played a dangerous and careless game — a game only mindless fools would find themselves partaking in — and for what? That was the question neither of the two women witnessing the melt-down of a man both had shared admiration for could find an answer to.

Unlike Mrs. Fins, Stelle recognized the name the good doctor blurted out in his nearly hysterical, tremulous voice — "Fisker."

"It was Fisker. He was so drunk, we all were. He couldn't see with the blindfold on." The doctor's words were hard to decipher as he spoke so quickly and kept gasping for air; but still, Stelle and Mrs. Fins understood enough to have cold chills running down their spines.

"We both were throwing up; it was like poison." The doctor took in a deep breath. "And weak — he was too weak to get a firm grip on those damn slippery rocks!"

Both women turned and looked into each other's eyes. It was then they realized they both had tears flowing down their cheeks.

"It was because of their god damned hazing, they forced us to drink until we were deathly sick and then —" The doctor composed himself in what both women observed was an eerily quick manner, before he proceeded in an even more chilling calm.

"And then it was over. The blindfold had fallen off and that's when —" At that moment, the full silence between the doctor's words weighed so heavily in the air, Mrs. Fins felt she would suffocate.

"It was then, I saw the last dimming glint of light in his eyes quietly swallowed by the cold, wet darkness — and he was gone."

There was not a movement made by any one of the three. The women sat like they were pre-arranged mannequins fulfilling their designated staged roles as the doctor stood motionless too. Everyone remained perfectly still as if caught forever inside of a photograph. Not even the air moved in the surrounding silence — that is, until a quivering voice broke through it.

"Can someone help me please?"

Mrs. Fins' guttural scream was nearly outdone by that of Stelle's shrieking howl. Combined, both of the women's sudden outbursts were so loud the doctor instinctively threw his hands up to cover his ears as he jumped backwards. Losing his balance followed, causing him to twist his right ankle eliciting a painful groan as he collapsed to the floor.

The voice breaking the awestruck silence was that of Dillard Bigley. By the time he had awoke from the drug-induced nap gratuitously provided to him by Dr. Marksdale's little pills, the side of his head and face were so swollen and bruised, he was barely recognizable. Feebly, he haphazardly leaned against the doctor's office door jamb. He looked as if he could, and most likely should, sleep even longer. He did not resemble the dashing gentleman everyone knew him to be and would have felt familiar with. Instead, his swollen and bruised face gave him the appearance of an unfortunate side act in a cross-country traveling freak show.

"Can someone help me to the couch, I can't seem to focus very well."

When getting up from the couch, Mrs. Fins did so with such a burst, Stelle found herself grabbing for the arm rest fearing she may bounce to the floor.

Mrs. Fins' voice assured, "I am coming Mr. Bigley, just stay still."

Dillard Bigley's sudden appearance was a jolt to both of the women and the doctor's consciousness. It was that jolt which made all three of them realize how deeply invested they had been in everything the doctor had been telling them, in particular, the last bit of information he had revealed. The two women could not have recovered from hearing what they had just heard, and most likely the doctor himself was still shell shocked from having told them.

Stelle managed to get out, "What the hell happened to him?" as she stood up and headed towards the doctor, who by now was using the back of a chair to assist himself to get up from the floor.

The doctor started with, "The sedative I gave him must have not been enough —" That was when the doctor's wife interrupted.

"What did you use? A bat? He looks like you used a bat." Stelle's face clearly showed the concern she did not attempt to hide.

"That is Dillard Bigley. He is one of my patients."

Before the doctor sat down in the same chair he had used as leverage to get off of the floor, Stelle walked around in back of him and in a low tone, questioned, "Is he dangerous?"

"Of course not!" Mrs. Fins entered into the conversation as she helped Dill to the couch.

"You met him earlier along with Mr. Jeffries."

Stelle searched her mind and though all the pieces of it were present, they were so jumbled up from the cumulative array of that morning's events, she found it nearly impossible to focus.

"You remember Mr. Jeffries, don't you? Mr. Bigley was with him when you came out of the lounge earlier this morning."

Mrs. Fins was giving Stelle the benefit of her trained psychiatrist's observational skills. She then offered a description which she was sure would ignite Stelle's memory.

"He was chewing a big piece of gum."

"Mr. Bigley was chewing gum?"

Mrs. Fins, allowing herself a brief respite from her customarily controlled manner, screamed inside of her own head, "So much for your observational skills, Mrs. Marksdale!"

Indeed, it had been a very long morning. After clearing her throat, Mrs. Fins raised her chin in that special way only her greatest admirer, that being Dillard Bigley, could fully appreciate. She then gracefully regained her composure and continued.

"No, it was Mr. Jeffries who was chewing the gum. Mr. Bigley was with him."

Helping Dill get situated on the couch, Mrs. Fins grabbed two throw pillows from one of the other chairs and propped them under his head. Then she lifted and swung both of his legs up onto the couch so he was fully stretched out. Dill made a few unrecognizable sounds and succumbed to unconsciousness.

"He swallowed the gum and we — Mr. Bigley and I —" Mrs. Fins turned to Dill to get clarification only to realize he could offer no support, as he was sound asleep once again. "We were quite concerned he may choke." With that, she went into the private lounge to retrieve a blanket which she covered Dill's peaceful, almost corpse like, body with.

"Wait — do you mean Bud?" Stelle questioned. "Yes, I remember him, of course."

"How could I not?" Stelle thought privately to herself. Considering she had just spent a good part of the morning sitting on the sidewalk with the man, for her, it was the least she could do after spraying the poor man directly in the face with pepper spray (though Stelle would prefer to say, if asked, "accidentally spritzed").

Yes, she knew who Bud was. But this man she did not remember nor did she recognize him. Silently, she entertained in a somewhat twisted way — Mr. Bigley probably wouldn't recognize himself either.

"Speaking of Bud, he and the others may be coming up here soon —" Stelle began to say — but stopped herself — when it occurred to her neither her husband nor Mrs. Fins would have any reference to what she was talking about.

Too much had happened in too short of a time span. The doctor had revealed so much — too much for Stelle to have had time to absorb it all.

"My God, all these people!" Stelle thought almost out loud. Except for her husband and Mrs. Fins, all these people she had spent the better part of the morning with were complete strangers to her. No one, Stelle was sure, would be able to keep track of all which had transpired that day without the assistance of a professional score-keeper.

"I asked them to give me a little time before they returned. I needed to talk to you, Phillip." Stelle turned to look at her husband who, by now, had a blank expression on his very tired face. His exhaustion would have been apparent — even to a non-informed observer. For Mrs. Fins, Stelle and the doctor, himself, the reason for it was well understood.

There were loose ends which needed tying up, and more details would come to fill in the blanks; but for now, the doctor was spent. He had let out what he had held inside for so long, and when he did, it poured out of him like pieces of a puzzle being poured out onto a table. What the final picture would ultimately be could have been anyone's guess.

*****

Ally, Bud and Percy were still sitting next to each other — allowing for the time Stelle had requested they give her — before coming back up to the doctor's office. Their conversation had covered all the "crazy," as Bud put it, which had taken place so far that morning.

Not one of the three of them knew why the good doctor had requested them to come to his office so early that morning, yet they all agreed it felt important enough to show up. And so, they waited.

The way they were sitting gave the impression they were huddled together. While they sat on the sidewalk, all three of them began to feel somehow smaller in some unexplained way. Perhaps it was the light of day which began an awakening, after which the city street rapidly came to life.

City buses had begun to drop commuters off at their corner stops, and the crisp morning air was beginning to fill with the scents a sleeping city reveals when it rouses into a new day. The exhaust from cars and buses was pungent, while a variety of perfumes, and periodically a hint of cigarette smoke, could be detected — wafting by the three of them, cutting through the otherwise fresh morning air.

As people made their way to their offices, passing by the threesome huddled together on the sidewalk did not seem to garner them any untoward attention. "They must have not appeared out of the ordinary," Ally noted.

In response, Percy added, "There are all kinds of strange and disgusting freaks out these days. We don't look all that out-of-place."

Bud was still suffering the ramifications someone faces when one's face gets in the direct path of a burst of pepper spray. He sniffed back hard and then made an attempt to clear his throat. When he felt he had done so efficiently, he spit a large wad of slimy mucus out onto the sidewalk in front of them.

"Ewww," was all that came out of Ally as she rested her forehead on her bent knees.

Percy turned slowly to look at him and with a roll of her eyes — a reaction which had become her trademark like Ally's shoes had become hers — she tiredly muttered, "Thank you, Bud, for reiterating my point."

"How long do you think we should wait?" Ally sounded like a tired child. "I'm getting really hungry and I have to pee."

"Yeah, me too." Percy looked around and then down at her watch.

"Seems like we've been here a long time, don't it?" Bud started rubbing his eyes.

"I don't think you should do that Bud. We should probably get you some more water for your eyes too." Percy started to get up.

"Oh man, my leg's asleep. It's gonna take me a minute." Percy leaned against Stelle's car and shook her leg a few times; but stopped, when she almost lost her balance, as a woman ran right past her almost knocking her over.

"What the hell? What's the freakin' hurry, lady?" Percy yelled out at the woman, as she continued to run up to the building the doctor's office was in.

Ally and Bud looked up, too, just in time to see the woman shoving an older couple out of her way, as she hurriedly entered the office building's main entry doors.

Percy looked down at both Ally and Bud before asking, "What the hell? Did you guys see her?"

"Yeah, she sure was in a hurry," Ally said as she too started to get up. "Ya need some help to get up, Bud?" She asked while she offered him her hand.

"Sure, I think I can do it, but my legs seem to be a little stiff." He took the hand Ally offered and put his other hand against Stelle's car door to assist him further.

"You know, I think I recognize that lady. I just can't place her." Ally's comment caused Percy to look at her with a quizzical expression.

"Strange, I think I recognize her too. But from where, I don't know," Percy replied through pursed lips.

"Wait a minute. I think I got it." Bud stood up straight and adjusted himself.

"Sorry girls, but the boys needed to shift around a little."

"Oh," was all the response he got from Ally.

Percy either didn't hear him or she chose not to encourage him. Maybe, she just didn't care.

"What do you got, Bud?" Ally asked. "You said you thought you got it."

"Yeah, I swear she — that lady looked like — well, I think she looked like Moronica."

Both women turned to look at Bud at the same time and in unison asked, "Moronica?"

"You know, the crazy — that crazy that got us into trouble with the judge — Moronica, Emma's wacky daughter."

"Oh yeah, her," Ally said, somewhat wistfully.

"You know Bud, you just may be right." Percy patted Bud on the back.

"I wonder what she's doing here? And she was in such a hurry too." Ally started to straighten and dust off her clothing.

"My butt's asleep from sitting on this hard sidewalk." Ally started to pat herself when Bud offered her his help.

"Down, big boy," Percy snapped, "We better go see what's going on."

"Why do ya think she's here?" Ally asked while continuing to smack herself.

"There's only one way to find out." Percy looked at Bud and Ally and then started towards the office building.

Ally and Bud had to quicken their pace to keep up with Percy — a task not easily accomplished with one sleeping butt and a couple of stiff legs.

"What ya think is going on?" Ally sped up while still holding on to Bud's arm, helping him along.

"After everything else that has already happened today, it's anyone's guess," Percy said over her shoulder and started walking even faster. It was getting harder for the other two to keep up.

Bud sounded like he was beginning to wheeze, and Percy turned back to look at him.

"You gonna be okay?"

"Yeah, just keep going."

"I'll help him, Percy, you go on ahead." Ally wrapped her arm around Bud's and they followed — now several feet behind Percy — Bud wheezing and Ally clickity-clackity-clicking all the way to the elevators.

The doctor and Stelle were in a quiet conversation, and Mrs. Fins stood above Dill Bigley straightening his blanket when — the outside office door swung open so hard the room shook. And, then, the door made a thunderous sound when hitting the wall.

"Where the hell are you? You miserable quack!"

The woman screaming at the top of her lungs looked frantic, as she came rushing into the doctor's office. Before anyone could react, she was grabbing Dr. Marksdale by his shirt and lifting him up off of the chair he was sitting in and began shaking him so hard his neck could be heard popping.

Shocked expressions were on both Mrs. Fins' and Stelle's faces. The unknown woman's face, grimacing and red, looked like that of someone who had gone completely off the edge.

Stelle jumped up and grabbed the back of her husband's shirt trying to pull him away from his attacker.

"Let go of him, you lunatic!"

Just as those words came out of Stelle's mouth, Ally, Percy and Bud had made it to the doorway. Again, all three were at a loss as to what was happening. When Bud caught what Stelle had called Monica (a.k.a. Moronica), he looked at Ally and offered, "She's a lunatic alright, Stelle just confirmed it. And she's a doctor, you know." Ally's eyes and mouth were wide open as she moved her head up and down confirming Bud's well-made point.

"Let my husband go! Let him go, you crazy bitch!"

Coinciding with Stelle's outburst — whether it was due to the raucous activity in the room or perhaps the meds were beginning to wear off — Dill Bigley sat straight up and slurred, "It would appear she's gone around the bend." After which he promptly laid back down, closed his one good eye and fell back into a deep sleep, his mouth fully agape.

Percy ran up and grabbed the woman from behind pulling her grip free of the doctor's shirt.

"Now don't make me hurt you, because I will." Percy sounded relatively calm but very assured in her tone.

"Now let's figure this out, what is the matter with you? What do you want from the doctor?"

Percy pulled the woman across the room and sat her down in a chair a fair distance away from Dr. Marksdale and Stelle who, by this time, looked to have fire coming out of her eyes.

Mrs. Fins had come up next to Stelle and had acquired a firm grip on her arm so as to prevent her from going after the stranger, although her own instinct was to do the same.

"That quack has ruined my mother's life! He's gonna pay, I tell you. He's gonna pay!"

"Who is this woman, Phillip?" Stelle implored.

"I have no idea! Who the hell are you? And who is your mother?" The doctor looked equally as confused as the stranger looked insane.

"Emma, you son-of-a-bitch! Emma is my mother and you've ruined her life!"

The woman lunged in the direction of the doctor, but Percy had too good of a hold on her for it to matter. Being as petite as she was, it did not seem to stop Percy from being quite a formidable opponent.

This was something Bud had never observed before. He had only been exposed to her abilities in the verbally abusive arena — an arena he was quite familiar with, and one he prided himself in having been a rather formidable opponent himself. Momentarily, he seemed duly impressed.

"Now, see here. I have done nothing to your mother, if she is your mother!" The doctor started to head towards the phone.

"I am going to call the police if you don't leave, and leave now."

"Go ahead, call 'em! I'll be glad to tell 'em what a quack you are."

"What on earth do you think I've done to your mother?" The doctor asked in a desperate tenor, the phone in his hand.

"You convinced her to follow her dreams, her crazy ass dreams, and she took off."

"What dreams?"

"You know, you told her if she believed in the love she felt, she should follow her heart — some shit like that." The woman was visibly shaken. The doctor could see that, and he gestured to Percy to release her hold on her as he set the phone down.

"Are you sure doc? She's unwound 'bout as far as you can unwind." Percy looked to the doctor for assuredness, this was what he wanted her to do.

"Yes, Percy, please let go of her. I am sure this woman and I can discuss whatever the issue is, rationally." The doctor looked at the woman and waved his hand towards a chair indicating he would like for her to sit down.

"I'm not here to get treatment, you jerk. I want you to pay for putting crazy ass thoughts in my mother's head."

"What is your name?" The doctor's voice had gone from sounding filled with fear and anger to a calm which seemed to be helping everyone in the room begin to feel more at ease.

"Monica, I'm Monica. My mother is Emma. And the crap you told her — got her to pack it up and take off yesterday." Monica, too, seemed to begin to calm down to some small degree.

"Where did your mother go, Monica?" The doctor queried.

"She took off to freakin' Utah! A place she's never even been to."

"What is in Utah that she is looking for?"

"A man — a god damn man — a man she doesn't even know."

The doctor's mind began the process of recall, and he did indeed remember Emma speaking of a man she had met, only once, a couple of years before she began treatment with the group. She had met him in, of all places, a hardware store.

Over the course of her treatment, Emma spoke often of missed opportunities in her life, her cautious nature keeping her from trying new things and seeking new adventures.

The doctor remembered, too, he along with the others in the group had encouraged Emma to break free of her old ways and let herself open new doors. Had his advice led his patient — the one patient he had special feelings towards — into harm's way?

This was something he would never be able to live with. He had lived far too long with deep regret, and after that morning, he knew he would never allow such a travesty to ever happen again, particularly on his watch.

"What kind of a doctor would tell a patient to chase a relationship they made up in their head?" Monica's screaming had calmed down to angry shouting.

Both doctors knew this was a marked improvement. But then, anyone awake in the room — whether trained in reading human behavior or not — was keenly aware Emma's daughter had started to cool down some from the raging maniac she had been moments before.

"I must interject, Monica, it is always my intention to create an atmosphere wherein my patients can feel a sense of self and —"

"Cut the crap, quack! I didn't come here to hear how great you are." Monica started to get up off the chair when Percy reminded her with a steady and firm pressure applied to her shoulders she was still standing right behind her.

Monica turned quickly to look up and behind her. "Who's this goon?"

"Ha! That's a good one. 'Goon' — I like it." Bud seemed pleased for the first time in quite a while.

"Shut up pepper breath!" Percy shot back, but, at the same time, seemed oddly amused. She then turned her attention back to her captive audience of one.

"Don't you worry 'bout who I am. You just stay in this chair and you'll be just fine."

"I really don't think we need to restrain her, Percy. Monica wants my help. Isn't that true, Monica?" The doctor asked while sitting back down on his chair.

"I want to help you, Monica, but you need to help me first. I need to understand better what has happened. Please fill in the details for me."

By this time, Mrs. Fins, having just released her hold on Stelle's arm, found herself pondering how the good doctor could be so calm after having been so hysterical not ten minutes earlier.

For Mrs. Fins, who would usually praise herself for her normal and rational approach towards the daily occurrences at her place of work, now found her mindset was being challenged by all the actors in what had become an increasingly absurd play.

"Thus far," she thought, "There were the regular players of which none were behaving normally, even for them." And then, there was all of the new information she had been exposed to and was still trying her best, admittedly under the most unusual circumstances, to sort through. She realized it did seem odd the only patient in the good doctor's group that had not made her entrance onto this, the most bizarre of stages, was Emma. Now, instead of Emma, her daughter Monica had hysterically presented herself. Transcending from all she was familiar with, Mrs. Fins reviewed the stage once again.

First, upon arriving at the office that morning, she found the good doctor deathly intoxicated and found his wife, Stelle, beside herself with a toxic mixture of disappointment and rage. Mr. Bigley made his first, and in Mrs. Fins' estimation at that early hour, an unsolicited appearance only to return shortly after she had firmly escorted him out. That second time he came back, he came with Mr. Jeffries — the two of them making a most unlikely pair. They arrived together, insisting it was in response to a personal request from Dr. Marksdale himself.

In addition, there was the matter of the unpleasant altercation between the two doctors resulting in Stelle making a mad exit and leaving her husband with a bleeding head wound. Mrs. Fins acknowledged to herself she was only concerned with the two doctors at the time — in particular, the wound Dr. Marksdale suffered — and not with the odd twosome of Bigley and Jeffries.

The recap dialogue of the good doctor's college years and his revealing of a truth so horrific she still had not fully absorbed it, Mrs. Fins felt she was at a disadvantage. Usually, she ran an efficient office and took pride in the thought her services to her employer were of the most fastidious nature. Now, as she looked all around herself, she not only felt she had lost any semblance of control, but she was quite aghast at what she saw.

Across the room on the couch lay Mr. Bigley — swollen, bruised and drugged. Mr. Jeffries looked as if he had been in some kind of a scuffle too. His eyes were blood shot, swollen and watery. And Mrs. Marksdale, well, she had never seen her in such a way. Her hair was disheveled along with her clothes which looked as if she had slept in them all night in some filthy back ally.

Then, there were the stains. The stains were the worst: dried blood and eye makeup which was now mixed all together and running down her once beautiful white silk blouse. Her normally lovely face now bore red-puffy eyelids, a result of her constant crying. Black mascara and eyeliner had left streaks down her cheeks and pooled under her eyes. Poor Mrs. Marksdale, Mrs. Fins observed. She had taken on the appearance of a ghoulish raccoon.

Percy had taken on a strangely masculine appearance, something Mrs. Fins was not at all used to seeing, as she held her prisoner steady in her chair (converted into a holding cell).

Ally retained the most normal appearance of them all. She almost looked like her usual self except for her deer-in-the-headlights expression. But then, that could have been a subject of controversy on any ordinary day (of which this was not), as some would argue she always looked that way.

What may have happened to all of these people escaped Mrs. Fins. She barely knew what had happened to her. Feeling a little light-headed and hoping to regain a semblance of balance, she chose to take a seat at the end of the couch, where Dill was still sleeping.

"Look, I don't have time to waste. I have to find my mother! You got her into this mess, you need to get her out of it." Monica was not altering her train of thinking when it came to the doctor's responsibility for Emma's decision to take off to Utah, according to her — in search of an imaginary man.

"She's in danger and it is all your fault! I can't afford to go after her myself. You're gonna have to go find her." The anger was diminishing in Monica's voice, and what sounded like real fear was rising to the surface, "You gotta help me."

"What do you mean, he has to help you? How dare you come in here and demand my husband —" Stelle, still visibly angry, confronted this additional stranger — adding to the motley mixture of strangers she had already found herself surrounded by that morning.

"What makes you think she may be in danger?" The doctor intervened.

"She took off after a guy she met once. Come on! She doesn't even know his name. He could be crazy!" At that comment, everyone except Dillard Bigley cast a quick glance at everyone else in the room.

"I don't know if the word 'crazy' is really appropriate at this —" Dr. Marksdale barely managed to get his words out before Monica started to cry.

"She thinks she and this guy are meant to be together. He doesn't know who she is, and she knows nothing about him!" Monica started to wipe tears off of her wet cheeks and started to stand up. Looking behind her, she saw Percy still standing guard. But this time, Percy backed up while not hindering Monica from moving away from the chair. Monica took a few sheepish steps away from Percy and then turned away from everyone, placing the palms of her hands down on the doctor's desk.

"Please, you gotta help us — my daughter and me. My mom is all we got." At that, Monica started to cry harder. Bud picked up a tissue box which was on one of the end tables and brought it to her.

Standing a full arm's length away from her, he handed her the box before taking a few cautious steps back. When he turned around, for the first time he got a good look at Dill's head and face.

In a voice which could only be described as several octaves higher than most men were known to reach, he blurted out, "What happened to him?" His head swiveled around until he made eye contact with Stelle. "Wha ja do ta him?"

Stelle's mouth fell open as she gasped, "Why do you think I did that?"

Bud shot his arm straight out with his hand fully open and fingers outstretched. He pointed first at Dr. Marksdale and then at his own face. Along with his incredulous expression, "Why wouldn't I think it was you, is a better question!" Bud had made his point.

After a long deliberation, Monica had calmed down a great deal and achieved getting her point across to the doctor — that her sense of urgency was not out of bounds. True, the doctor had surmised Emma was the most "normal" member of the group. The doctor also honestly had to admit, without clarification, as to why, from the beginning, he had a special affinity towards her.

Now this special member of the group may very well be getting herself into some dangerous waters. And, there was nothing about that thought which rested well with either of the Marksdale doctors.

This new development brought to bear another pressing issue. That issue was their court appearance was scheduled for the following week. All members of the group were required to be present, no exceptions. With one of the group's most stable member missing, the doctor again felt dread.

How, Dr. Marksdale wondered, was he ever to find Emma and bring her home in time? How was he to find her at all?

According to Monica, Emma was not answering her calls verbally — but only by text. That meant she was alive. At least, one would hope that to be true. It also meant Emma was not in the mood to talk to her daughter, something Monica — though painful to do — had to confirm. Another red-flag for her was in the last few days, her mother's normal behavior had reached far beyond those predictable bounds. Her strongest indicator to back up this theory was there had never been a time when she needed her mother, where her mother had not been there for her.

Monica made it clear her mother was "damned determined" to find this man she had become so emotionally ensconced with since their one-time meeting. She also made it clear she blamed the doctor and the group for putting irrational "garble," as she put it, into her mother's head.

Emma relayed to her daughter the therapy she had been undergoing had opened the doors to her very cautious life. She knew herself to be the one who would always do the sensible and right thing — always. However, her thinking had changed since the moment she had met this man — this nameless, and for Monica, faceless man. The doctor and the group, Emma admitted, gave her the strength to dare to think outside of her self-induced prison of propriety.

And with that, she was gone. Emma packed up what she thought she would need, and out the door she went. She left a quick note for both Monica and Lizzie telling them she was off to Utah to, as Emma put it, "find her heart." Monica put it straight to the doctor it was up to him to find her and convince her to come back to her family and to sanity.

How on earth was he to do that, he openly questioned. The answer came from the most surprising voice — the voice of Mrs. Fins.

"I will go with you, doctor; we must bring her home."

"Wait, if she's going, I wanta go too," Percy voiced next.

Ally perked up, "Hey, what about me?"

"Hold on now, this is not a laughing matter." The doctor cleared his throat, "We can't all just pick up and travel half-way across the country!"

"Why not, Phillip? After everything that I learned today, I'm ready for a long ride with you. We've got a lot to figure out." Stelle sounded very assured.

"I can use the van from our restaurant. It will seat six — if we push it, maybe eight." Bud was eager to add.

"Hey, my semi can carry three, and it has a sleeper and a great place to store food and supplies," Percy cheerfully contributed.

Monica looked around the room filled with strangers ranging in age and varying degrees of injury, "Really? You all want to go — why?" Her question reflected suspicion.

"Because Emma is a wonderful person, and she has extended to all of us, at one time or another, a hand of help or word of support and kindness." Though the words were somewhat slurred, they were clear enough, and all eyes turned to see Dill Bigley partially sitting up by propping himself up on one elbow.

"I will only need someone to assist me to my car. We should all go home and pack necessities for the trip and meet back here post haste."

"I agree," Bud said and went to the couch to help Dill stand up. Wobbly at first, Dill got his bearings when Mrs. Fins barked, "absolutely not! I will drive you home and assist you in packing. You are on heavy medication." With that and a roll of her eyes, Mrs. Fins was gathering her purse and Dill's arm in her arm.

"Okay then, I guess we all agree. We're going to Utah." Percy looked pleased.

"Let's meet back here in two hours, and we'll figure out who will ride with who." She looked around the room, and everyone seemed to be in silent agreement.

"I'm not sure this is such a good idea," the doctor stated.

Stelle surprised her husband with, "The more eyes, the better. Let's get moving. I'll call mother to get her to take the children."

"Oh, that reminds me, I have to go get my birds too." Ally started towards the door.

"Birds? How do you expect to carry them on such a trip?" Percy sounded indignant.

"In their cage of course." Ally replied coarsely. "How else do ya think I would carry them, in my purse?"

"How big is this cage?" Percy entertained.

"Don't worry about it. I got plenty ah room in the van." Bud offered with a smile.

"Better they travel with me." Percy pushed, already regretting what she said next. "I got a lot of space and they can stay safe and warm." Shaking her head, Percy asked herself in silence, "What the hell is the matter with me?"

"Oh, this is going to be such fun!" Ally giggled.

As each person managed their way out of the doctor's office after agreeing to meet in two hours, the doctors looked at each other and then away from each other. Most likely, they were both wondering how all of this was going to play out.

After the office was emptied of its occupants, the good doctor locked the door behind Stelle and himself. He turned and looked at all in the group who, by then, were waiting at the elevator. He reflected on how far his group had come — something he had done just the night before. That is, until the fear in his inner voice came gurgling to the surface — the same voice he silenced with the better portion of a bottle of scotch.

Looking at the group, all he could see was a most unlikely group of individuals to take on an endeavor such as the one they had just volunteered themselves to take on. To add to the mix, this group, in their current states of being, more likely resembled a circus of the inane than a group setting off on an important mission — one which was already leading them into the great unknown.

Yet, there they were, the good doctor observed, all of them minus one very important member: one with swollen eyes, still sniffling and coughing; another in her crazy get-up; and, one both bruised and sedated — setting off to rescue one of their own.

CHAPTER EIGHT

Two of the most unlikely people to agree on anything would be Percy and Bud. If someone were to wager a bet on which one of the two would be the testiest with the other one, some would place their bet on Bud. Others could argue a wager would be better placed if placed on Percy. Neither choice would be wrong. The main connection these two people shared successfully was their mutual hostility towards each other. That had been the case since their first encounter almost a year earlier, when everyone in the group met for the first time while in traffic court.

Ironically, the common thread which stitched the five members of the group together was the aggressive attack perpetuated on Dill Bigley by the arrogant James Elliot Jeffries, a.k.a. Bud. Without that most unsavory occurrence, none of the five members of the group — total strangers at the time — would have had any reason to begin any sort of relationship with any of the others.

On that fateful day several months earlier, Percy was the first one to come to Dill Bigley's aid. Having always found bullies' attitudes abhorrent and their actions even more so, Percy was prompted to run to Dill's rescue after witnessing Bud throw Dill Bigley over a row of chairs in court that day. Being as petite as she was, she felt the only course of action to be of any real assistance was to leap up on Bud's back. Emma, possessing a kind, giving and helpful nature had followed immediately behind Percy.

Bud was oblivious as to who had jumped on his back. He knew only his repeated attempts to pummel Mr. Bigley were being thwarted. The extra weight generated by the two women — both clawing and clinging to his arms in attempting to subdue him — stifled his ability to swing his arms. The irony of having two women, literally on his back, was lost on Bud. He gave a great "heave ho," thrusting the two women off of his back, and as her grip was the least secure, Emma went sailing off first. At the same time, from the corner of her eye, she saw Percy being flung backwards too.

Fearing Bud could be a mad man and may attack either her or Percy next or (worse yet) her daughter or granddaughter (both sitting like statues with frozen panic on their faces), Emma drew up all the energy she had in her and ran up to Bud, body slamming him into and over the chair in back of him. The force with which Emma pushed Bud left her off balance which sent her spiraling out of control towards the chairs where other people were still seated.

Witnessing this clown-like scuffle and realizing how uncomfortably close to her it was unfolding, Ally instinctively jumped up from her chair. She wanted to assist the other two women in their efforts to stop one man from beating another while, at the same time, she wanted to prevent Emma from falling on top of her. Unfortunately, one of Ally's spiked high heels (not the best footwear while performing heroic acts) got caught on Percy's pant leg, drastically altering both of their original goals.

In an instant, Emma was on top of Ally with a heaving mouthful of Ally's hot-pink feather boa trapped in her mouth, while a loud scream burst forth from Percy. Ally's frighteningly sharp high heel had gouged a two-inch-long layer of Percy's leg skin, as Ally, Emma and then Percy piled on top of each other, resulting in a mishmash of arms, legs and pink-dyed ostrich feathers.

The apple-shaped bailiff swiftly waddled (as swiftly as anyone can waddle) towards the squirming pile of humans lying on the floor. He waved his unholstered gun with his chubby hand, and his voice reached octaves higher than what would be expected to come from a man possessing such an ample girth as his. His commands — delivered in erratic spurts — sounded more like squeaky barks than orders coming from someone of authority.

"Cease — all of you! Cease — or I will shoot!"

This command, in and of itself, may have been an effective tool in convincing most people to take heed. It was, however, a command which did not have the benefit of time — to be tested.

While the over-zealous bailiff was wildly waving his gun above and about his head, it accidentally discharged emptying the chamber's contents across a wide swath of the ceiling above everyone. Along with the deafening sound which filled the room, a large area of the acoustic ceiling was affected which included insulation and a four-foot-long overhead light fixture which collapsed down on the heads of all those in the skirmish, as well as the bailiff himself.

No one in the courtroom was spared the ear-splitting pain the bailiff's gun discharging created. Innocent individuals sitting closer to the riot Bud had created — those who had not thrown themselves onto the floor when the bullets started to fly — also fell victim to the ceiling's untimely demise. Everyone in the courtroom was trying to clear their ears, while several innocent bystanders could be seen dusting off their sore heads. No doubt, some were rethinking their choice to appear in court that day. It may have been a better decision to have paid their traffic violation fines by check — via the U.S. Mail.

Judge Glib was now standing behind her bench pounding her gavel so hard the force caused it to break thus sending the flathead end hurling across the room which barely missed the bailiff's head and left her with nothing more than the handle dangling uselessly in her throbbing hand. She continued screaming at the top of her lungs, "Order! Order in the court!" Although, by this time, her voice was dry and hoarse, and the only real affect her screaming had was to make the veins in her neck shockingly visible.

"Order! Order! Do you hear me? Order in the court! NOW, DAMN IT!" Sadly, even if they had wanted to, no one could hear her demands due to the loud ringing in their ears.

After much ado about everything, Judge Glib ordered everyone in her court involved in creating, what she termed as, "a complete, inexcusable and unabashed fiasco," to enter into intense therapy — together — as a group. With a raw and raspy voice, she made it clear she was not, in any way, going to yield to anyone's complaints or objections, and no one would be excused — no one except the bailiff. He was promptly relieved of all his duties, and according to the newspaper reporting the story at the time, his new position was a filing job. The location of this filing position was rumored to be located in the basement of one of the county's older buildings.

There was nothing in the judge's orders which could be misconstrued or taken lightly. Anyone not in complete compliance would face severe fines along with serious jail time, too. And, everyone was dependent upon everyone else. If one person did not fulfill their obligation, everyone would suffer the full severity of the consequences — no exceptions.

Knowing the consequences for one was the same for each and every one of them, Emma going AWOL had serious ramifications for the entire group, if she did not return in time for their court date the following week. That, by itself, would have been enough of a driving force for all of them to consider, and no doubt all of them must have done just that. There was still something more to their putting aside their hostilities towards each other, and a couple of them found themselves reviewing what drove their rationale.

Dr. Marksdale was willing to accept accolades for his hard work with the group and pondered about graciously accepting the credit for everyone amicably joining forces. That was, until he succumbed to the fact, that, after having been knocked down a peg or two — there were other forces at play. Everyone's willingness to seek the same outcome in finding and bringing Emma home was in their best interest. The detail-orientated doctor found himself in agreement with, and able to take credit for, all of the hours and months of deliberate therapy he had guided. But then, there were those severe court orders his group had hanging over them and the weight those orders carried. Those pesky details, the doctor's thoughts now harbored, would no doubt come into play. It was then the good doctor found himself reflecting on Emma.

Emma was the one member of the group from their first meeting the good doctor was inexplicably drawn to. Everyone, including the doctor, had openly come to care for her — for what was obvious to the doctor: Emma had not wavered from encouraging everyone else to reach their goals. For her, it had never been a matter of just complying with the finite details of the court's orders — it was helping everyone to find a better place within themselves going forward.

Dr. Marksdale now recalled the numerous occasions Emma backed him up when he had said, "Since you're here anyway, you may as well take advantage of the free therapy and straighten out your heads." Dr. Marksdale never doubted all of their heads, with maybe the exception of Emma's, were in dire need of straightening. While he continued his internal struggle with whether he would, or could, accomplish such a feat, Emma's confidence in the doctor's capability never faltered. It was that kind of kindness Emma displayed to him and the members of the group which contributed to the good doctor's sense of gratitude towards her. In all honesty, her confidence in him was something that, at times, he did not possess in himself.

Perhaps the good doctor had more to be proud of than wary of. Notably, it was Emma who commented on the positive evolution she observed between the members of the group. During one of their more recent sessions, she brought to their attention that they all could attribute their personal growth and achievements to their having begun to work together positively; and as such, they all deserved to take equal credit for their accomplishments.

"This," Emma emphasized, "is in direct opposition to each of you still harboring resentments towards each other. Who knows," she had commented while addressing everyone — "truth may actually be stranger than fiction."

Percy, Bud and the ever-consummate gentleman, Dillard Bigley, had earned their respective hostilities towards one another beginning that first day in court, and their animosity had grown with great fervor ever since. Knowing that to be the truth, Emma still had encouraged them to find a way to bond. She reasoned, even if their hostility was the only tie between them, it was a commonality, and so, a position they could start from.

As natural as it seemed for Bud to pick a fight with any of the others in the group, it was Emma's nature to follow a positive path. She may have been one of those rare eternal optimists. Maybe, she was just a fool.

Percy found herself contemplating: If Emma were present, she may not have been as surprised as she had found herself to be, when it came to how quickly she and the others managed to put aside their mutual dislikes for one another. Emma, Percy deduced, would have had no doubt the group was more than capable of coming together for a bigger cause. Maybe it was not such a big deal Percy and Dill, or even Ally for that matter, had been able to cooperate with one another; but, for either Percy or Dill to be able to cooperate with Bud, that was a foreign concept. For some, they would have to see it to believe it — not Emma. Percy smiled knowing Emma, for some unknown reason, would have believed it from the start.

Percy and Dill found Bud to be nothing short of an obnoxious dolt, a name they both had used to address him with on so many occasions. And, whenever the opportunity presented, Bud was quick to use any tactless verbiage he could conjure up when he addressed either of them. For Emma, that would be a good starting point from which to work. As the events continued to unfold the way they did, her point had merit.

Now, it was Percy, Bud and Ally all agreeing to travel together, starting with going to one another's homes to pick up items each one would need. Surprisingly, all three found common ground and agreed it would save time, thus allowing them to meet everyone in good time to get on the road sooner — strange, unheard of and inexplicable behavior for any of them, let alone all of them at the same time — remarkable.

For Percy to be in the same room with Ally for more than a few, unbearable minutes without envisioning herself pulling out Ally's hair, all three colors of it, was a hallmark moment in and of itself. Thinking back, Percy was reminded of how Emma had interrupted Percy during one of her tirades involving Ally — her young and irritatingly effervescent nemesis.

"She doesn't have a freaking brain in her head!" Percy flared. "She shouldn't be allowed to walk among even the stupidest people!"

"Now Percy," Emma injected, "Even if her head were proved to be empty as you say, you have to agree, her chest is filled with a heart of gold."

Percy acknowledged there was something about her which prevented her from getting angry with Emma, even though she was repeatedly right. Not being a patient person, this was a scenario which would normally irk Percy to the point she would twitch. Maybe it was the fact Emma had, from the beginning, come to her rescue like she seemed to do with everyone. For Percy, it was an odd behavior to observe in anyone. Even more so, it was very rare to see such behavior exhibited between two strangers.

A critique of Dill's and Bud's relationship would have shown a gradual improvement over time. There was a slight but noticeable frequency, wherein each of these men had treated the other with a glimmer of civility. Indeed, it appeared more recently they had managed to bury the hatchet more often than not — and not in each other's heads.

Halfway through Seattle, Dill realized the shadowy figure he saw from under his swollen eyelid was Mrs. Fins. It dawned on him he was a passenger in her car. Then he remembered Mrs. Fins was driving them back to pick up what each of them would need for the journey. Not sure whether drugs were affecting his thinking or the mere fact he was a passenger in Mrs. Fins car, Dill was in no hurry to analyze anything other than the purity of the moment. His relationship with anyone else on the planet was not on his radar. Without shame or regret, he boyishly gazed (the best way anyone could gaze when faced with his current physical limitations) at Mrs. Fins' lovely profile. That was not an easy task, considering one of his eyelids was swollen from its earlier encounter with a doorknob and hard floor. The swelling of the side of his face and forehead almost completely covered one eye, and his neck had the tensile strength of a noodle due to all the sedatives pumping through his body. Mrs. Fins continued to plug ahead completely unaware of her admirer's attention. She was too busy weaving in and out of traffic on Interstate 5 hoping not to get stuck in the gridlock traffic which so often negatively affected any possibility of relaxed travel through the Emerald City.

The irony could not have been lost on any member of the group now, as everyone in the group, including the good doctor and his wife, had put aside their hostilities to join forces and find the one member of the group that had always over-looked their negative characteristics and, instead, pointed out the good in all of them.

★★★★★

Stopping first at the upstairs apartment where he lived, Bud gathered some clothing and other essentials before exiting through his family's bakery and restaurant located on the ground floor of the same building.

"Hey, hold on there. You just wait a minute!" Camilla ordered as she tried to catch up to Bud and the two women that accompanied him. Bud did not stop, nor did he slow down. Instead, he proceeded to walk through, what both Percy and Ally could not have avoided noticing, a bigger kitchen than either could ever have remembered being in.

Ally's eyes were so wide open from her surprise they looked like two, two-toned saucers. Failing in her attempt to muffle her verbal outburst, she blurted out, "Man, this kitchen is so big — it's freakin' diabolical!" Percy gave Ally a deliberate, albeit not too aggressive, shove when she ran into Ally's back after Ally slowed down to look around the room. Responding immediately to Percy's prompt, Ally picked up her pace; both she and Percy would remain close behind Bud, as he led them out into a parking lot.

"What do you mean you're going to Utah?" While wiping her plump hands on her flour-encrusted apron, Camilla's voice cracked when she took closer notice of the two women following her son.

Percy briefly glanced in Camilla's direction as Camilla, in turn, glanced towards her — neither woman seemed to be phased by the other. On the other hand, Ally and Camilla took noticeable double takes of one another. For Ally, it was a direct response to Camilla's shocked expression — an expression Camilla made no attempt to hide. Camilla's shock was in response to seeing Ally's eye and hair colors. After she took her second look at Ally, Camilla's mind began to swirl with a myriad of questions for her eldest son.

"It's no biggy, Ma. We just have to help one of the gals in my group. She went AWOL." Bud's answer came quick as he hurriedly unlocked the back door to a white panel van which had pictures and writing on both side and back doors.

Denoting superior accuracy, hand-painted renditions of a large mixing bowl, rolling pin and a few golden-crusted round and oblong loaves of bread festooned both side panels of the van. A basket with a red-and-white checkered cloth wrapped around a variety of fluffy muffins as well as a plate with some kind of pasta dish were painted on the back doors. Bold green letters spelled out the words "Nunzio's Bakery and Italian Eatery" and graced both the sides and back of the van directly above the mouth-watering, deliciously painted entrées and baked treats.

Standing no more than 4 feet 11 inches, Camilla Maria Santoro Jeffries, born to Italian immigrant parents, was a slightly rotund olive-skinned woman. To anyone unfamiliar with her, her size could be deceiving when it came to the kind of punch she may levy, if need be — not a punch in the literal sense (no one had dared to test that theory), but one delivered with great precision through the use of words and the weight those words carried.

Having been raised in Little Italy in the South Village, a well-defined community in Lower Manhattan, Camilla was tough enough to hold her own. Her brood of five children, four boys and one daughter, undeniably knew the fact of that.

"Wait son, what do you mean, AWOL?" Camilla pressed her son as she watched him toss a backpack into the back of the van.

"Emma, she's one of the gals in my group. She took off and her crazy ass —" The moment the word came out of his mouth, Bud caught himself and turned to the inquisitive little woman and corrected himself.

"Emma's crazy blanking daughter is all freaked out her mom has gone nuts and asked for our help." Knowing full well he was not being completely honest with his mother, Bud checked his pockets for something and then turned around and headed back into the restaurant — all three women, right on his heels, behind him.

"But —" she started, "Utah? You? Why not the doctor? And what happened to your eyes?" Camilla took a step back, her face revealing slight horror. When she looked up at her son's eyes, she saw the color red where it should have been white, and his eyelids were abnormally puffy.

Her line of questioning seemed fair enough to everyone. The reasoning behind Bud's choosing to take a side trip from the truth, and weave a web of fiction when responding to his mother's inquiries, left Percy somewhat bewildered.

"Maybe he's just in a rush to get back to meet everyone at the doc's office," Percy entertained. Bud's story telling did not seem to have any effect on Ally, providing she even noticed, Percy observed.

"If I weren't the wiser," Percy thought to herself, "I'd think Bud was single-handedly picked to find this rogue group member." But it was not just anyone listening to Bud's fanciful tale — it was Camilla, and Camilla was no one's fool. Sifting through a story containing both fact and fiction required a patient and decisive mind, and Camilla was a champion at gleaning partial truths from fanciful webs — particularly those weaved by any of her children.

Tradition dictated in an Italian family, the father was the head of the household, and the children were to pay close attention to him. As a young girl, Camilla learned to listen to what her father, Nunzio Santoro, had to say and all he had to teach. It would be Camilla's mother who often emphasized it was she who led her father to believe he was in charge. Camilla learned that may have worked between her parents and may have worked when she too became a wife; but as a child, she paid close attention to her father. That was what was expected of her.

Most of the lessons Camilla learned and applied through her life were learned from listening to her intuition, and she was not inclined to believe a good portion of the stories she was told. Thanks to her father, one of the most valuable lessons Camilla had learned, she held close to her heart. That lesson was to avoid being played for the fool, and for her to accomplish that just as her father had directed, it was up to her to be a careful listener.

"It is important," her father would teach her about listening, "to use both ears." Then Nunzio Santoro would smile at his little girl and say, "One ear to let words in, the other, to let some go. What stays, is truth."

With her own children — Camilla had honed her listening skills into a fine-tuned instrument. This was particularly true when her eldest son spoke. Camilla knew full well a lot of words would be entering, and a fair share of words would be exiting when James Elliot Jeffries did the telling.

"I see why you think you have to go." Camilla's voice was patient. "You'll need to eat something before you head out." Still quite uncertain as to what was going on with her son or how the two women that stood next to him were involved, she knew if she knew anything, it was her son rarely turned down a meal.

Bud looked at both Ally and Percy and finally introduced them to his mother.

"Sorry Ma, this is Ally and Percy. They're in my group, too." Turning to Ally and Percy with a nod of his head in his mother's direction, he added, "This is my mom, Camilla." In an unusual fashion for him, Bud finished with, "Guess you guys already figured that out, huh."

Without hesitation, Camilla immediately offered all of them something to eat.

"Come, sit at the table. It'll take no time to heat up some pasta. You like pasta? Who doesn't like pasta! Come — sit," Camilla directed. It is doubtful if anyone had wanted to object or if they would have dared to. The sound of plates clattering against one another had already begun as Camilla retrieved them from the cabinet.

Percy wanted to excuse herself, but once she saw what Camilla brought to the table, she eagerly joined Bud and Ally who had wasted no time in putting silver to ceramic.

"Oh my God! This is the most delicious food I've ever had!" Ally was ravenous and did not hold back her eagerness to dive into the food piled on her plate, of which she came close to inhaling.

Suddenly, Camilla did not find all the different colors the young girl displayed so shocking. In fact, upon now hearing the familiar sound of forks clanging on plates and after witnessing the speed at which Ally consumed the contents on her plate, she found this lovely young woman to be uniquely attractive. It did not hurt, either, Camilla found Ally's eating style to be similar to that of her own children.

Camilla loved to cook and loved to feed people too. What she loved even more was when the people she fed loved her food. And so, when sounds of ecstasy came first from Ally and then from Percy, Camilla welled up with great satisfaction.

Being nobody's fool, Camilla knew her son all too well. Once well fed, he would mellow enough to be more congenial and open to conversation and — the truth. Quietly amused, she kept bringing more bread and pasta to the table. As she expected — the more the food flowed, the more the words came.

In a relatively accurate fashion, Bud laid out the morning's events in between chewing and swallowing the pasta which was covered in marinara sauce his mother had ladled on his plate. When the fork piled high with pasta seemed not to satisfy his eagerness to quash his tremendous appetite, he scooped up as much as a slice of freshly baked French bread could hold and shoved that (which could fit) into his mouth — one heaping mound at a time.

Bud's capable display of being able to talk as clearly as he did while his mouth was completely full was quite a skill. He probably acquired the talent for eating this way by perfecting the practice throughout his entire life; but in all fairness, some of the credit for his smooth rhythm while masticating and conversing should have been attributed to his love affair with chewing huge wads of gum.

Once they had filled their stomachs to the point of aching and Camilla had heard Bud's synopsis of the morning's events — some in horror and some with cautious trepidation — she fell into agreement with her son which, it seemed, she was used to doing. She was sure of only one thing:

The group member who was missing meant a lot to her son. From what she could garner from her son's story, the missing woman had been a great help to him, and it appeared she had been of great help to all of the other members of the group as well.

Camilla felt a growing sense of pride arise inside of her, knowing her son wanted to participate in such an endeavor to find and bring home the woman of whom he spoke so fondly. It showed the less selfish side of his character — a side Camilla realized she was seeing with more frequency since he had started his therapy sessions. She did, however, have a real problem with one individual in her son's story. That individual was Stelle Marksdale, the doctor's wife.

Between shoveling pasta and bread into his mouth, her son described how this woman had sprayed him in the face with pepper spray thus answering his mother's question as to what had happened to his eyes. Even though her son clarified that he had put all of that behind him as he knew it was an accident, Camilla was not as willing to relinquish annoyance or concern in regards to this woman. Her protective nature was something Camilla felt she could not — and by personal choice, would not — let be brushed away so quickly.

With her dual-colored eyes slightly glazed over, Ally politely excused herself to visit the bathroom to freshen up. Appreciating, but rarely observing, good table manners, Camilla immediately took notice and was pleased by this oddity of a young woman, once again.

Percy thought she would do the same as soon as Ally returned. During the food free-for-all, both women had a fair amount of marinara sauce find its way to more places than their stomachs.

Once the clickity-clack of Ally's heels was out of ear shot, Camilla looked seriously at Bud. "Son, I feel good about you taking this trip. And I think it wise that Donato goes along with you."

Bud's jaw dropped. "Ma! No! Ain't no reason for him to go!"

"I would feel better knowing there were more men on this trip than you and the doctor. These ladies would feel more secure with the two of you together, too, I'm sure."

"But Ma, the English dude, he'll be there too!" Knowing his true feelings about Dill Bigley to start with, even though they had begun to mend some of the fences they had between the two of them, Bud knew Dill would be of little assistance in his current condition. And after describing to his mother some of what had transpired that morning — even though he did not know the full story of how Dill's physical condition had waned so dramatically — he knew Camilla was aware it had.

"From what you've said, the Englishman will be of little help," Camilla said in a serious and matter-of-fact tone. "In fact, he will need more help than anyone else, it would seem."

"Damn English!" Bud cursed in silence. Donato, his youngest brother, and he got along well, but Bud really did not want an additional passenger.

"You know, if anything happens to the van, Donato is the best mechanic too," Camilla continued.

Bud knew arguing with his mother at that point would probably be useless and would take up too much time. By then, he could see she had started to clear the table, and he recognized he was beginning to feel quite relaxed (the way one does) after having had a big meal. He bent his head all the way back and then to the sides (popping his neck); and surmised that, it may not be all that bad having Donato accompany him on the trip after all.

"You know, Bud," Percy interjected, "It would be good to have an extra driver. You never know what we may run into."

The stamp of approval coming from Percy caught Bud off guard. He was surprised as the two of them had originally argued over whether they should take both her rig and the restaurant's van. Percy felt, at the time, neither needed a backup driver, and both were perfectly capable of driving the full distance on their own. Had they chosen to go in that direction, Ally likely would have ridden with her, leaving Bud to take the bakery van by himself — a waste of space in both of their estimations.

If Mrs. Fins chose not to drive, Dill was certainly not in any shape to do so. That would leave the two of them needing a ride. Bud wanted to avoid Dill having to ride along with him, and he really had no desire for Mrs. Fins to tag along either. She could be and had been, albeit deservedly, harsh and abrupt with him on more than one occasion. Bud simply did not look forward to being in such close proximity to her perfectionistic ways. He would prefer it if "English" and "Mrs. Prim" would ride with someone other than himself.

"Yeah, I guess, it's just that —" Before he could finish, Camilla was calling out Donato's name.

When Donato entered from another room, he was wearing a white apron similar to Camilla's over a white T-shirt, and he too had remnants of flour on his arms, a few smudges on his face and a light dusting in his pitch black, loosely combed back hair.

Percy gasped. His olive complexion was just a little darker than that of his older brother, Bud, and his chiseled features along with his almost black eyes made him appear to be what she had always envisioned a Roman god would look like.

"Yes, Ma, what do ya need?"

Percy gasped again upon hearing Donato's voice. She had never heard a voice sounding, like it had a texture. For Percy, his voice sounded to the ear like velvet would feel to the touch.

"Donato, I need you to join your brother, James." Camilla made her way to her younger son's side and looked up at his six-foot two-inch frame. "James has to go on a rescue mission and needs you to go along."

"What?" Donato asked as he looked at Bud and then at Percy and then at Bud and back at Percy again — confusion written all over his face.

"I'm heading to Utah, Donnie. I will tell you all about it once we get on the road. These gals are going too." He casually pointed towards Percy who stood frozen in place.

"Gals?" Seeing no one other than Camilla and Percy, he looked back at his brother. As he started walking towards the table where Bud was still sitting, the clicking sound of Ally's high-heels could be heard as she entered the kitchen — at which point, she stopped dead still in the doorway.

Her chin dropped leaving her mouth wide open, "Whose are you?" Ally's words clumsily spilled out. "I mean — who are you?" Clearly breathless and just above a whisper, it was all Ally could muster as her cheeks began to turn crimson.

"This is my son Donato; he will be going on the trip with all of you." Camilla offered cheerfully.

Donato's eyes followed everyone's eyes in the room, leading them to the doorway. At the same moment he saw Ally, the tip of his shoe caught an uneven spot on the concrete floor which, in turn, caused him to lose his balance, and he clumsily fell down — hard.

After seeing Donato (Percy's first Roman god) sprawled with his legs and arms awkwardly going this way and that, she was jarred back into reality. Under her breath she muttered, "So much for that fantasy!"

"Oh great, here we go," was all that came out of Bud as he headed to help his brother up. Ally, being even faster (which was a pretty amazing feat for someone wearing high-heeled spiked shoes), beat him to his brother's aid.

"Here, let me help you up." Ally reached down to Donato, and he sheepishly took her hand rising quickly to his feet — his face now more crimson than Ally's.

"Are you okay? Come over here." Ally led Donato to the closest chair. "Sit here for a minute." Ally gently went through the motions of dusting off Donato's T-shirt when Bud assured her, "He'll be fine, Ally. We gotta get going."

"Not before I get some meatball sandwiches packed up. Donato, if you're okay, go pack. James, come help me," Camilla instructed while putting dishes into the sink.

Donato was still holding on to Ally's hand looking stunned. As he gathered his faculties, Donato's gaze became fixated on the young woman's eyes. It was apparent his fixation went further than the two different colors he saw. It was as if he were looking past the colors and peering deeper into her soul. Both he and Ally were enraptured by the other and lingered in each other's stare for what seemed longer than the moment it actually was, until it dawned on Donato his mother was speaking to him.

"Your brother says you'll be gone for a few days so pack enough for that, and be sure to take something warm."

Camilla shot Bud a glance while pulling several containers of food from the huge walk-in refrigerator.

"Doesn't it snow in Utah, son?"

Snow! In everyone's haste, Bud realized no one knew yet where exactly in Utah they were going. That detail could make quite a difference in the clothing choices he had made. Surely, that detail would be made available to everyone, once they met back at the doctor's office. But, just in case, he excused himself and ran upstairs to get more weather-appropriate clothing. While he was at it, he gathered some warmer garments for Donato too.

There is something to be said about the closeness of Italian families, even those who live in modern-day America. And, there is something particularly special to be said about Italian mothers. Camilla was no exception. They are nothing if not involved in their children's lives and attentive to their children's needs.

Being a woman of strong faith, Camilla also believed her faith spoke to her through intuition. She arrived at most of her conclusions through what she called her "mother's intuition" — another example of her faith's messaging methods. Her intuition was not something she took lightly either. If she had a feeling, she followed through with it — no questions asked. Her children and her husband, James Elliot, had learned long before this to never question her intuition. It made life a lot easier for everyone involved and (in its favor) had been proven time and time again to be a valid delivery system of inevitable events — a fact Camilla reminded her family of on a regular basis over the years, almost as regularly as she recited her rosary.

The reaction the girl, with three colors of hair and two colored eyes, had to Camilla's son Donato, and likewise his reaction to her, did not go unnoticed by anyone in the room — the least of which was Camilla. Though Percy's initial reaction to him was equally as obvious, Camilla had not witnessed it. It was of no consequence at that point anyway. Once she had seen Donato fall as if having a spasm of some sort, Percy's moment of titillation had passed.

A mother who was ever eager for her sons to marry, Camilla could hear her motherly instincts talking to her. Yes, Donato was indeed joining his brother on this rescue mission to Utah.

"After all," Camilla said to herself, feeling pride she had set the ball into motion, "It's the least a mother could do."

Donato had some loose ends to tie up before he could leave, so Bud, Ally and Percy proceeded on to Percy's house first to pack up the clothes she would need and a few other essentials (like an ice chest for the food Camilla was preparing). At Percy's suggestion, a quick stop at an automotive store provided them with a shovel and snow chains in case they got stuck in the snow. Then they swung by Ally's to get all of her necessities: several pairs of shoes including a "real cute," but sensible, pair of snow boots and, of course, her birds.

In short order, all four (or six if taking into account the birds) were waiting in the pre-designated spot for all of the others to arrive. Percy and Bud had already agreed, until his eyes were better, she would drive first. Knowing she was a professional truck driver, Bud felt more at ease than if either his younger brother or Ally were to drive the family's company van. He sat in the passenger seat and closed his eyes letting them rest, as they still had a way to go before returning to normal. Donato and Ally sat somewhat nervously together in the next row of seats in back of them.

"How long do you think it will take to get there?" Ally's voice sounded like a kid hyped up on sugar, ready for a vacation to Disneyland with the whole family — a fact which did not go unnoticed by Percy. This time, though, due to the mood she was in — as Percy loved to travel and was excited about the trip — she did not let Ally's impetuous nature bother her.

"If we have good weather," checking her phone, Percy began, "We could get there in about twelve hours. I can tell better when I know exactly where we are going in Utah."

With all the people in this group going, Percy thought to herself it could take as long as two or three days just for bathroom stops, alone. Percy's tone took a negative turn. "So many people going will only slow us down. It seems kind of stupid to me."

"I think it will be fun. Won't it, babies?" Ally turned in her seat to look at her two sparrows. They both appeared to be well secured in their cage in the space directly behind the back row of seats in the van. She began making cooing and clicking sounds in an attempt to communicate with her rescued baby birds.

"Besides," Ally turned back around facing the front seat. She had long ago proven she was not one to stop talking when she had a thought emerge. "We all could have so much more fun traveling this way, Percy!"

Percy kept her eyes looking forward while she tightened her grip on the steering wheel. Aside from Ally bringing her birds on the trip — which resulted in their needing a larger vehicle with all the other passengers too — she questioned herself as to her reasoning for having Ally ride with her instead of someone else like Mrs. Fins and Mr. Bigley who had not yet arrived.

The girl's chattering alone was a constant reminder as to why Percy felt almost immediate agitation whenever Ally was in her presence. Unfortunately, it made sense that Ally ride with her, especially if Bud and his brother were going to be in the same vehicle.

Bud was not known for his tact and never tried to hide his unbridled interest in the girl — actually, anything that looked like a girl for that matter. Percy still found herself perplexed by her decision to keep the goofball and her birds with her. She was aware she had no reason, as far as she could decipher, to try to protect Ally from Bud and had about as much interest in Bud as she did in developing hemorrhoids. Her thoughts were interrupted by a soft cooing sound Ally was directing towards the two caged sparrows that had begun to chirp noisily in response.

Cringing, Percy thought, "Jesus, I won't be able to take this all the way to Utah." She may very well have had a valid point, for at that moment, they had not left the doctor's office parking lot.

★★★★★

Dill Bigley's financial consulting business was doing quite well. That fact became evident to Mrs. Fins when they pulled into the parking garage reserved for the residents of the towering building in downtown Seattle where he lived.

Aware that Dill's gate was not yet steady, Mrs. Fins kept her arm wrapped around his, helping him to traverse the enclosed garage until they were safely inside of the elevator. When Dill told her which floor he lived on, Mrs. Fins pushed the button numbered "21," and the elevator began its ascent. The result — a jarring movement strong enough to cause Dill's legs to wobble beneath him — forced him to reach out towards the elevator wall. Normally, when Dill Bigley spoke, he did so in an astute and refined manner, so when an uncharacteristic and high-pitched "Whoa" escaped his lips, it caught both he and Mrs. Fins off guard. Struggling to stay upright, he began swaying back and forth — his legs feeling like they were liquifying beneath him.

"Those pills Dr. Marksdale gave you!" There was an undeniable trace of anger in Mrs. Fins voice. "They've had such a negative effect!" She maneuvered herself into a position under Dill's arm and against his side, firmly pushing him against the elevator wall for additional support.

"Oh dear, Mr. Bigley. Please hold on to me."

Without hesitation and with notable clarity, Dill released, "Of course, Mrs. Fins."

"Do you have someone I could call to come and stay with you, Mr. Bigley?"

Mrs. Fins, certain that Dill was in no shape to travel, did not feel she could leave him alone, either. It did not escape her it may not have been just the drugs affecting Mr. Bigley's senses. Even for a non-medical person such as herself, Mrs. Fins could see Mr. Bigley's head was quite abnormally swollen — causing her concern over the physical condition of his brain.

"Perhaps the swelling is responsible for some other ill side effects," Mrs. Fins considered, "aside from lending him the appearance of that poor soul, the Elephant Man, Mr. Bigley's thought processes must be all askew." Mrs. Fins was beginning to fret — something she did often and quite successfully.

Dill's response, "I don't," interrupted Mrs. Fins' thoughts.

Some may think when the answer to a question, such as the one Mrs. Fins asked Dill, replied as "no," it would indicate a sadness in relation to his or her life's circumstances. That was not the case for Dill Bigley. For him, in fact, it was quite the contrary.

Taking into account the circumstances he faced, he knew that even if he did have someone to call upon, it was imperative he convince Mrs. Fins otherwise. The only other choice than going with her on the trip was for her to stay with him, and that would only be until the drugs had worn off; at which point (he presumed), she would know he would be well enough to leave alone. This was an end result that, even in his drug-induced befuddled mind, would be completely unacceptable. No, Mr. Bigley had only one choice as he saw it, and that was to be able to accompany Mrs. Fins like all the others in the group would be doing on their trip to Utah.

"Oh dear, Mr. Bigley, are you quite certain? I don't think it's a good idea that you go on this trip in your condition." Mrs. Fins held herself firmly against Dill pressing him into the elevator's wall, and with growing trepidation, she watched as the elevator indicator light went steadily from the parking lot level and continued its ascent to the twenty-first floor. She quietly held out hope it would not stop before his floor; but just in case it did, she braced herself — positioning her feet firmly in place. Her biggest fear was when the elevator came to a complete stop, the effect of its deceleration would cause Dill to topple over. She did not believe his head could take anymore. She was quite certain — her's could not.

"I'll be alright. This medication will wear off soon." Trying to assure Mrs. Fins he would in no way be a burden to her or anyone else for that matter, he stated, "Once I gather my wits about me, I will be of great assistance to you and the others in finding Emma."

Dill Bigley faced his dilemma with staunch confidence. He derived that, true as it was — his head being very swollen compared to its normal size and his body being filled with sedatives and pain medication — his determination would win out over anything which would stand between Mrs. Fins and himself from being able to take this trip — together. He had to flush the drugs from his body, even if it meant the already present throbbing in his head were to increase as a result. Dill reasoned, if there was ever a time for him to exude the infamous British stiff upper lip, it was now.

Dill quietly contemplated how he could go about straightening himself up, both figuratively and literally. It would require all of the strength he could draw from down inside himself; nonetheless, he knew he had to do it to convince Mrs. Fins he was capable of traveling unassisted — and do it, he would.

As he deliberately attempted to take in a deep breath, his nostrils could barely expand due to his swollen face. He stood as erect as his self-inflicted mangled body could muster. With his lower jaw jutting forward — a physical act which instantly reminded him as to why pain was to be avoided — he sternly said to himself, "I can do this. I must do this. I will do this. Yes — quite . . . ." As the elevator doors slowly opened, wrapped in each other's arms, he and Mrs. Fins exited together.

In order to further facilitate his plan and prove his faculties were returning, Dill asked Mrs. Fins to give him back his keys which he had given to her in the doctor's office. Somewhat reluctant at first, Mrs. Fins obliged him. Without the full use of both of his eyes — one being swollen shut and the other with the lid only partially open — he used both of his hands to feel his way around the doorknob, until he was successful at inserting the key and opening the door to his high-rise condominium.

Up until that moment, the thought of Mrs. Fins being in his home had only been a daydream he visited with pleasing regularity. In that moment, he realized those thoughts were resurfacing and making him aware his breathing had become heavier and, Dill feared, noticeable. Knowing his daily thoughts always led back to Mrs. Fins, it did not strike Dill as anything to be concerned with, in fact, he preferred it that way. What other thoughts would be as uplifting or meaningful than any he entertained of her? For others, Dill was aware his constant thoughts of Mrs. Fins — as lovely as she was unattainable — may indicate he suffered from a deeply rooted psychological abnormality. And now Dill's fanciful thoughts were intersecting with reality, and his dreams were colliding with a world he chose more often, than not, to escape.

"How odd," he thought. "My lovely Mrs. Fins and I are finally alone, and all it took was my being physically mutilated beyond recognition."

For all that had transpired since he was in his condominium several hours earlier, the series of unfortunate occurrences were too foggy in nature for Dill's excessively compromised brain to grasp. "Perhaps," he found himself thinking, "to get out of this soggy swamp of grogginess, I must see what I can remember."

While he sat on the edge of his bed where Mrs. Fins had led him and instructed him to stay, she gathered the clothes he told her he wished to take on the trip, and Dill continued trying to remember the events of the night before.

First, he recalled there had been the opera, one of his favorites. He remembered attending it in the comfort of his living room. Then things began to get fuzzy again. There was his date — yes — his date — a bottle of his finest Port. He vaguely remembered consuming more than he had planned, and now, as he sat on the edge of his bed, he had to acknowledge his unbridled consumption of alcohol had led him into a self-inflicted drunkenness. Notably, it had been a rare and expensive bottle of Port he had ingested, but to the brain, the price or quality made no difference. The Port produced the same outcome rot-gut whiskey would have, had he consumed it in the same fashion. Under his breath, Dill chastised himself — "shameful."

Second, there was a phone call — yes, a phone call. Dill remembered it came in the middle of the night. It remained unclear why it came or what it was all about. He did not remember who he had talked to either. His only recollection was he needed to meet with Dr. Marksdale early in the morning. From there, only bits and pieces of light and unrecognizable faces and voices mumbling indiscernible words flickered behind Dill's swollen eyes.

There had been such an assault on his brain, Dill did not think he would be able to put all the events back into place; and some memories, he concluded, may be gone forever. At best, the rest would remain out of reach until the medication he had ingested wore off completely.

As the minutes passed, he began to feel some of the damage he had managed to inflict on himself. He carefully leaned to his side to see himself in the mirror hung on the wall next to the closet where Mrs. Fins was retrieving his clothes. What he saw made him gasp. His face looked like it had met with a dastardly event which left the flesh hanging in bruised layers barely clinging to his skull. Little did he know at the time, it was all of his own doing — a direct result from his bashing his skull about on hard and inanimate objects while eavesdropping on Mrs. Fins and the good doctor's conversation.

"Oh, Mrs. Fins!" Dill's voice cracked as he looked at her through the slit of one sorrowful eye.

Mrs. Fins saw the urgency on Dill's face, and, as she was accustomed to when seeing someone in need, she hurriedly went to his side.

"Oh, Mr. Bigley, what is it?" She sat next to him on the bed and took his hand in hers.

"My face — my God, Mrs. Fins! What a horror it is." Dill turned his face away from Mrs. Fins hoping to prevent her from seeing it. In a rather pathetic whimper, he added, "Please look away."

Gently squeezing one of his hands in hers, she raised her other hand to place underneath Dill's chin and turned his face towards hers.

"Mr. Bigley, you have had an accident, and all of this swelling and bruising will soon go away."

Dill looked into Mrs. Fins' soft, gray-blue eyes and instantly felt more at ease.

"What kind of accident, Mrs. Fins? What on earth happened to me?"

For the first time, Dill realized how truly far out of the loop he was. Having no memory at all of an accident, or any other misfortune which would leave him with such a dreadful malformation of flesh, he awaited Mrs. Fins' answer.

"We're not really sure, Mr. Bigley. We believe you took a hard fall in the doctor's office. Stay right here, I will get you some ice." Without further discussion she got up and proceeded to find her way into the kitchen.

Having never been in his condominium before, Mrs. Fins was taken aback by how beautiful it was but had no time to linger. What stood out to her above all else was how clean it was, something which impressed her a great deal. When she returned with a make-shift ice pack she was quick to comment on that fact.

"Your home is quite nice and so tidy, Mr. Bigley. I'm quite impressed."

She sat next to Dill and placed the ice-pack in his hand telling him to hold the pack against his forehead and eye. Making her way back to the closet, she gathered the last of Dill's clothes which she would pack for him. Turning her head slightly, she spoke to Dill over her shoulder.

"You'll be alright, Mr. Bigley. The swelling will go down soon, and I've no doubt you'll be back to your normal handsome self."

At first, the ice was shockingly cold to his skin causing Dill to take in a quick breath. The cold, he concluded, was a good sign. If his senses were returning, he surmised, maybe the trade for an increased degree of pain would not be such an unfair price for having some of his memory return.

The cold ice-pack and the fact he thought he looked like a nightmarish ghoul were not the only things causing Dill shock. Mrs. Fins' words, "your normal handsome self," continued to play over and over in the back of Dill's now disfigured face. Not one to dwell on how anyone may think of his looks, Dill found himself quite taken with Mrs. Fins' complimenting his "handsome self." But then, Mrs. Fins was not just anyone.

Stelle stuffed one more garment into her overstuffed suitcase which was lying on the bed and angrily said to her husband, "Why would you keep all of it from me, I just don't get it Phillip."

"It's not something I wanted to do Stelle." The doctor looked across the bed at his wife, "I think I've got everything I will need." He snapped his suitcase closed opposite his wife's. "I was sure everything that happened back then was all behind me."

"But it wasn't, and you kept it from me. I knew something was up for months." Stelle went into her closet one more time pulling out a stylish wool scarf which, with great effort, she stuffed into one of the sides of her already bulging suitcase.

"When you started to drink like a fish, I knew something was up. But you kept denying that anything was wrong whenever I'd ask." Shooting her husband an angry look, Stelle continued.

"I look like a fool — not knowing my husband was being blackmailed!" Stelle took the top of her lipstick off and applied one last layer before pulling out her blush brush and touching up both her cheeks on her freshly washed face before tossing both items into her makeup bag and closing her purse. She stood looking at herself in her vanity mirror — her face looking a good deal better than it had earlier.

"And for what? All you had to do was tell me. That is the worst part of it all, you were hiding it." The anger resonated in her voice, but as she and her husband headed down the long hallway towards the front door, she turned to him just before exiting their home — her tone having noticeably mellowed.

"We have to figure all of this out once and for all, Phillip. We must."

Due to his right ankle still being sore from his earlier fall, the married doctors slowly made their way around to a shiny Black Lexus parked in the closest of the five garage stalls, adjacent to their Medina mansion.

"I can't believe you kept so much from me all these years, Phillip." Stelle was quick to start as she pulled the car out of the garage. "We promised we would not keep secrets, and these aren't just any secrets!"

"I know, Stelle, and I'm sorry. I was afraid — just plain afraid." Shame could be heard in the good doctor's voice.

"Afraid? Afraid of what? Me? Don't tell me you were afraid of me!" Stelle's voice was raised as she pulled out of their long, horseshoe-shaped driveway and onto the main road. "I've never been anything but understanding!"

Knowing this was neither the place nor the time to question anything his wife may say, the doctor kept his voice — and his head — low.

"No, of course not. I — I — was only afraid of —" His voice began to trail off.

"Oh no you don't, Phillip! I meant it when I said I'd had all I could take — no more avoidances, secrets or lies."

Stelle's foot involuntarily pressed harder on the gas pedal resulting in the Lexus lurching forward, startling both of them. It alarmed Stelle enough to cause her to let up on the gas, but just enough to slow her down to a dozen or so miles per hour higher than the posted speed limit.

"I know. It was never you — it was him. It was always him and what he could, or would, do to us." The doctor swallowed hard before continuing.

"He always held it over me, the son-of-a-bitch! Finally, he called in his debt." The doctor squirmed from side to side in the passenger seat.

"Are you talking about Elan? If that is it, you have to be kidding me!"

Dr. Marksdale's face was so close to the window his words were muffled, and his breath fogged the glass. "He held it over me."

"What?" Stelle snapped.

Dr. Marksdale turned his face towards his wife. He did not feel he could say exactly what he wanted to, but knew he had to be open with her — more now than ever before. He had tried over the years not to show her how her prior relationship with Dr. Elan Glenn, though very short lived and over almost a year before he himself had met her, had always left a bad taste in his mouth. And though Stelle had chosen him and married him too, the arrogance Elan Glenn displayed when no one else was around had been a thorn in Dr. Marksdale's side. Worse yet, Dr. Elan Glenn knew it and gloated whenever he could, taking care to do it where no one else would see. And though Dr. Marksdale had a propensity to lean in the direction of what he himself would diagnose as mild paranoia, Dr. Marksdale was certain of and harbored no doubt of Dr. Elan Glenn's methodology.

Contrary to what his admirers would see, Dr. Elan Glenn was not always what his image portrayed. Over the years, whenever and however he could, he would needle Dr. Marksdale and goad him with the fact he had been with Stelle first. This event would leave the overanxious, self-conscious and ever striving perfectionist psychiatrist in a bad way. It was not that his wife had been with Dr. Elan Glenn, the man who had become his nemesis, but that this nemesis — whenever the opportunity presented itself — would re-plant a seed in the overly fertile imagination of the good doctor's mind. That seed was fear. And when that seed grew, it reminded the good doctor that if Stelle were to ever know the complete truth surrounding the hazing, the resulting death and his involvement in the subsequent grade changes, she would leave the good doctor and go back to the supposed "'good-doer" who had always promised to be waiting in the wings.

The good doctor knew that even though Dr. Elan Glenn was referred to as the good-doer, he knew if all those in Dr. Elan Glenn's fan club were aware of his darker side, his so-called friend would be in one hell of a hot stew. Quietly, Dr. Marksdale mused, "That is one pot I would love to stir."

"Phillip — are you paying attention to me?" Stelle's voice interrupted Dr. Marksdale's thoughts. "You didn't cause Leon Fisker's death, and no one can prove you did."

"He knew there was no one who would admit to their participation in the hazing, but —" Clearing his throat and sitting up straight, Dr. Marksdale ended with, "Elan had evidence — I changed the grades. I didn't want them to get away with what they'd done."

Dr. Marksdale's memory was only clear on some facts of that night. There was a total of six people involved: four older fraternity brothers who relentlessly goaded the two freshmen — he being one and Leon Fisker being the other. Both young men — barely past boyhood, really — held high hopes of being accepted into the fraternity. Neither understood, at the time, their acceptance had more to do with the clout and money their names would bring to the fraternity than anything the fraternity could do for them. Even after their bodies rebelled against the overdose of alcohol being forced into them by repeatedly emptying whatever contents their stomachs held, they were stripped naked and humiliated into drinking more. The last insult was to jump into the dark and cold water of the lake and stay in the water, until they could barely move their limbs.

Leon Fisker, suffering from alcohol poisoning, had reached the point of hyperthermia and could no longer grip the slimy rocks to pull himself onto the shore. Not one of the four frat brothers would assist him. In fact, they jeered at him while stepping on his fingers as he clawed at the mud and rocks. Dr. Marksdale lost sight of Leon once immersed under the water; and try as he may, having no feeling in his arms, he could not swim to where the other freshman had gone under.

The four older frats pulled him to shore where upon they hurriedly dressed him. He recalled being thrown into the bed of a truck; and after that, there was only darkness. Whatever the memories were (when he first awoke in the frat house the next morning), they were so convoluted it would take him years to piece them all back together. At best, they would be only a patchwork of drunken sounds and images. The only real emotion he could identify with was fear — a real fear of what the other four fraternity members were willing to do to him if he ever divulged what he thought he may know.

Leon Fisker's absence was noted by the school after a week of his missing classes, but that did not arouse a cause for alarm at first. That only began to emerge after two weeks had passed, when Leon's family members had not heard from him either.

Some time had passed before Leon's body was accidently and literally stumbled upon on a distant and sheltered shore of the lake by an unsuspecting fisherman. Due to the condition of his bloated and decomposing corpse, any sign of physical abuse was no longer apparent.

Young Phillip Marksdale knew the guilty parties would never have to face their crimes, particularly with him being the only living witness to the events of that night. At best, his fractured memory would never allow for conviction. And if their threats were to be ignored, he may not live long enough to testify against the culprits. "No," Phillip Marksdale concluded with what little memory he was able to piece together, his testimony would never be able to stand up to the four frat brothers' renditions of the events that night of horror held secret. And so, the young misguided Phillip Marksdale knew if any of the frat brothers were to pay for their horrendous crimes, it would be because of whatever he could do — and do something, he would. Once and for all, he made the decision to take it upon himself to be the responsible party's judge — and jury.

He knew those involved would stick together leaving the younger freshman holding the bag himself. He had always justified his actions of the grade changes under those terms, as it was only himself and the other foolish freshman, Leon Fisker, who were the victims of the older fraternity brothers' sinister acts. Unfortunately for the young Phillip Marksdale, his poor decision-making tools would prove to be operating at full throttle. When he decided to share these secrets with someone — someone he believed to be a friend and worthy of his trust — he not only continued on his path of pathological, bad decision making; but, he found out there is only one way to keep a secret — that being, to never reveal it to anyone — ever. Once a secret left one's lips, the young Phillip Marksdale came to discover, it belonged to the entirety of the universe. At the time, though, he felt none other than his trusted old college pal — Elan Glenn — would be better to share his secrets and thoughts regarding retaliation.

As Stelle pulled onto the highway heading towards the doctor's office, she questioned her husband further.

"You have to know that I have been faithful to you, don't you Phillip? I would never go back to him."

"I used to think it was just that —"

"What else, Phillip? Tell me — we don't have long before we get to your office."

The doctor started, "He knew about the hazing; and, he knew about the grades being changed." The doctor stopped and took a thoughtful breath. His replaying the events of that horrible night — when Leon Fisker drowned during the skullduggery practice of hazing — left the good doctor's body cold. "He is the only one who has proof it was me — that was a part of it all."

"So? He's not going to use it." Stelle was emphatic. "Even if he did, he kept it a secret, and that makes him just as involved as you." Stelle's hands gripped the steering wheel tighter. "Those involved would have been in more trouble if the truth had come out — a lot more trouble."

"There's more." The good doctor took in a deep breath and just let it flow out, along with the words he had dared not say for all those years:

"I changed your grades too. Please forgive me."

"You did what? You changed my grades?" What little color she had in her face rapidly washed away.

"I wanted both of us to graduate. I wanted us to be together so much. I thought it was the only way." His heart was pounding so hard in his chest, the good doctor thought it would burst through his ribs.

"Do you mean to tell me I was going to fail?" The pitch of Stelle's voice came close to breaking glass.

"No, you weren't going to fail, but, well, your grades weren't as high as they needed to be for us to go into residency together." The doctor cringed, thinking he was soon most likely going to be experiencing some kind of physical pain. When nothing happened and his wife was quiet, he turned in her direction to see her with a big smile on her face.

"What is it, Stelle? What are you thinking?"

"I think it's great! I'm a damn good doctor, so it doesn't matter. And we're rich so everything is okay!" She began to chuckle, leaving her husband flabbergasted.

All these years, he had kept this secret from her out of dire fear, and she could not care less about the truth. Had he misunderstood his wife all these years? He was sure she would explode with anger if this truth were exposed. Feeling she was okay with that news, the good doctor was sure, now, she would be okay with the final piece he had kept hidden. Feeling more at ease than he had been in more years than he could remember, he ventured further with, "There is the problem of lawsuits."

"What do you mean? What lawsuits? Who would sue?"

"Any one of them I changed the grades for, if Elan breaks his silence." The doctor felt more assured as the seconds ticked by.

"There is no way any of them will ever tell the truth about Leon, I know that for sure."

"So? What does that have to do with them suing? Suing who and for what, Phillip?" Stelle had stopped chuckling, and her tone and body language had morphed into that of a recoiling snake — ready to strike.

"Me — suing me — and for any number of things." Dr. Marksdale could feel his heartbeat begin to speed up at the mere thought of all of these events unfolding.

"If I told what I know, they would sue me for defamation of character." The doctor shook his head, "No one would believe me. I'm only one. They are four." The doctor let out a heavy sigh. "They'd sue because I ruined their chance at medical school and the level their livelihoods may have reached."

Taking in a deep breath and looking down at his hands which were clasped together on his lap, he finished, "Be assured, they'd do just as I said. And they'd stick together in their lies, like they always have."

Stelle looked fearfully at her husband. "They deserve to go to prison for letting him drown." Dr. Marksdale could see his wife had started to shake.

"Yes, if it could be proven. There's no way to do that, especially now."

The doctor turned his face away from his wife and purposefully and cautiously proceeded in a matter-of-fact tone.

"Our whole way of life — was — is — in jeopardy. Changing the grades, whether morally right or not, was illegal and can be proven." Dr. Marksdale looked back out of the passenger window unaware of the other cars they shared the road with.

"Do you mean to say that Elan, Elan has proof?"

"He always threatened he would expose me, and dumping the group on me was my ticket out of it all." The doctor reached over to his wife and laid his hand on her leg.

"He said if I didn't take on the group, he would expose me. He has a tape of my confession."

Stelle's eyes grew big and her mouth dropped open.

"That wretched vile rat! What did I ever see in him?"

The good doctor had pondered that on many occasions himself.

"We have to find Emma in time and bring her back for next week's court appearance."

Stelle was not worried about what her husband was saying or the ramifications of their not being able to meet the court deadline. Her mind was filled with anger towards him for not telling her about everything they were now facing. "His keeping these secrets," she continued to stew, "He may as well have just thrown us off a bridge. How dare he do this to me!"

Stelle's anger did not relent there. Her anger grew towards whomever the member of the group was who left for parts unknown, leaving her to have to take this impromptu trip — a trip she had not planned — to a place she had not chosen.

"Utah! What middle of nowhere hell is that?" The question reverberated in her head. Stelle knew how to plan a trip and knew just the right methods of traveling (like a private yacht). It was all she could do to not scream at the top of her lungs. And she was mad as hell at her old beau for holding her and her husband hostage to get what he wanted.

"Bastards! Damn bastards!" She repeated in her head over and over again.

While Stelle drove, she fumed internally thinking of the things she wanted to do to everyone involved — those unspeakable acts her mind was conjuring up — those acts she would act upon, if only given the opportunity.

"How dare all of them! Every last one of them, whoever they are. Look what they've done to me!" She cursed everyone — all of those she believed had put her where she now found herself. As these thoughts filled her head, an inconceivable horror suddenly dawned on her, and it was far worse than any other thought she had up until that moment. It was then everything the good doctor had said fully sank in. Her head swung sharply to the right looking straight at Dr. Marksdale's face, and she blurted out, "Phillip — sued? You don't mean to say that — we — we — we could end up poor? Do you mean that — Phillip?"

"Yes, that real possibility exists."

Stelle's gasp for air and her shaky breathing which followed were the only sounds either of them heard, as the doctor duo drove on in an otherwise heavy silence; until they reached the parking lot where everyone else was awaiting their arrival.

*****

"I'm pretty sure it's Parks — yeah. My mom said a while back that this guy lives in Parks, or was it Park City?"

"Great! Let's all just take off to a place that Moronica thinks it might be!" Bud's head swiveled around taking in the blank expressions on the faces of all those standing next to his restaurant's van. Everyone turned to look at him including the little girl who stood next to her mother, Monica. Monica turned to look at Bud, too, her expression revealing slight irritation.

Dill appeared to be slowly coming out of the cloud which held his senses, but he still remained with the door opened in the passenger seat of Mrs. Fins' modest, but distinctly sporty, older model BMW.

"Let me take a look at that map." Dill gestured to Monica to bring it to him. "I've done a fair amount of traveling. I'll look for the fastest route. We all want to be on the same page and organized."

"No need, Dill," Percy held up her hand to Monica. "I've got GPS and already know the best route to take — I do this stuff for a livin'."

"That makes a whole lot of sense, now don't it!" Reaching into his shirt pocket, Bud realized he had not brought any gum with him, and beads of perspiration began to form on his forehead. He had been so distracted up until then, he had all but forgotten he had swallowed the last of his gum hours earlier.

Bending down to get his backpack which he immediately started to rummage through in search of a pack of gum, Bud snapped, "Yup, let's just go wandering around the country. Jesus! Do we even know this guy's name?" His search for a pack of gum, even just one piece, was proving to be an issue with no resolve, and he started to break out in an all-out sweat.

As the two doctors parked their car, Dr. Marksdale noticed a young man unfamiliar to him standing next to Ally. He started to wonder how many people in attendance were planning on taking this trip. The number of individuals felt cumbersome to him and he turned to Stelle. She was sitting perfectly still and staring out the front window, expressionless.

Dr. Marksdale nudged his wife's arm with his. "We should reconsider how many people are going Stelle. I'm afraid there may be too many."

Stelle continued to gaze motionless out the car window. She was so still the doctor could not see her breathing, and he shook her arm with his hand.

"Stelle, what is it? Stelle, tell me what you're —" His words cut off as Stelle slowly turned to face him.

"I can't be poor. I can't be poor, Phillip." Her voice revealing growing desperation deepened and she repeated, "I can't be poor."

"You're not poor, Stelle. And if we can get Emma back here in time for the hearing, you won't ever have to worry about it." He tried to assure his wife, but his honest assessment of their situation teetered on fragile ground; and, as he looked into his wife's unblinking steely glare, he knew it.

"No, I said we'd take 90 to 82 East and then take 84." Ally was looking at the map she had spread open on the hood of Mrs. Fins' BMW, as Donato stood on the other side of the car observing her, as if mesmerized.

Ally was agitated with Percy for not being open to her suggestions, instead, shrugging off her suggestions, and with an indignant tone she snapped, "It's really simple Percy! Just come here and look at the freakin' map!"

Percy shook her head as she raised her right hand — her palm open and facing Ally — a gesture Ally interpreted as Percy telling her she should shut her mouth.

"I know what I'm talkin' about, Ally. I do long hauls back and forth across this country all the time!" Cold irritation was obvious in Percy's voice.

"So? That doesn't mean you're right!" Ally testily persisted. "Come and look at the map, then ya can tell me I'm wrong."

"I don't need to waste my time lookin' at anything on your map before telling ya, that — you're wrong!" Percy's squinted eyes exposed her growing disdain.

"Ladies — ladies, please! Let us try to keep in mind our mission. Though not imperative we get along, it would be advisable." Dill Bigley's voice was calm and clearer than it had been in some time, and Mrs. Fins nodded her head making clear she was in agreement with him.

"Ehhh — She's never going to agree with anything Ally says." Bud, while nervously rummaging through all the pockets in the clothing he had packed, shot his comments in Dill's direction. "She's as stubborn as a mule, even smells like one."

"And you'd know what a mule would smell like, figurin' your nothing more than a jack-ass yourself!"

The likelihood Percy and Bud's short-lived truce was nearing its demise was becoming increasingly apparent.

As the doctors approached the group standing around their cars, they could hear the rising discord. It crossed both of their minds that, as far as it had been flimsily planned, this trip was on tremulous ground as were their futures. In order for them to be successful, something had to change and fast.

The ultimate goal of finding and bringing Emma back to Washington was, to both doctors, one which had to be met. Blatantly obvious to both doctors, too, was the more feet on the ground looking for her, the better chance of finding her. And so, any alterations to their original plan needed to be inserted, and inserted then, if there was to be any hope their risky endeavor was to meet with success.

"Listen to me, Percy, I can see right here what path we need to make." Ally pointed to the map with a long, brightly polished fingernail. She saw the two doctors approaching but was not deterred nor was she going to allow Percy's harsh tone keep her from stating her case. Percy, however, was having none of it.

"We're not Lewis and Clark for Christ's sake! We're following a route — not making a path! And your path is not the right route!" Percy, noticeably agitated, turned to look at the doctors before countering Ally's suggestion.

"It's I-5 south all the way into Portland where we catch 84 and then —" Ally abruptly interrupted her.

"What? Why Portland? We're going to Utah! God Percy, I thought you were paying attention!"

Percy felt there was little left for her to say and bit her lower lip. The tension was too great, and before she thought better of it, she blurted out, "You're such an idiot!"

In unison a resounding "Hey" was heard coming from Dill, Donato and Bud, when the good doctor interrupted all of them.

"I've got a better idea than all of us driving such a long distance. I'll charter us a jet. It will get us to Salt Lake City in just a few hours."

Everyone's eyes turned sharply towards the good doctor standing a few feet away from Percy. Stelle swung her head in her husband's direction and back at the group.

"Phillip, that is an excellent idea. We're packed already, we just have to do something with our cars."

"We can park them at the airport. Mrs. Fins, would you make the arrangements?"

"Of course, doctor. I'll have to do it from the office, where I have all the numbers." At that, Mrs. Fins turned to Dill who was still resting in the passenger seat and asked him, "Will you be alright? This shouldn't take very long."

"Yes, I will be fine right here, thank you, Mrs. Fins. You are far too kind." Dill's faculties were slowly returning but, still, with Mrs. Fins attending to him, it gave him a sense he was in an alternate dimension — a dimension, Dill Bigley entertained, where he would love to reside.

"Wait a minute, I don't want to pay for airport parking doc. That would be way too much green, I'll take the van back." Bud made a good point.

"Not to worry, Bud. I will take care of everything. All we need to do is get to the airport and soon. Mrs. Fins will handle everything else."

"What about my birds? Can they fly?" Ally's eyes widened with concern.

"They're birds, daft one! Of course, they can fly!" Percy felt she was losing her mind trying to deal with Ally. Percy was sure all the hair dyes the girl had used had seeped into and damaged what little brains the three-hair-colors airhead had.

"Shut-up Percy! She means, can they go on the plane. God, everyone knows what she meant!" Bud turned his head around looking eagerly at everyone else while getting increasingly agitated.

"I need some gum! Does anybody have any blanking gum?"

A small and gentle voice said, "I do."

Bud looked around trying to find his small-voiced savior. That is when for the first time he saw the little girl. She was about eight-years old, or so, and she was walking towards him. When she got just a couple of feet from him, she reached up holding her hand out and offered Bud a full unopened pack of pink bubble gum.

"Who are you?" It was apparent Bud had not seen her earlier, or if he had, she had not registered in his frantic search for a gum fix.

The little girl handed him the gum and introduced herself, "I'm Lizzie."

Bud reached down and took the pack of gum and tore off the top exposing several, single-wrapped pieces inside. Like a shaky addict finally getting his fix, his hands shook as he unwrapped the first piece of the precious stuff. He shoved the first piece into his mouth as fast as he could and was just about to unwrap and shove the second one in, when he saw the little girl's big brown eyes staring up into his. For a moment, he stopped and then looked down at the gum in his hand and then back at the little girl's eyes. He swallowed hard, being careful not to swallow the delicious piece of gum he was delighting in and then proceeded to insert, with noticeable difficulty, the second piece of gum back into the pack.

With kindness, the small-voiced savior said, "That's okay, you can have that piece too."

"Are you sure?" Bud slurred as his saliva began to flow.

"I'm sure."

"And your name is what again?"

"I'm Lizzie. That's my mommy." Lizzie turned to point at her mother who was standing next to her small compact car which was parked next to Mrs. Fins' BMW.

Bud followed Lizzie's gaze and realized it led him to Monica, Emma's daughter — Moronica — as Bud referred to her (and one of Bud's least favorite people). He had blamed her from the beginning for his ending up in the group and under the court's orders to receive therapy.

Somehow, Bud had managed to evade his entire role in, or taking any responsibility for, his ending up where he was. It had started with a crude comment he had made towards Monica in traffic court all those months ago and his impatience with her taking too much time, in his estimation, to plead her innocence for a traffic violation. Dill Bigley heard such comment — a comment better left unrepeated here — and being the gentleman he was, Dill was unable to keep his disgust and outrage to himself.

"See here, young man, I cannot abide your vulgar mistreatment of this fine young woman. You must apologize to her at once."

Bud's face transformed into a horrible mass of red gnarled flesh as he headed towards Dill.

"I gotta do what? I'll show you what I gotta do!" In a split-second, Bud had made his way to Dill, and with a strength he was unaware he possessed, he had lifted Dill off the floor so fast one of his shoes fell off; and for a split second, Dill's foot was left twitching and dangling at the end of his pant leg. With a force driven by his irrational anger, Bud then hurled Dill over the row of chairs in front of him. Like a madman, Bud was on top of Dill doing his best to pummel him when Percy, Emma and eventually Ally all involved themselves in the skirmish.

The end result: months of court-ordered therapy sessions with the same people — none who Bud wanted to associate with. Ironically, that was the one thing he had in common with every other member of the group.

Now, he was being saved by the generous child of the woman he blamed for his entire situation. There she stood watching her little girl and Bud in their most unlikely encounter. From Bud's perspective, Monica seemed to stand and stare at them, almost expressionless, catching him off guard and leaving him feeling a little out of his realm.

"Thanks kid — I mean — Lizzie." Bud handed Lizzie the rest of the pack of gum and put the second piece, so generously offered to him, into his shirt pocket and then turned to see the good doctor talking to Ally.

"Yes, you can take your birds, we're all going. Now, I need to know how many of us there are." He looked around and realized there was indeed one more than he had counted.

"And you are?" The doctor addressed Donato.

"I'm Donato, James' brother."

"Well, Donato, would you enlighten me as to why you are here?" The doctor inquired.

"Our mother insisted I come with James on this trip."

"I see." The doctor turned to look at Bud, hoping to get clarity.

"She thought we were going to take the van." Bud pointed to the restaurant van a few feet away.

"Donato is a real good mechanic and, well, she thought it would be —" Bud could not complete his explanation as his brother interrupted him.

"Our mom thought it would be better if there were more men on the trip, you know, to help the ladies."

"Oh — I see." The doctor looked back and forth between the two brothers. Once he looked at Dill sitting quietly in Mrs. Fins' car, and once he saw how glassy Dill's eyes were, he could find no reason to argue.

The jet required for this trip would depend upon the distance traveled, any stops along the way and the total number of passengers and crew onboard. That being the case, there were going to be eight passengers and at least two crew members. A chartered jet which could accommodate that many people and go the distance they would need to go was going to be, at a minimum, in the high teens to the low twenty-thousand-dollar range. Understanding those facts, the good doctor questioned how one more, and particularly one more able-bodied man, would present a negative result. Ultimately, he concluded he would not.

"Okay, I'm going to go upstairs and see if I can help Mrs. Fins with anything."

"Hey Doc — What da we do once we get there? Utah, I mean. How will we get around?" Bud asked what everyone else was thinking.

"Mrs. Fins will set up rentals for all of us — we'll work in teams. It will take all of us looking, if we are going to find Emma." That was the good doctor's hope, anyway. He then turned to Monica and asserted what some would consider a semblance of authority.

"If we are to have any chance of finding your mother, you have to keep trying to contact her." He looked away from Monica for a moment and at her daughter, Lizzy.

"Anything you have to do," the doctor kept his gaze on Lizzy as his tenor remained calm but firm, "to urge her to know the priority of importance that she attend the upcoming hearing —" He quickly turned his gaze towards Stelle and kept it there before continuing — "do it."

After both doctors left the parking lot and headed up to the office, Bud turned to his brother, "It must be nice to have so much dough you could do somethin' like this and not even blink an eye."

What Bud and none of the others knew was the doctor was willing to spend an awful lot to save an awful lot more.

The jet was ready and waiting for them when they arrived at the Seattle-Tacoma airport. Once their cars were parked and each one of them, along with their luggage and all the food Camilla had packed for them, were securely onboard, their pilot awaited the final go ahead from air-traffic control.

Their final destination: Park City, Utah, via Salt Lake City.

With everyone seated and belted in, the jet engines began to roar. The supremely sleek aircraft picked up speed until her wheels lifted off the runway, and for the first time in their lives, Ally's sparrows took flight.

CHAPTER NINE

Lying on her lap, the page she had opened the magazine to revealed itself, but Stelle sat staring and saw nothing — no words, no pictures. The page may as well have been left blank as her mind was preoccupied elsewhere. Knowing the full story behind her most recent discoveries, few, if any, would disagree Stelle's mind being in a state of shock was understandable.

For Stelle, facing poverty was such a foreboding concept which even for a psychiatrist with her abilities, she found the dilemma before her — and the prospect of coping with such — out of the realm of her expertise. Thus, it was then she had to admit this doctor could not heal — thyself.

As she turned to look at her doctor husband seated next to her, Stelle quivered at the prospect of losing the only lifestyle she had ever known and felt her mind spiraling in a whirlwind of despair. He had reclined his seat and with his eyes closed, he had the appearance of sleeping peacefully. Mustering tremendous effort, Stelle stifled her incredible urge to smack him in the face with the now rolled up magazine she held tightly in her trembling hands.

Percy watched as Ally held her sparrows' cage up to the window and listened to her talk to her birds, as if they were perfectly capable of understanding what she was saying to them.

"And that's the top of the clouds! Look over there. They're so big! They look like cotton candy." Ally giggled with excitement. "That's what it would look like if you were flying. What am I saying?" Ally broke into a full laugh. "We are flying!"

Whatever it was which influenced Percy to keep Ally at some level of emotional distance from herself in the past, it would now be odd and strange that she felt a connection to this woman who, in general, remained more of a pain in her side than anything else. She could not help but observe the interesting twist to her general attitude towards Ally, and this bewildered Percy.

One of her observations led her to the conclusion, Ally was not bothered by anyone listening in on her conversation with her feathered friends. On some level, the reasoning behind it — still unbeknownst to Percy — left her feeling a new and strange closeness to this peculiar young woman. Their equal propensities to opposite attitudes was their one commonality up until then; and so, Percy found herself somewhat in awe of her own emotions during that most uncharacteristic moment.

Donato was eating a sandwich his mother, Camilla, had made. He made it look so tempting; that, even though he had stuffed himself a couple of hours earlier, Bud reached into the ice chest and grabbed one for himself.

The aroma of the meatballs was so tantalizing, Mrs. Fins turned away from her window, upon realizing she could not remember when she had eaten last — only that she had left the food remains in the waste basket at the doctor's office several hours before.

"May I have one of those, Mr. Jeffries?" She politely questioned.

"Sure, here ya go." Bud reached in and pulled another sandwich out and handed it to Mrs. Fins.

She reached for it and asked, "Are you sure there is enough?"

"Are you kiddin?" Both he and Donato exchanged quick glances at each other and laughed.

"Our ma never sends too little food!" Donato was quick to offer.

"Thank you so much, I had not realized how hungry I was. It smells wonderful." Mrs. Fins started unwrapping the large meatball sandwich thereby releasing more of its odoriferous effect on everyone in the plane.

"How about you, Mr. Bigley?" She asked gently. "Would you like to share this sandwich with me?"

Dill started to sit straightened up in his seat, and with a warm smile through partially swollen lips, he accepted her offer. The two of them sat and ate quietly — Mrs. Fins chewed in her much-admired fastidious fashion, while Dill had to draw upon his greatest strengths to chew with his battered face (still managing to heroically thwart his screams).

After a short amount of time, everyone had taken a sandwich and were in varying stages of devouring them, when Ally admitted she did not have any room left to put another morsel of food into her stomach but was driven by pure temptation and lack of resistance to anything which smelled that good.

A conversation had already begun as to their next step once they arrived in Salt Lake City, while the last one eating, Monica, swallowed her last bite.

"I keep getting 'message failed to send notifications' when I try to send texts to my mom. I'll have to wait until we land!" Monica sounded desperate but calmer than she had been earlier while in the doctor's office. When Monica grabbed Dr. Marksdale by his shirt and began shaking him so hard his neck was popping, Percy had seriously considered whether she would have to rough up Monica, as she believed Monica to be radically unhinged and dangerous at the time.

"Have you told her you have her granddaughter with you?" Mrs. Fins began while she neatly folded both her and Dill's napkins on her lap. "If she knew that, knowing Emma, she will re-think herself not responding to you."

"You make a good point, Mrs. Fins," Dr. Marskdale interjected. "Emma is quite responsible, really." He held out hope his notions would prove to be true. "Emma's concerns for her granddaughter would prevail over more selfish desires."

"Yeah, one can hope, but what da we do if she doesn't answer Mor-on-a?" Bud caught himself before the full word came out just as it passed his lips. Although he did not apologize, he quickly countered with, "I meant to say 'Monica.'"

"Yes, Phillip," Stelle joined in, "What do we do if she doesn't respond?"

"We start the search. Everyone here knows what Emma looks like."

"Excuse me, Phillip. I don't have a clue what she looks like."

"Yes, but you will be with me, and Donato will be with Bud."

"Okay, give it a try, Monica," Bud suggested. "Let her know Lizzy is with us and she's freakin' out. That kinda stuff works on our ma, don't it Donnie." Donato nodded in the affirmative.

Monica pulled her phone out and sent another text, as did the good doctor. They both continued to do so off and on for the rest of the flight with both receiving the same "message undeliverable" each time. No time was wasted, though, as everyone discussed what the plan would be once they landed.

Mrs. Fins reassured she had secured rental cars which would be ready at the airport with hotel rooms for everyone in Park City. The drive time from the airport to the hotel, depending on traffic and weather, would be a little less than an hour. She noted to everyone the odds were slim they would be able to begin their search when they got to Park City. Nighttime would be approaching, and they would be on Mountain Standard Time, an hour ahead of Seattle. If Monica had not heard from Emma by morning, they would already be in Park City and could begin at daylight. They were all working together — teasingly similar to rational human beings. Everyone noticed the fact, but no one dared say it out loud.

Appearing to chase the same shadows it created, the sun intermingled with the craggy peaks of the high desert Wasatch Range, as the group's procession of rental cars made its way into Park City. Nestled at 7000 feet between ranges reaching above 11000 feet high in a basin of the Rocky Mountains and being the first week in October, everywhere anyone in the group looked, they witnessed how the surrounding hills and dingles displayed a plethora of colors.

The raw beauty before them took everyone's voice away. It was hardest for those who drove, as they had to keep their eyes on the road ahead of them, while at the same time, wanting to succumb to being drawn into the mesmerizing topography.

Canyon maples along with scrub oaks harmoniously boasted their orange and crimson leaves; golden aspen groves and serviceberry trees and shrubs trumpeted brilliant reds, oranges and yellows. All of their leaves were locked in harmonious rhythm with the cool autumn breeze — each leaf purposefully holding tight until the very last moment before being torn from, or succumbing to, a pre-set time to let go of their branches — ending their dance with life. Joining the others would be their last deed. They would drift to the ground where together, they would form carpets of decaying color — eventually becoming one with the earth.

There was no doubt autumn in the basin in which Park City resided, and all of the mountains engulfing it that first week in October, was not going to go out with a whimper — indeed, not. Instead, it would make its departure in an exuberant uproarious blaze of color.

"I've never seen such colors before! Never in real life." Monica's eyes widened as she got out of the car — Lizzy right at her side.

Lizzy turned a complete 360 degrees next to their rental car in the hotel parking lot. "Mommy, it's so pretty here, I've never seen anything like it."

As they got out of their cars, each member of the group stood for a moment and then did as Lizzy continued to do — each of them turning a full 360 degrees in an attempt to take it all in. The air was cleaner and clearer than in Seattle. It was colder, too, as indicated by everyone pulling their sweaters closed or zipping up their jackets and, those who had them, pulling up their hoods and tying them snuggly under their chins.

The hotel Mrs. Fins had booked for all of them was a masterpiece in and of itself. The architecture was that of a log cabin and was not so much unexpected as was the monumental size of the structure. It loomed large, even in its grand setting. Surrounded by nothing short of the birth of color and nature, momentarily, everyone was left breathless.

"Wow Doc, you sure know how to pick great digs." Bud was the first to speak, and though the others may have picked different words, everyone quietly had to agree. "Let's get our rooms and get everyone settled," Dr. Marksdale said as he reached into his pocket and pulled out a money clip retrieving a couple twenty-dollar bills. He handed them to the hotel bellman who had already begun loading up his cart with the group's luggage.

Mrs. Fins had reserved individual rooms for everyone except for the doctors, Monica and her daughter. She felt everyone would like their privacy, and as had already been established, cost did not seem to be an issue — at least not until Ally brought it up.

"Hey, I don't mind sharing a room with someone. This is going to cost the doctor a fortune." Looking around at everyone standing in the lobby, she asked, "Who wants to room with me?"

Percy almost snapped her neck when she turned to give a stern look at both Bud and Donato. Without any words being exchanged, both men understood neither of them would be spending any cozy sleepover with Ally, not as long as Percy was in attendance.

"That's really not necessary, Ally. I've secured very nice rooms for all of us on the same floor, allowing for our close proximity and privacy too." Mrs. Fins assured.

"Yeah, but this is way over the top. I don't mind sharing a room." Ally appeared like she would be happier to share a room than to stay alone.

"Honest, I would like to be with someone." Continuing to look around at the others, it apparently was not an issue with whom she would share a room — just that she would want to.

"This kid is going to kill me!" Percy wanted to get a good night's sleep without the constant chattering of Ms. Ally — with or without her birds — but, as in the past, she was driven by her young nemesis to intervene and volunteer herself against her own wishes.

"Fine, I'll bunk with ya." Percy had a hard time getting the words out and felt queasy after doing so, but there she was — committed. "Humph, committed," Percy thought. That was a word she had come to reflect on quite often since becoming a member of Dr. Marksdale's group — and not just in reference to the others in that group. Her own behavior, such as at that moment, warranted her scrutiny. Volunteering to share a room with one of her least favorite people was something which made her question her own mental stability — yes, "committed." The truth is, she often entertained this word in reference to herself. Knowing she could be harsh at times, Percy knew she was harshest on herself.

"Yay!" Ally's smile was quite vexing Donato thought, as he saw how easy she was to please. He was becoming more smitten by the moment.

"Come along babies, we're going to spend the night with Percy. We'll have so much fun!" Picking up her birds' cage, the bellman placed it gently on his cart. He, too, witnessed how his simple action of being gentle while handling the bird cage pleased this strangely attired young woman. The only thing Percy was aware of feeling was a severe bout of indigestion coming on.

With the help of Mrs. Fins, Dill Bigley was getting his bearings in his elegant room which overlooked a perfectly manicured golf course. He, too, wished not to spend the night alone; however, knowing his lovely Mrs. Fins would be only a few feet away on the other side of the wall, he felt it may as well have been a million miles away. And yet, he had never imagined in any of his daydreams, or his boundless fanciful wanderings, he would ever be in such close proximity with the one and only woman who had won his heart so completely, as he had found himself at that moment — grateful. That is what Mr. Dillard Bigley was — unabashedly grateful.

"I feel like a princess, mommy! This is the most beautiful place!" Lizzy was bouncing on the bed while her mother kept sending texts to Emma.

"Don't jump on the bed, Lizzy." Monica had already lost the luster which had come over her when she first arrived in Park City. That luster had dimmed, and she could not enjoy the size or décor of the room her daughter was enjoying so much. She was immersed in worry as to her mother's whereabouts.

"Come on, mom. Answer me. Damn it!" Monica shoved the phone back in her pants pocket and started to pace.

"Mommy, it's going to be okay," Lizzy tried to reassure, "We'll find her and she'll be okay."

Monica could not help but see what a smart little girl Lizzy was. She wanted to believe what she said, but from her adult perspective where years of life had worn down the mirage of hopeful thinking, she could not help but think the worst. Her mother had told her time and time again to stop being so negative. She would remind her that life was too short to dwell in such places, and she must learn to pick herself up from the downtrodden places life's circumstances had led her to.

"Why?" Monica silently questioned, "Why can't I be more like either my mom or my daughter?" She felt tears begin to well up in her eyes, and she turned her face away from Lizzy, picked up the room card and told Lizzy to put on a movie and to stay put.

"I'll be back in a few minutes. Just stay here and don't answer the door for anyone. Do you hear me?"

"Yes mommy, but . . ."

"No buts about it, Lizzy."

"But mommy, what if it's my Nana? Can I open the door for her?"

"No! Your Nana doesn't know where we are, not yet. Do you understand me? Lizzy?"

"Yeah, okay — okay."

Monica closed the door behind her and stood with her back to it for a few long minutes. She wiped her tears away and called Emma instead of texting her. This time, she left a message with the name of the hotel where they were staying. She made a point to emphasize that not getting in touch with her was no way to treat Dr. Marksdale or any of the members of her group. Struggling to get the words out and controlling her urge to cry, Monica said all of her group had come along to help find her because of how much they cared for her. After giving Emma her room number and pleading with her to contact her, she hung up.

"Hey, sorry 'bout your mom. She'll be okay. She's a smart lady."

Not being aware Bud was standing a few feet away, Monica nearly jumped out of her skin.

"God! You scared the crap out a me!" Monica was indignant.

"Sorry — was just going to check the place out, you wanna come along?"

"I thought you hated me. Why would you want to go anywhere with me?" Monica began to curtail her urge to scream.

"Hey, I thought I did too. But I've been wrong before." Monica had to note Bud almost sounded sincere.

"You've been wrong before?" Monica inquired as she began to relax.

"Yep. There was that one time, it was a long time ago." Bud stood nervously with his hands in his pockets, awkwardly rocking on his feet. "It was when I thought I hated you."

Monica looked up at Bud, and for the first time, she felt she actually saw him; and, what she saw took her by surprise. Instead of the testosterone saturated, bull-headed bully she remembered from their first encounter in court months earlier, Monica saw this man's laugh lines were deeper than any others on his face. "I never would have thought," raced through her mind. What struck her most was the gentleness in his deep brown eyes — the color she had never, until that moment, even noticed.

"I guess I could go take a look around, but I don't want to leave my daughter."

"No worries, I want Lizzy to come too." Bud smiled, "For a kid, she's okay."

That was the moment Monica smiled too — something she had not done since Emma had left for parts unknown.

*****

"Phillip, how is your ankle?" Stelle questioned her husband as she came out of the bathroom brushing her hair.

"What? Oh that." The doctor looking down at his ankle realized he had twisted it several hours earlier. By that time, it seemed to have been days before, not hours. "It's getting better. In fact, I think it is doing quite well."

The good doctor was somewhat puzzled by his wife's sudden concern as to his condition. He had been taken by surprise by her mood changes many times before. But on that day with all of the events and the myriad of highs and lows of everyone's moods, he did not want to assume anything but humbly accepted what seemed to be sincere caring from his wife as to his well-being.

"Good, then if you can walk well enough, I would like to take a walk outside before the sun sets." Stelle grabbed jackets for both of them from the closet she had hung their clothes in.

"Alright, but I want to get everyone together for a light dinner, so we can go over our plans for tomorrow before everyone turns in for the night."

Prior to their leaving the hotel, Dr. Marksdale and Stelle stopped by Dill's room where they found Mrs. Fins helping Dill to unpack his clothes. They wanted to let them know they were going for a walk, and Dr. Marksdale suggested they all meet downstairs in about an hour or so for dinner in the hotel restaurant.

Inhaling those first breaths of the late-day mountain air caused both doctors to pull their jacket collars up around their necks, as they made their way out through the grand hotel's front doors which the bellman politely held open for them.

Once Mrs. Fins had finished helping Dill, she excused herself and went to her room next to Dill's. There, she contacted the front desk and instructed the concierge to inform the rest of her traveling companions about the good doctor's dinner request. It was not until then, that she stepped out of her clothes — clothes which she left lying on the bathroom floor, an act quite uncharacteristic for her. She then took a hot, relaxing and much deserved shower.

The clarity of Dill's mind was returning as the medication's strong effects were increasingly waning. Even some of the swelling had begun to go down. Holding onto the wall with one hand for balance, he proceeded with the other hand to undress himself. As his thoughts began to gain clarity, he was abruptly reminded Mrs. Fins was a married woman, and he had allowed himself to take far too many liberties involving the two of them throughout that whole day.

"Yes," his shaky voice broke the silence, "She is a married woman!" Removing his last sock, he knew his moral character was being tested; and, he felt the struggle tearing at him, as he saw himself flailing in the wrong direction. Reflecting on his unusually uncharacteristic behavior, he felt shame. In his own estimation, he had become an incredible and shallow brute.

Mrs. Fins was a married woman, and it was that painful truth which kept him at bay when it came to ever daring to ask about him, the husband — the one man in the world, no matter what his status or condition, Dill would have changed places with given the opportunity. No, he would not dare to ask about him, for that would be far too forward of an act on his part. Yet, he could not help but wonder why she never spoke of him.

"She never utters a word about him — why? Why indeed!" Dill's head, still sore from his unfortunate and forgotten fall, began to throb.

"Why does she not speak about him at all?" His puzzlement morphed into sadness as Dill had to acknowledge the reality he faced.

"She may never speak of him, but I cannot deny the fact he exists. The most fortunate of men — Mr. Fins."

After steam began to fill the bathroom and Dill felt the temperature of the water was safe, he gingerly stepped into the shower and began to relax as the hot water washed over him. It was then it dawned on him he and Mrs. Fins were doing the same thing, and taking yet another liberty, Dill presumed they were doing it at the same time. Although the images were brief, he could not help but chastise himself for conjuring them up and for the desire to linger on them in the secret recesses of his mind.

They were beautiful — those images of Mrs. Fins — the soap suds flowing over the loveliness of her soft curves. They covered the full length of her body, chasing after each other down and onto the shower floor, where they gathered in clusters on and around her bare feet.

"Bloody bubbles!" Dill shook his head as if by doing so, he could erase the images which danced relentlessly within.

"I must not think these things. What would she think of me if she knew?" He reached out to the shower wall and held his hand flat against it.

Deep from within, wherefrom wishful thinking is born, he questioned, "What are the chances — she may be thinking of me, too?"

With that thought in his mind, Dill Bigley envisioned his lovely Mrs. Fins' hand reaching up and placing it against his on the other side of the shower wall.

*****

"I'm gonna go downstairs and get a cup of coffee, if you wanna take your shower first, Ally." Percy looked at Ally as she reached for the hotel room card.

"Sure, I like to take a long shower, so take your time," Ally replied while rummaging through her suitcase, pulling out one item of clothing after another and tossing them into a pile upon her bed. Recognizing Ally appeared to be facing a dilemma as to what she would wear next, Percy said she would be back in a little bit but warned Ally she should not take too long of a shower. It would be her turn next, and they had to meet everyone at the restaurant at the designated time.

"Hey, hold up!" Percy hurried to the elevator which was just about to close its doors and begin its descent to the lobby.

Once inside she realized Monica, Lizzy and Bud were heading downstairs too.

"Are you guys going to the restaurant already?"

"Nope, we're gonna check out the place." Bud checked his watch. "We gotta a while still before dinner."

"Yes, we thought we'd kill some time checking this place out," Monica offered. "Do you want to come with us?"

Percy was not sure if Monica was inviting her to join them on their exploration for the experience, or if she was looking for a buffer between her and Bud; but decided, she had pretty much seen all of these people enough for one day. Truth be known, she had seen enough of everyone for a lot longer than just one day. When the elevator reached the lobby, she excused herself and went to the desk to ask where she could get a cup of coffee.

"There's a lounge just around the corner." With a white toothy smile, a tall slender young woman advised Percy she was just in time for "happy hour." There would be a variety of hors d'oeuvres served as well as two drinks — all on the house for all of the hotel patrons.

"Good timing is right," Percy thought. "This sounds just like something I need," and around the corner she went.

Taking a seat at the bar which looked more like an elegant piece of wood sculpture than any previous bar she had sat at, Percy recognized everything about this place was high end. Along with everyone else, Percy was beginning to understand nothing Dr. Marksdale did was anything less. She ordered a glass of red wine, and after taking a few sips, she knew this was not the average house wine she was used to getting in a bar or restaurant. This was the good stuff. And, she realized how she was really starting to feel this crazy trip she was on may not be as awful as she first imagined.

"Do you mind if I join you?" A man's voice interrupted Percy's calm. Turning around she saw Donato standing next to her.

"Sure, take a seat."

"Thanks," Donato pulled out the bar stool next to Percy and sat down. He, too, ordered a glass of red wine and remarked on how good it was.

"Being half Italian, we drink vino with everything, and this is good vino." He smiled and Percy saw the clear resemblance of the two brothers' good looks. For Percy, she had never really thought of his older brother as being "good looking," maybe because until, more recently, Bud and she were generally too busy insulting each other. She had to admit that while she and Bud were preoccupied with calling each other "rat's asses" and "butt faces," neither probably ever really saw the other person. Now, sitting with his younger brother and recalling the assistance she helped Bud with earlier in the day, Percy found herself seeing both Bud and herself in a slightly different light.

"Tell me something, Donato," Percy began. "Has your brother always been such a smart ass?"

Donato's body jerked back slightly, and his facial expression indicated surprise at Percy's question.

"Smart ass? Hmm — don't tell my ma that. She would never allow that from any of her kids." Donato took another long sip of his wine, "What kind of stuff did he do for you to ask that?"

Percy, too, was taken aback by Donato's reaction, as she could not imagine his not knowing his brother's general attitude. For her — she assumed that with the two brothers working so close to one another and on a regular basis — it would be nearly impossible for Bud to hide his obnoxious side. For Percy, that would entail every side of Bud.

"It's his attitude, the way he talks to everyone. He's, well, he can act like a real jerk a lot of the time." Percy turned to face Donato, "Are you telling me you don't see that side of him?"

"No, not really. I mean he can get angry about stuff like anyone. But, no —" Donato turned and looked directly into Percy's eyes revealing how dark brown his eyes were. "Our parents, 'specially our ma, expect us to be respectful. Has he been disrespectful to you?"

"Ha!" Percy had just taken a sip of her wine and almost spit it out.

"Disrespectful? Let me count the ways!" She started to laugh heartily leaving Donato looking bewildered.

"Before our dad died, he made us promise we'd do what our ma wanted us to — never speak bad of somebody and keep our language clean." Donato swallowed hard as if speaking of his dad were difficult to do without choking up, "Keeping our language clean and doing good for anyone we met were the biggest ones."

They were both quiet for a couple of minutes, before Percy asked Donato how long it had been since his father had passed away. He told her it had been many years, when he was just about twelve. When Percy pursued how old Bud had been at the time, Donato had to take a moment to think.

"I'm fifteen years younger than James. So, if I was still eleven, almost twelve —" Donato tilted his head and looked up in the direction of a massive, blown-glass chandelier hanging from the ceiling, "James would have been in his mid-twenties, I guess."

Donato continued to tell Percy how their father had been sick for a long time, and his older brothers and sister all pitched in to help with the restaurant — but no one more than Bud. He remembered Bud had dropped out of college to come into the business full-time when their father's health worsened. His mother did not want him to drop out, but he insisted. He felt the family was more important than whatever career he was pursuing. When Percy heard Donato say Bud had given up on his own dreams to save his parents, she was more than surprised — she was shocked!

"I didn't realize all that had taken place nor that your brother had made such sacrifices." Percy could not tell if it was the stories she was hearing about the man she had shared such an adversarial relationship with, or if it was the fine wine she was drinking (or maybe a combination of both) which made her feel light headed. She only understood something was causing it.

"Honestly, in our group sessions, he has never really given any real insight into his life. This is all new to me."

"James is quiet about his feelings, and when it comes to family, he keeps a lot inside. He pretty much took over everything, including raising us kids." Donato and Percy had both finished their second glass of wine, when Donato suggested they have another one.

"I guess so, but that will be enough for me." Percy was running her fingers over the side of the wine glass while the bartender filled another glass for both of them. She sat there quietly listening to everything Donato was relaying to her, and with each sentence, becoming more astonished by all Donato was telling her.

The man she had known only as her nemesis was someone quite different than she had ever imagined him to be — or imagined him capable of being. The wine had really begun to go to her head.

"He did what?" Percy found herself asking Donato to repeat himself several times, as he laid out a litany of good deeds his brother had done for others. She had him twice repeat his recollection of the time Donato said his brother had organized a group of people to help build a wraparound deck for a fallen fireman's wife — something he would have done himself but could not, as he died while helping to put out a fire in another family's home. And, there was the time he donated the money to buy a family in their neighborhood a newer car, when theirs was too old to repair. Donato said he had done that, so the father could still go to work thus enabling him to feed his expectant wife and three children. The list went on and on; and, Percy could see in Donato's face and hear the infliction in his voice, of how much Bud's younger brother admired, respected and looked up to his older brother.

Why, she wondered, would Bud represent himself the way he did in court and during her first encounter with him, or in the group's sessions? It was only in the past couple of months, she saw any improvement in his attitude, and, even then, there was no way to have known what the truth of his private life looked like. From what Donato was telling her, it sounded as if Bud had single-handedly held and continued to hold his family intact. Why, Percy wrestled with, would he have hidden the relevant facts of his life from everyone so completely.

Who was this man — Bud. Who was — the real James Elliot Jeffries?

"Don't say anything to James about what I told ya," Donato began. "He's really private about his feelings — sounds like he's been keeping a lot from you guys."

"No — not to worry." Percy sat back in the bar stool and looked down into her freshly filled wine glass. "No, I won't say anything." As she ran her fingers along the curved sides of her wine glass, she knew what she was about to ask. She silently asked herself why she would ask it in the first place, because as far as she knew, the answer would not matter to her anyway. It was Bud after all, at least in Percy's summation, who had created the problems which got all of those in the group in the trouble they were in. And why would she care anything about this same man who had consistently been a thorn in her side? He spoke so rudely to and about her, and most of the time, he acted like a complete "horse's ass" — one of the names she most commonly used when referencing or addressing him. And yet, it was earlier that same morning she had come to his rescue to assist him after, in her estimation, the doctor's crazy wife tried to blind him by shooting him directly in the face with pepper spray. So, what did she feel for this man — a man she had considered to be her nemesis for so long, and now who she felt strangely attracted to. When Percy finally spoke, her voice was so soft she almost sounded like she was whispering.

"Donato, tell me — does your brother have or, well, has he had —" Percy cleared her throat, "Has he or is he —"

"Is he what?" The voice was not that of Donato but of his brother, Bud. "Aren't you a little long in the tooth to be pickin' up my brother?"

Percy and Donato both jerked in their bar stools — neither being aware Bud was standing behind them. Both Donato and Percy had to have asked themselves the same question: "How long had he been standing there?"

"She's not trying to pick me up, James! We're just having a nice conversation." He looked up at the clock on the wall and realized they had been so deep in conversation; if they did not leave then, they would be late to the dinner Dr. Marksdale had arranged.

"Wow! I didn't know we talked so long. It's time to head to the restaurant."

"That's why I came looking for ya." Bud addressed his brother.

Percy looked down at her watch. "Oh my God! Where did the time go?"

Taking one last, long sip of her wine, Percy started to stand. As she did, she lost her balance, and both Bud and Donato reached out to her to prevent her from falling. Bud got a hold of her arm first, and Donato (half on and half off of his bar stool) caught her wine glass as it was flung from Percy's hand.

"A real light weight, huh?" Bud said with a teasing tone in his voice. "Anglos just can't hold their vino." He smiled broadly and continued to hold onto her arm.

"I can full well hold my —" Just as fast as she started, she stopped the direction her words were heading.

"Guess I had more wine than I thought. It's been a long day. I better get back to our room and get Ally." As she spoke, she could feel her face turn red and hot. Percy questioned herself — was the wine causing her temperature to rise, or could it have been attributed to something else?

Bud continued to hold her arm as she regained her balance. She had never been embarrassed by anything he had said or done before — at least, not towards her. There were those times she felt embarrassed for him and had wondered how he had not felt embarrassment for himself, but this was different. She could not look up at him. She could only say, "Thank you, I better go now."

"Sure you'll be okay?" Donato asked as he, too, got up while setting both their wine glasses on the bar.

"Yes, thank you, Donato, for the wine . . . and conversation, too." Percy turned and Bud let go of her arm just as she started to walk away.

Donato called behind her, "Thanks for letting me join you, and call me Donny, if ya like."

Percy turned and looked at him and nodded her head, "okay — Donny."

She smiled at him, and without thinking about it, she looked at Bud. When their eyes met, she immediately looked down and turned away from both of the brothers. Hurriedly, she headed towards the door to exit the lounge but not before underestimating the distance between herself and the door jamb. As gracefully as one could, after running smack dab into something directly in front of them, Percy moved just enough to the left of it so she could safely exit — hoping to have regained some semblance of dignity, though the chance of that was very little, she thought.

Whatever else may have been on Percy's mind was lost to her, as she felt making her way to the elevator posed somewhat of a challenge. Once inside and as the elevator began its ascent, she grabbed hold of the railing on the wall for balance. She asked herself how she had managed to get herself higher than the floor she was heading to.

Percy shuttered, "What the hell was in that wine?" As she made her way to her room and while fumbling to get her room card out of her pocket, she realized that although she was not feeling much, she could still feel where Bud had held onto her arm. Percy shuttered again.

As she entered the hotel room, she saw what she believed to be Ally's head lying on the floor at the edge of her bed. It had to be Ally. What were the chances anyone else would have spiked hair in three vibrant colors and be in her hotel room? Even so, what she saw did not make sense.

Why would Ally be lying on the floor? Had she fallen? Was she injured? Percy rushed to the side of the bed. When she got there, what she saw was too difficult for her to immediately derive any sense from. For there, at the edge of the bed, lying on the floor — without a head or a body — was Ally's hair.

"Where the hell is the rest of her?"

Percy screamed with such force, she staggered backwards and tripped over her own suitcase which caused her to do a complete backwards summersault over it. Just as she made an almost perfect landing, the bathroom door flung open.

Percy scrambled to right herself, only to see a young woman she did not recognize standing in front of her. This unknown, yet strangely familiar woman, had a towel wrapped around the top of her head, and she wore a white plush bathrobe with the hotel's initials embroidered in gold-colored letters on it.

"What's wrong, Percy?" Ally's voice sounded like a high-pitched whine which got her birds to start squawking.

"Why did you scream?"

Just then, there was a hard knock on the door. "This is housekeeping, is everything alright?"

Clearly shaken, both women could not look away from each other. Percy's widened eyes sought an explanation from the woman who, by then, stood above her.

Percy knew her voice sounded like Ally's, but she shared little, if any, resemblance to her. Without a trace of make-up, the young woman looked almost childlike, and her eyes, a soft bluish green, were both the same color.

"Yes, everything is okay," Ally responded to the housekeeper standing outside their door and then said in a much softer voice, "I think."

"Are you sure?" The housekeeper pursued.

"Yes, really, we are fine — had the TV up too loud — thanks." Ally looked into Percy's eyes and smiled a girlish smile.

Kneeling down in front of Percy, who had only managed to make it to her knees after her sudden and unexpected summersault, Ally put her hand on Percy's shoulder and gently asked, "What happened? Are you going to be okay?"

"I thought you were hurt or worse. When I saw your head — what I thought was your head —" Percy weakly pointed down to what she had believed to be Ally's head lying on the floor next to the bed.

"Ha! That's just my wig." Ally picked up her wig and flung it onto her bed. Percy grimaced.

"Sorry, Percy, didn't mean to scare you. I tell ya, though, your scream about scared the life outta me!" Ally got up, took Percy's hand and helped her up onto the bed where they both sat next to each other. It was then, when Ally began to chuckle. Within moments, her chuckle turned into a full-bodied laugh which was very shortly followed by Percy's own quiet giggle. Within seconds, both women's laughter had fully blossomed into throaty, tear-causing, stomach-aching hysterics.

Maybe it was the wine — maybe the wig. Most likely, it was a combination of both which led Percy to let go of her emotions. Both she and Ally lay consumed by the pain and pleasure hysterical laughter evokes, as each woman succumbed completely to losing control.

"Oh God —" Percy started to sit up while wiping tears off of her cheeks. "Wow, I can't remember laughing so hard, my sides ache."

"Mine too. That was so funny, you thinking my wig was my head!" Ally, too, wiped tears from her cheeks.

"I sure don't think it was funny." That was all Percy could get out before both women started to laugh again.

Percy had made it to the dresser and was holding on to the corner of it. "At least, not at first," was all she could get out between her laughter and her need to breathe. "I was pretty freaked out, really."

Ally walked around to the other side of her bed and sat on the edge of it. Looking into the mirror above the dresser and wiping her face, she too had not gained full control and continued to chortle.

"I'm sorry you got scared, Percy, but you have to admit, it is pretty funny now."

"Yeah, I don't often lose my mind like this." Percy, still laughing, made her way into the bathroom, where she continued to laugh heartily for a few more painful but pleasurable minutes.

Straining to gain a little control, Ally said, "I gotta stop laughing and crying like this. I won't be able to put my makeup on."

Percy splashed water on her face and grabbed a hand towel to dab it off. "Why do you do that?"

Ally removed the towel she had wrapped around her hair and started to use it to wipe away her tears. She looked away from the mirror and up at Percy who, by then, was standing in the doorway.

"Why do I do what?"

"Wear all that makeup!" Gesturing with her fingers, she pointed at Ally's eyes. "Different colored contacts and, God help me, that hideous thing?" Percy could barely bring herself to point at Ally's wig still lying on the bed — *"Ewww."*

"You think Madeline is hideous?"

"God, don't tell me you named it!"

"Well sure, she has to have a name. She has a personality, too, you know." Ally's expression looked confused, as if she could not understand how anyone would not understand her naming her wig. "How bizarre!" flashed through Ally's mind.

"I just don't get why you do all this stuff." Percy waved her hand in a circular motion around her own face. Before Ally could say anything, Percy blurted out, "You're so pretty just the way you are. And your hair — your own hair — fits you perfectly."

With that, Percy turned and went back into the bathroom. "I'm gonna take a quick shower. I know we're going to be a little late. Go on ahead of me if you want — no reason we both should be late for dinner."

"No, I'll wait for ya." Ally looked back into the mirror and saw a somewhat surprised expression on her face. "She thinks I'm pretty? Hmmm — just the way I am?"

Ally sat motionless for a few minutes, before she began running her fingers through her still damp and short, ash-blonde hair. Bending her head down, she shook her head from side to side. When she lifted her head back up, the different lengths her hair had been cut fell haphazardly around her head and face. Again, with her fingers, she jostled the hair in the front and on the sides of her face.

A slight smile grew across her face — "not bad — not great, but not bad."

After several minutes passed, Percy came out of the bathroom feeling quite refreshed after her shower. The effects of the wine had begun to wear off slightly, and she could feel her stomach needed food.

"Thanks, Ally, for waiting. I'll be ready in a couple ah minutes." Percy was busy getting dressed and was not paying attention to what Ally was doing at first. But then, out of the corner of her eye, she saw Ally appeared to be doing something with her eyes.

"You're not putting in those weird colored contacts, are you?"

"Nope, just putting on some mascara. I don't wear them all the time, ya know."

"No, I didn't know that. None of us — at least that I know of — have ever seen you without them. Has anyone in the group seen you without them?"

"Nope, just you — until tonight!"

Ally turned away from the mirror and stood up to face Percy who was exiting the bathroom and running a brush through her shoulder length blonde hair.

"Wow! You look great Ally — really, you do." Percy gave Ally the once over — her eyes landing on Ally's shoes. "And I love your boots!"

Percy was impressed with how truly lovely Ally was. She was wearing a light blue cardigan, dark blue leggings and two-inch heeled, dark-blue suede boots.

"Thanks." Ally picked up a tube of lipstick and did a quick roll over her lips, leaving them just lightly colored with a natural tint and a hint of shine.

"Ready Percy? I'm starving!"

"Yeah, I'm getting there too." Percy went to the mirror and did a quick fluff of her hair when Ally commented, "You're pretty too, Percy."

It was apparent by the expression on Percy's face she was not accustomed to hearing such things, or maybe it was because she was not used to hearing them from another woman. Being a truck driver, it was likely she was more familiar with hearing less flattering commentary from her male counterparts when it came to her looks. Whatever the case, Percy nodded a thank you of sorts towards Ally as both women headed to the door.

Never having been one for light chit-chat and never really having given any serious thought to making nice with Ally, Percy was beginning to feel a little uncomfortable with her and Ally's politeness towards one another. This whole day had been a completely different day than she had ever experienced before, and it seemed to be continuing on that path.

Percy sought out and found comfort in solitude, so becoming chummy with anyone — let alone this unusual young woman — left her feeling off balance. The fact she was actually beginning to enjoy Ally's company left her feeling vulnerable, an emotion she was not at all comfortable with. It started to dawn on her that on that particular day, everyone and everything seemed to be turned upside down.

Like everyone else in the group, she too had received a call in the wee hours of the morning from her therapist. Even though she found it difficult to understand exactly what it was he needed or why he needed her to be at his office first thing in the morning, she felt an obligation to be there.

From the point of arriving at the doctor's office, nothing resembled or took on any semblance of normalcy.

Although he had experienced an unfortunate run-in with a mad woman who wielded a canister of pepper spray, Percy still found herself perplexed over the fact she had done all she could do to assist Bud — a man who had deservedly won his place as her least favorite person. Then, without question or concern, she volunteered to fly half way across the country with a group of lunatics (her favorite description of the group) to rescue a woman she thought was kind, but in reality she hardly knew. And now she found herself beginning to feel comfortable — almost happy — about bunking with her second least favorite lunatic (and the lunatic's birds)!

After Ally had told her birds to be good while she was gone and assured them she would not be gone for too long, she covered their cage. As the two women headed towards the elevator, Percy had a sense that all she had seen, heard and felt that day had taken her emotions and shaken them like a bartender would do when mixing liquor and ice in a tumbler. Only in this case, she was left wondering what would eventually pour out.

"I do it because of the work I do." Ally's voice shook Percy out of her thoughts.

"Oh —"

"You know, I'm a backup singer with a grunge band, and I'm a cosmetologist too." Ally turned to look at Percy, "It's part of both gigs really. I just like to keep the image — know what I mean?"

Percy took a long look at Ally again and said, "You look so different. I really had to figure out who you were, you look so different — without the costume, I mean."

Ally laughed and blushed slightly. "Costume? I guess you're kinda right 'bout that. I just never thought of my dressing up like I do as a costume."

"Really? What did ya think it was?"

"Part of the gig, like I said. The salon where I work is really trendy, and everybody has piercings, tattoos and wild hairdos. The owner likes it like that."

"And the grunge group you sing with? Is it their preference too?" Percy continued her inquiry.

"Nah, they're just a grunge group — pretty much anything goes." Ally looked down at her boots as the women continued to make their way down the hall, "I just do it cause it's easier than tryin' out more than one style for both gigs."

"You seem to be very busy with two jobs — gigs, I mean." Percy corrected herself, "Do you need to work both, or is it just that you like both?"

By the time they reached the hotel restaurant, Ally had revealed she joined the band only because of the young man she had been dating and, until just recently, was living with. At some point, Ally told him to leave, but he had managed to get her to let him stay at her place again; even though, they no longer shared a bed. That was not for lack of his trying. Percy found out, too, all Ally really ever wanted was for the two of them to settle down. But, he had his own dream, and that was to create his own band, become famous and go on tour. If she really wanted to be with him, she had to be a part of his world. He had never shown any real interest in being a part of whatever was going on in her world. Ally liked him enough to give it a try and shyly admitted she was afraid of being alone.

Percy recognized a pattern in her and Ally's behavior, for she too had made poor decisions based on the fear of loneliness. Ally pressed on and admitted she convinced herself that, in time, she may be able to get him to think of more than just his band.

After being around the music for a while, she got into it and liked it enough to become a backup singer. She would not only see him more, but hoped he would see how good they were together; and maybe, he would want to settle down and start the family Ally craved. It was well into their relationship — both professional and personal — when she discovered her chosen one had chosen several other ones other than herself. This would explain the many nights he took so long to get home after doing a set, while she went home to their place to get the sleep she needed for her day job at the salon. His excuse was always that he and the other members of the band went out for something to eat.

Once she knew the truth, she told Percy, the pain she felt was unbearable; and, she finally had to make a choice. That choice was for him to leave. Even after he left, she continued to sing a couple of nights a week with the band. She did not want to let the others down, while they looked to find her replacement. Percy kept to herself what she thought — that what the bum really wanted was a free backup singer and a place to stay, and Ally served as both.

Ally continued to wrestle with his coming back to stay at her place, because she had lost any trust she once had. Once she lost that, she lost the better part of the feelings she once had for him too. She assured Percy she was working on getting another place for herself. She said she felt a little sorry for the guy, and acknowledged he could keep her place once she left. He would not have been able to afford to rent a place on his own with all the security and cleaning deposits having to be paid upfront. When Ally asked Percy if she understood, Percy had to acquiesce she did.

"I, too," Percy thought quietly to herself, "have been with my fair share of jerks." And it was then Percy began to understand better, why she may have found herself so at odds with this young woman and strangely protective of her at the same time. Ally may very well have represented a version of her own, younger self minus the get-up, of course, Ally was all too familiar with wearing. That was Ally's, alone.

Everyone was seated at the table when Percy and Ally entered the restaurant. Donato noticed Percy first and gestured with a wave for her to come to the table. As the two women approached, all of the men stood up while the two women were seated by a waiter — much to Percy's and Ally's surprise but most evidently to Ally's surprise. Percy was old enough to know, that was how gentlemen behaved in such a setting. Ally was confused and wondered if all the men were getting ready to leave.

"Ally?" Dr. Marksdale was the first to question the young woman sitting next to Percy. He thought it may be the dim lighting, as that is often the case in a fine restaurant; however, he could not help but think she looked somewhat familiar (albeit not completely).

Ally giggled as if she had pulled off a great joke, "Yep doc, it's me."

There were a couple of noticeable gasps, most likely from Bud and his brother. Dr. Marksdale immediately said, "You're a vision! You are very pretty, Ally. I hardly recognized you without, without . . . ." Stelle kicked him under the table and said, "You are so cute, really cute, and I love your hair that way!"

For the first time anyone at the table could remember — other than most recently when he swallowed a large wad of gum — Bud was unusually quiet.

"Man —" was all Donato managed to get out. Then he just sat across from the women with a broad smile on his face.

Once everyone was seated, Dr. Marksdale said, "Now that everyone is here, I hope you don't mind, but I've ordered some hors d' oeuvres and a couple bottles of wine."

Ally briefly looked back at Donato who had not taken his eyes off of her since she and Percy made their entrance, and she softly said, "cool."

Mrs. Fins commented, "How kind of you."

Dill Bigley nodded his still partially swollen head and reiterated Mrs. Fins' comment, "My sentiments exactly. Well done, doctor, thank you."

Three waiters approached the table. One started to serve plates of a variety of hors d' oeuvres, while the other two poured everyone a glass of wine — except for Lizzy who already had a tall glass with a red liquid in it and a straw. Once everyone had a full glass in front of them, Dr. Marksdale stood with his glass raised in his hand and toasted, "To our success in finding Emma." After the clinking of glasses being tapped against one another, a couple of voices could be heard saying, "here, here." It was then that Bud stood up, and while raising his glass, in a booming voice everyone was quite familiar with, he said, "Yes! To finding Emma!"

*****

Planning a search party requires some knowledge of who, what and where. Deductive reasoning and some sleuthing skills also come into play. Planning a search party when you have next to nothing was hard enough, but what the doctor was rapidly discovering — they had less than that in the form of information. This fact presented them with more than a few challenges. As the good doctor became more aware by the minute, this task they had all taken on was becoming more than a little daunting.

Monica offered what little insight she could into what her mother's plans were to find a man she herself had never met, and Emma had met only once. At first, when asked the man's name, Monica was sure her mother said she did not know it. But after some time and her wrestling to remember, she recalled, yes, her mother had said his name. The hurdle to overcome: Monica was sure her mother had mentioned it, but only once, and she could not remember what it was.

Already anxious about her mother's whereabouts and condition — add to that the guilt she felt for having not paid more attention to her mother all those times she spoke about the mystery man — Monica became flustered on top of her frustration. Dr. Marksdale knew he would have to calm her down, before he could draw out of her whatever information she may be able to offer.

During their dinner, everyone felt comfortable offering suggestions ranging from who should be teamed up with whom to which part of the city each team would cover. The ideas were sound enough, but the real issue could not be ignored. They had no idea what they were looking for other than Emma herself. Where was she staying? What kind of car did she rent? What does the mystery man look like? They had nothing: zip, zilch, nada.

As the group ate and discussed their skeleton plan, Monica's phone beeped. Hurriedly, she opened her purse and fumbled with its contents until finally finding her phone. Turning it over to get to the answer button, it slipped out of her hand and made a big splash, as it fell into her French onion soup. Thrusting her hand in the soup, she pulled the dripping phone out and began frantically trying not to drop it a second time. She was happy she had purchased a protective case for it in the event of an unfortunate situation, such as the one she was experiencing; and, erratically, she wiped it on the front of her blouse. Nervously, she tapped the answer button — but only after flinging a limp onion off of her finger which flew across the table and landed smack dab in the middle of Stelle's forehead.

"Mom?" Everyone stopped what they were doing — even Bud stopped his chewing. Stelle grabbed her napkin and removed the slimy object from her face and shuddered (still trying to maintain her upper-crust persona).

"Mom? Is that you?" Monica's face looked panicked as she grabbed her napkin and began wiping the side of her face, where the phone continued to drip onion soup on her. Turning her head in different directions while trying to hear the voice on the other line, she looked at the others sitting like statues around the table. Other than wide-eyed blank expressions on everyone's face, there was nothing anyone could offer her.

"Mom? I can't hear you. Hang up and call me back!" Monica sounded desperate, and agitation obviously could be heard in her voice.

"Mom! I can't hear you! Call me back, please!" The tension around the table could have been cut with a knife.

With a look of helplessness and desperation, Monica's eyes raced around the table once again. Her eyes were seeking any hint or suggestion of what to do. Dr. Marksdale shot up from his chair and rushed to Monica's side, where he then grabbed the phone out of her hand.

"Emma, this is Dr. Marksdale." Although his body language revealed unmistakable urgency, his tone of voice was calm and a credit to his professionalism.

"Emma, so that I may be able to hear you, please move to another location — Emma?" The doctor's head tilted slightly in the direction of the ear he held the phone to. He cupped the palm of his free hand over that ear, and it was obvious he was straining to hear. His eyes darted around the room giving the appearance he was hearing something.

"I can't understand anything you are saying, Emma. You're coming in, in bits and pieces." Looking around the room, it was obvious he was hearing something, but it was not discernable.

"Emma, I'm going to hang up and send you a text, maybe that will work better." With that, he ended the call.

"Monica," Dr. Marksdale said firmly, "Text your mom and tell her I need to see her — immediately." At that point, Monica's face, which had lost most of its color except for where the onion soup left a slight brownish residual, wore an expression of utter shock. Dr. Marksdale slowly took her shaking hand and put the phone in it.

"Monica, I need you to do as I instructed, and I need you to do it now."

After sending several text messages and receiving no response from her mother, Monica was clearly nearing another breakdown. The doctor observed that between the exhaustive hours of their first encounter earlier that morning — when she had violently shaken him as if he were nothing more than a rag doll — and their arriving in Park City, Monica had held her own and, to some degree, took it in good stride. He was, however, becoming increasingly aware her frustration was growing and recognized the signs she was lapsing into desperation. And, if the doctor knew anything, he knew desperate people would do desperate things.

"I'll try texting her myself from my phone." Dr. Marksdale could see his comment had a strong negative impact on Monica, and he knew from his professional experience he needed to address that fact immediately.

"Sometimes," the doctor started, "A patient responds better to their doctor than they would to a loved one." The good doctor hoped his comment would help to restore some positivity in Emma's daughter who looked, to him, like she was on the verge of collapsing into a puddle of tears.

Dr. Marksdale excused himself and proceeded to move to outside of the restaurant. He wanted to be out of earshot to the others — maybe even more so to Monica — as he could only try to put out one fire at a time. He knew he had to convince Emma to meet with him, thus revealing her whereabouts. He then had to convince her further to go back to Washington, hopefully, with him and the rest of the group.

Everything was riding on his having all of them appear before Judge Glib in a very short time. Gnawing at him was the fact he had used up all of his get-out-of-jail-free passes from her honor, so he had to be prepared to use any means available to getting them all there, together, and on time.

Everyone, as calmly as they were able to, went back to eating their dinners and exchanging small talk. Although no one said it out loud, Mrs. Fins and the members of the group were on the same wave length, interestingly. Monica was a ticking time bomb, and calm demeanors were the only diffuser. They chatted quietly amongst themselves about the food, the décor and atmosphere of the restaurant, how nice their rooms were and how beautiful the surrounding grounds were too.

Taking care of his wording and in a thoughtful manner, Bud said quietly to his brother, "I don't get it. Emma's always the stable one out of all of us." Immediately following that comment, the level of his voice raised just enough for everyone at the table to hear him say, "She kept me from losing my cool on more than one occasion."

Leaning back in his chair, he cracked his neck by turning it from side to side and followed that with a sucking sound he made by getting a piece of food out from between his teeth. That caught Percy's attention, but she stopped short of looking in his direction.

"Oh yeah, me too. She was like a calm mom to me — always saying something kind and, well, motherly." Ally fit the words in between bites of what was left on her plate with her usual air of, well, airiness.

Mrs. Fins stiffened as did Dill Bigley; but, when Monica did not seem fazed at all, it caused them both to, albeit cautiously, relax.

Percy took one last bite of her stroganoff, wiped her lips with her napkin and snuck a quick glance at Bud who by now was patting his stomach, indicating his appetite had met with satisfaction.

Donato was too involved in his observation of Ally to notice much of anything else. He thought to himself that for someone who left barely a trace of food on her plate — combined with his observance of how much she could consume since their first meeting only a few hours earlier — she should have been several sizes larger. He was grateful she was not and he was, yet again, impressed.

"Keep in mind, your mother has done something quite out of character for her." Sitting in her usual dignified pose, Mrs. Fins turned to face and listen to Dill Bigley. She recognized immediately, she felt complete trust in him with whatever he had to say.

"She always left all of us feeling she was quite well centered, and this may be a difficult time for her." Dill gestured with his hand indicating symbolically he was encompassing all of the group sitting around the table.

"We've gone through a long process together. She may be embarrassed by her most recent deviation from her norm." He looked down at his plate, and with his fork, Dill began to move the few remaining pieces of chewier meat and vegetables around in gentle circles. His injuries had reminded him of how difficult it was to masticate chewier foods with a battered and swollen face.

"What you must know is how important of a role your mother has played in my own personal growth during these very trying months. Others would likely agree." Looking up, Dill could see the other members of the group nodding their heads in the affirmative.

Mrs. Fins quietly thought, "He really is quite impressive — this Mr. Bigley — thoughtful, kind, quite lovely — really." She held her gaze on Dill until he looked up at her, catching her a little off guard. Feeling a bit out of sorts, she again corrected her posture, as she had let herself relax more than she was accustomed to; and then, she turned away.

"She's always been there for me and Lizzy." Monica put her arm around her daughter who was blowing little bubbles with her straw in what was left of her drink. "She really has been a great mom and grandmother. I just wish I knew where she was!"

"I do," the doctor said as he approached the table. "She told me where she is and has agreed to meet with me." He then took his seat and picked up his glass of wine.

"What?" Monica gasped — "Where? When?" Monica's screech almost lifted everyone off of their chairs.

Dr. Marksdale took a sip of his wine, emptying the glass, and then reached for the bottle. "Who would like some more?"

Flabbergasted, Monica's contorted face was oscillating between expressions of dire curiosity, exhilaration and complete frustration.

"Wait! You can't just come in here and drop that crap and leave me hangin'!"

Dr. Marksdale had to admit she did have a point, but was cautious in his reply.

"Emma," he started, "is safe and is willing to meet with me tomorrow for coffee." He looked around the table and stopped when he got to Monica's waiting glare.

"She is very concerned at how she has inconvenienced all of you, and me and especially you, Monica."

"Are you kidding me? I thought she could be dead. I thought I might never see her again! Inconvenienced?" Monica's lower lip started to quiver. "Where the hell is she, I need to see her — now!"

"Mommy, it's okay. She's okay." Lizzy got up from her chair and put her arms around her mother and held her as if she were the parent and not the other way around.

Close to hysterical, Monica continued — her mood increasingly growing with intense agitation. "Look doc, she may feel bad and all that shit, but she has some explaining to do — to all of us — but especially to me!"

"I'll have another glass." Stelle, who had remained quiet up until that point, offered her glass to her husband. "Fill it, if you don't mind, Phillip."

"Yeah, me too, I'm ready," Bud said as he reached for another bottle, closer to where he and his brother were seated.

"I'm okay," Percy shook her head back and forth, confirming she was okay with what wine remained in her glass.

Mrs. Fins looked as if she were contemplating having another glass but could not make up her mind. It may have been she was more concerned with how the doctor was going to address the already unsteady, and increasingly agitated, Monica. Dill reached for the bottle which had been placed closest to him and offered to pour some wine in Mrs. Fins' glass while leaning towards her and whispering, "I don't mean to be presumptuous." Mrs. Fins nodded her approval and returned her attention to the doctor awaiting his response to Emma's daughter, while Dill topped off his glass.

"What the hell is the matter with you people? How can you just go on like nothing has happened?" Monica started to shake, while Lizzy kept her arms around her mother.

"Monica, please trust that your mother is alright. We will all know more of her story after I meet with her tomorrow." Thinking better of it, the doctor chose not to make another toast at that juncture.

"I'm going with you when you go to meet her, and don't think I'm not." Monica was getting angrier by the second.

"I'm afraid that will not work." The doctor made a wide sweep around the table making eye contact with everyone and stopping on Monica. "Emma has requested I come alone. It was the only way she would agree to meet with me."

"That's crap! I'm her daughter, you're just her doctor."

"And that's the point. She knows she has upset — even hurt you. She wants to talk to me before anyone else. Please be patient, Monica." The doctor looked at Monica with his gentle eyes, and the sincerity in his voice could be felt by everyone at the table. Looking directly at Lizzy, "She loves both of you, and I think she regrets the way she has handled this matter."

Mrs. Fins, the group and even Stelle found themselves quite impressed with Dr. Marksdale's calm and collected manner. Everyone, except for Monica, felt more at ease with his ability to take control of the situation.

"Well, I'm going with you no matter what ya say." It was clear, Monica's spool was unwinding.

"Stop and think about that. If ya do, she could decide not to talk to the doc and split again. Just let the doc do his thing; he's real good at this stuff." Percy had a quick thought that Bud almost sounded wise.

Monica shook her head and started to repeatedly smack her own forehead with the palm of her hand. One of the waiters who was standing near their table walked to the back of the doctor's chair, leaned down discreetly and asked the doctor if everything was alright. Bud was quick to interject before the doctor could answer.

"For a bunch a nut cases, I'd say everything is just fine!" And though Percy could not entirely disagree with his summation, her next thought in regards to Bud was quite unlike the one that had preceded it.

"See English over there?" Bud addressed Monica as he pointed to Dill Bigley. "Well, if you don't wanna have your face look like that, you better quit smacking yourself." Bud laughed heartily at his own comment.

Monica first looked at Bud — then at Dill and again at Bud. "Are you all nuts?"

"That's what the judge asked." Percy mumbled under her breath.

"Hey, English, what did you do to yourself to end up like that?" Pointing at Dill's face, still laughing, Bud continued, "Don't tell me the other guy looks worse!" Bud laughed even harder.

"To be quite honest, I don't recall how I did it. For all I know, you could have attacked me!"

"Hey, I was nowhere near ya. You were alone with Miss Prim as I recall. Maybe, she did it to ya." Bud leaned towards the table and, with a boyish grin, continued to taunt Dill.

"Maybe you were gettin' fresh with her? Ya know how to get fresh with a gal, don't ya, English?" The comment could have been perceived as Bud being his old obnoxious self, but there was that boyish expression on his face; indicating, he may actually have been teasing Dill in a non-mean spirited way. Until a month or two prior to the group's trip to Park City, for Bud to act without malice — a behavior which had been his typical modus operandi in the early months of the group's sessions — would have been highly improbable.

"How dare you speak of her that way. You should show Mrs. Fins the respect she deserves." Dill's voice reached a level and pitch higher than he had expected it to, causing several of the other diners in the restaurant to look in the direction of the group's table.

"Mr. Jeffries, Mr. Bigley is nothing short of a complete gentleman — something I dare suggest you would do well to dabble in, on occasion." Mrs. Fins was as controlled as usual, but a hint of heated protectiveness was observed by all — most notably, by Mr. Bigley.

"I suggest we all calm down some. We've come a long way, figuratively and literally. Let's remember we're here to help Emma." The doctor kept his voice even, as he was known to do.

"Ah, I was just trying to rile him, doc." Bud sat back in his chair. "You know that, don't ya English? I do wanna know how you got so banged up though." He turned and looked at Mrs. Fins. "You were with 'em, the doc and English, you gotta know what happened, right?"

"I only know that we, Dr. Marksdale and I, heard a loud crashing sound coming from the main office. When we went to investigate the cause —" Mrs. Fins looked at Dill with a compassionate expression on her face — "We found poor Mr. Bigley sprawled out on the floor." It was obvious Mrs. Fins felt true sympathy for Mr. Bigley's most unfortunate condition. "Sadly, I can offer no further insight into how he incurred his injuries."

"What about you?" Bud looked serious. "English — you can't remember anything?"

Dill's face tightened, and he looked like he struggled with conjuring up any memory of how or what caused his face and head to look like they did. He took in a deep breath and slowly exhaled.

"Nothing, absolutely nothing." Dill shook his head slowly — perhaps at that point, that was the only way he could shake it.

Bud pressed on. "How 'bout you, doc. What were you doing when you heard the crashing sound?"

The doctor looked at Mrs. Fins. While in earnest, he did his best at recalling the events prior to hearing the referenced crashing sound. Mrs. Fins slowly looked at each of the three men, one at a time.

"You know," the doctor began, "I believe we —" Looking directly at Mrs. Fins and then at Dill Bigley, "I think we were talking about your husband. Yes, that was it, Mr. Fins."

Expecting to see some kind of reaction from Mrs. Fins — although for totally different reasons — Dill and Bud turned their gaze in Mrs. Fins' direction, where neither saw the slightest reaction of any kind. Mrs. Fins' expression did not indicate any emotion — negative or positive.

"That's right. We were talking about Mr. Fins, my supposed husband."

"Supposed?" Bud looked puzzled.

"That is correct — supposed. There is no Mr. Fins." Sitting straight in her most-admired perfect posture and remaining emotionless, "There has not been a Mr. Fins for a very long — no —" mid-sentence, Mrs. Fins corrected herself. "There has not been a Mr. Fins for a very long time — still, not long enough." A smile as beguiling as that of the Mona Lisa's gracefully swept across Mrs. Fins' face.

"Oh," Bud was not affected one way or the other by Mrs. Fins' comment, and the doctor nodded his head as his memory ignited.

"Yes, I remember. I do remember now, you were telling me about him — not a stand-up fellow, as I recall." The doctor's and Mrs. Fins' eyes met, and the doctor was not sure he dare go any further on the subject. Waiting for some reaction from Mrs. Fins which would indicate how or if he should proceed, everyone's calm was shattered by Dill Bigley's wine glass as it fell out of his hand.

There was a shrill, high-pitched sound the wine glass made as it crashed onto Dill's dinner plate — accompanied by Stelle, Ally and three other unsuspecting women diners screaming — causing more than just the group to jump.

The shattering of the fine crystal vessel as it crashed onto his dinner plate sent tiny shards of crystal and ceramic flying every which way, and the dark red Merlot the fine vessel once held splattered all over the white linen table cloth. The setting — for anyone not knowing the truth of the matter — presented quite a grizzly scene.

"Oh my, Mr. Bigley!" Mrs. Fins instinctively grabbed his hand so he would not get cut on the jagged edges of what remained of his glass and plate.

"Oh dear, Mrs. Fins, what have I done?" Nervously, Dill began to visually take in the mess which lay in front of him. He soon discovered that the mess he made not only made its way to the table cloth in front of him, but also literally spilled all over the front of his neatly pressed dress shirt.

"Please forgive me, I — I —" Dill's words stumbled out between his still swollen lips. "I feel like such a fool."

Little did anyone sitting at the table know how much of a fool Dill Bigley felt himself to be. And none of what had just happened — his dropping his glass, its shattering into hundreds of tiny sharp pieces, the shattered nerves of all of the restaurant's diners nor the splattering of blood-red wine — had anything to do with the feelings he was experiencing, either. All of the time that had passed and all of the emotions he had held at bay, because he believed Mrs. Fins was a married woman, came surging to the surface. He could not understand how he was so far off from the truth — a truth he could decipher from the words he had just heard come from Mrs. Fins — a truth he had dared only to dream of. So rapt with joy, Dill was unaware of the high level of activity all around him.

Waiters came from throughout the restaurant and rapidly gathered the broken shards of crystal and fine dinnerware which were strewn all the way across the table. They began removing all of the plates from the table for fear glass may have made its way onto them and into whatever food remained on them. The fact is, Dill Bigley was so absorbed in trying to pull his thoughts together, he was not even aware Mrs. Fins was holding onto his hands — something that, only mere moments before Mrs. Fins' revelation, would have been unheard of.

There was only one individual at the table who believed he was aware of Dill Bigley's predicament. If Dill had a choice of who it could be, he would most certainly never have chosen the person it was.

"Hey, English — looks like your luck is about to change." Bud snorted and, in his normal fashion, ended it with a smug sneer. "So, what da ya think of that? Ha! —" Bud shook his head.

"Mr. Jeffries," Dill made an attempt to lead Bud in another direction than the one Dill feared he was heading.

"I do not think that this is the time, nor the —" Dill did not get the chance to complete his sentence because, as was his regular behavior, Bud jumped in.

"Not the time? Not the time for what?" Bud's smile was across the width of his face.

A cold fear enveloped Dill and he felt his insides recoil. He knew that of all the members of the group, it had been Bud, and only Bud, who had in some uncanny way discovered Dill's secret passion for his Mrs. Fins. This was not the time nor was it the place, she should find out his longing for her remained the only fire which warmed his soul and gave his life a sense of purpose. No, she must not hear such things, and not from the likes of a man he was loathed to refer to as "Bud!"

Dill's mind was in a tailspin, and his mouth was suddenly so dry, he could barely open it. He sat frozen in place, paralyzed by his own fear. He could only imagine that any words Bud would use to expose his guarded and precious secret of his purest love for Mrs. Fins would, at the least, exemplify the deepest form of depravity and degradation.

"Mrs. Fins is not married! Whatever shall I do?" Dill, grappling with his fear and at the same time realizing his dreams may have a chance to meet fruition, came to understand that, in a split second, he had arrived at the intersection of his past, present and future — all at the same time.

"How could it be?" Dill asked himself, "That I, a man at this progressed age in life, have come to this point, where the entirety of my life may be in the hands of an obnoxious dolt?"

All the dreams which had lived in his daily thoughts from the first moment his eyes were blessed with her presence now stood the chance of becoming a reality. Dill knew he was duty bound for his own survival to stop Bud from saying anything further. But again, as Dill squandered his time in analyzing his predicament instead of acting on his instincts, it was easy for Bud's words to fill the void Dill's procrastination designed.

"You know, English, you probably heard what the doc and Mrs. Fins were talking 'bout. Maybe that's when you —" It was at that moment, Bud looked straight into the least swollen of Dill's two eyes, and whatever it was he saw, it would seem he saw it for the first time.

Something in Dill's eye stirred something within Bud. He stopped speaking just long enough to cause Dill's heart to skip several beats, and then Bud continued as if he knew beforehand exactly what he was about to say.

"That's when you, English, being the gentleman you like to be, wanted to let Miss Prim know you thought she deserved better." Bud then turned to look at Mrs. Fins who was still holding Dill's hands away from the table which the waiters were hurriedly finishing to re-set — as if she felt she still needed to protect Dill from further personal injury.

"English talks real good 'bout you like he does 'bout all you women in the group. I bet he tripped on somethin' and then, well —" Bud pointed to Dill's face, "That happened. And let's face it, English, you ain't the most coordinated dude."

Quietly, everyone at the table had to agree with Bud's observation. As attractive and well-mannered a man as Dill Bigley was, he had proven on more than one occasion — particularly on that day — that he did possess a tendency towards the unfortunate when it came to keeping himself out of harm's way.

Bud laughed at his comment like he usually did, but both he and Dill knew this was different. Bud actually stopped himself from throwing Dill under the bus. What his motives were, if he had any, Dill did not know.

All Dill could think of was he was grateful, Bud had not divulged his beliefs about Dill's feelings toward Mrs. Fins. But, still, Dill could not help but ask himself — why? Why would Bud do something kind in regards to him?

If he had not witnessed it himself and if he were to answer for the reason behind Bud's actions, Dill would have to say Bud had something up his sleeve. But since he did witness Bud's act of what Dill chose to believe was an act of pure kindness, Dill had to admit that if asked what the chances would be — that Bud would ever do something resembling kindness — Dill would have to say, "Those chances are pretty good."

CHAPTER TEN

Leaning in close, Stelle whispered into her husband's ear, "What time are you meeting that crazy girl's mother?" Dr. Marksdale swiftly turned to face his wife. His expression was stern and made Stelle pull her face away from his. Stelle immediately recognized her question was quite inappropriate, particularly for a mental health professional such as herself. She sat poised for some kind of deserved reprimand, but none came. Instead, Dr. Marksdale turned back to the table and finished the last few sips of his wine.

"This has been a long day. Feel free to enjoy after-dinner drinks and dessert if you like. I think it best for my wife and I to turn in for the evening." Dr. Marksdale then turned to address Monica specifically.

"This had been a difficult day for you and Lizzy. Please try to get a good night's sleep."

Everyone thanked Dr. Marksdale for their dinner and asked what time they should be ready to meet again in the morning. The doctor told them they should come back to the restaurant for breakfast, and emphasized they should feel free to order anything on the menu they wanted. He was adamant they understood everything on this trip would be on him. If they could meet for their breakfast around 8:30 a.m., he would be in contact with them as soon as possible after his meeting with Emma.

With that, Dr. Marksdale stood up from his chair, and while reaching for Stelle's hand to help her up from her chair, he continued to address Monica.

"I am sure I will have good news for you once I return from meeting with your mother in the morning, so please do not worry further."

As the doctor and his wife stood up from their chairs, Dill, Donato and surprisingly Bud, too, all stood up. Seeing this, Ally thought everyone was going to leave which did not make sense to her, after she had just heard the doctor say if anyone wanted dessert, to feel free to stay. Awkwardly, she began to stand too.

Percy observed her temporary roommate's dilemma which caused her to take a hold of Ally's arm, pulling her back down into her chair. Ally's puzzled expression caused Percy to say only loud enough for Ally to hear her, "It's a gentlemanly thing to do. I'll explain later." Percy wondered how much more Ally did not know about the customs Percy had been taught as a young girl regarding social norms.

"Jesus, I'm not that much older than her! Don't people teach their kids manners anymore?" Percy bit the inside of her cheek, "Shut-up Percy, now you do sound old!"

As is the custom, when the two doctors had risen from their chairs and began to leave the restaurant, the three men sat back down leaving Ally in a complete state of confusion. It was not a state she would visit for long, however, for once she knew she could order dessert, she called the waiter over and said she wanted whatever it was, "that lady over there got." Ally pointed to another diner a few tables away.

"I want what she got, it was huge!" Ally's eyes widened, and in her excited and breathless fashion, she went on to say, "It was tall with lots of layers — chocolate layers of somethin' and whipped cream between 'em."

Percy had not seen the dessert Ally was referring to, but her mouth began to water just listening to her description of it.

"Lots of whipped cream on the top and chocolate pieces all over that!" The waiter seemed to be enjoying Ally's animated gestures as was everyone else at the table. "Ya know what I mean?" Ally's eyes implored the waiter to respond.

"Yes, miss. I believe you are referring to our Chocolate Trifle."

"Okay, but are you sure it has lots of layers?" Ally was insistent it be what she had seen the other diner order.

"I'll just go ask the lady." Ally began to get up from her chair, but the waiter gently placed his hand on her shoulder getting her to sit back down.

"There will be no need for that, miss. I know exactly what you are referring to."

"Yeah?"

"Yes, miss. It is our chef's famous Chocolate Trifle. And, I must say it is a fine choice, miss."

"Ya sure it has lots ah layers of chocolate goodies and whipped cream?"

"Yes, miss. It has layers of the moistest chocolate and walnut brownies and in the middle — a rich, smooth and creamy chocolate mousse."

"Yeah, okay. That's the thing, and lots of whipped cream too, right?"

"Most assuredly, miss. And it is all made with our chef's secret, finest chocolate recipe."

"Including the shavings on the top?"

"Yes, miss — including the shavings on the top."

Ally wriggled in her chair, "oh goodie."

The waiter proceeded to take the dessert orders from everyone at the table. After Ally's mouthwatering description still fresh in their minds, it came as no surprise they all ordered the same thing — it was a round of Chocolate Trifles for everyone.

Both Donato and Bud were impressed with the amount of food Ally could put away, "She would make ma proud," Donato said between bites of his dessert.

"Yup, she would. Ma don't like girls that refuse to eat to save their figures," Bud added.

Percy reached a point where if she were to take another bite, she would not be able to swallow it; and if she dared to, she knew it would come right back up.

"I don't remember a time I ate like this and could still move." Percy put her fork down and leaned back in her chair letting out a little moan. "Oh, boy — that's it for me." She pushed her plate away as if doing so would make the overstuffed sensation she was experiencing go away. But, all she felt was how heavy her arm felt to lift it up.

Too much wine with Donato, too much information from Donato, too much food, too much of everything — Percy suddenly could only think of sleep, a long night of uninterrupted sleep. She looked over at Ally whose spoon could be heard clinking against the glass bowl she continued to scrape from — every last bit of brownie, chocolate mousse and whipped cream that remained. Chuckling to herself, Percy half hoped Ally would lick the bowl.

Observing Ally did not look at all tired, nor anywhere near ready to retire to bed, Percy privately questioned if Ally would fall asleep as soon as she herself wanted to, or if she would be up chittering with her birds until all hours of the night. She did not have long to wait to find out. Ally put her extremely clean bowl back down on the table with one final clanking of the spoon as it settled against the inside of it. Then she looked directly at Percy and asked, "So whada ya wanna do now?"

"God help me," was all Percy's brain could come up with.

"I got an idea," Bud piped up. "How's 'bout all of us go to the rec room. Monica and I found it earlier, and it has a bunch ah games to play."

Percy saw Bud was looking right at her. Normally, that would not have mattered one way or another. Under the new circumstances she faced after having heard so much about him earlier from Donato, she was more than a little uncomfortable — she was downright nervous. Finding a way to place Bud in any other light than the dimwitted half-brain she was used to associating him with, Percy faced quite a conundrum.

"Yay, that sounds like fun." Ally was quick to distract Percy's thoughts.

"Oh, can we Mommy?" Lizzy excitedly asked Monica. "I really, really want to."

"I don't think so, Lizzy. We have to get some sleep, you must be sleepy by now after such a day." Monica's mood had relaxed quite a bit from earlier that day, but there was still a hint of pensiveness in her voice.

"Mommy, please."

Looking at Ally, Donato offered, "Sounds like fun. Give us a chance to unwind before we head back to our rooms."

Ally got up from her chair and said, "Okay Bud, lead the way. You're coming too, Percy." Ally reached down and took Percy's hand in her hand. "Come on, you'll have fun."

With a quizzical expression, Mrs. Fins looked at Dill. "What do you think? Does it sound like something you would like to do?"

Dill Bigley felt like he was traversing in another dimension for most of that day. If he were to try something out of character at that point, he deduced it would seem to fit. In fact, it would seem to fall directly in rhythm with the almost twenty-four-hour period he had been experiencing. It was then the words escaped from his lips without his usual analysis and attention to planning.

"If you would like to accompany me, Mrs. Fins, I would be delighted to explore the idea." Dill gasped internally. "What? Had everyone else just heard me ask Mrs. Fins — my lovely, my most exquisite Mrs. Fins — on a date?"

Mrs. Fins' response was quick and precise, "Indeed, Mr. Bigley, I would."

Even though his eyes were compromised from his earlier run-in with a doorknob and the rock-hard floor, Dill saw Bud give him a "thumbs-up" from out of the corner of one of those eyes. That would be Dill Bigley's first "thumbs-up" ever received by him. And, although he had always felt it was a form of communication used mainly by crass simpletons, he did not find it to be completely untoward — knowing this most wonderful development!

Borrowing from Ally's first observation of the recreation room, it was "honkin' ginormous!" It had four pool tables, two snooker tables and a variety of other game tables, card tables, Foosball and the like, all spread out across the expanse of several thousand square feet of space. A small movie theater which looked like it could seat about 30 people was through a door at the far end of the expansive room. Everyone agreed they had never seen anything like it before. Bud added there was an adjacent room with an enormous pool — past that, several more rooms, spas and a couple of saunas with still more rooms which Monica, Lizzy and he had not been able to gain access to.

"Isn't this place a kick?" Bud was quite pleased upon seeing everyone seemed duly impressed with his earlier find.

"Don't believe I've ever seen so many games in one place before. Guess it would be good for those holed up inside during long winter nights," Percy noted, as she started to get what had to be her third or fourth wind of the day.

"Percy, come play shuffleboard with me!" Ally did not appear to be winding down in the least and was as giddy as a school girl which slightly chaffed Percy. Feeling a little miffed too, as old habits die hard, Percy assumed Ally's choice of games was directed at her age. She thought Ally picked the one game out of all which were available, because the majority of people who played it were old. Percy was pleased, however, to find this shuffleboard game was not on the ground but instead about four feet above it.

"Not the shuffleboard I was thinking of," Percy thought to herself. "I think I might just enjoy this." She put her hand on her lower back and rubbed it for a few seconds. "Maybe, I can play a game on this board without having to bend too much. My back has been acting up a little lately . . . ."

"Hey English, how 'bout us playing a little eight ball?" Bud, standing at the end of one of the pool tables, already had his cue stick picked out and was rolling it on the table assuring himself it was straight.

"I must admit, Mr. Jeffries, I have not played billiards or snooker in a very long time. Now that I think of it, goodness, it has been decades." Dill turned to look at Mrs. Fins who was nodding her head up and down and smiling.

"I would love to play snooker, I used to play it with my father when I was a little girl."

Both Dill and Bud looked at each other and then back at Mrs. Fins who had started to walk over to one of the snooker tables.

"I don't know how to play that game." Bud addressed Mrs. Fins personally. "I never learned that one. What 'bout you, English? Ya know how to play snooker?"

"I have not played snooker for a longer time than billiards." Dill looked in Mrs. Fins' direction and wondered if he should offer to play snooker with her. He was more familiar with the games of snooker and billiards than he was with eight ball, and he wanted to play anything Mrs. Fins wanted to play. Donato interrupted his thoughts.

"I don't know how to play anything but eight ball. Why don't we team up and play a few games against each other?" Donato looked to his brother for his response.

"I'm okay with that, Donnie. I don't know how to play those other games either. How 'bout it, English?"

"Mrs. Fins, would you like to be my partner?" Donato questioned.

"Oh." Mrs. Fins sounded surprised by Donato's request. "Well, I suppose so, young man."

Mrs. Fins chose not to look at Dill at that moment. Dill chose to look away from her as well and offered, "It looks like you and I will be partners, Mr. Jeffries."

"It's 'Bud. If we're gonna be partners, you gotta call me by my name, at least." Bud picked his cue stick up off of the table.

"Alright — Bud. I may slip on the name issue, but I will try."

"Very well then," Mrs. Fins spoke up sounding less formal than Dill had ever heard her sound before. "You'll have to refresh my memory on the rules for eight ball if you don't mind." She looked at Donato with a smile.

"You got it. It's real easy even though everybody goes by different rules. We'll just play the way me and James are used to, if that's okay." Donato looked at Dill, his brother and Mrs. Fins who, by then, were all standing at the pool table, and they each nodded their heads in agreement.

After a few minutes of explanation, the foursome reached an agreement as to the rules and goals of eight ball, at least the rules the Jeffries brothers went by. Bud gave Mrs. Fins her choice of heads or tails. She chose heads just as he tossed a quarter in the air. As it came back down, Bud caught it and quickly put it on the back of his other hand keeping it hidden from anyone's view.

"Are ya sure ya want heads?"

It was obvious Bud's giving Mrs. Fins a chance to change her mind gave her reason to doubt what she had chosen; although, it was only a few seconds which had passed, before she assured everyone she would stick to her original choice.

Bud removed his hand from over the quarter. "It's tails! English, you're up." Dill hesitated, then at his insistence, Bud took the opening break shot.

The loud sound of the cue ball hitting the other balls was loud enough it startled Dill, but still, there was a familiarity to it which raised Dill's spirits — not that they needed lifting. Mrs. Fins and he were playing a game of pool together, and she was an unmarried woman! No sweeter words had ever played over and over again in his mind: "Mrs. Fins was an unmarried woman!" The words had become as beautiful to his ears as any of his favorite arias.

He would have preferred being on the same team with Mrs. Fins, and at first it made Dill feel a little let down; but, when he saw the balls scatter and heard three of them going into the side pockets with Bud blurting out, "We're stripes, English," he felt titillation at the prospect he likely may have been on the winning team. The day may have started out in a very unpleasant (even horrific) way, but as it progressed into the night, the positivity of new developments was quite pleasing. Dill Bigley mused cheerfully to himself, "Quite pleasing, indeed."

Monica and Lizzy started to play Foosball, but like most youngsters, the short duration of Lizzy's attention span drove her to another section of the rec room which had a long row of arcade games. Her young impulsiveness was helping to distract Monica from her intense concerns regarding her mother's whereabouts, her mother's next move and how she was going to get her mother to come back to her senses.

When Ally heard the excitement in Lizzy's voice, she too lost interest in the more sedate shuffleboard game she and Percy were playing. Noticing Ally's interest wain, Percy said she would like to give the arcade games a try, secretly hoping they may help to finally tire Ally out. Percy longed so, to sleep.

The zinging, buzzing and dinging sounds of bells ringing are known to create quite a din in a normal arcade setting. However, that would prove not to be the case in the grand hotel's recreation room. The shear massive proportions of the room itself, married with its architectural design, were exceedingly successful in muffling the cacophony associated with the likes of playing any such noisy games. If it were not for the periodical screech from either Lizzy or Ally when either of them would get a high score or win a game, except for Donato, the others playing pool did not seem to be affected by their presence.

Periodically and with an air of casualness, Donato would attempt to act nonchalant as if he were haphazardly glancing in the direction of the arcade, but really, he wanted to sneak a peek at Ally. He knew next to nothing about her, but observed she seemed to glom onto one thing at a time in a single-minded way. He did not think she was slow witted, quite the contrary, but he did take notice she concentrated on one thing at a time intensely — but still, just one thing. As of that time, it did not appear that one thing had anything to do with him. Admittedly, he was drawn to the colorful and unique young woman, even more so, without all the color. At the same time, his attention was diverted from his interest in her, as it was his partner's turn to take her shot.

Carrying herself with the upmost tact and grace — qualities she was known and admired for with her lady-like presence always at the foreground — not one of the three men watching could believe or mentally grasp what they were witnessing. When Mrs. Fins began to chalk her cue stick, the men watched as she assessed the position of the balls on the table. Not one of the three men were expecting anything out of the norm. Not even the few loosened hairs which fell softly down the side of her face indicated, or prepared them for, what was about to happen.

With refined ease and in her most articulate fashion, before each shot, Mrs. Fins called the ball number and the pocket she planned for each ball to go into. Following that, she proceeded to clear the table with a few very swift, firm and precise shots.

To say Mrs. Fins had shocked Dill, Bud and Donato would have been an understatement. The fact is, she left the three men standing like statues — cue sticks in hand and mouths agape — with each radiating a distinct deer-in-the-headlights aura.

Not one of the men, at least not in any universe which made sense, would have presumed she, the controlled and exquisitely mannered Mrs. Fins, would have possessed the skills of a killer pool shark. Due to the fact he had only met her that day — a fact which gave him the benefit of not having been as shocked as the others — Donato was the first to speak.

"Where in the heck did you learn to play pool like that? I've never seen anything like it!" His face expressed his unabashed surprise.

"No, never. Not ever." Donato began to shake his head from side to side.

"No kiddin'! I've never seen nothin' like it, either." The bloodshot haze his eyes had suffered from for most of the day caused by the pepper spray encounter had cleared. By that time, they had returned to their original deep-brown and bright-white color which added humorously to Bud's erratically flashing them back and forth between Dill and Donato hoping to receive an explanation as to what they had just seen Mrs. Fins do. He received nothing from either of them.

"Gentlemen, I believe that is the way it is done." Mrs. Fins pulled the loose hairs back from behind her ear and looked at Dill with a widening smile. Dill could not get a sound to come out of his mouth while at the same time, as he squeezed tighter on his cue stick, "My oh my, Mrs. Fins!" was loudly echoing in his mind.

Donato broke the silence, "We gotta play again."

Mrs. Fins came back with, "Lovely, Mr. Bigley, would you be so kind and rack them up?"

*****

The likelihood two highly trained observers observing the same individual(s) being exposed to the exact same stimuli and set of circumstances would come to two completely different conclusions is higher than one may think. Each of their observations could leave them at odds with their associate's findings, and they could be aware they shared nothing more in common with one another than their differing opinions.

Case in point: The good doctor and his wife, both having been trained in the area of observation while pursuing their goals of becoming members of the psychiatric profession, found themselves at opposite ends of the spectrum when it came to theorizing the good doctor's group of patients. The good doctor assessed his feeling a sense of relief in regards to the group he had been treating was attributable to his patience, dedication and the particular style of treatment he preferred to use with them.

From her vantage point, Stelle, having observed the same group of individuals for only a brief few hours reached the conclusion they ranged from the ridiculous to the absurd; and, quite frankly, would have surmised none of the group appeared to have ever been under treatment of any kind. To Stelle, if her husband believed his treatment was somehow effective, she questioned his abilities to even make such an observation. Taking one step further, as far as her husband was concerned, she held him accountable for having divulged the most disturbing news to her just that morning, leaving her mind floundering in a state of chaos. If anyone expected her to be charitable towards her husband or his group of misfits, their expectations were surely to be met with disappointment. The only act of charity she was able to conjure up on that day — a day she viewed to be the worst day of her life — was put to the service of preventing her last raw nerve from untethering.

Starting with the walk Stelle and her husband had taken prior to meeting the others for dinner that night, more was revealed than the great outdoors. Not only was Stelle's emotional vulnerability and the shaky ground her mental stability was balancing on exposed, another equally serious matter was realized — one that the good doctor was ill-prepared to hear.

"I sense you are unusually upset, my dear." Dr. Marksdale reached over to hold his wife's hand which she sharply pulled away from his, as they headed down a neatly manicured path leading through the grounds of the majestic hotel.

"Upset Phillip? Upset? Ha!" Stelle's spittle could be seen spraying forth from her mouth before she pursed her lips.

"I know this has been a rough day —" The doctor barely got the words out, before Stelle turned and faced him with an angrier expression than he was familiar with.

"It wasn't bad enough you kept such a dangerous secret from me, no." Both of Stelle's hands were frantically waving, "On top of that, you have us traipsing all over the country with a bunch of hair-brained lunatics!"

"Now, Stelle —"

"Oh no you don't! You don't get to placate me."

"I can clearly see you are distressed, and you have every reason to feel what you are feeling." Hoping to find a middle ground where his wife and he could meet, he continued, "I'm so sorry for you having to go through this. I was wrong in not telling you sooner about the predicament I was facing."

"That's all I can take, Phillip! You aren't facing anything alone. It's on both of us, and if I'd known I could have saved both of us from any of this —"

"You are so kind my love, but no one could have saved me from —"

"I'm all too familiar with how dirty Elan Glenn can be."

Cringing at the words his wife had just said, as they reminded him of her dalliance with his nemesis back in their college days, he looked at her hoping she would clarify her meaning and wipe clear what he was envisioning.

Stelle was too angry to see her husband was reeling emotionally from her choice of words. She turned on her heal and began to run back towards the hotel. Speechless, Dr. Marksdale had to break out into a full run, too, to catch up to his wife. The only thing that slowed her down was her having to wait for the elevator to arrive, once they were back inside the hotel.

Fuming, Stelle looked over at her husband as they both entered the elevator. She could not help herself from entertaining the thought of witnessing his head getting caught between its closing doors.

"There is something I have to tell you — something I should have told you a long time —"

"Stelle, I don't know if I want to hear whatever it is, especially if it has anything to do with . . ." Stelle cut him off mid-sentence.

"That's too bad, you're going to!" Stelle led the way out of the elevator and waited for her husband to find the card to open the door to their room.

"If I'd known what Elan was up to, I know I could have stopped him by —"

The good doctor raised his voice and held up his hand signaling his wife to cease speaking.

"Stelle stop! I can't listen to this."

As they entered their hotel room, Stelle threw her purse across the room onto the bed and angrily began to remove her jacket and scarf.

"Can't, or won't listen? You put us in a place we could have lost everything, and it all could have been avoided." Stelle's growing agitation was palpable.

"All these months of not knowing what was going on with you — and the group — you would not have had to treat these bizarre people!"

Still afraid of hearing anything about her affair with Dr. Elan Glenn and at the same time very well aware he was not going to be able to stop Stelle from speaking her mind, he was resolved to hearing whatever it was his wife was so adamant to tell him; and it was then, he reluctantly succumbed.

"What do you mean?" Beginning to feel queasy, he sat on the arm rest of the love seat he was standing next to. "What do you insist on telling me?"

Stelle walked to the love seat and dropped her jacket and scarf over the other arm rest. With a guttural sigh, she plopped herself down on one of the two seat cushions.

"Elan assisted girls at our college to abort their babies." It felt like the air in their hotel room had been sucked out of it. Stelle sat motionless. The married doctors did not utter a word for what seemed like a very long time. Eventually, the doctor stood up from the arm rest and took a seat next to his wife.

"How is that possible?"

"Elan had access to mifepristone. That's the RU486 pill and he already had access to misoprostol. His dad was a doctor, but I don't know if —"

Dr. Marksdale looked at his wife clearly unsure of what she meant.

"The second drug, the misoprostol, is given one to two days after the RU486 pill to cause the uterine contractions which causes the abortion," Stelle said flatly.

"He was so smug when he said some of the girls didn't know they were being given the drugs." Stelle's voice remained monotone.

"I don't know if that part is true. They were girls Elan had slept with, and most always, he didn't even know if they were pregnant." Stelle looked straight ahead — her body stiff — and as still as a statue.

"Always sneaky, like a snake in the grass." Stelle took in a deep breath. "He said he put the meds in a drink or food without them knowing — the ones he had slept with, that is."

Dr. Marksdale felt like he was outside of his own body. There was a distinct disconnect from his brain's electrical functioning processes and his conscious thoughts. The sensation of a numbed brain mixed with distant and bewildered physical functioning capabilities made it close to impossible for him to speak.

"How? I mean — how did he — what girls? I'm lost." The doctor was at a loss for words, and those he found came out like letters in a bowl of vegetable soup.

"Abortion? Abortion was legal. Why would anyone go to him to get one?"

"Anonymity."

"What?"

"Complete anonymity."

"Why?"

"So that no one would ever know, Phillip — not their parents or their doctors — no records of it, anywhere."

"Why, why did he sneak it to the girls he slept with? I don't understand." Dr. Marksdale was pale and could feel his skin growing clammy.

"God forbid any of them would bring his child into the world. No, he would be sure no surprises would interfere with his own life's plan."

"Damn him. How did you find out about this?"

"I was one of them."

Stelle stood up from the love seat, picked up her clothes from the arm rest and quietly went into the bathroom closing the door behind her.

Sitting alone in their beautiful hotel suite, numbed and near deaf to any sounds outside of the dizzying sound in his own head, a few minutes passed before the doctor leaned forward and with his head in his hands, he quietly wept.

When Stelle came out of the bathroom, no one would have guessed she had just been in the state of mind she had been in only minutes before. She was dressed and ready to go to dinner.

"We have to hold it together, Phillip. While you get ready, I am going to call the children." Stelle was surprisingly calm, as she went to her purse and took out her cell phone. Within seconds, her mother answered her call.

"Hello darling."

"Hello mother, I am just calling to say 'hi' to the children and to see how everything is going." With that, Stelle continued to talk to her mother as if nothing unusual or out of the ordinary had just taken place. Her husband sat still on the love seat in a daze. He could not think of how Stelle, who was so close to unwinding earlier, was capable then of being in such good control.

Stelle handed him a dinner jacket she retrieved from the closet for him to wear. He took it in his hand when she handed it to him and stood to put it on but stopped himself and headed to the bathroom to wash his face first. When he came out of the bathroom, Stella said into the phone, "Here is your daddy."

After a short conversation with both their son and daughter, both he and Stelle said "I love you" to their children and hung up.

"Looks like you're ready, Phillip. We better get to the restaurant, or we'll be late." She bent down to put the shoes on she had chosen to wear for the evening. Then she took one last brief look at herself in the mirror above the bureau and headed for the door.

"Stelle, we need to —"

"No Phillip, we don't. He is exactly where we want him now, and there is nothing more he can do to us." Stelle gave her husband a quick kiss on his lips.

"Once you tell him what you now know, he'll know it too."

With the truth having finally come out, both doctors knew she was right. They had the good-doer right where they needed him to be.

Dr. Marksdale had questions, but knew his wife was the one to make the decision if she would ever allow him to ask. All of the emotions he was feeling as he and Stelle's elevator descended to the main floor were almost overwhelming, but he knew Stelle was right; they had to hold it together. And, through the entire dinner and even afterwards, they did just that.

As the others indulged in chocolate decadence and began their adventures in the hotel recreation room, the doctors retired to their room. Any conversation they had consisted of benign verbiage. When they retired to bed, the good doctor tossed and turned. It was only after his wife took his arm and put it around herself that he began to relax.

Stelle whispered, "We have him over a barrel and he's done."

"To be honest," Dr. Marksdale softly replied, "I would rather him be at the end of a barrel."

Stelle pulled his hand from where it lay around her waist and kissed it. The doctors cozied up closer to each other, and for the first night in months, they both fell into a deep and peaceful sleep.

*****

"Oh, mommy, I don't want to leave yet," Lizzy whined.

"We've got a long day tomorrow," Bud overheard her mother say. "Starting with meeting with your nana, and then we're going back home."

"But, mommy, Ally and me are still playing Mission Impossible."

"Yeah, and Lizzy is beating me!" Ally squealed.

"I'm sorry, Lizzy, but we have to go." Monica took Lizzy's hand and started to walk in the direction of the door.

Bud excused himself from the others playing pool and walked towards Monica, and when she was right in front of him, he stopped causing her to stop, too.

"You're not thinkin' ah sneakin' to follow the doc tomorrow, are ya?"

"What if I am? She is my mother."

"Yeah, but the doc really wants to meet with her alone. He said that was how Emma wanted it."

Monica looked directly at Bud. Taking in a deep breath and lowering her shoulders, she lowered her head next and said, "I have to get her to come home. That's the only reason I'm here."

"Right, that's why we're all here. Maybe those two meetin' alone is the only way she'll decide to come back." Bud looked at Monica hoping she would look back up at him, but she kept her head down.

"C'mon Monica. Don't be actin' like Moronica! We have a lot to lose if your mom won't come home, so does she. Let's let the doc do his thing." Bud was gentle when making his request. That was something Percy could not help but notice when she, too, walked up to Monica.

"How 'bout we all meet for breakfast like Dr. Marksdale asked us to, and wait — together. That way we'll be together when it's time to go home." Percy's tone was not condescending. In fact, between the two of them, she and Bud made their point(s) like a well synchronized team. This was something Bud took notice of.

Ally was jumping up and down when she finally won her game which did not add up to one of the greatest feats — in particular, taking into consideration her opponent had quit playing. Nonetheless, that did not stifle her sense of glorious victory.

"This is too cool! Finally, I won one. But my wrists are so sore from playing these games." She backed away from the game and started to rub one wrist and then the other.

Mrs. Fins was up and when Bud saw that, he said, "C'mon girls, you gotta see this." He walked back to the pool table: Ally, Percy, Lizzy and Monica right behind him.

Mrs. Fins was concentrating on the configuration the pool balls were in and looked quite serious for a few moments, but when she looked up at the group looking at her, she let out a laugh. It was nothing short of the most beautiful laugh he had ever heard — Dill Bigley was sure of it. And then she began what was to be a remarkable thing to witness.

Using her cue stick like a teacher's pointer, Mrs. Fins pointed as she spoke. "Okay, number two in the corner pocket," and ball Number 2 went into the corner pocket as did all the balls she called — one after the other in harmonious obedience.

Ally clapped and giggled. Percy's mouth dropped open. Monica's eyes widened while Bud stood shaking his head, and Donato had a smile that went from ear to ear.

After clearing the table, Mrs. Fins put her cue stick back in its rack and turned back to face everyone. "It is time for me to retire for the evening."

She started to walk towards the door when Dill Bigley said, "Please wait, I would like to ride up with you if you do not mind."

"Of course, I don't mind, Mr. Bigley. After all, you did invite me out for this little adventure. It is only appropriate you see me to my door." Mrs. Fins actually sounded playful making Dill's heart just about jump out of his chest.

Donato piped up with, "Hey wait up, I'll ride up with the two of ya." Putting his cue stick up in the rack, he grabbed his jacket and started to laugh while looking at Mrs. Fins. "You're the best dang pool partner ever!"

"Oh dread, must he?" Dill had not thought it through as to what he may or may not do when escorting Mrs. Fins to her hotel room door, but all hope of anything happening at all was dashed by, in his opinion, "that young and impetuous lad!"

"Yeah, me too — I guess I better get to bed, it is going to be another long day tomorrow." Although Ally still did not show any sign of being tired, Percy hoped her comment would indicate it was time to end the night.

"We all better hang it up for the night. Monica?" Bud inquired, "Would you like me to go with you when you follow the doctor to meet your mom tomorrow?"

Monica quickly turned her head — "I, I don't know what you —"

"Ah c'mon. I know you'll find a way to follow him, so I want to go with you."

Not being able to hide the look of guilt on her embarrassed face, Monica took Lizzy's hand and said, as she headed towards the elevator, "I guess so."

"Hey, wait a minute, if you two are going, I am too." Percy did not know exactly why she said it, but once it was out, she was committed to doing it.

"Now wait just a minute. You all heard what Dr. Marksdale said." Mrs. Fins no longer sounded playful.

"The doctor knows what is best, and I cannot condone such insubordination."

"Well then, Prim, come along, 'cause I know nothing is stoppin' this one from followin' him." Bud was looking directly at Monica as he put his hand out to stop the doors of the elevator from closing as he entered it.

"Oh my, Monica, you must abide by Dr. Marksdale's wishes. He is quite adept at what he does and has done so much to find your mother."

Monica looked at Mrs. Fins who, by this time, was beginning to fidget and looked at Dill Bigley and the others for any sign of support.

Dill did not disappoint by showing his support, "I will do whatever you think is best, Mrs. Fins."

"Hey, now that's ground breaking info and a real big surprise, English!" Bud scoffed.

"I'll do whatever Ally wants to do," Donato accidently let slip out.

"Oh, hell. Looks like we are all going to follow the doctor. You better hope he doesn't see us." Percy was the first to exit the elevator. "And if we have to get up that early, Ally, you have to go to sleep right away."

Crinkling up her nose, Ally said, "That's exactly what I was gonna say to you!"

Percy rolled her eyes.

Although he did not have any more of a plan than Dill Bigley had, any possibility of anything more than a quick goodnight to Ally, at that point, was all that lay in that night's possibilities for Donato.

CHAPTER ELEVEN

"Oh God — please tell me you're not wearing that thing today!" Percy had just come out of the bathroom after finishing showering to find Ally pulling her three-colored wig onto her head.

"I told you, she has a name. Say good morning to Percy, Madeline." Giggling, Ally removed the wig just long enough to wiggle it in front of Percy's face.

"Get that thing away from me!"

"I told you — this thing — has a name." Ally giggled harder while she held the wig in front of her own face, moving it like a hand puppet.

"Now, Madeline, don't let grouchy ol' Percy upset you." Pulling the wig onto her head again, Ally continued to talk to it. "She probably didn't get enough sleep last night."

Squeezing some clear gel into her palms, Ally began to run her hands through her wig pulling several sections straight up and out — creating a number of dangerous looking spikes.

"It has nothing to do with sleep — too much or not enough," Percy snapped. "I just think there is no need for you to wear that thing."

"Madeline — her name is Madeline. C'mon Percy, call her by her name, please?"

Percy thought that even with the hideous thing on her head, it could not hide the childlike and impish expression on Ally's face.

"No! I refuse to call that thing by any other name than, 'thing.'"

"Oh, don't listen to her, Madeline. She's being such a grouch this morning."

"Knock it off, Ally. I'm not being a grouch. I just think you're too pretty a girl to dress up like some — some —" Percy forced herself to stop.

"Like some, what?"

"Never mind. Let's hurry so we can be ready to leave when Bud calls us." Percy pulled up her pants and was buttoning them when she turned to look at Ally.

"No, damn it! I'm gonna tell ya. You're too pretty a girl to wear all that make-up or dress up the way you do. It makes you look like some kinda nut."

"The judge thinks I'm nuts." Ally turned to look at herself in the mirror. "Remember, Percy?"

"The judge thinks we're all nuts, Ally." Percy ran a brush through her hair and pulled her jacket on.

"Ya think so?"

"Yes, I'm sure of it."

Ally sat looking at herself in the mirror for a moment before starting to put her two different colored contact lenses in.

"Hey, Percy, do you think Monica will really call Bud to let him know when the doctor leaves to meet Emma — or just sneak off?"

"The only thing I know is Bud will be watching for when the doctor leaves. He doesn't want Monica to screw this thing up."

After applying lipstick, Ally puckered up her lips and looked at her own reflection. Out of the corner of her eye, she saw Percy was looking at her too, but she had a frown on her face and was shaking her head.

"Are you mad at me?" Ally asked in a soft voice revealing a touch of sadness.

"Why would that matter to you?" Percy questioned.

"I dunno. But I think, maybe, it would."

A moment passed before both women's eyes locked onto each other's in the mirror.

"Well, then —" Percy swallowed and took in a breath. "Well, then — no — now c'mon we have to be ready."

"Hey Percy, do you like Bud more now?"

"Why would you ask me that?" Percy's question was brusque.

"Oh, no real reason. I guess, just 'cause you used to be meaner to him." Ally had finished applying her eyeliner to her right eye with her trademark cat-eye styling and was beginning to do her left eye, when Percy's phone let out its loud, horn-honking ring tone causing both women to jump.

"Hello — yes — almost." Percy motioned to Ally to hurry up. Ally was busily wiping the excess eyeliner off the side of her face she had accidently extended too far, when she had jumped to the honking sound of Percy's phone.

Percy continued to reply to the caller, "Okay, we will. Yes, I will be sure to tell her — yes, right away — bye." Percy ended the call and started to lace up her hiking boots.

"Ally, we have to move."

Bud relayed to Percy the doctor had the rental cars returned to the rental company the night before, so Monica was waiting for a taxi. He had called for two more taxis for the rest of them to follow her, but to do so, they would really have to hurry.

"Go where?" With the precision of a skilled artist, Ally finished the application of eyeliner to her left eye.

Percy looked up at Ally's reflection in the mirror with disbelief written all over her face.

"Are you kiddin' me? We're going to follow Monica to meet Emma!" The high-pitched sound of Percy's voice even made her cringe.

"I know that, I just wondered where — that — is." With that, Ally slipped her foot into one of her spiked high-heels.

"No way in hell are you wearing those!" Percy found what little patience she had left had dissolved into thin air.

"Why not? They go with my outfit. And I like 'em," Ally concluded.

"Well, that's too bad. You have no idea where we're going and where we may have to walk. Those ridiculous things could cause you to break a leg!"

"I walk in these all the time, Percy. I can handle it."

"Well, I can't! Oh, hell — I don't have time to argue with you. We've got to get downstairs or the others will leave without us."

With one hand, Percy grabbed her purse and, with the other, Ally's arm and headed towards the door. As Ally opened the door, Percy said frantically, "Go to the elevator and press the lobby button, I forgot somethin'."

"Bye bye babies." Ally called out over her shoulder to her birds, as Percy pushed her out the door. "I'll be back in a little bit, babies."

"Get going!" Percy demanded.

Ally, wearing a blank expression, headed towards the elevator. Percy rushed to the closet and grabbed an extra pair of hiking boots she had brought with her and shoved them into the backpack which she had also brought along on the trip. Hurriedly, she slipped the backpack on over her shoulders. As she started to run to the door, she noticed Ally's jacket hanging precariously on the back of a chair where she had flung it the night before. As she grabbed it, she saw the hotel room card on the table by the door — something she nearly left behind. With automated precision, she nabbed it, too, and inserted it into her pants pocket, before the heavy door closed swiftly behind her nearly smacking her on her backside.

Ally had just made it to the elevator when Percy breathlessly caught up with her; and, with both women in the elevator, Dill Bigley's hand appeared between its closing doors.

"Hold on, we're here too." As the doors to the elevator reopened, Dill stood out of Mrs. Fins' way allowing her to enter first.

"Good morning, ladies."

In unison, Ally and Percy said, "Good morning, Dill." Immediately followed by their good mornings to Mrs. Fins and after the customary chitchat which cordial greetings include, Ally noticed Percy holding her jacket.

"Hey, that's my jacket."

"Yes, it is." Percy replied.

"Why do you have it?"

"Because you don't."

Ally's blank expression was now replaced with one of confusion, an expression Percy thought to herself was "ever so typical."

Percy handed Ally her jacket, and Ally quipped, "I guess I should wear this."

Percy came back with, "Only if you're cold."

"Well, yeah. God, Percy, that only makes sense," Ally giggled.

This was not the first time Percy had found herself in an elevator with Ally feeling overwhelmed with frustration, nor was it the first time she had asked for divine intervention. And so, as she looked up at the elevator ceiling and within the privacy of her own mind, she said, "I don't know if you're payin' attention, but just in case you're not, I really could use your help!"

When the elevator reached the lobby and the doors opened, Bud and Donato were pacing back and forth. As he turned and saw everyone exiting the elevator, Bud's chomping hard on a large wad of gum and the tenor of his voice left no doubt he was in a high-stressed state of mind.

"It's 'bout time! The doc left in a limo, Monica and the kid were right behind 'em, in a jeep. It aint gonna be easy to catch up with 'em." Saliva sprayed out from around his gum. "Let's go!"

No one stopped to question Bud, and in complete compliance, they all began to run to the hotel's main glass doors where two taxis could be seen waiting. Dill and Mrs. Fins were right behind Bud and Donato. Dill, in his casual, well-kept loafers and in chivalrous fashion, took a gentle hold of Mrs. Fins' arm, thus offering her the security he felt she may need as she began to run in her comfortable and sensible pumps. Aside from the black and blue parts of his face having become a deeper shade of each, the non-injured areas of Dill's face appeared to be moving closer to a normal hue.

Percy followed right behind them as Ally, in her spiked high-heels making their familiar sounds of clickety-clack, brought up the rear.

"Who's riding with who?" Percy asked as she began to open one of the back doors to the taxi closest to her.

"I'll ride with you and . . . ." Not being able to talk fast enough, Donato heard his brother's instruction.

"You ride with English and Prim. I'll ride with these two." Bud climbed into the taxi next to Percy and yelled at Ally, "hurry up, get in."

Without question, Donato did what his brother told him to do, and just as he was jumping into the second taxi and squeezing in next to Dill, he yelled out to his brother, "what color?"

Bud did not hear what Donato said and leaned over Ally and yelled out through the open window, "what?"

Donato responded louder that time, "what color? What color is the jeep?"

"Blue, it's dark blue!"

The taxi which Bud, Percy and Ally were in started to pull out first, and Bud instructed to the taxi driver through his slurps and swallowing the oversized wad of gum in his mouth, "You gotta catch up with the jeep and limo that just left." The taxi driver could barely see the back of the jeep just cresting the hill about a mile away from them.

"Once you do, you gotta keep far enough behind, so they don't know we're followin' 'em."

His face emotionless, the taxi driver took a quick look at Bud and then at the other two passengers through his rear-view mirror. That being the first time he got a look at the threesome in his back seat, he observed Bud was vigorously chomping his gum and cracking his neck while gripping the top of the front seat so hard his knuckles were turning white. His eyes landed on Percy who, by all intents and purposes, appeared to the driver to look relatively normal. Then, he saw Ally.

What caught his attention first was Ally's spiked hair with its dramatic colors. Next, the driver had to blink twice to be sure that what he thought he saw was actually what he was seeing: The same woman with the bizarre hair, and sitting next to the tense and noisy man in the middle, had boldly painted eye makeup on her eyelids which made them look like cat's eyes. And when she looked up and out the front window, the driver saw, to his surprise, one of her eyes was orange — and the other — emerald green. That was when the driver's face, which had started off as emotionless, had rapidly morphed into a face growing with apprehension.

Before their driver had a chance to speak, Donato burst out with, "Follow that cab." With a big smile on his face, Donato said, "You know, I always wanted to say that."

"Your destination, sir?" The driver questioned as he, too, started to drive up the hill to catch up with the other taxi.

"We are not sure, sir," Dill answered. "We need you to keep up with the taxi in front of us, which is trying to catch up to the two cars in front of it."

Dill's taxi driver caught a glimpse of the very attractive woman sitting directly in back of him and the handsome young man sitting on the other side of the backseat next to the door. It was when that same young man asked, "Hey, do ya mind if I call you Cabby?" that the driver took note of the man sitting in the middle.

Startled by Dill's appearance (the bruising on his face and general overall knotty swelling about the man's head) and the other passengers, the driver had to make a conscientious effort to keep his eyes looking straight ahead as he answered Donato's question.

"Sure, if you like, but my real name is Earl."

Everyone in Dill's taxi introduced themselves and shared light conversation for a few minutes, while their driver attempted to catch up with the other taxi up ahead of them. Barely able to see the back of the jeep and with the limo still nowhere in sight, Earl, a.k.a. Cabby, found himself incapable of tamping down his curiosity and finally asked, "What's up with the jeep, and why are we following it? And whadda that have to do with a limo?"

At that moment, Dill took it upon himself to intervene. Neither Mrs. Fins nor Donato and even more so Dill, himself, had any idea what Dill was about to introduce Cabby to. By the time Dill had finished weaving his fanciful web, Cabby believed everyone in the taxis, the jeep and the limo were members of a writing club, and as members of the club, a few times a year their assignment was to contrive a mystery — a "who-done-it" of sorts. Club members were divided into two teams: One would write the script; the other would set out to solve the mystery. The team which created the story would give the opposing team clues to use, but only a few. These clues were to be their only form of a lead in the resulting scavenger hunts.

Looking into his rear-view mirror, Cabby let out a snort, "What a kick!"

"Yes — quite," Dill injected before proceeding.

The on-the-spot, moment-by-moment and eloquently detailed fictional story that Dill created not only grabbed Cabby's attention, but it drew Donato and Mrs. Fins in too, especially Mrs. Fins. She had no idea how creative and convincing Dillard Bigley could be, until she found herself drawn into his fanciful tale.

Dill liberally took editorial license when conjuring up his tale and seemed to derive a bit more than a fair amount of pleasure from telling it.

The scavenger hunt that Cabby, himself, was now involved with included romance, intrigue and a mentally unbalanced woman. The more story Dill told, the more satisfied and pleased with himself he became.

Fascinated, Mrs. Fins watched and listened, as Dill's words flowed seamlessly from between his bruised and partially swollen lips. Her expression never revealed her mind was in a tailspin, as Mrs. Fins caught her breath and thought, "Oh my — Mr. Bigley — what a creative genius you are!"

Dill explained that the unbalanced woman in the story was the individual the scavenger hunt was created to find. It was this woman's psychiatrist who was riding in the limousine up ahead of them who was also trying to find the unhinged woman, before she could cause harm to anyone, including herself.

Regardless of whether it was truth or fiction, Cabby was intrigued by Dill's story which continued to draw him in, and his interest was honest and real even if the story was not.

Eagerly, Cabby asked, "What can I do to help?"

"Kind sir, we must remain undetected. You are a very capable driver and must remain so while intermingling caution and stealth."

"Wow — this is a hoot! This club sounds like a heck of ah lot ah fun. I'd love to be in a club like this. How'd ya all get together to start with?" Chuckling, Cabby looked back at Dill who appeared to be relaxing and done with his explanation. When Cabby looked at Dill's face again, he entertained, maybe it was a part of the story. "Maybe," he ventured, "The crazy lady had taken a blunt object, or perhaps a bat, to the poor man."

After a fleeting moment, wherein Dill's mind raced, he continued, "We met at a fundraiser for a local judge who was running for office in Seattle." Dill hid his surprise at his own quick response and added, "The judge wanted to start the club and was looking for people to join." Instantly, Dill smiled.

Mrs. Fins, beyond impressed with his story and quick thinking, smiled too. She took the liberty of patting Dill's hand which rested on his leg offering her approval and appreciation. Little did she know just how appreciative Dill was as a result of her appreciation.

"Well, I'm glad me and Benny got the call for you guys today. This will be more fun than we've had in a long time." Cabby sped up a little but still kept a safe distance from Benny's taxi in front of them, while they drove closer to the downtown area of Park City. Whether it was Dill's story or the beautiful countryside, everyone in Cabby's taxi was calm and momentarily quiet.

The atmosphere was a bit different in Benny's cab and for good reason. He was transporting the gum popper, the wild child (who, by then, was oblivious to anything other than the emery board she was using on one of her long sparkly nails) and the pretty blonde lady who sat quietly in back of him. Benny wondered what she would be doing with the others. He thought maybe she was married to the gum man, and the young one was their daughter. "People do make mistakes," he said to himself, "can't always hold it against 'em."

What Benny felt sure of was the pretty blonde lady looked to be a little annoyed, and he could not help but think it had to be due to the ever growing, agitated passenger sitting next to her. The snapping of Bud's gum combined with his blowing bubbles and loudly popping them along with his insisting Benny not lose the blue jeep or the limo up ahead of them was surely contributing to Benny's own growing agitation.

Poor Benny, he had picked up the wrong fares. If he had the other people who were in his buddy's taxi, he would have heard all about the club and the fun scavenger hunt everyone was on — just the way Cabby had. Instead, he was stuck with the fares he had, and so he dutifully plodded along; and, each time Bud would pop a bubble followed by, "Keep up with 'em man!" Benny would simply cringe. Pop, snap, pop! "Hurry man, don't lose 'em." Snap, pop, snap.

Percy looked out of the window and up into the clear-blue-morning mountain sky. Benny noticed her doing this through his side mirror and could not help but think, she was prettier than he had originally noticed. He would have had no way of knowing, she was praying again.

For someone who did not have a propensity for such behavior as praying, Percy was wondering if this whole experience — the group and, in particular, her association with the group over the prior twenty-four hours — was leading her to find religion.

"Nah," she said under her breath. She knew she needed a distraction from both Ally and Bud at different times and on this particular trip, more so than others. And, she knew if she did not want anything more than for Bud's gum to stop snapping, the distraction which prayer offered was something she was willing to do, even if the necessity for it came with a tiring redundancy.

The doctors continued to walk up the street past several specialty shops — the kind of high-end shops and boutiques which lure thousands of tourists in, tourists who frequent Park City all four seasons of the year. Upon reaching their destination, Dr. Marksdale opened the door for his wife, and they disappeared into the restaurant where Emma had agreed to meet with them.

From the perspective of those in the two taxis — both of which had managed to get closer to being behind Monica — it appeared the limo driver had let the doctors out to walk to their destination, while the driver then drove off in search of a place to park. This would not cause those riding in the taxis a problem; however, Bud sensed this development posed a problem for Monica, as it was not something she had taken into consideration when she decided to rent the jeep. He could see she was confused about what to do. This became more apparent as her brake lights kept going off and on, as she inched the jeep along. Quickly, he reached across Ally and grabbed the door handle. As he opened it, he ordered Ally to get out or pull her legs up so he could get out of the taxi.

If anyone in the group would have said Ally was known for her quick responses, they would have been wrong, for that would have been a rarity if not entirely unheard of. The situation being as it was, there was not much time for even the quickest of minds to react to Bud's order, as he was already climbing over her. He made it out of the backseat and yelled out to Percy, before Ally could even consider what was going on. "Percy, pay the driver and you two get out. Stay hidden and don't lose sight of where the doc goes!"

"Oh sure, stay hidden. Have you seen who I'm traveling with?" Percy angrily grumbled while she rummaged through her purse for her wallet. She paid Benny and thanked him for the ride and snapped her fingers in front of Ally's face.

Percy thought Ally may as well have been back in the hotel room chit chatting with her birds. She did not show any sign of urgency or any sign indicating she was aware, or cared to be, of anything happening all around her.

"Wake up, Ally, we gotta get outta the car!" Percy got out of her side of the taxi and went around to Ally's side; accordingly, she took a hold of Ally's arm and pulled it to get her moving.

"Okay — okay — I'm comin'. Jeeze, what's the rush?" Ally dropped the emery board into her purse and adjusted her wig, as Percy continued to pull her towards the sidewalk.

Upon reaching the jeep, Bud swung the driver's door open. The screams from Monica and Lizzy indicated he had startled them both. "Hop in the back, Lizzy, so your mom can move to your seat." Lizzy understood, as did her mother, what was required of them, and they both did what they were told.

As the second taxi caught up with the first, Cabby slowed to a stop and said while pointing his finger, "Hey look! Everybody got out of Benny's taxi. What should I do?"

For a split second, Donato, Mrs. Fins and Dill looked back and forth at each other — their eyes earnestly seeking suggestions from the others — until Dill said, "We will get out here." Realizing the driver needed to be paid, Dill asked Donato to go around to the other side of the taxi to help Mrs. Fins get out and to escort her to the sidewalk, while he paid Cabby.

"Sure, be glad to." Donato, just like Lizzy and Monica, understood what was required of him and was eager to oblige.

As Dill was waiting to get his credit card back, Cabby asked, "How 'bout me and Benny wait for all of you. You'll need a ride back to the hotel, right?"

Dill looked at him realizing he had no idea what was going to happen next; but indeed he knew, they would have to go back to their hotel at some point. Cabby could see, even with Dill's bruised and lumpy face, he was weighing his options.

"Tell ya what," Cabby pulled a business card from his jacket pocket which had his cell phone number on it and handed it to Dill along with his credit card.

"I'm gonna radio Benny, we'll try to wait." Dill could see Cabby's eyes showed his sincerity, "I might get called out, but you call me when you're ready. I wanna see where this thing goes!"

Dill was quick to answer, "You are so kind. That will be splendid, thank you." With that transaction, he too exited the taxi and met Donato and Mrs. Fins who, by then, were standing in the shelter of an art gallery doorway.

Bud swung the jeep around and went down a side street, where he easily found a place to park due to the early hours of the morning. They could not see the restaurant from where they were, so the three of them got out of the jeep and (as inconspicuously as they were able to) walked back to Main Street. Bud searched to find the others, as the three of them walked with their jacket collars pulled tight up to their chins — not only to hide their identities but to also fend off the cold breeze which had quite a bite to it.

When Bud caught a glimpse of Ally's wig from a distance, he pointed her out to Monica. The three of them headed down the street and started to cross it, just as Ally and Percy had made their way to where Dill, Donato and Mrs. Fins were standing.

In the doorway to the gallery, the eight of them huddled shivering together trying to shelter themselves from the crisp and cool, morning mountain air. The first one to speak was Bud.

"What's the idea of you tellin' me you were waiting for a taxi when you'd already rented that jeep?" Everyone looked at Monica and waited for her to answer.

"Look, I don't see how that matters now." Percy volunteered.

"Well, it does to me. Monica, I just wanna know why. We had an agreement." Bud did not want to let it go.

"Okay. I wanted to get here without all of you. I thought my mom would agree to come home for me and not for all of you."

"C'mon, let's not be hard on her. It's her mom." Donato's comment was reasonable.

"We are not going to accomplish anything this way. We are all here now, and we must figure out what to do." Percy was firm.

Everyone said "yes" at the same time which was followed by a heavy pregnant pause. Finally, Donato asked, "So, what's the plan?"

It was as clear as the lumps on Dill's face, no one knew. And that was when Dill said, "I have no clue."

Flatly, Donato responded, "Not a good way to start a scavenger hunt."

Everyone except Mrs. Fins, Dill and Ally (Ally for entirely different reasons than anyone else) had a puzzled look on their face in direct response to Donato's comment.

Imagine for a brief moment, if you will, the kind of imprint this small gathering of eight individuals would leave on an observant and rational mind — in particular, if you were to take into account that even Bud was affected by the vision of the eight of them squeezed together in the limited shelter of the gallery doorway.

"Look at us, if we don't make a scene, I dunno what would," he said while shaking his head. "We got English and Ms. Prim over there — talk about a wild couple!" Bud snorted while his head bobbed like a bobble-head doll.

Dill turned towards Bud attempting to raise his eyebrow to show his disapproval of what he considered to be another one of Bud's unsolicited and curt comments. Unfortunately, in the condition he was in, he fell short of his goal. The one eyebrow he tried to raise and most of the area surrounding it were already puffed up and raised from his run-in with a doorknob and hard floor. The only thing anyone may have seen was his neck stretching up and then sinking into itself on the way back down — a movement which did not stand out as a very threatening or disapproving posture from one man to another. Ultimately, his posturing efforts went unnoticed.

"Then we got none other than Monica." For each person he named, Bud looked at them directly while his head bobbed at least once.

"Then there's Lizzy, Ally, Donato and me." After four head bobs and with an obvious and exaggerated movement, Bud lowered his head. He wanted to deliberately emphasize their height difference, as he cast his eyes in Percy's direction.

"And let's not forget good ol' Percy."

"Ah jeeze, let's do. Please! Let's forget her!" Percy piped up with a bubbling enthusiasm the others rarely, if ever, witnessed coming from her.

That is when everyone noticed Bud was obviously amused by Percy's comment, as the smile on his face clearly revealed. Stopping mid-head bob, Bud's eyes squinted nearly shut and stayed fixated on Percy — a fixation she was oblivious to, as she stood shivering in the cold. Her attention was focused on where the two doctors had entered a restaurant farther up the street.

Standing higher than everyone else other than Dill and Ally, Bud completed his spiel with, "We're all crammed together like sardines in a can."

"More like escapees from a looney bin," Percy let out.

At first glance, nothing stood out as being notable or exceptional about the eight of them, nor would any of them bring about any specific attention by anyone who may pass by them other than Ally and Dill's appearance. Upon taking a second and more deliberate look at the group huddled together, that passer-by would possibly take note of the height and age differences. Most likely, it would be the group's suspicious darting of eyes going back and forth between each other and then looking in the same direction up the street — that would give the impression the eight of them were out of their normal element. The fact is, anyone knowing the group would know right off the bat such an element never existed. To be fair, any unsuspecting innocent bystander who would come upon the group and observe the suspicious eye darting — Ally with her hair and made-up eyes and then Dill's bruised and lumpy face — would be hard pressed to relinquish any other word than, "Whoa!"

As the eight of them remained huddled together in the doorway, none of them were concerned as to how they may appear to anyone else. All of them, except maybe Ally and Donato, were more interested in what was going on in the restaurant between Emma and the two doctors. It was not that Ally or Donato were uncaring, it was only that Ally was easily distracted and at that moment was observing her reflection in a shop window across the street. She had never given much thought to how tall she appeared compared to the others in the group when she wore her high heels and spiky wig. She pondered whether or not she liked it. As for Donato, he too was easily distracted. And in that same moment, he found himself not only distracted by but attracted to Ally's reflecting on her own reflection.

*****

"You must think I'm an awful mother, Dr. Marksdale, and it would seem I owe you an explanation; but, I'd like to start off with an apology." Emma's voice was calmer than the doctor thought it would be, although he did not know why he would have expected otherwise.

From their first encounter, the doctor had believed Emma, for the most part, appeared well grounded. Even then, sitting across the table from both himself and Stelle, the doctor could not read anything out of the ordinary into Emma's demeanor. At that point, it seemed appropriate to question why he, with a panic stricken urgency, had chartered a jet to fly ten people including himself almost nine-hundred miles to find her.

"You do not owe me anything. I am somewhat concerned, Emma, as to why you felt the need to leave so abruptly if, indeed, it was abrupt." The good doctor felt the need to choose his words wisely. Whatever opinion he may have developed, he had to keep in mind that no matter what rendition of the events Monica had presented, he would not be delinquent in his actions by forgetting the old saying, "There are three sides to a story: his side, her side and the truth." Up until then, the doctor had only heard one side of the story — which was Emma's daughter's side.

If memory served him well, the doctor's recollection of his and Monica's first meeting was more along the lines of being violently assaulted by a raging psychotic. Trying to get Monica to release her violent hold on the doctor's shirt, as she realigned his neck and spinal cord (while thrashing him about), was par with trying to escape a den of angry vipers. Therefore, her side of the story, the doctor contemplated, could be in question as to its accuracy.

Once the waitress brought their coffee to the table and each of them had taken a sip, they picked up their conversation where they had left off. Both doctors listened to Emma, as she gave them a rundown of her actions over the prior forty-eight to seventy-two hours and her reasoning behind them. Stelle, being unfamiliar with Emma and her history, sat quietly sipping her coffee while listening.

The time passed quickly as Emma revealed what drove her to do what she had done. She was not comfortable with beating around the bush, but it was more her nature to get to the point without frill.

During the course of her therapy sessions with the group, she had mentioned she met a man a couple of years earlier; and, for reasons she herself could not explain, she believed she was meant to be with him. Unbeknownst to the doctor or members of the group, she set out to find him. When she finally did find him, that search led her to Park City. That, however, was not the only driving force which led her to leave when she did — for that, she had an additional motive.

Once Emma was finished explaining her reason for leaving as abruptly as she did, the doctor sat back in his chair. He appeared to be delving into deep thought as he cupped his chin in his hand. Both Stelle and Emma remained quiet and sat motionless. After a brief respite, the doctor began to slowly nod his head up and down. He then looked up at Emma and said thoughtfully, "I believe I understand now."

"I never meant to involve you in this situation, but now that you are here, what do you suggest, doctor?" Emma questioned.

"It is my belief that truth is the best route, Emma." The irony of his words escaped neither him nor Stelle.

"I can see that you are in a difficult position, but your daughter should now hear the truth." The doctor deliberately did not look at his wife after making this last comment, considering both he and Stelle had spent their entire relationship with their own dark secrets kept well hidden.

Although Dr. Marksdale sounded quite sincere, and a part of him actually was, he still held onto a thread of fear. He had to convince Emma to go back to Washington in order for her and the others in the group, along with himself, to appear in front of the judge the following week. Being aware of the new revelations which had emerged over the previous nearly forty-eight hours, the doctor did not feel comfortable leaving anything to chance. He was determined to get everyone in the group to court on the designated day and stand before the judge with them while trying to maintain a semblance of normalcy and decorum for at least as long as they were there.

Once the judge released all of them from their court ordered therapy, he would finally be free — free from them all, including the vile and reprehensible Dr. Elan Glenn. Even with what Stelle had on him, Dr. Marksdale did not want his or his wife's past to be in any way comingled with Elan. That past his wife shared with Elan — and the truth about it which Stelle had just revealed to her husband — would have to be proven to carry weight or to be of value. Up and until such a time it would be proven to be true, even if it were possible to do that, it would be her word against Elan's, and the exposure in the doctor's mind was far too risky. The simple words, "Just get me across the finish line!" resounded in his mind.

"Emma, I'd be happy to mediate a meeting between you and Monica if you like. I think that may be advisable." The doctor was reticent to let Emma know everyone was there in Park City, but Emma informed him she already knew that. She may not have replied to Monica's "bombardment" of phone calls, but she had listened to the voice messages and read the dozens of texts her daughter had sent her.

"At least," the doctor kept to himself, "They're all back at the hotel and not skulking around the corner."

Dr. Marksdale thought highly of what he believed was his exceptional intellect and relished the idea of his being in control. As it had turned out over the prior day-and-a-half, Dr. Marksdale had been — and appeared to have remained — in the dark more often than his exceptional intellect was aware.

Emma knew she and her daughter had shown spectacular inadequacy when trying to resolve their issues on their own. "If you think that is best, doctor, I would like you to contact Monica and set up a meeting between the three —" Emma looked at Stelle sitting next to the doctor. "Or the four of us sometime this afternoon. I just don't know how I will tell her the truth." Emma's voice sounded resigned and flat.

"The truth of the matter is I've made such a mess of things. I never should have lied to Monica in the first place. I was just so young."

"Your intentions were good, Emma. It's time the truth comes out — for your sake as much as hers." The doctor's tone was soothing.

"How do I start? I can't just blurt out I've been lying to her about her father's leaving for all these years?" Emma put her hands over her ears as if she could stop hearing the scream happening in her own head.

"How do I tell her — her father was not the heroic soldier I'd told her he was?"

"Emma, he was not a soldier — now, was he?"

"No."

"Did he not leave both you and Monica to join a traveling circus?"

"No, he left us for a sleezy acrobat. God, when I hear that out loud, it almost makes me sick. How could I ever expose Monica to it?"

"Wasn't the reason behind your leaving specifically to get Monica to move on, now that her own husband left her and Lizzy for another woman too?"

"Yes, but I —" Emma started but stopped and looked at the doctor with tears in her eyes. "I don't think I can do it. Your father took off with his lover — an acrobat in the circus!" Emma's eyes flashed back and forth between the two doctors.

"I can hear her asking me, 'Was my dad an acrobat too?' Afraid not, honey, he was just an aimless clown! 'Why wasn't he an acrobat?' He didn't look good in tights!"

Both of the doctors' training and personal control were being put to a test. Fortunately, due to great effort on both of their parts, they passed by managing to keep straight faces.

"Let me remind you, Emma, what you revealed to me just a few minutes ago." The doctor leaned forward placing his arms on the table and looking straight into Emma's eyes. Slowly and softly he said, "Your reason for leaving was to force Monica to face her new normal beginning with telling Lizzy the truth about her own father leaving."

Emma was at first resigned, but then her voice had a noticeable lilt to it.

"Of course, you're right. I have avoided this for so long. But first, I insist you meet someone."

Emma turned in her chair and waved at a handsome man with dark eyes and silver hair sitting a few tables away. Then she gestured for the man to join them at the table she shared with the doctors.

"So —" As the handsome man approached them, while trying to hide his surprise, the doctor's inner voice exclaimed, "He does exist!"

*****

All of the other participants in the make-believe scavenger hunt remained uncomfortably squished together in the cold doorway a hundred or so yards from the warm restaurant, where the doctors made pleasantries with Emma and the handsome man introduced to them as "Jack."

With her impatience evident, Percy broke away from the huddled mass and made her way to the sidewalk. "I've had about all I can take. I'm gonna get closer to the restaurant. I gotta find out what's happenin'."

"Wait Percy! Wait for me." Ally came out of her self-absorbed coma and squeezed herself out from between Dill and Donato, making her way to the sidewalk edge just as Benny's cab came into view. He had driven around the block a few times, before he saw Percy with Ally right on her heals. He came to a stop and yelled out to Percy through the taxi's open window, "Ya need a ride?"

"Hold on now. Everyone — please —" Mrs. Fins was eager to get hold of the situation, "We must not let Dr. Marksdale see us. He would be quite upset with our having followed them." Mrs. Fins turned first to Bud and then to Dill apparently seeking some back-up to her reasoning.

"Yes," Dill quickly offered, "We must stay together while keeping our distance from the doctors and Emma."

Percy was halfway onto the front seat of Benny's taxi when she turned and responded to Dill's instruction.

"You all can stick to each other if ya want, I'm closing in on the doc."

Monica tried to bolt free of the group, too, when both Bud and Mrs. Fins each grabbed a hold of one of her arms.

"No way," Bud let out before Mrs. Fins' comment followed.

"I must insist you oblige Dr. Marksdale's request, young lady. He is doing all he can for you and your mother, please be mindful of that."

"Yeah," was the entirety of Bud's contribution.

To no one's surprise, Donato made the decision to follow Ally and Percy. He was fast enough to make it to the taxi in time to hold the back door open for Ally, before he too jumped in taking a seat next to her.

"What the —" Bud's face was a combination of anger and surprise.

"No worries," Donato yelled out to his brother, "I got this, James, everything will be okay."

Benny pressed the accelerator and looked over at Percy, "where to?"

"Just go slow up this street. I want to get a closer look at that restaurant." Percy pointed towards the restaurant she had witnessed the doctors enter earlier.

"Oh goodie," Ally piped up, "I'm really hungry."

"Me too," Donato added — apparently having already become absent minded in regards to his self-imposed duty of keeping everything "okay."

Percy's head whipped around to see Ally and Donato sitting in the back seat, "What do you two think you're doin'?" while privately thinking to herself, "You're nothin' but ah couple ah unwelcomed interlopers!"

Benny was thinking something along the same lines, as being alone with Percy was not something he had expected to happen. He was not averse to the possibility, and his willingness for such an occurrence seemed more likely to happen when he saw Percy heading towards his taxi. That possibility, however, was quickly dashed when Benny saw the girl with the wild hair and makeup chasing after Percy — and chasing after the wild haired girl was an obviously overzealous young lad.

Percy knew there was no time for getting food. "I'm trying to get a better look at what is goin' on with the doc and Emma. Remember, we're not supposed to be here!"

"Oh yeah," Ally turned to look at Donato who was already looking at her.

"That's right." Ally looked back at Percy. "But I'm still real hungry." Her whine made Percy cringe and the hair rise on the back of Benny's neck.

"Me too," Donato nodded his head and absent mindedly took the liberty of patting Ally's leg, as he said reassuringly, "We'll get somethin' pretty soon."

Percy turned back to look out of the windshield. She thought to herself Donato really did seem to be a sweet kid; and assessed, she had come to that conclusion the night before, as they shared good wine and conversation. After she observed Donato's inability to take his eyes off of Ally, however, Percy acknowledged that sweetness did not equate to intelligence. As for Ally, Percy had long before concluded that, although the kid drove her to distraction, she was just as dumb and sweet as Donato.

"Hell," she thought, "They deserve each other."

Percy was again at odds with herself. This was something she realized she had experienced with a repetitive pattern more often than not since her very first encounter with anyone in, or associated with, the group. She unwillingly came to the conclusion that, although it had become an increasingly common occurrence, it was never something she relished. Why could she not just dislike all these people and be done with them?

"Pancakes, I want a huge stack of pancakes with oodles of syrup." Ally licked her lips.

Donato eagerly offered, "Me too — lots of syrup — my favorite is Blackberry."

"I could eat 'em every single day," Ally gleefully announced.

Percy turned to see Ally looking at Donato as she asked him, "How 'bout you?"

"Yeah, me too!" Donato's voice sounded like they had just discovered a rare and wonderful similarity in the universe which was just between the two of them.

Percy tried not to let them distract her further but could not help but think, "If I were to add both their IQ's together, it wouldn't add up to a two-digit number!"

Benny arrived at the restaurant and began to slow down.

"No! Don't stop. Just drive by slowly and keep going." Percy's sudden outburst startled Benny which initiated him to ask, "Is this where the hunt ends?"

Percy looked at him, confusion written all over her face.

"A hunt? Are we on a hunt?" Ally perked up.

Quick thinking made Donato realize Ally, Percy and this taxi driver had not heard the story Dill told to the other taxi driver. Donato jumped into the conversation and quickly asked, "Oh, wait, Cabby musta told you about the scavenger hunt, right?"

"Yeah, if ya mean Earl, he did. That's why we kept driving around the downtown area — just in case ya all needed us to take ya somewheres else."

Ally and Percy were in the dark, although it may have been a touch darker where Ally's mind resided.

Donato was quick to interject, "Remember how our writers' club decided to take our scavenger hunt to a place far away this time, Percy?"

Percy turned around once again just as Benny drove past the restaurant and saw a look in Donato's eyes indicating he needed her to go along with him. Percy was really puzzled but felt she could trust Donato. Ally on the other hand could not contain her enthusiasm.

"I love games and a scavenger hunt sounds like so much fun. Can we stop and get something to eat first?"

Percy turned around to see they had passed the restaurant before she could get a peek into it.

"Damn!" She shouted out. "Please go around the block again."

"No problem, miss." Benny headed up the street where he turned right at the next intersection.

"Hey, here they come." Monica said as she saw Benny's taxi coming up the street again.

Taking a hold of Monica's arm once again, "Whadda ya think you're doin'?" Bud asked.

Monica took a hold of Bud's hand with hers, and when she could not get loose of his grasp, she dug her finger nails into his wrist and stomped on his left foot at the same time.

Bud released Monica's arm and let out a scream, as his face took on the appearance of having just taken a bite out of a sour grape.

"Why'd ya do that? I wasn't tryin' to hurt ya. I was tryin' to help ya!"

"If you wanna help me, leave me alone!"

Bud had just lifted his left foot off the ground in an attempt to get some relief from the throbbing which had begun, when Monica pushed him away with such force, it caused him to lose his balance. He hit the brick wall, which encased the gallery doorway, so hard his jacket could not prevent his shoulder from being scraped. He would have suffered an even worse injury to his shoulder had it not been for his head taking most of the brunt of his fall.

"Here, let me help you up." Dill reached down and helped lift Bud back to a standing position.

"Stop her!" Bud screeched as he saw Monica with her hand on Lizzy's arm pulling her along as they ran up the street.

"I'm afraid she's too far ahead," Mrs. Fins broke in. "She is already almost to the restaurant. This is dreadful. Dr. Marksdale will be so disappointed in all of us."

While Dill helped to keep Bud steady, he offered him his handkerchief.

"Use this to dab the blood," Dill advised.

"I'm bleeding?" Bud seemed a little out of sorts.

"Yes, old boy, blood is beading up on your temple."

"What's wrong with that woman?" Bud implored as he held Dill's handkerchief to his head. "Man, my head hurts and my foot! She really can stomp; I think she broke my toes."

"Looks like we'll look like twins pretty soon," Dill said as he observed Bud's temple swelling.

"Is that your idea of a joke, English?" Bud snapped.

Dill smiled broadly, "Yes — Yes — it is rather, old boy."

CHAPTER TWELVE

"Human beings," Dr. Marksdale observed, "are interesting creatures." After having treated a myriad of individuals ranging in various stages of neurosis, he had quite a repertoire of stories he could tell; but, of course, his profession prohibited such an act. If someone were to doubt his ability to keep a secret, they would need to go no further than to ask his wife, Stelle.

During his time as a practicing psychiatrist, the doctor had treated a fair share of patients. Generally speaking, in his high-rent high-rise office, his patients consisted of extremely wealthy women — actually, bored housewives — that had almost as much extra time on their hands as money and lacking the imagination to figure out what to do with it — the time — not the money.

Shopping escapades could only go on for so long, before even that grew tiresome for many of his patients. They complained of their husbands being gone for far too long and too often. They complained about all that was expected of them befitting the high social rank they fit within, and they complained about other wealthy housewives with such vigor, the doctor often felt he was listening to a competitive sport being relayed to him.

To assist in their filling up time, most of these women became members of several organizations and clubs which raised money for one charity or another. These activities gave them a sense of importance and purpose.

The doctor was not unfamiliar with these types of clubs and organizations or the type of people who became members. He and Stelle were members of several, themselves. The charitable events both he, Stelle and his patients involved themselves with offered all of the philanthropists an opportunity to openly practice — philanthropy. These elaborate events also served as places to show off the designer clothes each had acquired on one of their many trips to specialty shops on both the West and East Coasts — specialty shops which are famous for catering to, and pampering, the wealthy elite. Disappointingly, however, these women offered little, if any, challenge to the doctor's chosen field of psychiatry.

The fact of the matter is the doctor had honed his skills to influence his patients, which he and he alone could provide the perfect place for them to get the emotional boost they all seemed to crave. The medications he prescribed for them made them feel even better than his luxurious office atmosphere could. And so, the combination of the two brought the women back once, sometimes twice, a week to prattle on about their boring dysfunctional lives. The combination of the positive environment and the meds he prescribed to them allowed these women to open up to their inner feelings and needs. The doctor had them convinced, it would behoove them to continue their sessions with him.

In other words, he had figured out a way to keep the hefty fees he charged them and to continue their coming in on a regular basis. If the women were aware of, or bothered by, his trickery, none of them canceled treatment because of it. They seemed quite comfortable with their symbiotic set-up with the good doctor, and the doctor planned to keep it that way. As far as he was concerned, none of his patients needed to know what was really on the pages of the notebook he appeared to write in (with earnest) during their sessions. The fact most pages in his notebook were filled with cartoon characters performing any number of mundane (and, on occasion, lascivious) activities would remain a private matter.

For the most part, Dr. Marksdale's practice had served him well in providing a constant flow of income — although it did not come to him without a price. Underneath his expensive clothes and looking past his extravagant life style, the good doctor did not feel he was reaching his potential. He had already acknowledged this feeling within himself, but that fact was amplified on his trip to Park City with the group of patients he never asked to treat nor ever really wanted to treat. The doctor was aware he had grown more agitated with the realization he was stuck with all of them, until the judge would release them from her order to receive therapy. Between occasional bouts where he had to draw upon his own internal strength to squelch the primal urge which surged through him to want to strangle the life out of, or beat, James Elliot Jeffries with a club, he had developed a strange sense of attachment to all of them — including Mr. Jeffries — in a most peculiar way.

While learning more about the life circumstances of each member of the group, Dr. Marksdale began to understand how they may have ended up creating a mess for themselves when, at a pivotal point, all of their paths crossed. He dared, on a rare occasion, to entertain the possibility he may have actually helped some of them achieve a healthier state of mind.

During the time they had been receiving therapy, each member had, in one way or another, revealed something personal they had experienced in maneuvering their way through life. These revelations helped the doctor in determining his approach to their treatment, as it would to any conscientious psychiatrist, and thus allowed him to flex his therapist muscles and his ever needy ego. Though he did not ask for these patients — and at times desired the capability of wishing them away — he found his treatment of the group let him exercise his capabilities more than his treatment of any of his other patients.

As is true of any therapist's practice, there are patients who pose more challenges than others. In Dr. Marksdale's case, more often than not, his biggest challenge was James Elliot Jeffries, a.k.a. "Bud." His constant noisy chomping and the insidious snapping of the large wads of gum he stuffed into his gaping mouth drove the doctor to distraction.

The doctor compared Bud's mouth and his gum chewing to a rodeo arena: his tongue, the cowboy's rope; the gum, the bull his rope is trying to lasso. It gnawed at the doctor's sensibilities and pushed him to pursue what the reason was which lay behind such an incredibly obnoxious act. Somewhere in his training, the doctor knew if he could draw out of him the actual causation behind Bud's obsessive gum wrangling, he eventually may be able to help the man — as the doctor often reckoned to himself, "I'm going to cure him or kill him!"

"It eases the tension I got on me, doc," Bud blurted out more than once.

"It stops me from crunchin' somethin' hard on people like ol' English's head!" The group and the doctor had heard him say that on more than one occasion, and they had to jump in to prevent Bud from doing just that to Dill Bigley.

The reasoning behind Bud's tension was a deeper issue Dr. Marksdale surmised. The doctor believed he had begun to unravel the twisted twine of James Elliot Jeffries' mind even before they left for Park City. He believed that somehow it tied into Bud's restricting himself from using foul language of any kind. What caused that restriction and why was it in place? The doctor had spent many hours trying to get Bud to reveal it to him. But most of all, as any psychiatrist worth their own weight would want, he would see Bud reveal the reason to himself.

The doctor was keenly aware, that while Bud was able to control himself in some ways, he had no self-monitoring mechanism in other areas of his behavior. Without that impulse control, Bud could — and had — flown off the handle with regular frequency and abandon.

*****

While Emma's friend, Jack, was sharing a little history of Park City and what impact its hosting the 2002 Winter Olympics had on the beautiful Rocky Mountain city, the doctor's eyes drifted past Emma and Jack and out through the restaurant window. Abruptly, he began to blink rapidly giving the appearance he had something in his eye. This was the first idea which came to him: He wanted to distract the others at the table from seeing the shock he was experiencing. What he thought he saw through the window was what appeared to be the back of Percy's head in the front seat and the side of Donato's face sitting in the back seat of a taxi, as it slowly drove past the restaurant. Hoping his rapid blinking would suffice as a mirage and hide — "What in hell are they doing here?" — that he was screaming in his head.

The doctor did not have to distract for very long. Within the next few moments, the restaurant door swung open, and Monica came rushing through it. Like a rag doll, Lizzy, red-faced and out of breath, was swinging back and forth behind her mother — Monica's hand tightly gripped around her daughter's wrist.

"There you are, Mother!" Monica's voice was so loud everyone in the restaurant turned to see what was going on. Even the cook looked up in surprise, and he was in the noisy kitchen at the back of the building.

Emma barely had time to turn around in her chair, before her daughter had made her way to the table and was standing alongside her. Stelle's mouth dropped open, while Dr. Marksdale's knee jerk reaction forced him to stand up and take a cautionary preemptive position in the likely event the need for an intervention between the two women were to arise. An exceedingly rotund man appeared at the table seemingly from out of nowhere and in a guttural tone asked, "Is there a problem here?"

"You better believe there's a problem, and if you don't wanna even bigger one, you'll get the hell away from me!"

Ah yes, it would appear that the Monica both the doctor and his wife remembered had returned. Dr. Marksdale tilted his head to one side which resulted in a popping sound in his neck, reminding him his neck was still a little sore from the sound thrashing Monica had visited upon him the day before.

"See here, young woman," with stern conviction in his voice, the unidentified jiggly cheek faced man shot out, "You will need to keep it down, or I will have no choice but to evict you from these premises."

"I'll take care of this sir. We apologize for any interruption to your other diners." The doctor took a gentle but firm hold of Monica's arm and guided her to his chair.

"There has just been a little misunderstanding, everything will be alright." The doctor assured the man who apparently was the owner or manager.

"Well, you better take care of it or I will. We don't want any trouble in here." The man's corpulent girth was quite enough to quell the situation as far as the doctor was concerned. Dr. Marksdale avoided confrontation at all costs, especially when it involved a man of such bulky proportions and vinegary temperament.

The doctor had long viewed himself through a lens of utter refinement, and any suggestion of a confrontation with the likes of the slovenly man who was standing above him (breathing heavily and omitting an odor resembling a mixture of souring meat and an ashtray) was, simply put, not as distasteful as reeking from personal degradation.

"Of course, I assure you we don't want any trouble, either." The doctor sounded confident and sure of himself, but inside he was swimming in a pool of emotional uncertainty, and hoped the perspiration he could feel beginning to wet his face would not be interpreted as a glowing sheen of fear.

As angry as Monica originally presented herself, she obliged Dr. Marksdale's moving her to his chair and sat down without further fuss. The doctor pulled two chairs from an empty table and invited Lizzy to sit in one and he in the other. Lizzy chose to sit on Emma's lap which the doctor thought was a splendid idea. He was not sure of what Monica would do, but he felt a little less trepidation with Lizzy where she was. Knowing Monica was a loose cannon, he did not think she would do anything which would hurt her own daughter. Matricide, on the other hand, briefly crossed his mind.

The other diners began to go back to their private discussions and continued eating, but the atmosphere in the room had changed. There was a sense of quiet caution throughout the room and inside of Dr. Marksdale as he calmly began the conversation.

Stelle found herself to be quite impressed with her husband's commanding demeanor. She was not all that familiar with what his protocols for treating his patients were. She only knew most of them were similar to her patients — rich, snobby types — the kind of individuals who were willing to pay someone good money, the more the better, to sit and listen to them rattle on aimlessly. They were somehow convinced that if they forked out a vulgar amount of money to a professional to listen to their droning on about their minor and inconsequential neuroses, it would make them more relevant as human beings.

Stelle had never run into or had patients like the people she had spent the better part of two days with.

"Now these people" — Stelle said to herself while keeping a mindful eye on Monica's every move — "These people are twisted, especially that one!" Stelle's eyes stayed keenly focused on Monica.

The conversation started off with Dr. Marksdale calmly addressing the reasoning behind Emma's departure, and when he introduced Jack to Monica, her mood noticeably mellowed. Perhaps it was the fact the man she had believed to be nothing more than a figment of her mother's imagination proved, indeed, to be real and was sitting straight across the table from her.

All the pleasantries aside, the conversation quickly began to address Monica's biggest fear — that being, her mother was abandoning her. Like a surgeon would use his or her scalpel, the doctor used his words skillfully as he proceeded with caution to tell Monica her mother was not abandoning her but moving forward with her life in seeking a partner to share it with — a partner who, the doctor pointed out, was sitting right before her in the flesh and garnered no threat to either her mother or herself. In fact, the good doctor emphasized, this man named "Jack" may very well add dimension and positivity to both women's relationships with each other.

"Damn, he's good!" Stelle was caught off guard as to how well her husband was handling the situation; and Monica seemed to be relaxing more and more, as the good doctor's words were obviously soothing her fractured nerves.

Meanwhile, the rest of the group were in a bit of a frenzy. The taxi containing Percy, Donato, Ally and Benny kept circling the block with Percy continuing to try to get a peek into the restaurant window and hoping to catch a glimpse of the goings-on with the doctor's and Emma's meeting. Ally continued to kvetch about her building hunger pains, and Donato grew hungrier with every one of her whines.

Tucked in the gallery doorway, Bud had some complaints of his own as his temple and toes continued to swell.

"What's the matter with women these days? Seems they're all tryin' to kill me!" Bud's growing exasperation was quite apparent to Dill and Mrs. Fins when both, shivering from the cold, spotted Cabby's taxi. Dill let out a whistle which could shatter glass trying to get the driver's attention. The ear-splitting whistle made Mrs. Fins jump and slap her hand against her chest, and she breathlessly gasped, "Oh my — Mr. Bigley!"

His whistle did the trick, and Cabby turned sharply, stopping right in front of the threesome and waved for them to get into the car.

Hearing his whimpers, Dill and Mrs. Fins each took a hold of one of Bud's arms and helped him as he limped into the front seat of the taxi, before they both hurriedly sought refuge from the cold in the back seat.

"What the hell happened to you?" Cabby looked over at Bud in the seat next to him and grimaced at Bud's bloodied and swollen face. He turned around seeking some explanation from either Mrs. Fins or Dill, when Dill saw Benny's taxi had just passed them and was heading up the street towards the restaurant. Dill, startling everyone, shouted, "Follow that cab!"

"Are ya sure?"

"Yes man, move!"

Mrs. Fins was not sure if the chill she experienced was from the cold, or if it was something in Mr. Bigley's taking control of yet another most unfortunate circumstance they both had found themselves in. She could not remember ever having such a sensation quite like that before; hence, when she realized how delighted she was with the effect it had on her, she felt her face flush and her breath slightly quicken and thought, "Oh, my."

Cabby, responding to Dill's order, stomped on the accelerator to catch up to Benny's taxi which was already several yards up the street. Not able to hide his concern for the moaning passenger sitting next to him with an obvious bleeding head injury, Cabby turned to look at Bud.

"Do you need to seek medical help, sir?"

"No!" Bud snapped as he continued to think, "I've been gettin' medical help for 'bout nine months an' see what it got me!" Bud leaned his head back slightly and continued to hold Dill's handkerchief against his temple questioning which was worse — his throbbing head or his throbbing toes.

Cabby was startled by his passenger's angry response and kept his head turned just a little longer than what generally would have been advised. It was at that exact moment when Cabby had turned his attention back to the road ahead of him, that he was able to be his own eyewitness to the front-end of his taxi running smack dab into the rear-end of Benny's.

Airbags serve an important purpose, and those in Cabby's taxi lived up to their expectation of providing safety to the taxi's passengers. They did indeed prevent both Cabby and Bud from hurtling through the windshield. Unfortunately, the force with which Bud's face was hit by the air bag, or vice versa, was intense enough to cause him to wield a nasty blow to his face resulting in a bloody nose. His eyes, bulging from shock with blood from his temple, coupled with his profusely bleeding nose — his whole face (at this point) covered with a white powdery substance released when the airbag exploded — rendered Bud with the appearance of either having been a victim of a demented madman or a deranged slasher in a horror film.

Mrs. Fins and Dill did not have the benefit of airbags, so when the two taxis collided, they were thrust forward; consequently, both of their foreheads met with the back of the front-seat headrests with a great force, before they were flung backwards into their seats again. Everyone in both taxis were in shock, and it took a few moments before anyone knew what had actually happened.

Mrs. Fins' head was spinning, her thoughts were jumbled and unclear. Before it dawned on her she had been in a car accident, she looked in Bud's direction as he turned around to look at her. What Mrs. Fins saw was an unrecognizable bloody face, and she screamed so loud it could have woke the dead if anyone fitting that description were to be near. Fortunately, no one was close by. Instead, in direct response to her chilling scream, a chain reaction of sorts took place. Dill, bloody Bud and Cabby all followed suit. Their combined screams were so loud in the calm morning air, dogs began to howl. If anyone in close proximity had not heard the crunching of metal when Cabby's taxi plowed into Benny's, the blood-curdling screams which followed would have mothers grabbing their children and running for shelter.

Everyone in the restaurant heard and some witnessed the accident, as it happened directly in front of the large windows facing the street. This included everyone sitting with the doctors. Because they were both medical doctors prior to becoming psychiatrists, they immediately went outside to see if they could be of any assistance to the accident victims. Neither had any idea of what they were about to find.

Benny's trunk lid had been forced open by the crash and was haphazardly bent and contorted in such a fashion, it was doubtful it would ever close again. However, that point was likely moot, as the trunk itself was smashed almost up to the back seat; indeed, looking more like it could have been a large soda can crunched by the hands of a giant.

Cabby's hood was opened, but instead of being in an "up" position, it took on the appearance of a mangled accordion. A geyser of hot steam escaped from his radiator and hissing sounds (the source not certain) could be heard. Under his engine compartment were different colored liquids draining onto the street below.

"Is everyone okay?" Benny asked as he wiped blood from his lip and began taking inventory of his passengers.

"What happened?" Percy was pale in color and looked disoriented, as a small trickle of blood started to run down her forehead and down her cheek. Her face, like Benny's and Bud's, had white powder all over it.

"We got hit." Donato sounding sleepy at first turned to Ally who just looked stunned. "How 'bout you? Are you okay, Ally?"

A moment past with no reply — "Ally?"

"Yeah, sure, I'm okay." Ally's voice was barely above a whisper, and she started to feel around the top of her head.

"Where's Madaline?"

Donato looked puzzled and wondered if Ally had hit her head so hard, she did not know where she was. He knew he was having difficulty orientating himself and could feel his own pain on his head from hitting the headrest attached to the front seat.

"Ally?"

"Yeah?"

"Are you sure you're okay?" Donato's concern was evident.

"Sure, I'm okay, how 'bout you guys?" Ally started to fidget around a little as if she was looking for something.

"I'm okay," Donato replied. "How's 'bout you two?" He gently put his hand on Percy's shoulder. It wasn't until he saw both Percy and Benny had blood on their faces that he realized he too was bleeding from cuts right above both of his eyes. Then, Ally opened her door and spit out some blood. Donato, beside himself, began to dry heave.

"Oh my God, Ally, you're really hurt! Oh my God, I've gotta get ya help!"

"Nah, I just bit my cheek." Ally turned to see nothing shy of unbridled fear in Donato's deep brown eyes. Even in her disoriented state of mind, she instinctively knew this young man was showing true concern for her. That was a feeling unfamiliar to her. Most people in her life wanted something from her and would shamelessly use the guise of caring for her to get whatever that was. She could not think of any time in her life where she had felt the sensation caused when someone really had her best interest at heart, and she liked the way it made her feel. She liked it very much, and, without a doubt, she recognized it was Donato's sincerity which had created it.

As the doctors made their way outside and headed to the taxis, a crowd had begun to gather. The seriousness of the accident victims' injuries was unknown to the doctors; however, their adrenaline was in high gear, and both were ready to jump into action. Several people were already calling 911.

Suddenly, both doctors heard loud screams and excessive vulgar expletives coming from what they believed to be one of the taxi's passengers. It was a man's voice they were both certain of. It rang familiar to the good doctor, and his wife, Stelle, felt she recognized something about it as well.

"What the hell? What in the hell is happenin'? Who the shit has got it in for me? Jesus! They're tryin' to kill me, all of these freakin' mothers!"

As the two doctors got closer to the taxi, they saw the source of the yowls which sounded more like they were coming from a wounded animal than a human, and in a way they were. They were coming from Bud. His language censoring dam had burst.

The doctor bent down and looked into the car, and once he saw Dill and Mrs. Fins, he was aghast. What were they all doing together, and there, right in front of the restaurant? He was absolutely certain he had not revealed the location to anyone. There was no time to try to decipher the reason — whatever was happening was happening. Bud's cursing and expelling every vulgar word known to man was shocking enough to the doctor, but the blood on everyone's faces made the possibility of serious head wounds a real one. Any thoughts he had other than to check on Bud's physical condition first were suppressed. Bud was either not aware or did not care that the doctor was checking his vitals, as he continued to rant and spew.

Other than a few swelling bumps, several areas of his face beginning to bruise, a couple of lacerations and a bloody nose, Bud seemed to be in fairly good shape to the doctor; although, when placing his fingers just below Bud's wrist, he could tell that Bud's heart rate was quite a bit higher than the doctor would prefer.

Bud suddenly looked up to see Stelle standing next to her husband, and he screamed like a banshee. This, in turn, startled Mrs. Fins and Dill and they too screamed. The crowd that was beginning to assemble and draw closer subsequently withdrew a bit.

"Get her the hell away from me, she's a screwed up crazy, crazy ass bitch!"

Stelle raised her perfectly contoured eyebrows and asked, "What? I beg your pardon! What have I done to you?"

Bud attempted to get out of the taxi, but Percy who had managed to make her way to where Bud was reached between the doctor and Bud and placed her hand on Bud's shoulder and gently pushed down on it.

"You better just sit for a little bit," Percy said as she handed the doctor some clean tissues. "Maybe he should put some of these in his nose to help with the bleeding."

Dr. Marksdale thanked her and showed Bud how to put them in each side of his nose, but Bud was still too agitated to pay the doctor any attention. The doctor realized who the other taxi's passengers involved in the accident were — the rest of his group — and his head was swirling with questions. But, what was more pressing, was his trying to get Bud to calm down, so he could attend to the other victims while they waited for the paramedics.

"You, you crazy bitch! You and that Moronica started all this shit. You're both crazy! And I've had it with both a ya!" Bud tried to get out of his seat, but both the doctor and Percy kept him in the car.

"You better just go away, Stelle," Percy advised.

"Why? I don't understand why he is so angry with me!" Stelle was indignant which was lost on everyone due to her whining tone and her pouting.

"Please just go help the others, Stelle." Dr. Marksdale addressed his oblivious wife and pointed to the other taxi; alternatively, he got Bud to sit back down while he checked on one of Bud's burgeoning wounds.

"Their tryin' to kill me, doc! These crazy bitch women — especially that Moronica — she's gone completely nuts!"

Bud shifted his position so Dr. Marksdale could check out his temple injury further. As the doctor accidently put pressure on the foot Monica had stomped on, Bud let out a cry of pure anguish.

"Oh God! What is it?" Percy screeched.

"My foot! My god damned foot! That damn crazed bitch broke my toes!"

"Your toes?" Percy questioned as she and the doctor both looked at each other.

Bud had lost the color in his face except for the bruises and blood streaking down his face and looked as if he was about to either throw up or pass out. Percy thought to herself — maybe both. She knew that she felt she may end up doing one or the other herself.

The doctor felt assured that Bud was ultimately alright, but with all of his injuries and the accident too, it would be best if he was observed in a hospital setting, and he offered the suggestion. He knew the paramedics would be arriving shortly and wanted to observe some of the others' conditions while they waited, and he thought it may calm Bud down a little to know he was going to be okay and well taken care of. It was a wise choice, as Bud did seem to come down a few levels from the high-wire hysteria he had been experiencing.

Dr. Marksdale was pleased to see Bud was not injured to any great degree. Privately, he was at odds with his emotions though. In one way, he was shocked to hear the dam of Bud's control break, but, in another, he was glad it had. Part of him intensely wanted to take credit for it, but he had to acknowledge it probably had little to nothing to do with him. Considering his wife Stelle's earlier attack on Bud and that which Bud had conveyed to him about what Monica had done to him right before the accident, Dr. Marksdale believed those actions had more impact on Bud's meeting his final straw than anything the doctor had done for him. Either way, Bud had experienced a break through, and the good doctor would not mind taking full credit for all of it. No, he would not mind doing that at all.

"Percy, would you please sit with Bud?" Dr. Marksdale asked her for her assistance after looking at her head wound and inquiring as to how she was feeling.

"Sure, I'll keep him here. You just keep your wife and Monica away from us."

The doctor nodded and said, "agreed, thank you," and walked around to the other side of the taxi where Dill and Mrs. Fins were standing.

Cabby and Benny were standing together flailing their arms as if they were frenetic traffic guards, obviously blaming each other for the accident.

"If you'd a not slammed on your brakes!" Cabby belted out.

"Oh no ya don't! If ya would'a paid attention to where the hell ya was goin', ya wouldn't ah ended up my ass!" Benny clearly was having none of Cabby's excuses.

While Stelle was trying to identify who Madeline was and why Ally needed to find her, Donato sat with both of them trying to console Ally who seemed unnaturally preoccupied with the top of her head. He watched the bump on Ally's forehead start to bruise and wondered if the one on his own forehead looked as blue.

A short period of time passed before the sirens could be heard. After the paramedics had checked everyone out, it was suggested they should all go to the hospital to have their head wounds checked out — just to be on the safe side. They all agreed they would go, and Dr. Marksdale said he would see to it that they got there. Only one accident victim was taken by paramedics on site — that was Bud.

The paramedics believed his erratic behavior could be a sign of a deeper brain injury brought on by the several blows to his head. While removing Bud's shoe and receiving direct glass-shattering and vile condemnation for doing so, the paramedics could see his foot and some toes could very well have been broken. The fast pace of swelling was of concern, too, increasing the urgency for him to get medical help and the sooner the better. In order to keep a close eye on him while in route, an ambulance would be the chosen mode of transportation. Dr. Marksdale said he would ride with Bud, but Percy offered to do so in his place. The doctor was caught off guard by the strange development and was not sure how he should interpret it, but when Bud agreed with her offer, the doctor acquiesced.

Cabby offered to call a couple of taxis for everyone else to go to the hospital, but the doctor said he had his own transportation for the group and offered Cabby and Benny a ride too.

After calling the driver and being assured the stretch limo would accommodate all of them, it was only a few more minutes before the majority of the group and the taxi drivers were all piling into the limo.

The police who arrived on the scene seconds after the paramedics arrived agreed to take statements at the hospital and would follow the limo. Ally wanted to know if she could ride in the police car which surprised the officers slightly. These kinds of requests usually came from children. Donato said he wanted to ride with them, too, and wondered if they could turn on their sirens.

"Oh yeah! That would be fun — can ya?" Ally seemed to have lost her interest in Madeline's whereabouts at that point.

The two officers agreed and after guiding their willing passengers into the secured back seat, they looked at each other over the top of their cruiser, and both shrugged their shoulders when one said in a low voice, "out-of-towners."

When one of the officers had finished talking to the tow-truck drivers securing the mangled taxis, he came back to the cruiser and pulled it behind the limo.

As the limo driver held the door open for each of his passengers, he could not help but observe all the bumps, bruises and bloody tissues being held up to the faces of most everyone getting in. When he closed the door and walked around to the driver's door, he made a clicking sound with his tongue and said to himself, "rough crowd."

Emma held Monica and Lizzy back, and the three remained in the restaurant when the doctors and her friend, Jack, ran outside to assist the accident victims. Not knowing the condition of those involved in the accident, Emma thought it best to keep Lizzy and Monica at a safe distance. The three of them watched nervously through the windows as did several other restaurant patrons. Although Emma was aware her therapy group had come to Park City with the purpose of finding her whereabouts, no one was more surprised than Emma; now, when she saw who the people were who were getting out of the banged up taxis.

"My God! What's going on?" Emma turned to Monica.

Monica, beginning to realize the gravity of the situation, her voice breaking, "They were following me, mother. They thought I would screw everything up, and I proved them right." A tear ran down Monica's cheek.

Emma took Monica by the arm and led her back to their table.

"Sit — both of you — sit down and listen to me." Emma sat next to her daughter and taking both her daughter's and Lizzy's hands in hers, she began:

"I didn't mean for things to go this way, I apologize. We're together now and we'll work it out — I promise." Emma took a tissue out of her purse and handed it to Monica who, by now, was quietly crying.

Jack was returning to go back inside the restaurant, as everything was under control. Everyone was headed to the hospital, when he saw Emma in deep conversation with her daughter and granddaughter. After interrupting briefly to let them know everyone was going to be okay, he said he would give them some privacy and turned around and went back outside. He stood there for a good amount of time, until he noticed a specialty toy store a couple of blocks down the street. Fidgety at first but then with resolve, he went back inside the restaurant and asked if he could take Lizzy for a walk.

Monica's first reaction was to be flabbergasted by this stranger asking permission to take her daughter anywhere, but her mother assured her everything would be fine. Emma thanked Jack for offering to intervene and for allowing Monica and her mother some time to talk. For the first time, Monica saw clearly the connection Jack and her mother shared. It was that sense of connection which she witnessed that allowed her to feel more at ease with the idea. In that moment, she thought this would give her a chance to get out more of what she had wanted to say, too, but her mother made it clear she would have to wait. As everyone else in the group were making their way to the hospital, Emma talked, and for once Monica listened.

Emma did not start off with the fact Monica's father had left her mother for an acrobat, nor did she immediately address the fact he had become a clown in the same circus to be nearer to his limber lover. She also held back the fact he was not the long suffering war hero she had portrayed him to be. What she desperately wanted to get across to her daughter was — her father had not left Monica — he had left his wife, Emma. Monica brought up the cold hard truth that when he left, he left both of them — no matter what his root intention was. Emma did not dispute her daughter's right to her raw emotion.

The words flowed with more ease than Emma had imagined they would have. She told Monica if her father had discovered he had made a mistake, she would not have taken him back anyway. In telling her daughter that, she wanted to make the point clear, both women had the right to make such a decision for themselves. She hoped it would give Monica the incentive to move past her own husband's bad choice when he left her. Monica would have to make her own choices too, and Emma wanted to put the emphasis on the fact a mother's choices are difficult; and, some are certainly more difficult than others. Ultimately, whatever decision she made would be alright. She really wanted to get into Monica's head who she had to take a stand with — her own wayward man. When he walked out on Monica, he walked out on his choice to be with her again. Only Monica would have the option to decide if she would allow him back into her life.

Holding back what Emma was thinking about of the man who hurt her daughter, she chose her words wisely. She knew releasing the venom which had built up inside of her for him (as she often wanted to do) would not serve anyone well if she were to expel it at that moment in time.

"His leaving you did not render you weak, it is your freedom call and chance to exhibit your strengths."

Emma then addressed the major point she needed to get across to her daughter: She was not going anywhere, and she would always be there for both Monica and Lizzy — as long as she had the ability and capacity.

Monica, Emma believed, had to recognize the similarities in the life experiences they shared, and it was time for her daughter to understand it was up to both of them to make choices on their own and to seek the happiness they both deserved. Finally, Emma told her daughter the truth about Jack, and how she had felt an indescribable drive to find him; and subsequently, how she was driven for two long years to search for him. The only lead she had was remembering the first and only time she and the unnamed man had spoken, when he told her he lived in Park City, Utah.

Emma was keenly aware her story sounded like it came from outer space, but it was true. She could not help but quote the familiar saying, "stranger than fiction," when she filled her daughter in on the details. Emma admitted she had kept Jack a secret for a longer period of time than she had originally said, but she believed her reasoning was sound. After all, she had once been in love with a man who turned out to be a clown.

Even as enamored as Emma and Jack were with each other and after the hard and long search to find him, it was Emma who held back from meeting him in person again. Neither Jack nor Emma were immune to the pain caused by unrequited love, and the love and intensity they both felt for each other had only grown deeper over the many months they had taken to get to know each other — and always, caution had prevailed.

Their relationship consisted of hours and hours of phone conversations which covered a span of many months. The calls started in the early morning hours while both were still in their separate beds and before they each began their day. They would pick up in the evenings as they ate their dinners alone but were together in conversation. Then, after their nightly showers, they would pick up one more time before saying good night from their separate houses in two different states with hundreds of miles between them. The next morning, the whole process would start again. This ritual continued for several months prior to Emma's finally agreeing to meet Jack in person. He offered to go to Washington, but she had insisted on going to Park City instead.

Emma's face could not hide the raw truth both she and Jack had known months before she got off the plane — they were unequivocally meant to be together. Emma believed something so pure as the love they felt for each other could endure the test of time, and she could have gone longer keeping things as they were. Jack had been the one who said he could barely take it any longer, and he was sure by the time Emma let them meet in person, he would have gone completely bald from having to wait so long.

"You know, the first time I saw Jack again, he was waiting for me on the ground floor of the airport watching as my elevator descended." Emma's face lit up, and she started to giggle as she put her fingers to her lips for a few seconds.

"There he was, as wonderful a sight as he was the first time I saw him. And, sure enough, when he took his baseball cap off —" Emma with a broad smile shook her head from side to side as she relived the obviously happy memory. "He pointed to the top of his head." Shaking her head back and forth even harder and laughing louder, "Sure enough, he had a fair loss of hair since I saw him last!"

She continued grinning from ear to ear while telling Monica that Jack then took a hold of a few hairs on the side of his head and said, "You got here just in time. This is the little I have left!"

Monica vacillated between understanding and doubting that her mother's choice was what was best. Her mother had always seemed so well grounded, and Monica could not help but feel that because it was so out of character for her mother to act in such an impromptu fashion (bordering on an overly smitten teenager), she worried her mother may be going down the wrong road.

Emma told Monica she knew exactly what she was doing — maybe, for the first time in her life. More importantly, she wanted Monica not to repeat the mistakes she had made. Emma assured her daughter that she never regretted choosing to stay single while she raised her, but she did not want to see her necessarily do the same.

Emma emphasized to Monica she had to pick up and move on. True, her husband did leave her, and life as she had known it would never be the same; and maybe, that was not a bad thing. Her and Lizzy's lives were not over — they were only at a crossroads. She urged her daughter not to close down or build walls too high for anyone to get over as she had done, because she knew she would find love again and deserved to.

The two women sat for what seemed like a very long time, when Monica turned and looked at her mother and quietly asked, "Did you do this to help me to see that I needed to 'move on' as you say?"

A slight smile grew across Emma's face. "Partially, but mostly, it was to finally be with Jack." Emma was still not being totally honest with her daughter. She absolutely wanted to meet with Jack, but at the same time, she knew her daughter needed a real jolt to get her life back together — they both did. She wanted Monica to see that she could do what she needed to do — on her own. Emma compared it to a strong, electric-shock therapy treatment but without the smell of burning hair. Both women sat quietly again for a few moments.

"Was my dad really a clown?"

Emma, Dr. Marksdale had noted on many occasions, was very adept at keeping her demeanor on an even keel. In fact it was one, in the good doctor's observations, of her greatest attributes. It was at that juncture, sitting across from her daughter and hearing the question come out of Monica's mouth, that Emma struggled to keep her keel in any semblance of balance at all. She wanted to answer truthfully — something she had not done for most of her daughter's life in regards to her father — but hearing the question out loud made Emma realize how ridiculous it sounded. It was all she could do to stop herself from breaking into laughter, let alone, in trying to quell her smile.

"Yes dear — he was."

Then something happened which her mother had not witnessed since Monica's husband had left her. Emma heard a distinct light-hearted lilt in her daughter's voice.

"I always thought clowns were creepy. So —" Monica tapped her lower lip with her index finger several times before pressing on.

"So, he left you for an acrobat, was it? It sounds like a joke." Monica looked directly at her mother.

"Yep — yep — he did. And no, it wasn't a joke."

Slowly, both women began to giggle and not unlike the walls of a dam having reached its fullest capacity — straining, but failing to keep captive its irrepressible burgeoning contents — their giggles gushed out in torrents of hysteria.

Monica held up her index finger as if she were about to make a point.

"Yeah, it's a joke alright. A clown and an acrobat walk into a bar —" was all she could get out, before she was bent over in her chair holding her sides.

Monica had tears welling up again which her mother took note of through her own watery eyes.

The opulent man who had been keeping his eye on both of the women came over to their table to see if they were going to be alright, for all he saw was they both had tears running down their cheeks.

"Are you going to be okay?" Although it would appear he did not mean to, he still sounded gruff like he did when earlier, he had threatened to evict Monica from the restaurant.

Emma was grateful the man was not ordering them to get control of themselves, as she knew that possibility did not exist. All she was able to do was to nod her head up and down, indicating to him they were actually okay.

"We continue to learn all of our lives," Emma thought to herself. "And this is one of the biggest lessons for me yet."

For most of her daughter's life, Emma had used her strong sense of motherly protectiveness to keep the truth from her. She thought the story she created about the man who had fathered her was better than letting her know who the man really was and what he had done — the choices he had made which ultimately changed all of their lives and for a long time — and not for the better for Emma and her little girl.

Looking across the table at her daughter, Emma felt a strange sense of pride rising up inside — pride in herself for finally taking the chance to find her own happiness — but especially, for pride in her daughter. Her fears Monica would not be able to handle the truth were unfounded; and, in fact, Monica showed her mother she could not only hear the truth but meet it head on. What her daughter could not deal with was the uncertainty of her mother's mistruths — not anymore and never again. She could not help but wonder if the stories she had created were more to protect herself than to protect Monica. Mother's guilt was apparently alive and doing well.

Seeing her daughter be hurt so badly by her own husband, she reflected on her past pain as a young mother left by her husband. Afterwards, she created a man who was a hero in many ways. In her mind, it gave Monica someone to look up to and, for herself, it helped to protect her from looking for love again. Thus, she would not expose herself to the possibility of ever being hurt again — a perfect set-up for both herself and for Monica. It seemed to work all so well for all too long. That is, until she began to understand if she wanted to protect Monica, she would have to do it with the truth. That would be the only way to prepare her daughter for what may lie ahead and, with any luck, protect her from having to live alone for decades in denial.

Emma reached over to wipe some of the tears from her daughter's face. She looked into Monica's eyes and with a broad grin said, "This is a new beginning for both of us." As she wiped her daughter's cheeks, Emma, while still laughing but softer now, then said, "These — these tears are the only kind we should ever shed."

Monica looked up and saw her daughter coming through the door holding a stuffed giraffe in one hand and Jack's hand in the other.

"Mommy, mommy, see what Jack got me? I named him Cuddly Spots Spuggy! Isn't he the cutest thing you ever saw?" Lizzy was glowing as she ran and was welcomed onto her mother's lap.

"Look at him, and feel him momma, he's so soft."

While obliging her daughter and feeling her newest soft and spotted friend, Monica caught out of the corner of her eye that Jack had sat down next to Emma and had taken her hand in his before gently kissing it. At that point, it was quite evident to Monica, and anyone else observing them, Lizzy was not the only one glowing.

CHAPTER THIRTEEN

When everyone was finished being seen by the emergency room doctors and all of their police reports had been completed, they headed in mass towards the waiting limousine. As he watched the procession of his battered, bruised and limping patients from what he hoped to be a safe distance, Dr. Marksdale thought to himself, "I could become famous simply by writing about the events of these past two days in one of the mental health journals." Immediately, his thought process made a 180-degree pivot and he shook his head, "Wake up Phillip, that will never happen. No one would ever believe you." He continued to speak in the second person.

"It's this damn group, I tell ya!"

And then as casually and comfortable as it had recently become, he spoke in the third person.

"You've got that right, Phillip."

Dr. Marksdale was not entirely unaware his talking to himself had evolved from simple commentary into more complex conversations. He acknowledged that, on occasion, he may have taken to talking to himself in a fashion which perhaps was more conducive to behavior coming from one or more of his patients and not entirely appropriate for that of the therapist, and yet — here he was — talking to himself.

Attempting to familiarize himself with his new crutches and knee-high boot cast, Bud was doing his best to keep his balance. He suffered an additional encumbrance, as one of his eyes was covered by part of a large, gauze-padded white bandage which wrapped around the top and side of his head. He took on the appearance of a freakish, bobble-headed accident victim figurine, as he wavered and wobbled to the curb.

As she observed all the padding on one side of his bandage, Percy thought briefly, "My, Bud, you wear that lop-sided look — oh so well." She was careful not to stare for fear she would not be able to control her urge to laugh.

These thoughts, Percy recognized, slightly aroused a sense of guilt. She did not allow herself to dwell on where the guilt came from, or why it would be present at all. Instead, she held Bud's crutches for him and prepared to help him break his fall, while he cautiously maneuvered himself — repeatedly and pitifully moaning — into the back of the limousine.

Donato's and Ally's foreheads along with Mrs. Fins' and Dill's had raised and bruised lumps protruding from the direct blows they had received in the accident. Everyone, except for Stelle, her husband and the limousine driver bore some type of injury. And, although Percy had the benefit of an airbag, her eyes were beginning to blacken like the rest of those in the accident too.

During his call to Emma, Dr. Marksdale established that during the few hours it took to have everyone give their reports and be seen by the emergency room doctors, Monica, Lizzy, Jack and Emma had gone back to Monica's room at the hotel to await word from them. Emma relayed she and Monica had worked everything out, and their plans were to return to Seattle in the next day or so. The doctor was not happy with that decision and told Emma, the one or two extra passengers would pose no problem to the pilot or capacity of the private jet which he had secured.

Emma explained to the doctor that Jack needed a couple of days, as he had to close up his place before taking the trip. It made sense for all of them to stay in Park City and then travel to Washington together. She encouraged the doctor to carry on with whatever travel plans he had in mind for himself and the rest of the group. She thought it was a good idea Monica and Lizzy begin to acquaint themselves with Jack. The doctor could hear the certainty in Emma's voice; she and Jack were going to be together for the long haul. The circumstances the doctor found himself in, with the hearing looming over his head and all of his most challenging patients in various stages of battle fatigue, would not allow him any sensibility for Emma's new found love; although, if pressed, he would have to say, she was his favorite of the motley patients he had been treating.

Beside himself at that point, Dr. Marksdale felt as if his intestines were twisting into knots. Not willing to take the chance on leaving Emma and

Monica in Utah together fearing something — anything — could happen which would keep Emma from returning to Washington in time for the dreaded hearing, he absolutely had to come up with a better plan. The doctor had no doubt he had to get Emma to return with the rest of the group.

"But how, Phillip?" He asked himself.

"I've no idea." He answered.

"What do you mean you don't know? You buffoon — you should!" He raged.

He chastised himself. "Knock it off! We've got to get this together."

Over the phone, Emma insisted she would be back in time for the court hearing, and she would not let the good doctor down — she promised.

"What if I can get everyone to agree to stay another day? Would you consider flying back with us then?" Dr. Marksdale could hear the urgency in his own voice and hoped Emma would not notice.

"Oh doctor, no — I can't put all these people out that way. The simple fact that they're here now is almost more than I can bear."

"Let me talk to them, please Emma. They have been through a lot with the accident and all." The doctor was tiptoeing as gently as he could but was determined to get Emma to go along with his wishes.

"It may be best they get a full day's rest before traveling again." It was not a complete lie on his part, but the doctor knew it was not his top priority either.

"I just don't want all of this on my conscience, I'm sure you can understand doctor."

Although the doctor felt he was losing ground, he refused to give up. He had put too much into the group — too much time — too many hours of therapy. He deduced he had put so much into them, and they had taken even more out of him — so much so he felt like an empty vessel which he had continued to try and fill for the past several months with high volumes of pricey scotch. He must not, and would not, relent.

"Please, Emma, it is very important to me. Please let me talk to the rest of the group before you make a final decision."

The silence coming from Emma's phone was nerve wracking, and the doctor could hear and feel his heart racing until finally, in a tone reflecting acquiescence, Emma said softly, "okay."

The doctor sighed a true sigh of relief.

"Thank you, Emma. I'm sure everyone will appreciate the extra day of rest and relaxation."

"He sure knows how to lay it on when it serves his purpose," Stelle thought to herself. Standing next to the doctor during his and Emma's conversation, she knew there was little she could do at that point to try to derail her husband's plans. All she wanted was to get the whole distasteful and bizarre situation over with. If they had to stay another day, she would find a way to cope. Shopping came to mind.

"Yes, shopping will pass the time." Stelle pulled out her cell phone and within moments had found three stores which piqued her interest.

Before the doctor and Emma ended their conversation, the doctor signed off with, "Even with you and Jack, our plane is capable of handling a couple more passengers, so it will be no problem at all."

"Good, if we go that route, there will be one more passenger I didn't mention — Cuddly Spots Spuggy," Emma chuckled.

"Who?" The startled doctor asked.

"Cuddly Spots Spuggy — don't worry doctor, he will be sitting on Lizzy's lap," Emma said girlishly as she hung up.

Dr. Marksdale grumbled to himself.

"Jesus, did they get that kid a pet? What the hell, just add it to Ally's birds and the rest of these nuts, and we've got ourselves a traveling circus!"

*****

"I've got to eat something!" Ally was more ravenous than usual. It had been a long day, and although they all had been given a muffin and a small cup of juice in the hospital, that would not put a dent in her or Donato's appetites.

"We're almost back to the hotel. Just go to the restaurant and order anything you want." The doctor's tone was more chipper than it had been in some time and for a good reason. Emma had called him back while they were on their way to the hotel to let him know, if everyone was going to stay another day, then, they would be willing to go back to Seattle with the rest of the group. The doctor assured her they were going to stay the extra day, even though he had not mentioned it to the others. If he had to drug and hog tie them, he was determined no one was going anywhere, unless they were all going together.

When he finally addressed the group regarding their staying an extra day, the doctor was pleased to hear they were all fine with the idea. And as Percy reminded the doctor, finding Emma was only a part of their taking the trip. Find her — they did. Bringing her home was the ultimate goal. Needing Emma to be present at their upcoming hearing was imperative, and the challenge, then, had not yet been met. Of course, there were some in the group who had other ideas in their heads or — as some may refer to them as — ulterior motives or agendas.

Dill Bigley for one — he simply wanted to spend any amount of time with Mrs. Fins and in any capacity he could. That evening before he dressed for dinner, he had nervously asked Mrs. Fins if he may escort her to dinner. Although she had thought it a bit grandiose for the occasion, she accepted with a slight flush to her cheeks. She had just begun to observe Mr. Dillard Bigley was more attentive to her than she had noticed prior. She questioned herself, for perhaps she was only just imagining it.

Donato, in less than twenty-four hours, had become so smitten with Ally, he could not take his eyes off of her. Ally was having fun, as she often did, and did not seem to mind the attention Donato paid to her; however, it was not all that clear she was aware of how special that was.

Bud did not entirely mind Percy helping him, and he really did need it. Donato was somewhere between the clouds and heaven adoring Ally, so it was Percy who assisted Bud in and out of the car and elevators. She made sure he was as comfortable as he could be by putting pillows under his leg with the boot cast on. When Percy suggested it may be easier for him if she ordered room service for his dinner, he asked her to stay and eat dinner with him — somewhat surprising, she agreed to. After they ate, they talked late into the night about things neither of them would ever have presumed to have talked to each other about. Not once did either of them call the other any humiliating names. In fact, after a good dinner and conversation, Percy made sure Bud was comfortable and sat next to him on his bed where they talked like two civil human beings for a substantial amount of time, until they both fell asleep.

When Donato came back to his room well past late night and into the early hours of the morning, he woke Percy up. She seemed somewhat startled and disheveled to find she had fallen asleep. She looked over at Bud who was still deep in sleep and held her index finger up to her lips indicating to Donato to be quiet and to not awaken his brother. Gently and quietly she got off of Bud's bed. As she was leaving the brothers' room, she wished Donato a good night. Although it was thoughtful on Percy's part, Donato did not need anyone's wishes at that point. Donato had already had a good — no — Donato, up and until that time, had the best night of his life.

Between dinner and playing assorted games in the recreation room with Ally, the hours they had spent together were the best he could ever recall having spent with anyone. His favorite part of the night was the time they spent together sitting under the glass pool enclosure.

A clear night sky in the Rocky Mountains is so black, those observing are able to see trillions of brilliant stars splayed out before them. Lying next to each other on the pool lounge chairs, they counted stars, and then Donato pointed out and explained all the constellations he could see to an eagerly listening and completely mesmerized Ally.

As Percy made her way to Ally's and her room, she experienced an involuntary shiver when she remembered she and Bud had agreed to take in some sights the next day — if only Bud's bruised foot with the two broken toes would allow them to. It was in that moment Percy realized the new day had already begun.

"What the hell is happening?" Percy said softly, albeit out loud, as she entered her hotel room.

"What are you talkin' 'bout Percy?" Ally asked cheerfully as she sat on her bed combing out Madeline.

A little startled, Percy answered quickly, "um, nothin'."

The truth is — it was something. Percy knew it too; she just did not know what "it" was.

As for Stelle and the good doctor, they had eaten their dinner with the others the night before and had excused themselves quite early. They stopped off at the hotel lounge to enjoy a night cap. After that, on their way back to their room, Stelle instructed the hotel concierge to purchase a high-end suitcase for her and have it delivered to her room that evening.

She would need it to carry the items home, which she would be purchasing on her shopping spree the next day. She had the concierge set the plans into motion providing her a private limousine to take her where ever she wished to go. The words flowed over her lips with such ease, it was as if she had been saying them all of her life. The doctor having carried his brandy with him from the bar finished off the last remaining drop.

"Put it all on our tab."

Dr. Marksdale, never tired of handling business, set the brandy snifter down on the hotel front desk and escorted his wife who, to him, was the most effervescent woman — Estelle Cummings Marksdale — to their room. It was there where they both slept soundly through the night.

CHAPTER FOURTEEN

Occurrences of a curious nature take place all of the time, and after having spent the better part of a year with his group — a group the doctor would periodically compartmentalize as misfits, lunatics and imbeciles — it would seem a bit out of character for him not to expect the unexpected. Would it not?

After a leisurely breakfast, the doctor and his wife said their good-byes before Stelle's limousine driver escorted her from the hotel. Once the doctor saw she was off for a day of shopping, he began to wonder where the group was. It seemed to him at least one or more would have come down for their breakfast by that time. He waved to the waiter and requested another cup of coffee and asked if the waiter had seen anyone in his group that morning.

"What?" The doctor's shrill voice cut through the comfortable atmosphere causing several of the other diners to jump and turn their attention to the doctor's table. He was already up and out of his chair and heading towards the door, as the waiter followed on his heal trying to soothe the harried doctor.

"I'm sure everything is alright, sir. Each couple left after their taxis arrived."

"Each couple? What do you mean, they didn't all leave together?"

Storming out into the lobby, the waiter still following close behind, Dr. Marksdale confronted the young woman standing behind the reception desk.

"Young woman —" The doctor's voice was still shrill, "Where did the people in my group go?"

The woman's face revealed her surprise at the doctor's aggressive behavior and looked quite taken aback by the blustery stranger whose tone of voice could be interpreted as a verbal assault. The waiter intervened and was able to bring the unsuspecting young woman up to speed.

"I was not at the desk yet, sir." The woman looked down at the desk and shuffled some papers in front of her before she responded, "It seems that three taxis were called, and six individuals left in them."

"It seems? See here, young woman, I must know where the hell they are!" The doctor was beginning to perspire profusely.

"I'm sorry, sir, I have no idea. Perhaps they went downtown — to sight see?" The young woman was fidgeting and noticeably uneasy.

A man with a large build and rather stern presence came out of a door in back of the reception desk; and, once he had established the doctor was not a mental patient himself, he gave the doctor the information he was seeking. This man of large stature could not help but be concerned for the patients' whereabouts, particularly after seeing how their attending psychiatrist was behaving. What this man, of a sizable presence, did not realize — it may very well have been the doctor himself who was the one to be more concerned about.

One heavy block of absurdity piled on top of another had left Dr. Marksdale feeling like the weight of it all was bearing down upon him. He felt threatened and he recognized his fragile mental apparatus, and the stability of the hinge which kept that apparatus clinging to his sanity was dangling loosely by one remaining screw — a screw which was rapidly being stripped bare of its threads. When entertaining the thought that a snug jacket — a jacket of which its single purpose was meant to hold him in a tight and inescapable hug — did not set afire fear in him, it led the good doctor to wonder if those threads may have already been laid bare.

The waiter, the young woman and the large man all stood pensively awaiting a reaction from the doctor, when he finally wiped his sweaty face with the palms of both hands and took a large breath in through his nose. In a calm and controlled manner, he thanked everyone for their assistance and politely excused himself. He then headed towards the elevators leaving the three hotel employees standing silently with puzzled expressions on their faces.

Dr. Marksdale had reached a plateau. He understood, as he had never understood at any other time in his life, what he could and could not control, and he knew exactly what he had to do.

Once he was in his room and with an internal calm he had not felt since prior to the college hazing he had so adeptly managed to squelch from his conscience for so long and with a resolve and conviction he was unfamiliar with — he began to compose a letter. When he had finished that letter, he began writing another. When that one was completed, he penned his third and last letter. After addressing each envelope, he summoned the concierge and instructed him to provide the proper postage for each. The concierge offered to post the letters for the doctor; but, Dr. Marksdale made a point, he would be mailing all of the letters on his own and in due time.

The doctor requested all three letters be secured in the hotel's main safe and only given to him upon his request, to which the concierge politely interjected, "There is a safe in your room sir. Perhaps you would prefer to make use of that."

The doctor assured the concierge he was aware of the safe and its whereabouts in his room but did not want easy access to it. He emphasized he needed the letters to be kept at a distance from himself, and at a later time when he was ready, he would request they be returned to him. The concierge, without further question, assured Dr. Marksdale his wishes would be respected.

"Now Phillip," the doctor addressed his reflection in the bathroom mirror after drying his freshly washed face, "I think it's time we have some fun."

In the closet, he found a comfortable and warm casual jacket with a hood. Appropriately, Stelle had insisted he pack the jacket along with gloves and a heavy scarf designed for weather, which the cold Rocky Mountains may require. After putting on the jacket, he rang the concierge again and requested a taxi for himself.

"Of course, sir, may I tell the driver where you would like to go?"

"Yes, you may. I'm interested in taking a gondola. I would like to ride up to a lodge, I have read about in your hotel brochure."

"Oh sir, yes, a fine idea. May I schedule a lunch at the full-service restaurant at the top, sir? It really is a remarkable lodge and the food is superb."

"You may. That sounds quite nice."

"Splendid, sir." The concierge was ever eager to assist.

"Yes — indeed — splendid." The doctor agreed.

"How many will be in your party sir?"

"For this party, there will be only one — just me."

The doctor barely recognized the feeling he was feeling, as he wrapped the thick scarf around his neck while riding the elevator down to the lobby. He was comfortable, even relaxed. He noted the sensations he was feeling came without the assistance from any libation, either — neither plant based nor pharmaceutical medication.

"Phillip, I vaguely remember feeling like this. I quite like it."

To which he replied, "Yes, old friend — it has been a long time."

The young woman behind the reception desk looked up as the doctor exited the elevator. As he headed towards her, her muscles started to tense up. Instead of being confrontational as the young woman anticipated he would be, she observed the doctor appeared to be nothing like the wild-eyed man she had encountered earlier. Instead, he was calm and displayed a demeanor of casual nonchalance.

"What's he on?" She silently questioned. "Whatever it is, I want some of it."

"Dr. Marksdale, sir, your taxi is here." The concierge's voice interrupted the young woman's thoughts. "Is there anything else that I may do for you, sir?"

"That'll be all. Thank you." And with a nod of his head, the good doctor strode calmly out into the cool morning air.

The hour-plus taxi ride to the gondola where the doctor had chosen to ride (out of all those offered), was an eye-opening and enjoyable experience for him. His taxi driver was a retired dentist who had made the decision to get out of the big city of San Francisco and move to the Rockies some five years earlier. He was financially comfortable, so he could afford to retire earlier than most people. His need to get away from the hustle and bustle was strong enough, he believed, so that even without the means, he would have found a way. After several months of "just plain goofing off," he wanted something to do, so he started driving a taxi part-time. The dentist explained to his attentive passenger (a passenger the dentist had no idea was a psychiatrist), he did not get the part-time taxi job for the money.

He got it to help fill his need for human interaction without having to get too involved with others. Most of all, he liked the idea of being able to be a witness to the beauty which was abundant all around him. The human interaction was important, but second in his order of priorities.

The doctor listened with earnest interest, as the retired dentist told him how his moving to the outskirts of Park City had saved him. Having been so wrapped up in his work, the dentist relayed to the doctor he had lost sight of his own life. The dentist was an affable fellow and offered the doctor quite the tour, introducing the doctor to a plethora of information about the area.

All of this was a welcomed respite for Dr. Marksdale who had for so long thought only of his own circumstances and periodically — but more recently to his dismay — of his patients.

For the first time in his recent memory, the doctor was not thinking about his former or current patients. He was not distracted by thoughts of how much money he and his wife had or how much more they wanted. In fact, he did not think about himself — at all. As he listened to his delightful taxi-driving tour guide, he became more and more mesmerized by the exquisite raw beauty of which he found himself engulfed in.

When he arrived at the resort where he would take a gondola to the lodge for lunch, the doctor thanked his friendly and talkative driver and handed him a sizeable tip. To his surprise, the driver said it was far too much in addition to his fare.

"It's only money. I want you to take it, please." Hearing those words come out of his mouth, the doctor thought how estranged he had become with the average man.

"It's only money," played over and over in his head as he headed towards the gondolas. "If it's only money, Phillip, then why have you put such an emphasis on it all your life?"

The snows had yet to come, but that did not diminish the doctor's experience when riding in the gondola which he shared with a young family visiting Utah for, as they told him, their second time. They loved it so much, they had come back to visit the mountains in the fall before the big crowds of snowboarders and skiers would arrive. The doctor shared that he had never been there, and while his wife was off on a spending spree, he thought he would take a ride up to the lodge located at almost 9000-feet elevation just to take in the view.

The ride was shorter than he would have liked for no other reason than he wanted more. Wanting more came as no surprise to him. He always wanted more. This time, however, the more he wanted was not for a thing or for money. He wanted more of the beauty — the irrepressible beauty of the mountain peaks with their shadowy crags and the vistas stretching out below him with unfolding carpets of yellows, greens, reds and oranges.

And the sky — he wanted more of the sky with its brilliance. In the crisp thin air, the morning sun shining through the sky's blue hues made the sky so bright — looking up into it was almost blinding. Taking in deeper and deeper calming breaths, he thought, "This must be what heaven looks like."

It was all too much — all too fast. So, instead of getting out at the lodge, the doctor rode the gondola back down only to repeat the ride back up again. He continued to do this for the better part of the morning and into the early afternoon. One element which impressed him during his repeated rides was that, as the sun's position changed, so did the shadows and highlights of the grand mountains surrounding him and the valley below. The beauty kept changing, adding new dimensions to the already indescribable canvas which mother nature continued to paint on.

CHAPTER FIFTEEN

Taking into consideration the individuals involved and the varied circumstances they have found themselves in throughout this story, if someone were to ask, "What are the chances?" It would be a fair assumption the answer would be, "The chances are pretty good."

*****

"Oh God! Look!" Ally was pointing in a different direction than Donato was looking. The simple reason was that while Ally was rapt with the view she was witnessing outside of the window, Donato was equally enrapt with his most recent and favorite focal point — Ally.

"Donato!" Ally's voice raised higher, "Look! It's just so beautiful! All the colors — all the everything!" Giggling with pure delight, Ally's eyes were sparkling — eyes which were not made up in their usual cat-eye disguise, and she was not sporting Madeline on her head either.

Percy had become a bit harsh early that morning in retaliation for Ally goading her on about her having spent the night with Bud. Percy tried repeatedly to explain to Ally her spending the night with Bud meant nothing, and although they slept on the same bed, that was all they had done — slept.

Ally's girlish giggling and taunting aggravated Percy to the point she lashed out by saying, "Jesus Ally, you're not goin' to wear that awful thing again, are you?" Ally, unaffected, continued to comb her wig out.

Then, in her girlish way, Ally giggled and teased, "Percy, say her name. C'mon, you who spent the night with Bud, say her name!"

"It could be God Almighty for all I care! It's god awful! And it is beginning to smell like a thrift-store shoe!" Percy thrust a judgmental finger at Ally's wig while unable to stop from stammering and feeling like a teenager trying to explain to her parents how she innocently spent the night with a boy after having fallen asleep on his bed.

Ally was not swayed nor was she convinced with Percy's rendition of the night she had just spent with Bud, but she decided maybe Percy was right about Madeline needing a good shampoo. She took Madeline to the sink and began to give her a thorough scrubbing.

"The girl has an uncanny ability to hop from one single thought to another — but only one thought at a time." Percy kept to herself, "Give her two things to pay attention to and her head would blow up."

Madeline had not dried out by the time Ally and Donato made plans to meet up for their day of exploration, so Ally went as her rarely seen, simple but beautiful, unmade-up self with her loosely cut, pixyish style ashen-blond hair falling naturally around her pretty young face.

In the early morning hours after Ally's third-degree interrogation of Percy, they both had decided it made sense, all of them should stick together — both of the women and the brothers — and thought it was a good idea if Mrs. Fins and Dill joined them too. They knew they wanted to do something, but at that point in time, they just did not know what.

Percy made a call to Mrs. Fins' room, and found she was in agreement and on board with the idea immediately. Her sense of protection for Dr. Marksdale had not waned, and although new developments had merged onto the scene for Mrs. Fins — developments she was not quite sure of but was nevertheless interested in how they may affect her own future horizon — she thought it was best if someone were to help the doctor keep an eye out on his group.

Mrs. Fins told Percy she and Mr. Bigley had made plans to eat at a restaurant in downtown Park City and were getting ready to head out when Percy called her.

Percy suggested, "Hey, how 'bout we all meet up at that restaurant and decide what to do today, together." Mrs. Fins agreed.

Percy and Bud would have to take a separate taxi from that of Ally and Donato due to Bud's need for extra room with his crutches and boot cast, but Percy insisted they would not be too far behind; and, it was then, everything was set in motion.

While having their breakfasts, they all agreed that because of the conditions both Dill and especially Bud were in, they would be limited to some degree in whatever they decided to do

Ally pulled a brochure out of her purse and said, "Look here. I read about this ride you can take. It goes way up a mountain, and there's a place at the top you can eat, goof off, shop or just chill in the lodge."

"Yes," Mrs. Fins replied, "I, too, read about that. You ride in a gondola. It sounds really quite lovely." She looked in Dill's direction to peruse his reaction.

"I think that is a jolly good idea, Mrs. Fins."

Keeping her thoughts to herself, Percy said smugly, "Surprise, surprise — Dill likes something Mrs. Fins likes!"

"We could get a real bird's eye view," Ally was quick to offer. Her bluish green eyes were surprisingly darker that morning — similar to the blue of the Pacific Ocean — and they sparkled as she was clearly tickled by her own quick wit.

And so, the group had come to a mutual decision. Even Bud, who was known to quibble over the smallest suggestion by the others, was in complete agreement. In fact, he sounded happy that he — in his disadvantaged condition with his lumpy head similar to Dill's and his cumbersome cast and crutches — would not be a liability to their adventure. Even more surprising was his offer to pay for everyone's gondola tickets and lunch. When Dill offered to pay half, Bud did not object nor did he interject any snide commentary. He just politely accepted Dill's offer — strange, strange developments, indeed.

Mrs. Fins took a quick peek at Dill when he made the offer and thought to herself, "Of course Mr. Bigley would make such an offer, he is nothing shy of a complete gentleman."

"Wow, you guys are so nice," Ally said brightly.

Percy, on the other hand, thought everyone's good natured comradery stemmed from the thinner air at their current elevation.

Taking a shuttle together made more sense than everyone taking separate taxis, and Ally surprised all when she said, "I'm already on it." She was very adept at researching information and using her cell phone. Within a few short minutes, she had secured a shuttle which would pick them up right in front of the restaurant.

Being the one in the group who had no compunction about showing her excitement, Ally was the most eager to get started. Her youthful and uninhibited passion for excitement did not go unnoticed by anyone within her realm, and her exuberance did not go unnoticed by two strangers riding with her in Percy, Bud and Donato's gondola either. But no one was more aware of Ally's unbridled free spirit than Donato. With each of Ally's giggles and exclamations of excitement, Donato sat in utter amazement of her pure and unbridled joy.

Donato smiled broadly while quietly asking himself, "How is it she can be so completely happy?"

Following in the gondola right behind them were Dill and Mrs. Fins, and although their observations and reactions to the same view were a bit less animated, neither of them were any less exhilarated with what they were seeing. For Dillard Bigley, the view of Mrs. Fins' profile was exactly that — exhilarating — and Dill thought to himself, the view just outside the gondola's windows was pretty spectacular too.

Everyone, including the bruised and battered Bud, felt a sense of relaxation which none of them had felt for a very long time. A man known for his quick temper and angst towards almost everyone and everything, Bud, on that day, found himself at ease in his surroundings. In particular, Bud surprisingly found himself more relaxed around Percy whom, on most occasions, he found himself at odds with. He was not the only one feeling off-center and somewhat perplexed.

Percy asked herself if Bud's startling and graphic release of pent-up hostility — while using the most vile and abrasive language even for a truck driver such as herself — had eased Bud's inner turmoil to the degree he may actually have begun to, on some primal level, become more human. She began to see clearer, at that point, how Donato could feel the feelings he felt for his older brother. The combination in which she and Bud had spent hours in conversation the night before — where they had both behaved like civilized human beings along with the day which followed — allowed Percy to get a glimpse into the man Donato had described as a caring and giving soul. The feelings it aroused in her — feelings she had pushed down over the course of many years — now began to come into view. Those feelings made her feel girlishly light-headed and dizzyingly wary all at the same time.

Every one of the doctor's patients were experiencing an array of different sensations that day. For some, they were new sensations. For others, they were sensations they had not felt for such a long time, they had dangerously approached being forgotten forever.

The same was true for the doctor who was experiencing elation while he rode peacefully in his gondola. All of the years he had hidden his dark secret had taken a large toll on him. He had come to understand that day — that which he had sacrificed was so much of his inner self — the part of a man that made the man. He had become a shadow of the man he wanted to be by fearing his truth would emerge — leaving him raw, exposed and unworthy of his professional position and social standing. How foolish he thought himself to have been. He had wasted valuable time placing a high priority on superficial things, and in due course he lost an immeasurable amount of non-refundable peace of mind. On that particular day, however, things would prove to be different.

Of the three letters Dr. Marksdale had written, one was addressed to the president of the college which he, Stelle and Dr. Elan Glenn had attended. Once Dr. Marksdale committed pen to paper — within that letter — he chronicled the secret he had held onto for so close for so long. The contents of the letter were precise and to the point, and he did not wince at the fact who, upon his return to the hotel, he was going to mail that letter along with a second letter to. The second letter he composed was written with determination and conviction, and he had addressed it to Mr. and Mrs. Fisker — Leon Fisker's parents.

Dr. Marksdale rode in the gondola for hours that day — up nine-thousand feet and down again to the valley below — feeling sensations he had not felt since he was a young boy. In his mind's eye, the doctor could see that young boy swinging on a rope swing just outside his childhood home, where he could hear his mother's voice calling out to him, "Phillip be careful. Phillip — don't go too high!"

The recollection was so vivid, he could smell the lilacs which bloomed and hung over the front porch. He knew there would be ramifications and consequences to his prior actions, but on that day, he felt only the sensation he was floating over the top of the world.

There was no sensation of being pulled every which way, a sensation which never left him — not until that day. Nor was there any dread from the fear of looking over his shoulder — quite the contrary. On that day, he finally met with and confronted his truth, and, in doing so, he granted himself irrefutable absolution. Dr. Phillip Marksdale was free.

Stelle found herself in an interesting mental space too. She realized she was enjoying looking out of the limousine window instead of dialing in all of her attention to her usual social media distractions, as the limousine driver shuttled her from boutique to boutique. Most curious to Stelle was that she found herself liking what she was seeing, and when she had visited all of the high-end shops in Park City (and purchasing surprisingly very little), her driver suggested they travel to Salt Lake City where, he assured her, they would find a plethora of trendy shops — shops which would wet the most parched lips and quench the thirsts of the most avid shopper. Stelle most unfamiliarly found herself thinking of how beautiful the ride would be instead of entertaining how much more shopping she would be able to indulge in.

At first and with trepidation, Emma and Jack observed the emotional altitude of Monica's overall mood, and once they saw how calm Monica had become and witnessed how receptive both Lizzy and Monica were to Emma's being with Jack, they both sighed — relief.

Emma and Jack had more than desire driving them to find each other. Acknowledging the almost unsurmountable odds of that ever happening were against them so much so, that when they did find each other, they concurred it was as if some magical wind kept whispering to each of them, "keep searching." And search they had, and beating the odds they did.

As the gondola Ally and Donato were riding reached the drop-off platform, Ally giddily took Donato's hand in hers and with great enthusiasm said, "C'mom, Donato, let's go!"

Ally's eagerness could not be ignored as she pulled him along behind her. "Hurry, let's go."

Donato could barely believe what was happening. His hand was in the hand of the girl of his dreams, and the best part of that was — he was wide awake. His heart raced faster than his feet could as he eagerly tried to keep up with her.

Bud and Percy had their own challenges. Bud's crutches were proving to be more cumbersome than he had expected, and with his younger brother almost out of sight as Ally held a firm grip on Donato's hand pulling him along, it was up to Percy, once again, to come to Bud's aid.

"Let's get you out of here first," Percy offered placing her shoulder under Bud's arm. "Then you can use the crutches." Bud agreed as he leaned on Percy's shoulder, while she wrapped her arm around his waist for better support.

"I'll carry the crutches, you just hop." Percy had Bud on her right side and carried the crutches in her left hand, as Bud maneuvered himself into an awkward-in-appearance-but-balanced position.

"You're not so bad, Percy." Bud said sounding somewhat sincere.

Percy smiled slightly as she, herself, worked to find her balance as they made their way off of the gondola. There were only a few *"ouches"* followed by a couple of *"ahhh's"* and every few wobbly steps an *"ewww,"* as they hobbled their way towards the lodge.

"Ya think you're ready to try out the crutches?" Percy asked in a raspy voice as she tried to adapt to the thinner air and the awkward, unbalanced weight on her right side.

"Not yet, I feel wobbly and a little dizzy — probably the elevation," Bud replied.

Percy stiffened her back and stood up taller while she looked ahead trying to calculate how many more feet or, if left to her back and shoulder to measure, how many more miles it was to the lodge door. For a quick moment, Percy's mind flashed the thought, "Bud always managed to get on my back — one way or another." For a while though, a short while, Percy relied on one driving force. That force was her hope a chair would be in close proximity to the entrance where either she or Bud, or perhaps both, would be able to collapse, once they had reached their destination.

Knowing she was in better condition at that point than Bud was with his bumps, lumps and cast, she put one foot in front of the other and tried to sound encouraging when she said, "Okay, let's just keep movin' Bud. We're almost there."

Mrs. Fins and Dill Bigley pulled up to the platform next, and as one could safely assume, their exit was more controlled and sedate in comparison to that of Donato and Ally's. However that act, in and of itself on either of their parts, was not necessarily a willful one.

Neither Mrs. Fins nor Dill Bigley would allow themselves to openly exhibit as frolicsome a behavior as Donato and Ally may. Secretly, they both wished they could. To do so would require them both to openly express their inner desire to abandon what they believed to be the proper comportment in a public setting.

Dill had offered his hand to assist Mrs. Fins from the gondola and she had accepted. Sadly, though, once she was safely on the platform, they both released the other's hand causing both to feel pangs of regret for allowing themselves to be driven by such stifling, straitlaced etiquette.

If this trip were to bring about any change or awareness to anyone, it would surely be how Mrs. Fins' feelings had begun to change towards Mr. Bigley. She had always seen him in a separate light than the rest of the group, but this trip had shown a narrower, more definitive, light on the handsome and proper English gentleman. That new light warmed the diminutive Mrs. Fins, she had come to discover, quite a bit more than slightly. As for Mr. Bigley, the effect of the trip on him only encouraged the exponential growth of his silent love for his most perfect Mrs. Fins, magnifying his continued ache and longing.

Unfortunately for both Mr. Bigley and Mrs. Fins, their shared propriety for decorum proved to be an unwelcomed and intrusive culprit.

✭✭✭✭✭

The lodge was beautifully decorated and just what one would assume the inside of a high-end mountain ski lodge high in the Rockies would look like — but better.

The wooden structure itself — the enormous fireplace open on all sides and the crackling sounds the burning wood made, combined with the aromas coming from the kitchen — awakened the senses of everyone entering the lodge. Besides providing relief from the chilly air outside, the lodge emitted an inviting ambience, as each member of the group entered through the large glass doors. Immediately and spontaneously, each one found themselves to have smiles on their faces.

Dr. Marksdale was no exception. He had ridden the gondola for a few hours, when he decided to disembark, peruse the lodge and shops and maybe get some lunch. Immediately upon exiting the gondola, he could not escape the crispness in the air and settled his scarf tighter around his neck, as he headed for the lodge. Upon entering the building, he began to take in the massive interior of the room and thought to himself, if the huge structure could speak, it would probably say, "welcome friend."

"Hey, there's Doc!" Bud shouted out causing Percy to turn her head away from the fireplace she was warming her hands in front of.

"Yeah, I see him. Let me wave him over here." Percy began to wave to get the doctor's attention just as Dr. Marksdale saw both herself and Bud, and he started heading towards them.

"Well now, this is a nice surprise." The doctor said cheerfully — a tone Bud and Percy were not all that familiar with coming from the doctor. During their sessions, he had tended to be more serious in his general, overall demeanor.

"Yeah, a surprise — we're all up here to check out the place an' didn't 'spect to see you." Bud was the first to respond to the doctor.

Having seen the doctor entering the lodge from through the shop window directly across the street, Ally grabbed Donato's hand and began to run to catch up to him, but not before the doctor had reached Percy and Bud.

"And to ride the gondola!" Ally was saying in her joyful way, catching her breath, as she and Donato made their way to the three of them.

"The gondola ride was a trip! It was so beautiful. I want to do it again," Ally breezily giggled while looking delightfully excited. Donato's face turned red from the cold air and his running to keep up with Ally. His facial expression could have been described as dreamy, but Percy could not stop herself from thinking his expression bore more like the appearance of a grinning idiot.

The five of them stood in front of the fireplace sharing congenialities as if they were old friends. Everyone was eager to speak about what they had experienced on their ride up the mountain, but none more so than the doctor himself. Not one of the members in the group, he was standing with, could recall seeing him so lighthearted and at ease.

After a few minutes of friendly chitchat, Dill and Mrs. Fins joined them. They had spoken to the manager and acquired an electric scooter for Bud to ride, thinking it would be easier than trying to lean on his crutches or Percy's shoulder. Bud was openly pleased when he saw what they had done for him but not nearly as happy as Percy was, as she sighed while rubbing and rolling her shoulder up and back a few times.

"Wow," the doctor began as he bent his head back and turned it side to side taking in the interior of the lodge. "This place is something else, don't you think?"

"Sure is," Bud began, "But you probably see places like this all the time."

Dr. Marksdale smiled and while looking into the one eye which was not black, blue and swollen, he said, "You would think so wouldn't you, Bud. But, no, I have never seen anything like this, not through these eyes." The doctor continued to take in his surrounding environment, as everyone could not help but notice an almost euphoric presence lighting his face.

"It took me," the doctor started, "It took me having to lose my mind before I got a true view of the world." He took in a deep breath and exhaled slowly.

Standing somewhat awkwardly, everyone kept quiet while looking at the doctor. His tone had changed, and he did not sound like the man they were used to. He sounded soulful and philosophical. These were not the emotions his group of patients were used to hearing coming from him.

Percy pondered, "I think something has happened to the doctor, but what?"

Bud was not sure what to think. He was glad Dill and Mrs. Fins had appropriated a mode of transportation for him. Although, while in the back of his mind he thought of these types of scooters as "old-man wheels," he was happy to have one. At the same time, he could not shake the feeling of concern for the doctor. Because of the call he had received from the doctor in the middle of the night a couple of nights earlier — the phone call which would set all of the bizarre actions into motion and lead him to where he was at, at that moment — Bud had found himself feeling varying degrees of anxiousness. Pensively, he surmised everyone else in the group must have been feeling somewhat the same while wondering what may happen next.

Donato did not give the doctor's comment much thought at all and chalked it up to typical psychiatrist type lingo. Besides, he was single-mindedly focused on one person, and that one person was not the doctor.

Dill Bigley reflected on the fact, most of the group's interactions with the doctor had been in a therapeutical and clinical setting. Only recently, their sessions had become less chaotic, thus enabling the doctor to be more communitive with the group on a therapist-to-patient basis rather than spending an inordinate amount of time, as usual, refereeing skirmishes of both a verbal and physical nature. The skirmishes, Dill embarrassingly had to admit, had always started between Bud and himself. Dill preferred to place the responsibility for the mayhem on Bud's combative caveman-like temperament. A moment passed when Dill felt he had to acknowledge, on more than one occasion, he too had contributed to the loutish behavior the two men had engaged in. The fleeting thought was of the time Dill had deliberately poked his foot out to cause Bud to trip which — causing his body to hit the floor with a loud thud — was not something Dill was proud of. Although at the time of the occurrence, he had reasoned his motivation was a source of self-preservation — the "get-him-before-he-gets-me" mentality.

Mrs. Fins questioned whether Dr. Marksdale's finally opening up to Mrs. Marksdale about the secret(s) he had kept from her had really eased his tensions enough, to where he had released his guilty feelings and constant underlying trepidation.

Ally felt she understood precisely how the doctor was feeling. Her experience riding in the gondola and witnessing the view was for her as it was for the doctor — transformational.

"The view," Ally thought to herself, "was spectacular." It was in that moment she thought of her birds.

"Being birds —" Ally quietly contemplated. "And being able to fly and see all that I got to see today all the time would make me so happy, I would burst!"

Almost as quickly as Ally's sparkle of delight filled her face, it also disappeared along with the joy in her eyes. This was something no one other than Donato would see, as they were all still looking at the doctor.

Ally's expression mirrored her realization, her precious baby birds had never flown outside of the cage (she had kept them in); since the time, she had rescued them from their fallen nest. Only Donato would witness the bittersweet moment. Though he did not know what exactly had transpired behind Ally's beautiful eyes to cause such an expression to waft over her lovely face, it triggered in himself, too, a pang of sadness due to his growing love for her.

Of all the experiences these "misfits" had experienced over the nine months of their treatment, none may have been more profound or life altering for everyone than those actions happening in the prior two (going on three) days, including for the doctor — perhaps more so for him than anyone else.

*****

Chased by dancing shadows on the mountain's crags and peaks, the sun moved across the azure sky. As the hour of the day drew closer to late afternoon, the temperature began to drop rapidly. No one inside the lodge seemed to notice the chill.

People were gathered in groups. Some groups were small, some larger. All were involved in sharing quiet conversation.

The doctor and his group had indulged in a delicious and filling lunch, gratuitous of Dill and Bud's offering. Afterwards, the doctor acquired a hot cup of coffee with a swirl of whipped cream and caramel on top and comfortably secured himself a soft overstuffed chair by the crackling fireplace. Besides having their own desires to entertain themselves, members of the group instinctively knew to leave the doctor alone. All were pleased to see he appeared to be relishing in his relaxed and quiet contemplation.

Mrs. Fins and Dill Bigley were discussing the Pacific Northwest Ballet and an upcoming opera which was set to premier the following weekend at the McCaw Hall in Seattle. They shared an almost giddy enthusiasm over attending it — together.

Neither Dill nor Mrs. Fins were sure who had broached the subject first as to their attending the event in tandem, but they were both quite satisfied with the end result. They found humor in the ease and comfort with how it came about. It was natural, uninhibited and unquestionably an easy conclusion to reach.

Bud and Percy picked up where they had left off the night before discussing Percy's job as a long-haul truck driver and the long hours it took her away from whatever was known as home to her, and Bud made clear his dedication to his family's bakery business. The two of them conversed calmly and continued to learn a good deal about each other. Both began to see the personal sacrifices each had made to accommodate their professional lives.

Percy revealed she had learned to like what she did, but it would not have been her first choice. She started to do it on her own after her ex-husband left her for another woman. He left her with an enormous amount of debt, including her having to pay off the truck which was their only source of income to begin with. Not having any other real experience other than driving the "rig," which was what she had done with her ex before his departure, Percy felt the circumstances she was thrust into did not lend her many choices.

Bud asked her about children and whether she had or wanted any. She admitted, although she had wanted them, it was mostly of her own volition — she never had any. She told Bud her ex had convinced her that having a family in their line of business did not fit, at least not in the typical sense.

Percy found herself opening up to Bud, about how she did not harbor ill feelings towards her ex for walking out on her; as much as, she was resentful of how, "He up and started a family with the tramp! He said he didn't want kids. Guess the truth is — he didn't want 'em with me."

Bud looked at Percy after what she said and saw what he thought was more sadness than anger on her face.

"Ya know, we don't have to talk 'bout this," he kindly assured her.

"It's okay, I don't care 'bout him anymore an' haven't for a long time." Percy looked seriously into Bud's good eye and said, "They're truckers too, and he doesn't have a problem traipsing all over the country with their little bastards!"

Bud uncharacteristically chose his words carefully. "If you met someone new would you want to start a family now?"

Percy took in a deep breath and tilted her head to the side appearing to be deep in thought answering, "At my age, maybe not. It would probably be better if I just played with other people's kids and then sent the little nose pickers home," prompting them both to laugh.

Bud picked up the conversation and opened up about his feelings of being the oldest child and the responsibility which that bore upon him — more so than any of his siblings. Percy remembered that Donato had told her how Bud sacrificed his own dreams of finishing college to instead coming home and taking over the restaurant and bakery business for his aging parents.

Percy watched and listened and was struck by how easy she and Bud could talk about such personal matters without calling the other unflattering names even once. She took note how Bud was telling his story. He was no longer the arrogant or egotistical, bombastic brute she had been familiar with.

This Bud — the Bud who had been pepper sprayed a mere two days earlier and bludgeoned by a water bottle, a brick wall, the back of a taxi headrest, in addition to being stomped on by a mad woman leaving him in a boot cast — was somehow now revealing glimpses of kindness and even compassion.

For Percy, listening to him talk about taking care of his family was easy. He admitted he had brief encounters with a few women along the way, and acknowledged he would have liked meeting someone he could have become seriously involved with; but, with his priorities, neither the women nor the time ever seemed quite right for it.

Percy wondered if that was why Bud presented himself the way he did. If he could keep everyone at arm's length — and in his case and with his behavior, it would be safer to be at a football-field length — then he would not have to ever know if someone would be able to accept his choice in life or not.

"It would take somebody real special to fit into my life." Bud continued, "She would have to be okay with my taking care of the whole family, and that wouldn't be easy."

Percy kept to herself, "not to mention, all your other little ticks and idiosyncrasies!"

Hearing a girlish giggle, Bud and Percy turned their eyes towards Ally and Donato. Percy opened with, "They sure have taken to each other," and then ventured further, "With his looks, he must be a real heartbreaker."

"You'd think so, huh, but nah," Bud started sounding quite assured, "Not Donnie — he's real shy." Then in a thoughtful tone, "He's pretty scared of 'em — girls that is."

Bud and Percy both took a long, serious look at Donato who had moved to sit closer to Ally in front of the lodge window. Huddled close to each other looking out at the view, Donato turned his head to look at Ally revealing his profile — a silhouette against the mountain backdrop.

Thoughtfully, Bud added, "I gotta say, though, I've never seen him like a girl like this before — not ever."

Percy turned to look at Bud who was looking forward exposing his own profile. Percy had never really paid any attention to the lines and cut of Bud's face before. She was struck in that moment of which, even with Bud's swollen eye, the similarities he shared with his younger brother's facial features were uncanny. They looked so much alike, it made Percy draw in an extra breath.

"God, they look so much alike!" Percy tried not to show her surprise.

Bud turned his head just in time to see the expression on Percy's face and immediately questioned her, "What is it?"

Caught off guard by her own realization and then by Bud seeing the look on her face, Percy tried to compose herself.

"Well, James, I never noticed until now how much you and Donato look alike."

"Did you just call me James?"

Another candid and unexpected expression flashed across Percy's blushing face.

"I think — I guess — yeah I did."

So surprised at herself for calling Bud by his real name, Percy's mind raced to find an explanation. She could attribute it simply to their talking about Donato, and that is how Donato addressed his brother — it just slipped out. Still, "caught off guard" was not a place Percy liked to be, so she hurriedly looked down at her lap and actively began to use her hand to give the appearance she was dusting something off of her pant leg.

The only response from Bud was his taking in a breath and leaning his head back a little. He did not go ballistic as anyone in the group would have presumed he would. Instead, he straightened his head back up and looked at his brother and Ally who sat huddled together in their own private world.

"You don't think she'll hurt him, do ya?" Bud's voice was soft and led Percy to believe she heard a sincere sign of deep concern for his younger brother's well-being.

"I don't know. I hope not. They're both still so young. It's a chance they take, I guess."

Percy knew what she said was as true as anything she could ever say, but in that moment, she had wished she could say something more — something encouraging which may provide comfort to the man sitting next to her who, she could clearly see, actually cared about someone other than himself. Seeing him in that light made her want to, in some strange and not so familiar way, shelter him, as she felt he was exposed and vulnerable.

"Not just young people get hurt," Bud added as he adjusted himself in his chair.

"You got that right," Percy agreed. "That's the truth — for sure."

"Guess ya have to take a chance every once in a while, though," Bud said barely above a whisper.

Struggling to prevent her voice from faltering — her words jittery and barely audible and in a broken voice — Percy eked out, "Yeah, maybe ya do, once in a while."

CHAPTER SIXTEEN

Imagine the surprise the doctor experienced later that evening, while at dinner in the hotel restaurant, when he was met with a boisterous round of rousing disapproval upon announcing he was dissolving the group. He merely told them there would no longer be a need for the group to continue their therapy, and the last time they would need to be together would be at the upcoming court hearing. The doctor had not anticipated such a response from anyone in the group — least of all from Bud — particularly not from Bud. Nevertheless, it was Bud who lashed out the loudest, as if he had received another physical injury to add to the ones he had already incurred.

"Wha da ya mean, doc? We aren't ready!" Bud exclaimed, his voice cracking, while his head swung back and forth, as the look of desperation darted forth from his one good eye. He looked at the other members of the group seeking some kind of back-up, when the doctor began to calmly explain his reasoning.

"You have all come so far. Look at you." Dr. Marksdale panned everyone at the table — his eyes meeting with everyone in the group — slowly, methodically and one at a time.

"What I have witnessed over the past several months and in these past couple of days is nothing short of a solid victory." The doctor took a hold of Stelle's hand as she sat quietly next to him.

"Look at how you all came together for a shared purpose." He looked down at his hand which was holding Stelle's and then lifted his head and said softly, "You do not need me any longer."

Smiling softly, he turned to look at Stelle before turning back to everyone else to say, "You are ready to go before the judge with pride to show her all you have accomplished. And then —" The doctor looked back into his wife's eyes. "You will be free to go back to your lives."

"Accomplished? Ha! I ain't accomplished nothin'!" Bud was inconsolable.

"Yeah, ya did." Ally was quick to cheerfully offer, "You don't try to bop Mr. Bigley in the head so much anymore."

"Yes — Jeffries, Ally is correct," Dill interjected.

Mrs. Fins, along with the others, smiled at Dill's comment and nodded in agreement.

"And don't forget how you blew your top and cussed up a storm! And ya didn't hit nobody while doin' it," Ally added. "I don't think I ever heard some of those words, and I sure haven't heard 'em all at one time, for sure." Percy candidly contributed, "I think it helped you to do it, ya know, lettin' out all that anger."

"You have become quite a bit less aggressive and actually, on occasion —" Dill cleared his throat and sat up straighter in his seat, "And on occasion —" Dill cleared his throat again, "You have been quite helpful and expressed generosity and kindness."

"That don't mean nothin', English! I just been helpin' the doc and all ah you out." Bud searched the faces of the others imploring them to offer a reason — any reason which would derail the doctor's suggestion the group be dismantled.

Feeling a sense of defeat, Bud slumped his shoulders and grumbled, "At least that's what I was tryin' ta do."

The doctor's voice, still soft but loud enough to hear, followed — "precisely."

"I don't see why we gotta stop our meetin's," Bud pressed further, "I just got used to comin' to 'em."

"I like them too." Emma began, "They have helped me more than I realized. Our sessions helped me find my internal courage." She smiled and looked at Jack and then at Monica and saw they too were smiling.

"In all honesty," Dill started, "I'm not sure that I am ready either." Hearing those words as they came out of his mouth — just as everyone else had — left Dill somewhat rattled.

"At first, I did not think there was any reason for my attending the sessions, but then . . . ." Dill's voice trailed off.

"But then, what?" Percy questioned as she turned to face the doctor, "I know I don't feel quite right about this either, doctor." Looking directly at the doctor she hoped to see something — anything — which would help appease her sudden discomfort with his having said they were ready to, "Go back to your lives." For a moment, Percy felt out of sorts with the doctor for breaking up the group.

Since she had been ordered to attend the unbearable sessions with unbearable people (as far as she was concerned, at that time), Percy could hardly have waited until the day she no longer had to attend another.

"So why is it?" She wondered — when it looked like her desires had been met, and she would be free from having to attend another session — did she say to herself, "I feel a strange sense of emptiness."

"I can see my announcement has come as a shock to some of you." The doctor said in a kind but authoritative voice. "It is not unusual for you to feel a sense of loss at this time, but I assure you it is a temporary condition."

The doctor knew from the instant he had met the group, he could barely wait for the day in which he would stop meeting with them. On that night, however, his usual keen ability to size up and judge a situation did not calculate into his equation the sum of this group of patients' responses. It was not that he was surprised some members of a group receiving therapy together would have grown fond of or, in a strange way, dependent upon the others. He just had not expected this result from this particular group of people.

Taking into account his training, Dr. Marksdale realized he had lost sight of some of the basics of his teachings and some of the most common occurrences between those receiving therapy and those providing it: transference and countertransference. He did not believe either was the case in the current situation, but he could not deny a strong bond had not only been built between himself and his patients but also between the members of the group for each other.

In his usual fashion, the doctor wanted to pat himself on the back. He had accomplished more than he had set out to do, but now, he found himself faced with having to make another assessment. This particular group of misfits had him wringing his hands many times throughout their arduous months of therapy. But, in that moment, sitting at the table with them and seeing their worried faces, he felt not only for himself, which was a usual reaction for him, but he surprisingly felt something for them too.

None of these individuals chose to receive therapy or had chosen him to provide it. All of them being thrown together was not on any one of the individuals' wish list, in particular, the doctor's. Yet, somehow in the time they had been forced together, a unique bond had formed.

Dr. Marksdale found it ironic who, of all the individuals in the group, the least likely to him to have formed such an attachment to anyone including himself would ultimately be the loudest one in protesting and objecting to the breaking apart of the group. Still worth noting — what, with the objections and sad long faces — the doctor was not going to allow any one of them to throw a wrench into the machinery. Once he had decided to end the blasted sessions — sessions which had kept him on pins and needles for months — he was not going to reverse his decision.

"Like any therapist worth their weight," he told himself, "I psychoanalyzed myself." He did this while making his repeated ascents and descents above the valley floor and up the mountain side. He had to take into account all that had transpired throughout the prior several months. He delved into his early college days, too, and what he saw was not a life he relished living further — not the way he had lived it up until then.

Although it was easy to blame the soulless Dr. Elan Glenn for holding the hazing, which ended so horrifically, over his head for the better part of two decades, his honest attempt to delve into his own psyche had led him to a place he could no longer avoid facing. Dr. Marksdale recognized he too, like the hundreds of patients he had treated over the years, was a victim of his own circumstance.

Later in the day as he relaxed in the lodge, Dr. Marksdale had begun to hear a sound resembling gentle frolicking in his head. It was a sound he could not ever remember hearing before, but one he hoped to incorporate into the library of his mental playlist. Once he heard the frolicking in his mind, he knew he had done all he could for the members of the group, and he no longer had to worry about ramifications from the threats his evil nemesis, Dr. Elan Glenn, may have held over his head. He indeed had the "goods" on the good-doer doctor, and any problem he thought he could cause for Dr. Marksdale would ultimately be a problem for himself only. As he sat by the fire in quiet contemplation and watched how the members of the group were interacting with one another, he had no doubt he had done his job well.

The good doctor was indubitably pleased the nightmare he had been living was looking smaller and smaller in the rear-view mirror of his mind, and he felt safe once again welcoming his old friend — honest self-admiration — back into his psyche. Looking at the group and at how far they had progressed — the way he was feeling about himself now was well deserved.

The letters he had written would be mailed soon, after which he faced the possibility he would have some questions to answer. This was, however, a bridge from his old life to his new one and he was not afraid. In fact, it was a bridge he was eager to cross.

For now, there was only one task left at hand. Dr. Marksdale needed to tie up a few very loose ends and go before The Honorable Judge Eleanor Glib — wherein afterwards, he would be able to wish everyone a sincere and fond, but affirmative, farewell.

As the doctor saw it, everything which had taken place in his life up until that night could be broken down into several acts of one long play. The curtain was just about to come down on the act which included his college years up until that very moment, including his association with the group. For a change, Dr. Marksdale was determined — when the curtain rose again, it would be he who would consciously author that act.

The frame of mind he was in led him to feel self-confidence and assuredness, traits he often pretended to feel — but that night, he truly did feel. It was the naked truth of those raw emotions which would help him to overcome any trepidation he may have regarding his next act — an act which would entail his approaching Stelle to broach the subject of making an utterly complete lifestyle change.

Sitting next to his wife, he attempted to squelch the concerns members of the group kept presenting — reasons they believed made their opposition valid to his ending their sessions. Dr. Marksdale remained calm and not just on the outside, but on the inside too.

"This is as unusual as the group is!" He thought. "Normally my guts are in a knot."

The good doctor knew exactly what caused the knots, too — he did. He had always been his own worst enemy. That is, until he had written the letters and taken the spectacular gondola rides on that enlightening and wonderful day.

That night, as he fended off the negative suggestions as to what would happen to all of them, the group was met with a positive and uplifting response from the doctor. It was encouraging as to how well they had been doing and how far each of them had come. He taught them to look with happy and hopeful eyes to what their futures would hold. When they acted as though they would miss the connections which they had become used to, he made the point there was no reason their futures could not include each other.

In the back of his mind, he was patting himself on the back again for a job well done. At the same time, he knew his next step would not be an easy one. Like the bridge he may have to cross from his past to his future, he was ready for it. All that was left for him to do was to convince Stelle to cross it with him.

CHAPTER SEVENTEEN

Coming out of the bathroom carrying shampoo and conditioner bottles in one hand and, in the other hand, a bottle of face wash with a loofah sponge, Ally could see Percy was sitting on the floor next to the birdcage. She made her way to the bed where her suitcase lay open, and she could hear Percy speaking quietly to the birds. Ally knew her birds, and when she turned around to see that both birds had their heads tilted, Ally knew they were listening to Percy.

Softly, Ally said, "Your turn, I'm all done in there. Be sure to check to get all your stuff, I almost forgot my loofah sponge."

Percy looked up at Ally and then back at the birds before asking her, "What do ya think ya'll do with 'em?"

Ally set her toiletries down inside of her small suitcase and knelt down on the floor next to Percy. She laid her hand down on the top of the cage and moved it back and forth so gently, it was as if she were stroking her baby birds' feathers.

"I've been thinkin' 'bout that a lot, Percy. I know you want me to let 'em go. I just don't think I can."

Percy looked up to see Ally's face had a tear slowly making its way down her cheek.

"They're my family, Percy."

A chill ran down Percy's spine, and she found it difficult to swallow. She realized she knew very little about Ally's life, other than what she had told the group. Being totally honest with herself in that moment, Percy had to admit she had paid little attention to what the girl had shared during all those sessions.

While sitting on the floor in their hotel room that morning, the memory of Ally telling the members of the group she had been on her own for a long time flashed its way across Percy's mind. There was something else too — something about her grandmother being the only family member she had kept in touch with. More importantly, as Percy recalled, she was the only family member Ally really cared about. As Percy concentrated harder, there was a flicker of recollection — Ally had said something about her grandmother being the only family member who cared about her.

Another memory managed to forge its way into Percy's mind, and this time the chill it induced left her cold. Trying to shake off that chill, Percy remembered Ally's grandmother had died about a year before the group was formed. That left Percy to presume the girl had no family left — at least, no one Ally was willing to acknowledge as such. As Percy had learned in her own life — one's perception is one's reality.

An overwhelming sense of sadness for Ally came over Percy coupled with anger towards herself. She had to ask herself if she either did not want to care, or did not care enough, about this young girl (kneeling but a mere foot from her) to have paid attention to her. Had she been so self-absorbed for all those months through all those sessions? Was Ally's life of such little importance to her, she did not bother to listen to Ally's truth?

"Had Ally listened to me?" Percy questioned herself further.

"I droned on about crap — oh, 'woe-is-me' crap. I never thought she had brains to bother with, or was it always me who didn't bother to listen?"

Percy felt somehow obliged, if nothing else, at that point to respond in some way to the girl. She concluded Ally may be in a fragile state. It never occurred to her that, perhaps, it was she who was the fragile one.

"I don't know that I want you to let them go, Ally. I want you to do whatever it is that you want to do." Percy having been so guarded for so long was not sure what provoked her to get up on her knees, too, and put one of her arms around Ally. When she did, Ally leaned into Percy's side and started to cry softly covering her face with her hands.

"Oh God, what have I done?" Percy asked herself while struggling to decide what she should do next. Keeping a safe distance between herself and — well — everyone, had worked just fine for her. In fact, Percy thought it had worked right up until that day in court when, for whatever reason, she decided to defend Dillard Bigley against his mindless unhinged attacker — the notorious James Elliot Jeffries.

"Curses!" she had yelled at herself time and time again since the day she had rued more than any other. "Why didn't I just pay the damn ticket and been done with it? I'd ah never been in court that day if I had!"

The months of talking about her feelings and having to act like she was listening to the others in the group when they talked about theirs was all too much. Percy had successfully managed to be on her own: no ties, no commitments and no emotional encumbrances of any kind for a considerably long period of time. She had done quite well without anyone to muddy the waters. The last thing Percy saw herself needing was an emotional tie of any kind. From her experience, they always ended — and ended badly.

"And now this damn impromptu and hairbrained trip!" In her head, Percy cursed again.

"Why did I answer the god damned phone the other night?"

Percy replayed the events as they happened on the night of the intrusive phone call which started and ended with Dr. Marksdale's slurring voice being barely decipherable. It had not dawned on her the doctor may have been drinking, as her own voice was difficult to decipher, too, having been more than half asleep at the ungodly time of night he called her — "a call the doc doesn't even remember making." "So —" Percy stiffened, "So much for him knowing the reason for making it — Damn him!"

Fast forwarding to the scene in front of the doctor's high-rise office building early that same morning, Percy found herself running to Bud's aid after, "That wild 'n crazy broad attacked him with pepper spray!" Percy had feared the worst, of which that attack may have rendered him permanently blind.

"The doc's call was just a prelude to this whole freak show," Percy chastised herself.

"I volunteered myself!" Percy shuddered, "To join the rest of the group, including that same, crazy mace-wielding nut case to take off in a private jet —" Taking in a long deep breath, she exhaled heavily, "To a place where we may or may not find someone who may not want to be found."

Percy shook her head, "If that ain't proof positive I need therapy, I dunno what is!"

All of these scenes continued to unfold behind Percy's eyes, while she kept her arm snuggled around Ally's shoulders as she cried.

Starting in the doctor's office and continuing over the prior few days, Percy had experienced feelings she had lost touch with for so long, she did not recognize them or their intention. She did not "do" emotions. In fact, she prided herself in her capability to display exemplary self-control in all areas of emotionally charged events.

Shortly after Percy arrived in Park City, she reasoned the group was used to living close to sea level, and now they had been exposed to a much higher elevation resulting in their breathing thinner air and receiving less oxygen. This, in her mind, was the best way to address the high intensity of all the damnable emotions everyone seemed to be experiencing.

Clearing her head of a mishmash of thoughts, Percy tried to assure Ally.

"It's okay, Ally. You don't have to make a decision now; besides, they don't know how to fend for themselves. Maybe it's best you do keep 'em."

Ally moved herself away from Percy's embrace and stood up. She walked to the vanity where she pulled a few tissues out of a tissue box. After wiping her eyes, she turned and leaned against the edge of the vanity and crossed her arms across her chest before speaking in the most adult voice Percy had ever heard her utter.

"Ya see, Percy, I know it's 'cause of me they're helpless. I did it to 'em. I fell in love with 'em and —" Ally looked down at the cage where her birds were happily preening themselves, "I held on too long." Ally sniffled and went to the bed where she continued to pack.

"It's 'cause of me," Ally sniffled while she tossed various items of clothing into her suitcase which had been strewn onto the bed into untidy piles. "They might never get to feel what I got ta feel yesterday."

Grabbing a hold of Madeline, Ally took a moment to run one hand through the varied colors of the wig before, to Percy's amazement, she tossed it into the waste basket next to the bed.

"Because ah me, they will probably never fly free like birds are supposed to."

Percy got up off of her knees and stood perfectly still for a couple of minutes, before she walked over to where Ally was standing and put her hand on Ally's back and rubbed it gently.

The two women were quiet for a few moments longer, until Percy broke the silence.

"If they're lucky enough to have you, they'll never miss what they've never had."

*****

"Grab that bag over there, will ya?" Donato asked Bud who was managing fairly well to get around with his boot cast.

"Sure, ya wanna pack it or carry it separate?"

The day before when Percy and Ally had wanted to go into a shop to look at, as Bud put it, "girly things," the brothers had stopped into a shop themselves and picked up some souvenirs of their own, before they all took their last gondola ride down the mountain.

"Sure, are ya gonna give it to her before we leave?" Bud asked Donato as he handed his brother the bag.

"No, I'm not sure when, maybe after we get on the plane. Do ya think she'll like it?" Donato opened the little box exposing a delicate necklace chain with two birds snuggled up to each other on a tree branch.

Bud shook his head while replying, "I think anything ya give her, she'll like."

"Really? Do ya think so? You're not kiddin, are ya?'" Donato's voice revealed his nervousness.

"Heck yeah, she'll like it. It's from you, ain't it?" Bud shook his head again, as he hopped over to the bed where he finished packing his own things.

"Whadda ya think ma will think of her?" Donato asked shyly.

"She's already in love with her, Donnie."

"What? How da ya know that?" Donato's face showed his happiness.

"I saw her looking at the two ah ya lookin' at each other at the house. Bet she's already got the invitations addressed!"

Even Donato's olive complexion could not hide his blushing cheeks.

"Get outta here." Donato tossed a pillow at his brother and laughed. Bud caught the pillow in mid-flight and tossed it back at his younger brother.

"Hey James, whadda 'bout you and Percy, now that the doc is stopping the sessions?"

"What 'bout us?" Bud replied.

"Well, ya know, will ya keep seeing each other?" Donato pursued.

"Why would ya ask that? We're not even friends." Bud zipped up his bag and tossed it at the hotel door.

"Whoa, James — who's kiddin' who, now!"

Donato picked up his and his brother's bags and headed to the elevator. Bud hopped to his crutches which were leaning on the dresser, and once he had them confidently under his arms, he hurried his hopping to catch up with his brother.

"Good morning," Mrs. Fins greeted them both as she was already waiting at the elevator.

"How are ya doin'?" Donato was quick to respond to her cheerful greeting.

"I'm doing splendid, how about the two of you?" Mrs. Fins was eager to offer.

"Splendid, huh — sounds better than just okay," Donato quipped back revealing a wide smile.

Mrs. Fins tilted her head to look behind Donato and saw Bud maneuvering his way towards them.

"It looks like you have got the swing of those crutches now, Mr. Jefferies. How do you feel?"

"Okay, I guess." Bud's voice was flat. It was neither downtrodden nor uplifting.

"Wow, James, Mrs. Fins is doing a heck of a lot better than you. She's doin' splendid!" Donato continued to smile.

"Oh my, Mr. Jeffries, you have had so much to deal with these past few days. I can only imagine how much you are looking forward to going home," Mrs. Fins had just finished saying, as she saw Dill Bigley coming out of his room and heading towards the three of them. Her cheeks immediately took on a flush of a fine rosé wine.

"Hold up there, please." Dill hurried towards the elevator.

"How is everyone this fine morning?" Dill asked while catching his breath.

In unison, the brothers gave their own answers — Bud's was "okay," while Donato's response was "great." Then, Donato again made the remark, "No one was doing as well as Mrs. Fins was doing, because she was 'splendid.'"

One would have had a difficult task having to choose between Dill Bigley and Mrs. Fins — as to whose cheeks turned from a rosé- to crimson-colored complexion the fastest. This should not have posed a problem, because just as the elevator doors opened, Percy and Ally (with her birdcage swinging next to her) were in a quick jog also heading towards the elevator.

"Hey, wait for us!" Ally yelled out.

Dill held his hand against the elevator doors, as Donato ran to Ally's aid and took her birdcage — offering to both women, that he would carry their suitcases for them too.

"Don't worry 'bout it, Donnie," Percy said. "We can carry our bags, but thanks."

"Ya remembered to call me Donnie," Donato said cheerfully.

"Yep, I did and it fits you," Percy replied as she entered the elevator.

As the doors closed, everyone in the crowded compartment was left to establish his or her own narrow spot to stand after each person — albeit briefly and very nearly verging on the abrupt — shared morning salutations with the others.

Standing next to Percy, Bud looked down as she looked up at him. In a hushed but clear voice, he addressed her specifically, "Hello, Percy."

Percy quickly looked away from Bud and directed her eyes at the elevator door. In a low hushed voice, but still loud enough for Donato to hear, she responded, "Good morning, James."

Donato's head turned towards his brother, and when their eyes met, Bud immediately diverted his gaze away — just as Percy had done to him.

Donato grinned from ear to ear while saying to himself, "Yeah! Who's kiddin' who!"

No one made the slightest movement or gave any indication they were even breathing, as they descended to the hotel lobby; thus, lending to the impression, more than dinner had been shared by the elevator's occupants. Percy may have been right in regards to the thinner air in Park City, but on that morning and in that elevator, the air was thick enough it could have been cut with a knife. It was unclear what may or may not have taken place during the prior night, but the tension being felt in that elevator clearly originated from something — with a titillating bent. Without a word being uttered, it was apparent no one was going to divulge the truth of what events had taken place the night before. By not speaking, those confidences would remain as such and would forever be relegated to the darkness of that night.

"I think doc said some guy will take our stuff before breakfast." Bud was the first to speak as everyone got off the elevator.

"Yeah, that's right. I don't know, though, 'bout somebody takin' my birds," Ally commented. The doubt she felt could be heard in her voice.

Trying to calm Ally's concern, Percy offered, "Oh, I think they'll be fine. The doctor wouldn't let anything happen to 'em."

"Can't be sure of that!" The decibel of Bud's voice was elevated.

"He could open the door and say, 'Get out! It's time ya fly.'" Still quite apparent, was Bud's sense of abandonment.

The group was making their way to the registration desk, when they saw Dr. Marksdale coming towards them from the direction of the hotel restaurant.

"Good morning everyone. Monica and Jack have secured a table for us, and my driver is ready to relieve you of any items you are taking home." The doctor's demeanor that morning had taken on a firm air of authority. He waved at a man who was standing in the foyer of the hotel and motioned him to come over to the group.

"Yes sir," the man addressed Dr. Marksdale.

"Please take everyone's belongings to the limousine, and be especially careful with this birdcage." The doctor gently took the birdcage from Ally and handed it to the man, before she had a chance to say anything. Percy patted Ally's arm and nodded her head in an attempt to put Ally's mind at ease.

"Yeah, be extra careful with 'em." Ally said to the man and then spoke directly to her birds.

"It'll be okay, I'll be with you in just a little bit." Then she made soft cooing sounds and blew kisses towards them.

Donato quickly thought to himself, "lucky birds."

Looking directly in the man's eyes, Ally questioned the man, "You'll be careful with 'em, right?"

"Absolutely, miss, I will take very good care of them." The man took the birdcage in one hand and propped Ally's suitcase under the other arm, before he began to reach for Percy's suitcase. That is when Donato stepped in and offered his help.

"That is not necessary sir." The man began, "I've got this."

"Nah, no problem. I can help." Donato took a hold of Percy's suitcase, and when he reached for Mrs. Fins' suitcase, Dill was quick to intervene.

"I'll be happy to get that, and I can take Percy's too. Why don't you take care of both you and your brother's luggage?"

A young man from behind the reception desk broke into the conversation, as he wheeled a luggage carrier towards them.

"Let me be of assistance. We can load everything onto this."

Dill nodded his head in approval while remarking, "splendid."

Donato put the suitcases he had onto the cart and thought to himself, "There's that word again — splendid. I like it."

As Ally stood silently watching the driver place her birds onto the carrier, Donato observed her pressing her hands against her lips. It was only after the driver had arrived at the limousine and had placed the cage inside, that Ally lowered her hands which exposed her turned down lips thus revealing her sad expression.

Donato's heart skipped a beat feeling a pang in his chest. "They'll be okay and we'll be with them right after breakfast," he assured her.

Ally's bluish green eyes immediately twinkled, and her turned down mouth turned upwards into a gentle smile.

Upon seeing that his comment gave rise to Ally's smiling, Donato felt his whole body instantly warming, and he thought to himself, "Now, that's splendid."

CHAPTER EIGHTEEN

"This breakfast was scrumptious." Dill nodded in agreement to Mrs. Fins' comment.

Ally was quick to add, "I love food! I think I could eat myself to death!"

Donato and Bud looked at each other knowingly — that could very well have been a dream of their own. The brothers knew their Italian mother, Camilla, had come close on more than one occasion to making that dream a reality. What, with her serving one course after another of her homeland's traditional cuisine, both brothers often wondered why they were not the size of a house. Although the food had been exceptional on their trip to Utah — starting with their mother's meatball sandwiches — the brothers were ready to go home. Their traditional Italian cuisine, which they were both very adept at preparing themselves, was hard to beat. Donato felt compelled to make that point to Ally.

"Wait 'till you try some of my cookin'," Donato looked directly at Ally. "You'll think ya fell in love!"

Both of the Marksdales could not help but notice everyone at the table except for themselves, Monica and Lizzy — blushed. To add to his embarrassment, Donato was aware both Ally and Stelle saw his eyelids had literally fluttered at his own comment, drawing more attention to his lush black lashes — something he would have preferred to avoid.

"I think it's time we head to the plane." Dr. Marksdale, not all that interested in what was going on with everyone, knew he was breaking into the noticeably uncomfortable moment.

"Yes, of course." After getting to his own feet, Dill assisted Mrs. Fins to hers.

Everyone except for Bud was up and ready, when Percy said she would help him with his crutches. She suggested everyone else should go on ahead of them, and they would catch up shortly.

"Very well," Dr. Marksdale said, and then he stopped for a moment — his body language indicating he had just realized he had forgotten something.

"Go on ahead, I'll be right behind you."

Percy handed Bud his crutches as the others headed out of the restaurant, and the doctor went in search of the concierge.

The driver, along with the warmed interior of the limousine, was waiting for them. He got out of the car and opened the door for Ally and cheerfully addressed her.

"Your birds are fine, miss. They are very sweet and friendly."

"They really are so sweet." Ally smiled and leaned down to let her birds know she was right there with them. She then moved to the farthest side of the seat by the door cozying up to their cage, and Donato squeezed in next to her.

Dill, being the consummate gentlemen, felt duty bound (with so many traveling together) to make sure there was enough room for everyone to fit comfortably. So, he cozied up to Mrs. Fins. He assessed it was the only fair thing to do — for everyone involved, of course.

Monica and Jack had secured their seats, and Lizzy said she would sit next to them once they left. Until then, she chose to sit on the floor next to Ally's birdcage, and along with Ally, she would talk to and be entertained by the precious sparrows.

While the limousine was full of activity, a car pulled up right in front of the hotel just as Percy and Bud were exiting it. A man who neither recognized got out of the car and headed towards them. It was not until the man was closer, when Percy realized the man had been their taxi driver.

"Oh, hello. How ya doin'?" Percy inquired.

Bud looked at her — his face showing confusion.

"Actually —" The man's voice broke, "That's why I stopped by. I wanted to see how you were doin'." The man, known only to Percy as "Benny the cab driver," fidgeted slightly while looking nervously back and forth at both Percy and Bud.

"Oh, well — I'm — we're —" Percy looked up at Bud and back at Benny, "We're all doing okay. How 'bout you — how 'bout your car?"

Bud, who remained clueless — thus the blank expression on his face — leaned on his crutches trying to assess the situation. While his one good eye darted back and forth between Percy and Benny, Bud concluded this man seemed to be acting very odd. That was saying something coming from Bud.

"Car is okay. Well, it's totaled, but other than that, it's okay," Benny answered, knowing his answer made him sound like a fool.

"Yeah, I thought it would be. Hopefully, you'll get another one soon." Percy stood next to Bud not knowing what she should do next.

"Well, it looks like you're goin' somewhere so I'll be quick." Benny looked more nervous by the second and then blurted out, "I been by twice hopin' I'd find ya. I dunno if you two —" Benny looked back and forth between Percy and Bud.

"I dunno if you two are together."

Bud looked down at Percy as she looked up at Bud — both with that deer-in-the-headlights expression on their faces.

Bud thought to himself, "What is goin' on? Just look at us, we're standing right here — together. What's up with this guy?"

Bud squinted a couple of times with his one good eye. It was still not quite clear to him what was happening, and then it hit him.

Benny wanted to be with Percy, Bud thought. He was interested enough to confront them both to see if they were "together."

Percy did not catch it quite as fast as Bud would have liked her to or, from his tone, would not have liked her to.

"Well, I was thinkin'. If you're not together, then I just wanted to know if — well, if maybe I could — if maybe you would, like — well —"

Several seconds passed (though it seemed like minutes to Bud), before he interrupted the pregnant pause with a harsh and sharp tone. Percy and Bud were familiar with Bud's capacity to send chills down the spines of those near him during one of his rants, still, neither had heard as sharp and harsh a tone as at that moment.

"He's hittin' on ya!"

Percy's eyebrows lifted as her eyes got bigger, and she started to say something when Bud snapped, "I gotta go."

He pressed down on his crutches and thrust his legs forward so hard, the force came close to causing him to lose complete control. Miraculously, he managed to re-establish his balance — barely — and not enough to prevent him from looking like a flailing boneless acrobat.

Sadly, the momentum and velocity his body had reached rendered him at a loss of control by the time he had reached the limousine — thus, his running into the heavy metal object resulted in his crutches clanking against the side of the car before flying out of his hands in opposite directions. This mishap was followed by an even louder thump, as his body slammed into the side of the limousine.

For Bud, the saying, "For every action there is an opposite and equal reaction," was soon, above all, to be proven accurate. A loud "humph" escaped Bud's mouth as the wind was being knocked out of him, when his body was thrust into the side of the limousine — after which he was forced backwards and onto the hard concrete sidewalk. The law of physics was not to be denied.

Benny and Percy witnessed the events unfold, as if everything were happening in slow motion. Upon witnessing Bud's unprovoked altercation with the side of the limousine, Benny anxiously asked her, "Do you think he needs help?"

"I'm sure of it!" Percy yelled to him over her shoulder, as she ran to offer aid to Bud once again.

"Oh James, let me help you up." Percy bent down to assist him.

"I'm fine." Bud snapped as he pushed Percy's hands off of him. "I'm fine!"

Percy backed away just long enough to recognize she was actually experiencing emotional pain — something she had not felt for a very long time. She tried to push the feeling down inside, before she took a hold of one of Bud's arms against his will and got him to his feet.

Once he was in the car, she gathered both of his crutches and handed them to Donato who reached out of the car to take them from her.

"Aren't ya gettin' in?" Donato asked her.

"No, not just yet," Percy replied to Donato's question. She turned away from the limousine, and headed back to where she had left Benny with his mouth agape. When she reached him, she put her hand on his arm and started with, "You seem like a nice guy. But I, well — I'm not sure what — I'm not sure about anything right now."

Percy thought to herself she was too old to behave like a foolish girl and too young to not want to be a woman in love. These thoughts were not foreign to her, but were thoughts she had not entertained in a long time.

What had taken place in Park City caused her to begin to think of, and question, why her emotions left her feeling raw and vulnerable. And, what had really happened in Park City begs the question: What had happened to both herself and Bud over those last couple of days? Part of her was afraid to know the answer, while another part of her was afraid to not know; likewise, another part of her was just plain afraid. She wondered if Bud may be thinking these same thoughts, and that made her wonder why — if he was, would it matter to her?

A tear ran down her cheek, and Benny gently reached down to wipe it off.

"I'm sorry, I didn't mean to cause you trouble. Really, I just think you are so nice, I would like to get to know you."

Percy looked up at Benny and wondered to herself what she was doing. What could she possibly have been thinking? How could she have thought several hours of talking to Bud and a couple of nights spending time together would have changed anything between them. It was clear to her — she was the one who needed help.

"Look, I don't know about anything right now — but, maybe somewhere down the road —" Percy knew she did not want to give this man — a man who actually spoke to her kindly — the wrong impression.

Feelings — his or her's — were too important to be exploited or taken lightly. She had just had an unpleasant crash course reminding her of that fact.

Benny reached into his pocket and took out his business card which had his name, phone number and address on it. When he handed it to her, he said, "Maybe I'll come to Seattle soon and we could, you know, do somethin' if ya'd like to."

"Maybe — yeah, maybe —" Percy looked up at Benny and saw his deep blue eyes for the first time. He was a good-looking man and seemed to have a gentle nature about him.

"Yeah, maybe some time." Percy took his card and put it in her pocket and shyly offered, "I don't have a card with me now, but if you can write it down, I'll give ya my number."

Benny's face lit up and he smiled broadly.

"You can just tell me your number, I gotta great memory. I won't forget it."

Feeling like she had been swept up into a whirlwind of emotion, Percy thought, in that moment, maybe it was time she took a chance.

"Okay, here it is."

When everyone was in the limousine and the driver had started down the road, Stelle looked over at her husband and asked, "What did you forget to do, Phillip?"

"Oh, I didn't forget anything. I just had to drop something in the mail." He patted Stelle's leg and leaned back in his seat, while Stelle went back to her cell phone to either check on her social media connections or to order a delectable bobble of some sort which had caught her keen shopping eye.

Once they were all secured in their private jet, Donato and Ally sat quietly next to each other, while Lizzy combed her giraffe's coat as Monica looked on. Dill periodically looked over at Mrs. Fins and wondered what she could have been thinking while she looked out of her window.

Jack and Emma had their seats leaned back and were holding hands, while Bud and Percy, like two wounded souls, sat alone on opposite sides of the plane silently staring out of their windows.

If the doctor meant what he had said about ending their sessions, then once they landed in Seattle, they would all go on their own separate ways until the court hearing. And, if all of that went as it should, no one in the group would have any reason to meet with each other again.

By all appearances, for a couple of passengers, it was going to be a long flight home. For some of the others, that same flight would be far too short.

Just as the jet left the tarmac, Ally squealed, "Look everybody, it's snowing!" Her face was beaming with delight.

Lizzy put her giraffe down and pressed her nose against the window — smiling from ear to ear.

Monica scooted closer to her daughter and put her arm around Lizzy's shoulders. "It is, isn't it, baby girl."

"Oh mommy, it's so pretty." Lizzy said softly.

Donato leaned closer to Ally to get a better look out of her window before saying, "It sure is snowing. Dang, and we just missed it."

Percy thought to herself, she did not miss it at all. She hated snow. Interestingly, seated across on the other side of the plane, Bud was thinking the exact same thing.

In just minutes, their private jet was high enough, nothing could be seen but gray, and the ride started to get a little turbulent — a common occurrence experienced when flying through clouds. The attendant offered everyone something to eat and drink to which everyone declined. Even Ally declined, at first. After she and Donato decided on watching a comedy (while Lizzy and Monica chose a Disney production), Ally thought something sweet sounded good. Lucky for her and Lizzy, there was a variety of candy bars to choose from.

Ally excused herself, before the movie started, to use the lady's room, allowing Donato's rapt attention to be diverted towards his brother instead. Donato saw that Bud sat as still as a statue appearing to be looking out of his window. That encouraged Donato to get up and take the seat next to him.

"Hey, James, what's up?"

Bud turned his head towards his brother and, at the same time, took a quick glance in Percy's direction — a glance Donato took notice of.

"Nothin' — nothin's up." Bud tuned his face back to the window.

Donato knew his brother and could easily see he was upset — even sad. This was not something he was used to seeing from his oldest brother.

"James, tell me what's goin' on with you and Percy."

Bud swung his head around and barked at his caring youngest brother, "Go back to your seat!"

"Ah c'mon, James." Donato quickly responded to Bud's order and was, as quickly, responded back to — "Now!"

"Okay, okay," Donato stood up from his seat, and before he started to walk back to where he and Ally were seated, he left his brother with, "Okay for now, but this isn't over."

Bud figured if nothing was started, there was nothing to be over with. It was then he realized he had not chewed any gum in almost two days — a realization which was surprising to him to say the least. He thought to himself, "What could I have been doing or thinking of to not notice I wasn't chewing gum!" The lack of understanding as to what he was feeling was unsettling.

He waved at the attendant who was happy to oblige him in his search. As he sat alone opening the pack of gum the attendant had provided him with, he almost drooled. Upon inserting two pieces of gum into his mouth, he told himself it was the most pleasure he had felt for most of his trip, and then he slurred the words, "this ungodly trip!"

The gum was not soft, and his mouth was not up to its regular agility due to the various prior impacts leveled on his head. He thought he would close his eyes and let the gum soak in his mouth to soften it — imagining the sensation would feel like he had found an oasis on a desert island. Unfortunately, the sensations chewing his gum usually gave him were starkly absent.

Bud sat with the small wad of gum soaking in his mouth and became overwhelmed by the lack of joy he felt. The joy he had hoped to experience had instead been overcome by joy's unwelcomed interloper — bleak disappointment.

Thumbing through her schedule she kept on her phone, Percy checked to see the upcoming dates for her next "drop and hook" assignment. This was her specialty, because this kind of trucking did not require her to handle any cargo. She would haul a loaded trailer to a designated destination and drop the trailer off and hook onto an empty one. She would then go on to the next destination, where she would repeat the action. It was not uncommon for Percy to travel a few thousand miles a week and have a need to stay in hotels along the way. On those longer trips where she needed to catch a nap or inclement weather had her stopped alongside the road, the sleeper bed located behind the seat sufficiently accommodated her needs.

From what Percy read, she was going to be fairly busy for the next week transporting several loads. This realization perked Percy up a bit, and she appreciated the opportunity to get sidetracked from her dwelling on the confusing and unpleasant emotions she found herself experiencing. Work had always been a good distraction for her. By its very nature, it kept her from other commitments of a more personal inclination — something which, until the present moment, Percy had not paid any mind to.

Sitting alone in that private jet, Percy silently asked herself if, perhaps, it was why she had chosen to stay in the long-haul profession. Realistically, she could have moved onto something which took less of her time and would have helped her to develop a more stable and stationary location. Instead, she had preferred not to be in one place for very long and thought she was happier zigzagging her way all over the country. After her ex hit the road with "gutter trash," a.k.a. "the other woman," Percy felt safer in her line of work, because she did not see truck drivers as an attractive or viable option for any kind of intimate encounter. It was not until the trip took her from Seattle to Park City, that Percy realized she had not given these thoughts any real attention.

Maybe it was a deliberate act driven by her subconscious — she had to keep herself on the move. She did have to acknowledge it was indeed hard to hold onto a moving object, and Percy perceived herself as that moving object. It had always been her go-to, to excuse herself from becoming involved in a messy long-term relationship — something she prided herself in being able to avoid.

Quietly, Percy questioned herself, "If it's not fear of me holdin' onto someone, is it fear ah someone holdin' onto me?"

The momentary reprieve — the distraction of checking her schedule provided — had passed for Percy.

"What am I supposed to get from all this thinkin'?" Percy shifted in her seat, and while doing so, she took a sneak-peek glance in Bud's direction.

His face was still turned towards the window, but from Percy's seat, she could see his good eye looked somewhat glazed over and did not appear to be looking at anything — just staring blankly. What did stand out to her more: His still swollen and bruised face wore an expression of unmistakable sadness.

Angrily chastising herself, Percy thought bitterly, "I don't want these thoughts! So fool — just stop thinkin' 'em!"

With that, she tossed her phone into her purse and forcefully lowered the back of her seat while slowly exhaling her breath. She put the ear buds in her ears the attendant had provided to her (and everyone else on the plane) and tuned to a radio station she thought she could relax to. Turning up the volume up to an almost uncomfortable level, she hoped to drown out the sounds of everything around her — but mostly, her own thoughts.

Not until the jet made its descent to the Seattle airport tarmac and the g-force was strong enough to rouse her, did Percy wake up. Although it was in itself a blessing, how she could have fallen into such a deep sleep remained a mystery to Percy.

The music that drowned out the world around her along with her own thoughts had suddenly, upon her awakening, become a source of agitation and annoyance as it blared in her ears. Percy attempted to turn down the sound and to remove the ear buds with fumbling fingers which were struggling to coordinate with her still groggy mind.

"Jeeze, I was out like a light." The ear bud cords had become entangled with each other, and as she tried to untangle them, Percy felt her ears building with pressure as the plane touched down making it harder to hear. She thought for a brief moment, she may never hear the same again due to the volume of the music she had directly piped into along with the pressure building in her ears. First, one ear cleared and then the other, allowing her to hear a voice; moreover, this voice had an unmistakable familiarity to it as it rang through her head.

"Percy, we're home!" Ally, more cheerful than usual, continued, "You gotta drive. Donato an' me had too much vino — an' Bud can't cuz ah his foot."

Percy raised the back of her seat up and turned around just enough to see, that Donato and Ally were leaning into each other as they sat side by side. More than likely, it was the over indulgence of wine consumption the young duo had partaken in which made both of their smiles appear somewhat off-center by a degree or two. Percy wondered whether it was that or just the youthful exuberance they expressed over just about everything. Their smiles took on the appearance of resembling animated characters. She could not help from thinking, the two of them with their crooked smiling faces and glassy bloodshot eyes could easily have been mistaken for a couple of happy imbeciles.

As her thoughts became clearer, Percy remembered that to get to the airport a few short days ago, she had ridden with the brothers, Ally and her birds. Unable to conjure up a sound reason why she could not ride back with them, Percy begrudgingly succumbed to driving the van with the Jeffries brothers and "miss cheery cheeks" back to their starting point, Nunzio's Bakery and Italian Eatery. After that, she would call a taxi if she needed to, to get back to her own home.

Taking a page from Ally's playbook, Percy mimicked a facial expression she would be happy never to have to witness again and rolled her eyes up towards the sky. Her words fell silent to everyone's ears, but they resounded with a depth and clarity which would not be ignored by her own.

"I musta raised some kinda hell in my last life!"

Normally, Percy would not entertain the thought of reincarnation or any belief which resembled such a theory. Searching her mind for a rational explanation as to why she would have been thrown together with the group in the first place — and all those months later finding her involvement growing deeper — she could find no other rational explanation as to why. Perhaps she had lived a prior life. If that were true, to her best understanding, she must have committed some dastardly deeds. Her proof was the damnable group and her involvement with them, and, at which point in time, old bugaboo karma had come a calling giving her notice that payment was due.

The pilot came on over the intercom, welcomed everyone back to Seattle, and told them they would be taxiing for a few minutes, before they would come to a complete stop; at which time, they would be free to disembark.

"Mrs. Fins was kind enough to secure us a ride to our cars. When we do stop, let's gather our things expeditiously." The doctor's voice indicated he was in a hurry to be on his way once they landed.

"Our driver will attend to your luggage." Dr. Marksdale sounded quite professional and almost emotionless, particularly when he added he would have Mrs. Fins contact each of them in the next few days with the exact date and time for their impending court appearance.

If anyone had any doubts or second thoughts about the doctor's intentions to not continue with future meetings for the group, both his words and tone put an end to those concerns. The doctor made it very clear the group, as it once was, was to be no more.

A chill came over almost everyone in the therapy group, everyone except for Emma. She was singularly the group member who was grateful for its inception, yet she did not feel ending it was a negative action. She had always felt the group's purpose was to be punished for those who had wreaked havoc in the judge's courtroom. Being one to always try to see the upside of a situation, she concluded she had benefitted greatly from being a part of the group — something she openly admitted. She believed, too, the others in the group, in their own separate and individual ways, had also benefited from their sessions. By that time, though grateful, she was able to walk away with that which she garnered from the experience. She could say with confidence she was ready to embark on a whole new chapter in her life. She shared with everyone, she believed they were all capable of doing the same.

Ally did not indicate ending the group was of any great consequence to her, either, as she had already decided she would keep in touch with members of the group on her own. It was evident she had grown especially fond of Percy — no understanding on Percy's part whatsoever. Having grown a unique attachment to Percy, Ally had every intention of making her a permanent part of her life — particularly after their trip to Park City. All of this was to Percy's chagrin.

Dill was feeling more than a little apprehensive. Although he and Mrs. Fins had made plans for the upcoming weekend, he would have no excuse to see her on a regular basis after that — if ever again. All of these thoughts made his heart beat faster, and he started to breathe in short and rapid breaths; meanwhile, the better of his two eyes began to twitch.

Bud was feeling worse than before about the sudden decision to halt the sessions. In fact, poor Mr. Jefferies was feeling quite glum, indeed. He could not rationalize why he should be feeling so out of sorts — even for him — his stomach was in knots, and his head was made even more sore from his chewing gum. He had to spit it out after only a few brief minutes of chewing it. It was to no avail, for he replaced it with the clenching of his jaw. Taking the soreness of his face from his unfortunate mishaps out of the equation, he found himself perplexed as to why the gum he had always turned to for comfort was neglecting to provide any.

He was sure it was a fool's errand on the doctor's part to end the sessions. It made no sense at all from his perspective. Bud surmised they were finally serving a purpose, though at that juncture, he was not able to narrow it down to precisely what that purpose was.

Bud reflected on the earlier event when his imaginary dam walls came crashing down, and when they did, they allowed years of pent-up emotions to gush forth in the form of a myriad of expletives. For a brief time he felt some relief, but when the doctor told everyone he was ending the sessions and reiterated that point just then (before they were to disembark the plane), Bud did not feel relief. Although in a contradiction of terms, it was at that point the poor, sad-sack Mr. Jeffries was filled with emptiness. He sensed there was more for him to do.

"But what?" He questioned himself.

"Is there more to let out?" — possibly.

"Is there something to open up to?" — maybe.

He had no idea of how to do whatever it was which needed to be done. He felt a desperate longing, yet was not sure what he longed for. He truly believed the answer he sought would be found by attending the group's meetings. The only resolve was for the group sessions to continue! Bud privately anguished over his own question.

"Why doc? Why now?"

Percy tended to keep any emotions and thoughts at bay — something she had become quite successful at for a fair amount of her lifetime. Managing to keep her thoughts on — "getting home with as little interaction as possible with anyone" — to get back on the road was her only conscious intent.

". . . Okay, and I'll get his other arm," Donato said to Ally as they helped his brother get off the plane.

"I'll get the van warmed up." Percy took the keys from Donato and headed to the van.

"You sure ya wanna drive?" Donato yelled out to her. "I can do it if ya don't."

"Not a good idea, Donnie. We've been drinkin'," Ally interjected. Percy had to admit to herself, Ally sounded like a sensible young woman at that moment, not the scatterbrained airhead she was used to.

"Yeah, you're right." Donato seemed like he would be happy with whatever Ally suggested.

"Not so fast, Donnie." Bud chastised his brother, "I can't go that fast with this cast."

Percy looked back and felt the urge to offer her assistance but turned back around and continued towards the van.

"He's done just fine without me all along. He'll do just fine without me from now on." Percy said this to herself without clarifying whom she was referring to — Donato or his brother, Bud.

CHAPTER NINETEEN

The bailiff did not mince his words. He articulated loud enough for everyone, including those seated in the back of the room, to hear. His instruction was as clear as it was unmistakable.

"Please rise. The Court of the Second Judicial Circuit, Traffic Division, is now in session — The Honorable Judge Eleanor Glib presiding."

When the judge entered the room, her body language told everyone present all they needed to know about the level of assuredness and comfort she felt with the authority she wielded.

Mirroring a well-choreographed dance, her movements were methodic and deliberate. Only after she was seated and had placed several files down in front of her did Judge Glib, without once looking up, address the still standing occupants in her courtroom. Her matter-of-fact, no-nonsense tone held true to someone possessing an austere persona. The mood of everyone in the courtroom rapidly grew from being mildly uneasy to being full-blown discomposed, before the judge finally and with razor sharp precision stated, "You may be seated."

Her chilly voice penetrated the ears of all who heard it, making the judge's statement sound more like a royal pronouncement. Without looking up from the bench or out into her courtroom — her tone never wavering — Judge Glib leveled one additional instruction.

"Bailiff — you may proceed."

The bailiff read aloud who was to be the first case on the docket, while Dr. Marksdale attempted to distract from the apprehension he was experiencing by meticulously rearranging his files on the table in front of him. Admittedly, over the prior several months, he had played the scenario in his mind of going before the judge — someone, he had never met before. Each time he played it out, Dr. Marksdale had managed to convince himself, no matter how many possible glitches he may face, he could overcome them. The good doctor would acknowledge he may have, on rare occasion, wavered from his opinion, but as a general rule, he usually thought very highly of himself and his capabilities.

Feeling he had done all he could prior to that long-awaited day, Dr. Marksdale believed everything he could do with the group and his recording of their progress, while under his care, had been done. Possessing a tendency to be an overthinker, the doctor had to, out of shear survival instincts, believe he had resolved all of the imaginary obstacles he had conjured up to a satisfactory end. But on that morning, even though he was operating on autopilot and was determined to singularly focus on the individual moment as each moment presented itself, the mere commanding presence of Judge Glib was formidable and unnerving.

Three additional extensions for their hearing date had added exponentially to Dr. Marksdale's anxiety. Fortunately, those extensions came directly from the direction of the court and had nothing to do with either himself or the group. Still, the extensions forced pushing the date of their appearance out an additional five weeks, something which was not at all easy on him.

The day had arrived and the doctor believed the stars must have all been aligned, when he saw everyone had arrived at the agreed upon time. He shared cordial but limited conversation with them before entering the courtroom. He took a seat at the table designated for lawyers and their clients, for he already knew their case was first on the docket. Along with members of the group, there were so many other people waiting for their cases to be heard — the courtroom gallery was completely filled.

By all appearances, it was going to be a full day for Judge Glib, and Dr. Marksdale breathed relief knowing his case was the first to go before her. Members of the group sat directly and quietly behind the doctor in the first row of the gallery — everyone, that is, except Percy.

Contrary to what Bud assumed when he saw Percy was not present, the doctor briefly explained Percy had not gone AWOL. Although if asked, Percy's answer would likely have been (over the five weeks since their return from Park City), she had strongly considered it. With each notification their court date had been moved, her normal patience level, which had always been in the low range, dropped even lower.

Earlier that morning, Percy contacted the doctor to let him know she would be a little late due to a traffic snarl she had hit the night before coming through Las Vegas on her way to Seattle. She had been on another one of her multi-state runs — the kind of trip she used to look forward to — as they were a great way to kill time. Since returning from Park City, they were becoming more grueling and were something she was liking less and less of with each trip. The doctor comforted Percy's concerns about her being late, because she had assured him, it would only be a few minutes later than expected. Percy had promised she would not let him or anyone else down.

Bud sat next to Emma who sat next to Dill Bigley. Ally sat on Dill's right-hand side and placed her jacket and purse on the space next to her, reserving it for Percy.

Dill Bigley was dressed in as fine a fashion as any reputable Englishman would have dressed in. But for his face, which still bore witness to his knockout folly with a door knob and hard floor, he looked very much like he did at his first court appearance. His bruises had almost healed by this second court appearance, and most of the swelling had subsided; but like Bud, there was discoloration and still a few lumps where the majority of the black and blue swelling had been.

For one not to notice either of the men's facial abnormalities would be, in itself, an aberration. The doctor, having a moment to observe the judge, was sure she would be keenly aware both men's heads and faces had tangled with a ghastly adversary of some sort, thus leaving him to hope Judge Glib would not venture an explanation from either man.

Ally would take the title as the most least recognizable one in the group if compared to her first appearance. She was not wearing a wig (with or without a name), nor was she wearing contact lenses of any color. She had come to court this time as her natural self.

Bud was dressed like any normal man. He was not wearing garish belts or shoes with buckles nor was he chomping and popping a wad of unsightly gum, and his thick black hair did not resemble an oil slick. Dr. Marksdale was relieved to see both of them had changed their appearances from when he had first made their acquaintance. Whether it was just for the court or something of a life change for both, the doctor did not possess the inclination to delve into their choices.

Dr. Marksdale's only willingness to associate with any members of the group, after they arrived at the Seattle airport five weeks earlier, was to follow up with the court ordered hearing. For him, it was as it had always been. His only remaining goal when it came to the members of the group was to be done with all of them, as soon as the judge said he (they) were free to go their separate ways. Anything which may have transpired since their trip together was of no concern to him.

When he and Stelle had left the group in the parking lot of the Seattle airport, he was happier than he had been in a long time, and watching them disappear in his rearview mirror had been both a figurative and literal desire from the moment he had met them. However, for the members of the group, their own personal stories were to take a different path.

Percy drove the bakery van to the brothers' bakery after Ally, Donato and Bud were all loaded into it. When they arrived at their destination, they were met by the brothers' mother, Camilla. She greeted all of them as if they had just returned from war, and her eldest son's appearance fit the part of the wounded soldier perfectly. The explanations everyone offered to her as to how her son had incurred his injuries seemed to satisfy Camilla to a degree, but she had to add the name, Monica, to her growing list of women who had attacked her son — a list that anyone, knowing Camilla, would not want to be on. That list had to be temporarily tucked away, for Camilla was immediately aware that something else, something more profound, had happened to both of her sons while they were away.

Mother's instinct is a powerful phenomenon, and Bud and Donato's mother (being highly in tune with and diligently responsive to her own) was struck in some way, both of her sons had changed. Being an astute woman, it was not long before Camilla believed she knew the reason why, and it was then Camilla knew she made the right decision in sending both of her sons on the trip.

Having always possessed an uncanny way of seeing into the future, or maybe just into her wishes for the future, Camilla knew her boys' changes had everything to do with the two women who accompanied them. In her left hand, she clutched her rosary beads and pressed them against her ample bosom and whispered quietly in Italian under her breath, as her long black lashes fluttered. With her right hand, she waved the two women and her sons to come to the table where she instructed them all to sit.

"Such a long trip, you all must eat something."

Percy wanted to run and gave it an honest try, but Camilla would have none of it. Percy was no match for the quick, little rotund woman who had already wrapped her arm around her and was holding her close. She walked with Percy to a chair and once there, she instructed Percy to sit.

"Everybody's gotta eat! Whatever ya have to do, ya have to eat!"

Ally did not need any coaxing, as her voracious appetite seemed to have no boundaries. However, she did take a moment to run it over in her mind. She deduced her wine high was wearing off, and she thought it would be a good idea if she did indeed eat something before she headed home.

"Yeah Percy, everybody's gotta eat," Ally giggled.

Percy sat down without any objection or struggle. Whether she did not have the energy to argue or the desire, she succumbed to Camilla's wishes — "more like demands," she thought to herself.

"We can help ya, if ya like," Ally offered and was followed by Percy's agreeing.

"Not this time. You must be tired from your trip," Camilla was already at the stove. Between the banging sounds from the pots and pans, she went on to say, "tell me, I wanna hear everything that happened. Did you find the lady you went lookin' for?"

Camilla, giddy as a school girl, kissed her rosary beads before tucking them securely between her bountiful bosom. As she went about fixing a batch of Pasta Puttanesca, she questioned and listened to all of them, including the two women she was convinced were going to be in both of her sons' futures. Camilla was in more than her kitchen — she was in her element.

Donato and Ally could not sit still and were up and about in the kitchen too. Ally followed Donato's lead in gathering dishes and silverware. Once Percy reached a decision where she refused to be a bystander, she joined them and helped to set the table — a decision which Camilla chose not to challenge.

"Set it for ten," Camilla said. "My other two sons will be ready to eat and *due dei miei nipoti* — two of my grandchildren will be eating too."

Never having learned Italian, she understood only part of what Camilla said, but Percy did as she was told. She could not help but wonder how often Camilla prepared meals of such a size and with such ease for her family, in addition to overseeing a restaurant and bakery. Bud sat quietly as his mother insisted he do — his boot cast propped up on a chair which she had Donato place in front of him.

Camilla could see Donato was bursting with obvious affection for the young and lovely Ally. She was tickled to see Ally's affection towards her youngest son was reciprocal and, by all appearances, seemed to be sincere. For the first time, she could actually see the young lady's real eyes, and their natural sparkle could not be missed. At the same time, she was keenly aware her son, James, and the pretty and petite, Percy, were struggling with their emotions — quite unlike her youngest son and Ally.

Her sixth sense ignited, Camilla recognized both Percy and her eldest son's emotions had been bruised in some way. Due to their age and those circumstances life had thrown in each of their paths, it was very unlikely either of them could have avoided ever being exposed to emotional pain. Even so, she could not help but consider her beloved first born was likely to have recently added to Percy's discontent in some way.

Camilla kept to herself, "Disappointment and heartbreak builds walls, and sometimes the walls seem too high to see to the other side." She knew it took a lifetime to get to where they were, and what she saw in Percy was a great deal of what she saw in her eldest son, James. She understood the wounds both of these young people bore were wounds derived from deep cuts, and it would take more than one of her fabulous meals to provide all which was needed to heal them.

"But," Camilla thought to herself while straining the pasta, "I know what I see, and I see something between them. They have a chance."

Always being one to hold onto hope and steadfast to her deep and abiding faith, Camilla saw in her emotionally damaged son's dark eye, he not only needed but was finally ready for a life's partner. She could see, too, that Percy and her son were careful not to be seen by the other, while they both stole painful glances at each other. Their obvious fear of the other was the same, and Camilla did not need coaxing to intervene.

There was a heat between the two of them, Camilla told herself. Although it had been some time since she had felt the full intensity of the flame she shared with her deceased husband, she had a lifetime of memories to keep their flame burning for the rest of her life. Her memories were sure to provide that to her, and she was quite adept at recognizing the flame between others when she saw it. What she saw and felt between James and Percy was as real as any emotions she had ever witnessed before. Albeit, it was a flickering flame, and it burned with noticeable fragility. The flame was alive and Camilla, compelled by her strong instincts, was determined to protect that fluttering flame from going out.

Having recognized her son's attending the therapy sessions for several months had brought about some positive changes in his overall demeanor, she also acknowledged his sessions may have contributed, in part, to her eldest son's most recent emotional development — emotional development which, for whatever reason, had been slow to come but successful nonetheless. For that, she was grateful.

Being Camilla came with specific requirements as far as she was concerned, and she was not about to relinquish her role in the perpetuation of catapulting any of her children into the arena of *amoré*. Knowing her eldest son was stubborn in all aspects, she knew the task which lay before her was not an easy one and would require calling on the big guns.

Placing her hand to her heart she whispered in Italian, "*Beata Madre Maria, dammi forza*" (Blessed Mother Mary, give me strength).

*****

"We could stop and get something to eat before you take me back, if you like." Dill was not just thinking of his stomach with his suggestion. He had hoped Mrs. Fins would spend more time with him before she dropped him off at his apartment.

"Well, I'd rather just pick something up and fix us dinner if you don't mind. I have had enough restaurant food for a while," Mrs. Fins replied.

"Of course, you and me both," Dill honestly agreed. Even though the food had been quite extraordinary on their trip, he looked forward to some home-cooked food too. It took a couple of minutes as they drove down

Interstate 5 for it to dawn on him, Mrs. Fins said, "fix us dinner." At that point, even his thoughts were stuttering.

Dillard Bigley had his own life's history, and that history may or may not have been any more complicated than anyone else in the group. Still, like everyone's history, Dill Bigley's was pertinent to his own story.

He was born to a very well-to-do family in London, England, and during his early childhood and against his mother's wishes, he was sent to attend boarding schools. They were the best boarding schools money could buy; but still, they were boarding schools which kept him away from his family.

The winters were long and lonely for Dillard, but those early summers were spent languishing on any of a number of beaches on both the east and west coasts of the United Kingdom. He happily spent that time with his mother and sister, and those were his favorite memories of his childhood.

In Dillard Bigley's mind, his father was a low-life degenerate philanderer who left his mother little choice but to divorce him and fend for herself, something she did quite sufficiently. Eventually, she met and married a charming American college professor who was working to earn his doctorate at Oxford University. This new man in his mother's life embraced both Dillard and his sister as if he had fathered them himself, and Dillard grew to love and admire this man immensely. In the early 1970s, just as Dillard entered his teens, his parents decided to move the family to America, and Dillard had nothing but high hopes.

Being desperately unfamiliar with the American life style, other than what he had seen on television or read about, Dillard exposed himself to suffer almost daily humiliation and bullying from many of his new school mates because of his strong accent and his name. This made him withdraw to a great degree. At the same time, he grew a determination within himself to overcome the daily torment by outdoing everyone else in achieving academic excellence. His new father was a strong influence on Dillard's diligence and was always there to encourage him to keep true to his birthright by keeping a stiff upper lip, and he repeatedly told Dill to "never let them get you down."

Dillard Bigley was determined to be better than the rest of the hooligans who shared his age group. He tried to ignore their existence, but to his discontent, these barbaric cretins fell into the category of being his peers (thus, continuously forcing them to be together). Even so, his determination to outdo them drove him on. And outdo them, he did. He not only excelled in all academics put in his path but far outranked most other young fellows in the athletic arena. All of this made him quite interesting to the young ladies. They found that, combined with his natural good looks, his accomplishments and self-confidence made him extremely attractive.

One would think this would make him a very happy young lad. It was not that he did not appreciate being appreciated, nor was it that he disliked the attention the opposite sex was willing to adorn him with. What it came down to was he had made plans, and they were big plans — plans which would take him to big places. Those plans did not include being coerced into activities of a more primal nature by the frivolous and flirtatious behaviors of his admirers. He refused to let his plans be stifled and was determined to make something of himself. He believed when he had accomplished that, he would make time to pursue the more ethereal and physical aspects of relationships involving his young manhood and his admirers from the fairer sex.

Unfortunately for Dillard Bigley, with all of his effort and forethought, things did not go the way he reckoned they should. No matter how hard he had refused to be influenced or sidetracked by the wiles of the young temptresses seductively sashaying themselves in his direction, there was one cheeky young damsel who was able to steal his heart away. Sadly, with all the efforts he had so diligently tried to protect himself with, she not only stole his heart, but she promptly — and with expert precision — broke it too. It was only after allowing himself a reasonable amount of healing time, before he picked himself up and proceeded with a new zeal to meet with the success he had always desired.

Indeed, Dillard Bigley had accomplished what he had set out to do and was a wealthy and successful man, and up until the prior several months, he had been in complete control of his emotions. There was the rare occasion he dabbled in a dalliance of sorts, but he never let anyone get close enough to be able to steal his heart again, nor did he desire to give his heart away. That was up and until he witnessed the vision of his life-long dream of the world's most exquisite and perfect woman — to be precise — Mrs. Marlene Fins.

Contemplating the dread of not being able to see Mrs. Fins — even if only briefly — at his group sessions which were abruptly ended, Dill Bigley found himself caught up in a whirlwind of surprise for the first few days after returning from Park City, starting with the dinner Mrs. Fins prepared for the two of them that first night back in Seattle.

Dill's description of that dinner pleased Mrs. Fins, and she played it over in her own head. "Heavenly" was the word she remembered him saying. Having not cooked for anyone other than herself for a very long time and recalling that when she did cook, it was not appreciated in the same way as Mr. Bigley's expressed pleasure, Mrs. Fins was stirred by a desire to do it more often.

The stress and concern Dill Bigley harbored, regarding the possibility he would not have the opportunity to see his long-adored Mrs. Fins (once the group therapy sessions ended), was quickly dashed and dashed by none other than Mrs. Fins, herself. She had always presented herself with exquisite manners and a sublime etiquette and continued to do so. As she grew more familiar and comfortable with him, she felt no compunction to offering Dill Bigley a myriad of things they could do and places they could go — together. Her free spirit was coming out and was a breath of fresh air for Dill Bigley, and on more than one occasion, it literally left him breathless.

Being the lady Mrs. Fins was, she did not taunt nor did she tease Dill Bigley. She was above all, a lady; and he was, of course, the consummate gentleman. Neither made mention to the other as to any physical tension which may have existed between the two of them. As the weeks wore on, they were becoming more comfortable with each other, like a pair of old bedroom slippers — minus the bedroom.

Anyone observing the two of them would take for granted their relationship was one of shared normal intimacy, as they appeared to be a "couple" in all other aspects. Not once did Dill attempt (in any fashion), nor suggest (in any manner), to move their relationship in a direction which would propose intimacy possessing a physical bent. This left Mrs. Fins to wonder if she was unattractive to Mr. Bigley — though all indications other than the aforementioned would suggest to the contrary. Truth be it known, as the weeks ticked by, Mrs. Fins found herself musing over the two of them engaging in activities of a physical nature. Each time this transpired, she tried not to linger too terribly long within the fantasy, as it caused her breath to hasten along with her eyelids to flutter and her heart to race.

The truth is Dill Bigley's attraction to Mrs. Fins was frightening and pitifully close to unbearable. The titillating sensations he had felt towards her were growing, and were sensations he could not remember ever having felt with such intensity before. His fear of making any advancements towards Mrs. Fins too early in their courtship was so terrifying, it was almost crippling. It further fostered his thought, if he were to make the wrong move, he could face fracturing whatever building blocks had been laid in their relationship. He held strong to the belief that in a truly loving and life-long relationship, the courting never ends. It would seem — that time was now due for Dill Bigley, in some way, to share his thoughts with Mrs. Fins.

Dill Bigley was totally unaware Judge Glib had begun to address Dr. Marksdale, for he was engrossed in thoughts of the next rendezvous to be later that same afternoon; whereas, he planned to invite Mrs. Fins to accompany him to a ballet a few short months away in — of all places — Paris, France.

The thoughts running through Ally's head were not as grand as those which ran through Dill Bigley's, but she was not paying attention to what the judge was saying either.

Bud was preoccupied as well. His thoughts were centered on why Percy had not arrived yet. He surmised she certainly should have reached her destination by then, and as tactfully as he was able to, he kept turning his head when the courtroom door opened and closed. His frustration had been building since he had not seen her from the time they came back from Park City, on the day they returned from their journey to find Emma; and then, she only came to the bakery to pick up something she had left behind.

Interestingly, the item Percy came by to retrieve was something she could very well have done without or could have readily replaced if necessary. That fact was not lost on Camilla — nor was it lost on Ally who, along with her birds, had been spending most of her time with Donato and the Jeffries. Ally agreed to let Donato build a large aviary for her birds in the Jeffries' lovely courtyard in back of the restaurant; and, it had come to be, the only time she was not with Donato was when she was working at the salon.

Try as she may, Ally's trying to encourage Bud to make contact with Percy fell on deaf ears. He was not going to have any of it. But Ally was not that easily dissuaded, and she continued to push him up and until Camilla looked at her and gently shook her head from side to side while putting her index finger to her lips to indicate that she wanted Ally to stop speaking. Ally had heard more Italian in those five weeks than she had heard in her entire young lifetime, and although she may not have known what any of it meant, she had no problem picking up on Camilla's body language. Camilla did not have to be aggressive in her approach. She had Ally's respect and that was all she needed. At one point, Camilla took Ally aside to let her know James was not one to be handled, although she had her own plans on how to do just that.

"All in good time," Camilla told Ally — "all in good time."

For the first time in Ally's life, she was surrounded by loving and giving people, and she felt the wealth of love she had always desired in the ambience of the Jeffries family's love — all of whom welcomed her in with open arms.

A lot had changed in Ally's life over the prior several months and especially over the five weeks before the hearing. She had given up her second job as a backup singer, and once and for all, she had given up the deadbeat drummer too. Both of these changes could not have made Donato any happier. However, it would be hard to see how he could possibly have been any happier than he was, just being in Ally's company. Donato's rare good looks had been taken over by a blissful googly-eyed, goofy-faced boy in love.

Taking what Percy had told her into consideration, Ally began to believe she did not need to always make herself up or dress up in, as Percy put it, "crazy-ass getups!" It was a whole new place she found herself in, and she liked believing what Percy said when she told her, "You're pretty just the way you are."

Emma sat quietly listening to the judge begin by stating she appreciated Dr. Marksdale's making his case files regarding the group available to her (to peruse prior to the hearing if she cared to). But, as he was already aware, the judge did not take him up on his offer.

Dr. Marksdale began to speak once he was given the floor, "Your honor, my patients are able to meet the challenges they face without issue." He turned to look at the group sitting behind him.

"I am confident that each of them is now able to communicate and express themselves without losing control of their faculties."

Emma watched as the judge panned the group sitting behind the doctor with a scrutinizing eye. Then Emma saw the look on the judge's face change, while she looked back and forth between Bud and Dill's faces. It was apparent Judge Glib had become aware of the men's head injuries.

"What is this?" Judge Glib questioned the doctor. "Why are these men's faces in the condition they are in?"

The doctor feared that either Dill or Bud may say something, so he immediately ran "interference" and calmly addressed the judge's query with, "These men had some unfortunate accidents — none of which were caused by . . . ." The doctor was unable to complete his explanation due to the judge's interruption.

"Looks to me like they ran into each other's fists — which would indicate nothing has changed!" Judge Glib's voice was sharp, sending a chill down Dr. Marksdale's spine.

"No, your honor, these gentlemen had run-ins with inanimate objects — purely coincidental and not associated with each other in any way." Dr. Marksdale still felt he could handle the situation the judge's question posed. That was until Judge Glib did exactly what the doctor had hoped she would not do.

"Stand up, gentlemen." The judge's voice continued to carry the weight of someone who knew they were in charge.

When neither Dill nor Bud stood up, the judge's voice cracked through the air like a wrangler's whip.

"This is the last time I will say it. Stand up — both of you!" Judge Glib's face contorted like she had taken a bite out of a lemon, and her eyes, barely more than piercing beady slits, darted back and forth between Dill and Bud — each, still engrossed in their own thoughts.

Emma used her elbows to jab both men on either side of her (at the same time) and said firmly under her breath, "The judge wants you to stand up — right now!"

"Did I ask for your assistance?" The judge directed her glare at Emma.

Emma responded flatly and while out of the judge's vision, she pinched both Bud's and Dill's thighs, hoping to get them to pay attention — "no, your honor."

At this point, Ally's mind had come back from wherever it had wondered off to. She elbowed Dill in the side while bending down and leaning forward to peek around Emma, hoping to get Bud's attention — which she did. He saw Ally's eyes were opened wide, and that is when she used her facial expressions along with the movement of her head to pantomime her intent — that intent being to get him to stand up.

"What is the matter with you people?" The judge's boiling anger unmistakable, "I do not need help from either of the two of you." Judge Glib's eyes went back and forth between Emma and Ally with the precision of a heat seeking missile.

Emma knew better than to cross the judge as did Ally, but in her mind, Ally could not help but say as if she were talking to the judge, "I dunno, lady. I kinda think ya do."

"Is there something wrong with you two gentlemen? Are you not capable of comprehending a simple instruction?" Just as the judge was about to say something more, both Dill and Bud had made it to their feet — their faces revealing nervous confusion.

"Dear God," the doctor began to pray silently, "Please don't let them screw this up!"

A man whose natural propensity was to lean more towards science than religion, Dr. Marksdale had found himself calling on a higher power more often in the several months leading up to the hearing than he ever had in his lifetime. In that courtroom, and on that day, it would soon come to light, Dr. Marksdale would find out how close he would come to his God.

Standing still, albeit awkwardly, Dill and Bud were aware, from her bench, the judge was looking at them both up and down. An uncomfortable and decidedly long duration passed, before the judge broke into the strained atmosphere with an order she directed at Dill.

"You will tell me now, how you incurred your injuries, sir."

"I — I — well, I'm not exactly sure, your honor." Dill swallowed hard, and before he could get another word out, the judge — her lips pursed and her eyes almost closed as they were squinted so tight — ordered Dill in a chilling voice, "Tell me exactly how you incurred your injuries, or I will hold you in contempt. Do you understand?"

"Yes, your honor, I — I understand. The problem I face is that I am not sure how I hurt myself, as I have no recollection of the event."

Feeling as if he were watching a train wreck in slow motion, Dr. Marksdale believed Dill Bigley's only hope in dealing with the agitated judge was to interject himself into the conversation.

"If I may, your honor, the accident happened in my office and . . . ."

"No! You may not!" The judge grabbed a hold of her gavel and slammed it down. "Sit down, now."

For anyone who was not paying attention — they were now. Dill was no exception. He was nervous, but he knew he could only relay what he was able to recall. He was grateful for the doctor's attempt to appease the judge who was becoming more unhinged by the second, and he understood what she wanted to know; moreover, it was up to him to settle the matter. Whether it would satisfy the judge or not, the only way Dill could think of to go forward was to tell her the truth.

"The doctor is right. I was in his office at the time, but, due directly to the accident and the injuries incurred, I have no memory of it."

Judge Glib possessed zero tolerance for anyone who would create any type of upheaval in her courtroom. Knowing what she knew about them already, she harbored an unhealthy resentment towards "the group." As much as the doctor had dreaded going before the court to somehow validate his patients' readiness to be released from their court ordered therapy, the judge, herself, had not relished the idea of having to deal with the same imbeciles again — the same imbeciles who had caused her former blundering bailiff to leave her courtroom in utter shambles.

With a glare which could burn a hole through stainless steel, Judge Glib turned her ire towards Bud. "Did you do this to him?"

"Who, me?" Bud looked at Dill and then back at the judge. "No way, no, I didn't do that."

"What happened to your face?" Judge Glib leaned forward in her chair — her eyes never veering away from Bud's — "And do not dare tell me you do not know."

"No prob." Bud's head bobbled assuredly.

"I ran into a brick wall and the back of a taxi's front seat headrest."

Bud seemed to be quite satisfied with himself, as the nodding of his head up and down would indicate. Overall, his body language revealed his confidence of the feeling he had just given the teacher the correct answer to her question.

Judge Glib sneered, "Oh, yes, I remember you. You're the cocky one. Now tell me this, genius, why would you run into a brick wall?"

The left side of Bud's mouth curled up and he lifted both of his arms up which had been hanging at his sides. Using his hands to help express himself, his fingers facing the ceiling, he obliged the judge with his honest answer to the question she posed.

"That's easy ma'am, someone was stompin' on my foot, and then she started body slammin' me in my chest!"

In that exact moment, Judge Glib's mouth dropped open. Her attention was diverted by sounds and activity outside of her courtroom. As she looked away from Bud and towards the back of the courtroom where her bailiff stood, the door opened and Percy walked in. Before the door could close completely, someone's running footsteps could be heard getting closer, along with shrill screaming voices coming from somewhere off in the distance. The urgent screaming voices were ordering someone to "Stop and drop it!"

Mere seconds passed — too few — for the sounds to register as anything ominous to Percy, for she continued to make her way towards the others sitting in the front of the gallery. Suddenly, the closed courtroom doors flew open, and a tall well-dressed man barged through them. In his right hand, he wielded a gun.

Everyone towards the back of the courtroom was aware there was a ruckus, and as the noise level rose, it caused everyone in the gallery to turn around too. As they did so, they all became witnesses to the man with the gun strike the shocked bailiff in the head with the butt of that gun, subsequently knocking him to the floor. Everything was happening so fast, so no one could do anything but watch, including Percy who had stopped in her tracks in the aisle and was not moving. The man with the gun moved so rapidly, he made it to where she stood motionless and threw his arm over her shoulder. He wrapped it under her right arm and literally lifted her off of the floor — all before she had any idea what was happening to her.

In a horrifying and bellowing voice, the armed man held the gun to the right side of Percy's head and ordered the injured Bailiff, who was staggering to his feet, to lock the doors and for everyone not to move. He threatened them that if they did, he would shoot his captive in her head.

Ally turned around in her seat like everyone else in the courtroom gallery had done. It took a few seconds for it to dawn on her, it was Percy whom the man had in his violent grasp. At first she felt shock, and then Ally felt an overwhelming sense of dread. All of her thoughts were mixed together and nothing seemed real. In fact, nothing which was happening made any sense, but she felt she recognized the man with the gun. Dr. Marksdale had turned in his seat to see the man holding Percy off of the ground, and it, too, took him another second to realize what had just become apparent to Ally.

The man holding Percy captive and with a gun to her head was none other than — Dr. Elan Glenn.

CHAPTER TWENTY

"Scalpel" — The surgeon's assistant placed a scalpel in the surgeon's waiting, opened hand.

Addressing his surgical tech, the surgeon informed her he was ready to use, what he termed, "the arm." The C arm, which is its common name, is used to connect the x ray source and x ray detector to one another and is used primarily for imaging during surgical emergency care procedures. The surgeon was keenly aware how invaluable a tool it would be in assisting him in the procedure he was about to perform.

The surgical tech had everything ready for the surgeon, just as she should have, for that was part of her duties. Once he was satisfied with what he saw, the surgeon made a steady and precise incision just above the left ear and the entry hole the bullet had made in the side of Dr. Marksdale's head.

The surgery to remove the bullet, alone, would not have taken so long; but, due to the repair required to the surrounding shattered skull bones, it was several hours into the surgery, before the surgeon was satisfied he had repaired, to the best of his ability, what he could. He then left the operating room and removed his surgical gown, mask and gloves, and once down to his scrubs, he went out to the waiting room to meet Stelle with the news.

A part of his job was to explain to the families of loved ones in similar situations the outcome of their loved one's surgery. It had never been a favorite part of his job, but the surgeon was good at explaining to Stelle, the bullet in her husband's head could not be removed without presenting more risk to his life than if he had just left it in place. Everything which could be done to the surrounding area was done, and at that point, it would be a matter of hours — perhaps days — to see what the outcome would be. He had a lot of pressure on his brain and, thus, had to have a part of his skull opened up to relieve that pressure. Stelle tried to take it all in but caught only the word "craniectomy." As of that moment, though, the surgeon assured Stelle that Dr. Marksdale was still in critical but stable condition. Time would tell if any permanent damage had been done to his temporal lobe where his short-term memory, speech and musical rhythm were located.

In another area of the hospital, all the members of the group were waiting in one of the surgical waiting rooms along with Mrs. Fins and a large number of the Jeffries family. Camilla was pacing back and forth — her short, round frame nearly trembling.

Donato had his arm around Ally for a few minutes and spoke to her in a hushed voice. He then got up and went to his mother and began to pace right alongside of her, his arm secured tightly around her shoulders. As for Percy, well, Percy sat in a chair against the wall with a blank stare on her colorless face.

Ally went to her side and pulled a chair up next to her. "He's gonna be okay, I just know it."

Percy turned to look at Ally — her face was expressionless. Then she turned away from Ally — her head facing forward again. She continued to stare out into the blank space in front of her — by all appearances, numb to the world — in shock no doubt.

Perhaps that was the best place for her to be at that juncture — in shock.

The reality of what all had transpired was a lot to handle for everyone, but for Percy who had been held captive with a gun pressed to her head, playing it all back — the sudden physical attack against her and being lifted off of the ground and used as a hostage for a madman — was like visiting an experience someone else had lived. The madman wanted only revenge and cared not for who may get in his way. This was a concept too hard for her to comprehend at that point.

She had managed to escape her capturer by using her heel to kick him in his groin, and as he bent over in agony, she broke his grip on her and ran towards the group and into Bud's arms. Bud grabbed her and swung her around while pushing her to the floor; subsequently, he immediately threw himself on top of her, just as everyone heard the eardrum-breaking sound of three gunshot rounds going off in rapid succession.

Percy managed to escape the whole ordeal without any visible injury with nary a scratch on her — quite unlike Dr. Marksdale or the shooter, Dr. Elan Glenn. And Bud — well, Bud did not fare so well either.

Percy sat in the waiting room having no idea how bad his injuries were or how long he would be in surgery. She was only well aware the injuries he incurred were incurred while he was saving her life.

Sitting in her numb state, the irony of it all was not lost on Percy. She saw the absurdity of Dr. Marksdale — his being a head doctor having been shot in the head. And Bud, poor Bud — his being the ass in the group being shot in his —

A few hours passed — for his mother, it felt more like days — before Bud's surgeon came out to update the family on his condition.

"The surgery was a success. Your son is in fair condition and in recovery. You should be able to see him in an hour or so." The surgeon spoke softly making it difficult for Camilla to hear her, but her youngest son was there to assist.

"James is gonna be okay, ma," Donato told his mother through his smile — a smile which Ally could not help but observe was beautiful.

"Ma, he's gonna be okay."

The surgeon was an extremely intelligent woman. When she spoke, she used more medical terms and jargon than perhaps would be fitting, if she hoped to achieve a good bedside manner with her patients and their families. Donato did his best to be the go between, between his mother and the surgeon which was not all that easy of a task, considering, he had his mother's emotionally frantic state of being to contend with. Adding to that, half of the time Camilla spoke too fast in English and the other half, too fast in Italian — never leaving Donato a slow lane in between. However, his challenges did not end there as he would soon discover. While trying to describe what she had to do during Bud's surgery, the surgeon's heavy East Indian accent added to Donato's difficulties.

The trajectory the bullet took and the subsequent surgical procedure the surgeon performed were very descript and graphic, even to a layman such as Donato. The best he was able to decipher from the conversation was the bullet had entered at the top on the back side of his brother's thigh and ultimately lodged into Bud's right-buttock cheek.

Feeling slightly squeamish, Donato continued to repeat to his mother what the surgeon was relaying to him. That information included the fact Bud had sustained extensive deep muscle damage, and he would require physical therapy once he had healed sufficiently. The surgeon felt his mother should know, too, the bullet had nicked a main artery in her son's leg resulting in the need for a transfusion of several liters of blood during his surgery.

Donato had held up pretty well until that exchange of information. He had done his best to relay the information while, at the same time, he tried to stop himself from passing out — a situation which was apparent to Ally who was standing directly next to him. Sensing Donato was about to have a face-meets-the-floor encounter, she put her arm around his waist and helped him to the closest chair which was about two feet from where they stood.

Camilla, clearly exasperated with all that had happened to her eldest son, showed signs of needing to sit down too. Ally helped her to another empty chair, where she sat down and released a noticeable deep sigh. Clutching her rosary beads to her chest, she gave the sign of the cross and then closed her eyes and began to quietly pray. Before leaving, the surgeon asked Camilla if she thought she would be okay. Camilla nodded in the affirmative and took a hold of the surgeon's wrist and whispered, "bless you," before releasing her grip. The surgeon smiled at Camilla and gently squeezed her shoulder before taking her leave.

Percy, having heard everything the surgeon had said, looked at Camilla and felt an overwhelming urge to hold the woman. She picked her chair up and made her way to where Camilla sat, pulling her chair close to hers. Camilla turned to look at Percy and reached out to her with an open hand. She responded by taking Camilla's hand firmly, but gently, into her own. For the first time in hours, Percy felt emotion — along with the tears which were slowly rolling down her cheeks.

"I will find out how Dr. Marksdale is doing and be right back." Mrs. Fins got up and started towards the door.

"Wait, I will go with you." Dill was following right behind her, but first stopped and put his hand gently on Camilla's arm and said softy, "We are grateful to hear about your son. Is there anything we can do for you?"

Camilla looked up at Dill with her watery brown eyes and thanked him, her voice slightly cracking.

"How kind of you — no thank you — I am fine."

As they made their way into the hall, Mrs. Fins stopped and leaned against the wall for a moment.

"Thank you for calling the office and letting me know about the shooting, Mr. Bigley. I would have hated to hear about all of this on the news." She leaned against the wall for a couple of moments longer, before she began to walk down the hall.

"Absolutely — I did not want you to hear about it in that fashion either. I am still finding it hard to believe any of this is real."

Dill kept to himself on how dismayed he was at times with Mrs. Fins still referring to him as Mr. Bigley. They had been spending a lot of time together, gradually growing closer. Although their relationship was not of a physical nature, he had convinced her to call him Dill on many occasions, and she had insisted he call her Marlene. Not being able to pinpoint the reasoning behind his reluctance to address her as anything other than Mrs. Fins or goddess, he would oblige her (of course he would oblige her — she was Mrs. Fins!) and nervously and dutifully call her Marlene. But he, too, found himself reverting back to referring to her as Mrs. Fins. The causation was unknown to him, although it just seemed proper and appropriate in some way.

"I should not be considering such things now," Dill said to himself, "This is a terribly difficult time. It is best I overlook such trivial matters."

If the truth were to be known, Dillard Bigley would not care what Mrs. Fins called him — just as long as she called.

*****

The news Stelle imparted onto them about Dr. Marksdale's condition was more difficult to take than Mrs. Fins had anticipated; and sadly, she found herself incapable of being the staunch and firm right hand to either of the Marksdales she once was.

She felt sick, sad and frightened — all at the same time. The anger she felt towards Dr. Elan Glenn was close to being unbearable. It was only then both Mrs. Fins and Dill Bigley found out that the shooter — the doctor known as the good doer, Dr. Elan Glenn — would not be doing anything for, or to, anyone ever again. He was dead.

"Dead?" Mrs. Fins shrieked.

The heads of everyone sitting in the waiting room turned sharply towards her.

"Yes, dead — just as he should be. I only wish I were the one to have pulled the trigger!" Stelle raised her voice. Her tone was vehement, and the faces of the strangers in the waiting room wore expressions of horror. Mrs. Fins and Dill Bigley — each sitting on opposite sides of Stelle — looked up at each other, their eyes wide with surprise.

Stelle proceeded to tell both of them the sheriff had come earlier to question her about the relationship between her husband and the shooter. That was when Stelle was made aware of the shooter having been Dr. Elan Glenn. It was after he had questioned her, the sheriff relayed to her Dr. Elan Glenn was not as fortunate as her husband and had not survived the gunshot wound he received at the hands of one of the sheriff's deputies.

While Mrs. Fins and Dill Bigley looked into each other's eyes with disbelief, Stelle proceeded to tell them, that the sheriff asked her why they would find a letter in the deceased's suit pocket addressed to the deceased — from her husband.

Knowing Mrs. Fins knew more about her husband's communications with other professionals than she herself would, Stelle ventured the query as to whether or not Mrs. Fins had any idea of the letter or its contents. Mrs. Fins was oblivious to both, and like the rest of the events of that day, she felt like she was more in the dark than ever before.

Under normal circumstances, Mrs. Fins would have liked to entertain the idea she would have had some inkling as to what relationship existed between Dr. Elan Glenn and Dr. Marksdale.

"Normal . . . ." Mrs. Fins found herself pondering. "What is normal?" After these past many months, I have no idea!"

What she did know, and had come to ascertain, was that after all of the years she had worked for Dr. Marksdale, Mrs. Fins did not know her employer as well as she once believed she had. At that pivotal point, she would not dare pretend to be sure of anything involving him again, and "normal" was only a word.

Stelle began to ask Mrs. Fins for her assistance with Dr. Marksdale's upcoming appointments, but before she could finish her request, two detectives came into the room. They expressed their desire to speak with Dr. Marksdale's wife privately. Dill and Mrs. Fins politely excused themselves but not before letting Stelle know where they would be in the event she needed them for anything.

After standing and before they could leave, the detectives stopped them. They informed both of them they would be interviewed next, along with anyone else connected to Dr. Marksdale who had been in court earlier that day. They understood everyone had been interviewed briefly after the incident, but those interviews were conducted by the sheriff's department. These detectives were from Homicide and had their own questions to ask.

"Homicide?"

Mrs. Fins heard herself say the word, just before she felt herself losing her balance and falling backwards. Fortunately for both of them, the ever chivalrous Dill Bigley was right behind her. He thrust his arms around her and, just as quickly, pressed his body up against her to prevent her from falling.

Up and until that moment, everything had happened so fast, there was little time to think about anything. Both Dill and Mrs. Fins had only been successful at functioning due to being on some kind of emotional autopilot. Neither Dill nor she had thought about the fact if Dr. Marksdale or Bud, for that matter, had not survived their injuries, that is exactly what it would have become — a homicide.

*****

An atmosphere of intense fear engulfed the group. Everyone's face, including Camilla and Donato's, bore shocked expressions as Dill and Mrs. Fins relayed Dr. Marksdale's extremely serious condition to them. Then Dill, drawing from his polished tact, informed them Dr. Elan Glenn — better known to them as "El," — had met with his demise.

No one uttered a word. Instead, they all sat rigid and quiet with all of their eyes locked in empty stares — all except Camilla. Unlike the others, her eyes were squinted and her jaw was noticeably clenched. For her, it was obvious the man who shot her son and his doctor got exactly what he deserved. Once again, she gave the sign of the cross and was only slightly comforted by her belief the deceased would be dealt with in good order and in good time from a higher court than any which existed on earth.

For everyone else, they had to have been questioning — how any of what had just transpired could have actually happened. But, the most pressing question everyone must have had on their minds would have had to have been — why?

The members of the group had known Dr. Elan Glenn as "El" and believed him to be a very personable doctor — a kind and attentive therapist. That was how he was remembered. At least, that was the persona he presented when he oversaw their therapy sessions. He had told them he felt they deserved the best therapist to oversee their court ordered sessions, thus, his insistence Dr. Marksdale take his place.

The raw fact was that El never had any of their best interests at heart. He had revenge and blackmail only on his mind — a revenge which had lingered within the darkest caverns of his deranged mind. Finally, Dr. Elan Glenn met with the opportunity to call a debt due which Dr. Marksdale would have been loath to pay but feared more — not to.

The sense of power Dr. Elan Glenn derived from his lording that debt over Dr. Marksdale was a powerful and diabolical force. It was that same sense of power which gave him pleasure to watch his victim sweat with fear. The hunger for that pleasure became his obsession.

These thoughts played over and over in his increasingly fragile mind. The thoughts his old college pal had the mansion, the cars and the notoriety — and he had Stelle too. This made Dr. Elan Glenn writhe in a stew of his own making — a poisonous stew of unbearable jealously.

He had always thrown women aside once he was done with them; and worse, Dr. Elan Glenn aborted their unborn children without their knowledge or consent. His nickname as the "good doer" was staggeringly misplaced — better the moniker, "evil doer," for the real Dr. Elan Glenn. Somehow, in the contorted twists of his mind, he had convinced himself that — although he was a serial and notorious womanizer — Dr. Marksdale had won Stelle, the only woman he had ever loved. Sadly, the odds of his being capable of loving anyone were nil, at best, when it came to Dr. Elan Glenn.

These thoughts burned a hole in the soul of Dr. Elan Glenn. When the opportunity to procure his ounce of flesh from his nemesis came, he never took into consideration: Dr. Marksdale may arrive at the conclusion he would rather face his fears than to live another day under the thumb of his sinister blackmailer.

Dr. Elan Glenn did not foresee his power wielding obsession may be his own undoing. As with many who become hypnotized by the aphrodisiac of power, he saw himself as all too mighty to believe his opponent may have a weapon of his own with which to duel. What he carelessly did not take into account was Dr. Marksdale's choice of armament may be something as difficult, yet as simple, as the truth.

You see, when in Park City, Dr. Marksdale found something more than Emma — he found himself. Several weeks earlier, before he rode the gondola over and over again and witnessed inexplicable beauty, he had written three letters: One was addressed to the president of the university he had attended; the second was addressed to Leon Fisker's parents; and, the third was addressed to Dr. Elan Glenn.

In the first two letters, he told the truth regarding the events of the night he and Leon Fisker were victims of a cruel and dangerous college hazing — a hazing which ultimately led to Leon's death.

He kept the best letter for last, the letter to Elan Glenn. In that third and final letter written to Dr. Elan Glenn — Dr. Marksdale was the diabolical one.

The letter addressed to Dr. Elan Glenn from Dr. Marksdale was simple and to the point. It said only that he was sorry to hear El was going to be leaving the Seattle area. It went on to say he would be missed. Anyone reading the letter would think they were dear old friends — exactly the impression Dr. Marksdale intended to portray.

Imagine Dr. Elan Glenn's surprise — and rage — when he read the letter knowing Dr. Marksdale had turned the tables on him. Dr. Elan Glenn was keenly aware he had been sabotaged when he read it.

The letter Dr. Marksdale had written left no room for doubt as he had made it abundantly clear, Dr. Elan Glenn's career in Seattle was over. The last few sentences stood out in particular.

"Stelle and I will miss you, El, but we understand that you have to move on. Stelle and all of us . . ." This is the point where Dr. Marksdale inserted the list of names of the women El had administered the medications to without their knowledge and which had caused them to miscarry. The coup de grâce of Dr. Marksdale's scheme to reap his revenge was to give the impression Dr. Elan Glenn would always be welcome to visit if he were to be in the Seattle area in the future.

Clearly, it was with a bit of vengeance from within his own soul, Dr. Marksdale's final cut meant to go deep when he signed the letter, "Your old pal — Phillip."

This left Dr. Elan Glenn with nothing else to hold over Dr. Marksdale's head. In fact, he now had to wonder how much Dr. Marksdale knew about his performing unsolicited pharmacological abortions on all of the women named in his letter — all of those years before.

He was finished. Defeat was all Dr. Elan Glenn had left — defeat and his blackened heart.

Both men had always felt they were above the average man and would not have guessed, nor could either have foreseen, what the other was capable of doing.

Some may ask both of them, "Was it all worth it? Their answer most likely would have been, "no," as the end result was one lost his life, and the other was left fighting for his.

*****

"Yes, that'll be all for now, but I might have more questions for you later."

The homicide detective — an attractive man who appeared to be around Percy's age — stood up, and while putting his note pad and pen back into his jacket pocket, he looked directly at Percy and asked, "You weren't planning on leaving town were you?"

"Well, I have a pickup Thursday that'll take me to Wyoming and then Boise for a drop. So yes, I'll be on the road for a few days."

Already having decided to cancel the trip due to both the doctor's and Bud's physical conditions, Percy found her response to the detective puzzling and did not know why she answered him the way she did. The actual truth, however, was her inability to mentally deal with what was happening to the doctor and Bud — especially to Bud.

At the same time, she was even further from being able to confront her own assault or how it may have been affecting her. It had been only a few hours since she had been taken hostage and had come so close to death. She deduced that, maybe with the detective hinting he needed her to stick around, it may be just the excuse she required to clinch her decision to take some time off.

"If we need you for more questioning, I guess we could wait a few days. Take care of business and check in with me when you get back."

The detective took out his business card and reached out to hand it to her. Percy was uncomfortably aware of the way he looked into her eyes, and he was acting more interested in her than in questioning her. In fact, she sensed he may have been using further questioning only as a segue to seeing her again.

The detective's hand first brushed hers, and Percy had no doubt he meant for their hands to touch in the way they did. When he did not move his hand away and let it linger longer than what would have been expected or appropriate, she thought to herself, "Why all of this sudden interest in me? First, Benny, and now this guy!"

Scheduling herself as many jobs as she could safely do over the prior five weeks, Percy was left with an abundance of time on the road to think. It was unmistakably bothersome she found herself thinking about one thing. To be precise, she found herself thinking about one person in particular.

In the beginning, the thoughts she had were convoluted. They filled her head and perpetuated a high level of stress. But, to her surprise, Percy observed (what she would normally describe as a bombardment into her otherwise peaceful mind) her thoughts continued to morph into daydreams which, for some inexplicable reason, she found herself looking forward to having.

Repeatedly, and often bitterly, she chastised herself, "I must be going mad!"

Percy could think of no sane reason the thoughts she was having should have been taking place, and she was painfully aware her daydreams had moved into every space of unoccupied real estate in her head. At times, it all seemed too much to bear and was becoming a full-time occupation for her psyche.

Surely, if anyone would have told her all those months earlier her head would be filled with thoughts of James Elliot Jeffries, a.k.a. Bud, she would have begged for an intervention. Finding herself comparing her new day dreaming obsession to a drug, she considered how drugs can sometimes have side effects. However, Percy discovered not all side effects were negative. Eventually, she resigned herself to the compelling truth the side effect for her was to like daydreaming about the man — the kind, caring and (on occasion) delightfully funny man, James Elliot Jeffries — the man she had spent many hours listening to and talking with while they were together in Park City.

Not Bud — no — James was a universe apart from the gum chomping, oily haired, pompous, swaggering, bombastic jackass Bud so relished portraying himself to be. Over time, however, Percy not only became familiar with each: She had come to understand the personas of both Bud and James.

Bud insisted upon keeping up the act — he was about as unbearable of a person as anyone could stomach with the single-minded intention of keeping everyone at arms-length away from discovering the James who was actually a giving, gentle and vulnerable man. To Bud's credit (Percy mused), for the most part, it had worked.

In the beginning, Percy would not have minded keeping more than an arm's length between Bud and herself. It was only the necessity to be in each other's company for their required therapy sessions which kept them together. If it was up to her, she would have insisted there be a couple of continents of distance between them, and even that would prove to be closer than comfortable — or necessary. Once the therapy requirement was not the predominant causation for their being together, Percy's mind and heart had taken on a change in perspective. Ultimately, that change in perspective changed her perception — opening her mind up to new possibilities.

Arm's length had become their common ground as to similarities between Bud and herself, and arm's length was precisely the distance Percy found herself most comfortable with in relationship to the proximity between herself and anyone else. It was only after the absurd events which had led her into that waiting room — and a lifetime of obscuring the light with which she chose to see herself — did Percy finally see she was closer in personality to the one person in the group she had most disliked.

While in the hospital waiting room, whether it was a deliberate attempt or not, to distract herself from meeting head on with all which had transpired that long and horrifying day, Percy began to reflect on her life. In doing so, she had to acknowledge and consider her twisted set of circumstances.

First, there was Benny. He was the good looking, sweet and attentive taxi driver. Percy could see he was more than just a little interested. He was really quite smitten with her. The fact he called her almost every day, after they had met in Salt Lake City for lunch a few weeks earlier, was a dead giveaway as to the level of his interest. The time they spent together was pleasant, but Percy deduced it was only lunch — nothing more. Even though his phone calls always lifted her spirits and their conversations were fun, Percy had to acknowledge, they often interrupted her preferred daydreaming.

Next, she thought, "And now this not-so-slick homicide detective is putting his not-so-smooth move on me."

Percy shook visibly while she continued to take into account her most recent relationship offers and options.

"And let me not forget the drooler . . . ." Percy's face reflected how unpleasant an affair it would have been with a fellow truck driver, if she had taken him up on any number of his less than gentlemanly proposals.

"While drool, mixed with tobacco chew, ran down his chin and onto his oily t shirt right after he spit an ungodly slug like substance on the ground," she shuddered, "The things he offered to do to me — Jesus! If they aren't illegal, they should be!"

Immediately, her brain flashed a picture of James in front of her eyes. The direct effect was for her mind to swiftly spin around — making a complete 360-degree circle — leaving her dizzy.

"I start feelin' somethin' for a guy, an' all of a sudden I got dudes comin' outta from under rocks!"

Percy found herself in quite the predicament. She had not been looking to find a man or to get into any kind of relationship with one. With all the interest from even more men than mentioned, she considered the possibility she may be putting off some kind of scent. The problem, as she saw it, was the one man she could not get out of her head must have had a stuffed up nose, because that man had not reached out — or uttered a word to her — in weeks.

She looked around the waiting room and saw all the people from his family who loved him and were worried about his condition and, just like her, were hoping he would awaken soon. Percy considered maybe she should not be there, but at the same time, she knew there was no way she would leave.

Up and until then, she had not realized how chilly the waiting room had become. Percy crossed her arms over her chest and pulled her sleeves over her hands up to her fingers. Once she felt snuggled within her own arms and felt herself getting a little warmer, she closed her eyes for a few minutes and thought to herself, "He did save my life, and he took a bullet in his ass doing it. I suppose that says somethin'."

Opening her eyes for a moment, she pulled her legs up to her chest and placed her feet flat on the chair seat. Wrapping her arms around her legs, she laid her forehead on her knees. Not yet realizing how exhausted she was, she thought, "Maybe his actions speak louder than his absence of words," just before her body succumbed to the involuntary action of nodding off into a few brief minutes of sleep.

With a jolt as if initiated from an electric charge, her body jerked so hard she nearly fell out of her chair. Awkwardly fumbling to right herself back into balance, Percy took in a shaky gasp of air. Whatever dream had made its way behind her surprised and pale face, it had not settled well with her; but, in that sudden awakening moment, she had no recall as to what the content of that dream was.

"You'll be alright dear, you just had a bad dream," Camilla's voice was comforting as she patted Percy's leg.

"Oh — wow — I didn't even know I'd fallen asleep." Percy took in another more controlled breath, and while remaining seated in her chair, she stretched her back up and her legs out before her.

"It is understandable. You've been through a traumatic experience." Ally pulled her chair up to where both Camilla and Percy sat.

Blinking rapidly a few times, Percy looked at both women and shook her head from side to side, as if the action would help her to reorganize her thoughts.

"We've all had a traumatic day," Percy turned to look at Camilla, "Especially you, is there anything I can do for you?"

Camilla looked back and forth between Ally and Percy. A soft smile warmed her tired face before she said, "You're doing it."

"Huh? What is she saying?" Percy asked herself.

"Ya know, Percy," in a girlish voice, Ally interrupted Percy's thoughts, "He talks about you a lot — always askin' if I've heard anything from you."

"Who's asking 'bout me?" The second the words left her lips, Percy felt like an idiot. Ally's expression left no doubt to Percy, Ally thought she was acting like one too.

"I don't know why he'd be asking about me. He hasn't talked to me since Park City."

Camilla was quick to offer. "He does indeed talk about you a lot. And my James doesn't talk a lot about anything."

CHAPTER TWENTY-ONE

As the effects of the anesthesia wore off, the process of going in and out of consciousness left Bud groggy but coherent. His doctor let the family into his room, and when Bud opened his eyes and looked around the room, he saw two of his brothers and their wives standing next to a chair where Camilla sat while looking down at her folded hands in her lap. Standing near the window, he saw Ally and Donato huddled together.

"Hey — how'd I get here?" He started to ask with a slight slur. "How's —" As his voice drifted off, Bud appeared to succumb to the anesthesia remaining in his system.

Startling everyone in the room, one of Bud's younger brothers shouted out, "He's awake!"

Everyone moved towards Bud as Donato helped his mother up out of her chair and to her eldest son's bedside.

Camilla began in Italian, *"Oh figlio mio, sei tornato da noi!"* Which Donato translated for Ally, "Oh, my son you've come back to us!"

"Ma —" Bud started before his eyes opened.

The nurse came in and gently moved the brothers and their wives, including Ally, away from the sides of Bud's bed.

"Let me check out James, please." The nurse took his pulse and checked his IV. She then poured a small amount of water into a plastic cup, added a straw and offered Bud a drink. Somewhat clumsily, he attempted to get his lips around the straw before he could finally take a sip.

"How are you feeling, James?" The nurse asked as she raised his bed a few degrees.

Bud nodded his head slightly and took another sip of the water she had offered him. After checking on a couple of machine readings which were in some way attached to him, the nurse asked how he was feeling again.

He slurred, "I guess — I'm okay."

"That is good to hear. I will be back in a few minutes to check on you again with a warm muffin. Would you like orange or apple juice to drink?"

"Orange — no — apple, no — orange."

With a wide smile, she turned to leave and said, "I'll bring you both."

His head still hazy, Bud made several attempts to ask about Percy. Where was she? How was she? When could he see her?

Donato and Camilla told him she was okay and had been waiting the whole time right along with them, while he was in surgery and recovery; however, the investigator had just come in and taken her into another room for a few more questions — right before they were all allowed into his recovery room.

Mumbling something inaudible at first and then saying something about a pain in his butt, Ally and Donato looked at each other with the same questioning expression on their faces. Was he referring to the actual pain in his butt he must be feeling? Or, was he referring to Percy? Knowing of their more than tenuous relationship, it was a question neither Ally nor Donato could easily have answered.

After several days of being closely monitored and recuperating in the hospital, Bud was told he would be released. He could continue his recovery at home, as long as he agreed to follow the doctor's orders and continue with his physical therapy; of which, he had started while he was still in the hospital. He wanted out of the hospital so bad, he would have agreed to just about anything. Even with members of his family bringing him home cooked meals every day, the seven days he was in the hospital had taken their toll on him — along with several members of the hospital staff.

Dr. Marksdale was not as fortunate. His overall condition — his brain swelling and an infection he contracted — left him laid up for an additional six weeks. He was put into an induced coma, so he was not aware of the many times his group members had come to see him and were seeking to know how he was progressing with his recovery.

On different occasions, Dr. Marksdale's feelings towards the group were ambiguous, and although he at times may not have felt fondly towards them, they had nothing but good feelings towards him. This is something Stelle had observed on their trip to Park City, but during the course of her husband's hospital stay, it was crystal clear how much they had cared for her husband. Having been through a myriad of emotional upheavals — more than she had ever experienced in her life — she had also had her mettle, so to speak, tested to its maximum strength. Through all of it, she found herself honestly feeling grateful for the group's attentiveness and sincere concern for her husband. This was something, she could say, she did not feel towards any of her or her husband's friends.

Their "friends" and fellow associates who shared the same professional field as they did made their initial calls and expressed concern in the beginning. Their attention to his condition, or hers, waned sharply — becoming non-existent over the many weeks of his hospitalization — something of which Stelle was keenly aware.

In good time, the investigation into the shooting and the shooter was completed — except for the questioning of Dr. Marksdale, and that was dependent upon his questionable recovery.

For all intents and purposes, Dr. Elan Glenn was believed to have somehow lost his mind due to any number of possible contributors — none of which had anything to do with Dr. Marksdale. It was assumed at some point during the investigation, Dr. Elan Glenn may have had a self-induced rivalry towards Dr. Marksdale, as the latter had done so well with his career. Even when the truth came out from the letters Dr. Marksdale had sent to both Leon Fisker's parents and his university's president, by his admitting his involvement in decades-old crimes, his letter to Dr. Elan Glenn revealed nothing but a strong friendship. In fact, his letter to Dr. Glenn thanked him for the encouragement to come clean about the earlier incidents. Nothing untoward could be derived from Dr. Marksdale's letter to Dr. Elan Glenn.

Once he had lost control of his faculties and forced his way into the courthouse, no one knew the existence or the extent of Dr. Elan Glenn's fragile mental state.

If and until Dr. Marksdale could be interviewed, it was presumed Dr. Elan Glenn's obsession with him was for reasons only he knew of, and those he took with him to his grave. They would remain a puzzling mystery resulting in a tragic ending — and Stelle had it in her mind to keep it that way.

The doctor's slow recovery was a challenge which weighed heavily on his wife. Whenever she was faced with anything of any consequence, she had Dr Marksdale to lean on to help her through it. Feeling the biggest challenge of her life was foist upon her as her life's partner lay unconscious with no guarantee of his waking up — and if he did, how much of who he once was would be left — Stelle felt an aloneness she had never known.

Her mother helped with the children, which was a blessing, as she spent almost all of her time at her husband's bedside. But it was the group members visiting at least once, sometimes twice, everyday to see how both of the Marksdale doctors were doing which fed her hope. And it was not just hope that she was fed.

Everyday Camilla came with a plate of food for Stelle along with some tidbit of old-world wisdom which she would pass on to her. For Camilla, the act of Christian kindness was at first a little difficult to extend. After all, she knew it was Stelle who, in Camilla's opinion, had almost blinded her eldest son; additionally, it was fortunate for Stelle that Camilla's strong faith (which taught her to forgive) won out over her urge to bat the woman about with a rolling pin.

All of these charitable actions combined helped Stelle to know she was capable of being the strength both she and her husband needed to get through. And as millions of women had done before her, Stelle met each new day with the hope and strength required of her.

There were some times alone when Stelle found herself staring at Dr. Marksdale in his hospital bed and observing the many hoses and tubes going in and out of him. It was on a few of those occasions, she would feel an overwhelming urge to just let go and smack her husband — and smack him hard — right up alongside his bandaged head.

"How could you do this to us?" She would ask her comatose husband. "Keeping those secrets all those years, you should have known we could fix it. We would have done it — together."

Then she would cringe at her own inhumanity and tear up, because she understood how much she really did love the man who lay so helpless and, at that point, incapable of performing even the simplest of functions.

Sitting by her husband's bedside for all of those weeks, Estelle Cummings Marksdale found humility. Something — even if she were to use all of her money — she could not buy.

✭✭✭✭✭

"We don't know how he will respond; and, we need you to understand, he may not know who you are at first. Please have patience." Her husband's doctors were gentle with Stelle while, at the same time, they wanted her to know what to — and what not to — expect.

The day had finally arrived which, along with everyone else, Stelle had longed for. Dr. Marksdale's condition had improved. The bone flap which had been removed to relieve the swelling of his brain had been fitted back into its rightful place in Dr. Marksdale's skull. All indications of any infection were gone. His craniectomy had been a success, and those physicians attending to his treatment felt it was safe to slowly bring him out of his coma.

Moments after arriving at Dr. Marksdale's room, Ally and Mrs. Fins were asked to wait outside in the hall, as they were in the process of bringing the doctor back into consciousness. Trading in her six-inch heals for the more sedate and comfortable, brightly colored running shoes she now adorned her feet with, Ally began pacing nervously. While she typed out a group text to all of the members of the group, Mrs. Fins waited for Dill to answer his phone.

"Yes, that is what his nurse said." Unable to sit still herself, Mrs. Fins spoke quickly but softly to Dill who was shooting off one question after another on the other end of the phone.

"I will, yes. Oh yes, Mr. Bigley, I would like that very much." Mrs. Fins hung up just as Ally completed sending her group text, and immediately, Ally's phone was sounding off indicating she was receiving responses to her notification.

The door to the doctor's room stayed closed for an interminable period of time until, finally, one of the nurses came out and quickly headed down the hall and out of Mrs. Fins' and Ally's sight. Both women looked at each other with surprised expressions but neither said anything.

Members of the group, as well as Donato and Camilla, began arriving at the hospital in response to Ally's text message. Together, they waited in the hall outside of Dr. Marksdale's room. Donato brought four chairs from the waiting room just down the hall, and after being sure to seat Camilla in the first one, he offered one to each of the women left standing.

Emma thanked him and said she would prefer to stand as did Ally and Mrs. Fins. Like everyone else, Emma's idea to stand evolved into more of an exercise in pacing. The only two members of the group who had not arrived yet were Percy and Bud.

Due to the extensive deep tissue and muscle damage Bud had sustained in his right leg and right buttocks, he faced one setback after another. He would have liked to have been at the hospital with the rest of the group, but his recovery was slow. He was not yet able to ride in a car for very long nor could he stand or sit for any length of time, so it would take both himself and Percy longer to get there.

Although he had agreed to continue outpatient treatment in the form of physical therapy, he had not kept up to his end of the agreement — certainly not to the degree his attending physician would have favored. It became apparent Bud was very close to being incapable of sitting for any length of time which rendered him unable to meet the majority of his appointments. It was assumed it was for this reason, he was granted in-home sessions with a physical therapist. At the time, that seemed to be the best solution for everyone.

A somewhat predictable situation arose a couple of weeks into the home treatments which, interestingly, led to Percy becoming Bud's main source of physical therapy — outside of the actual physical therapist's office. It was to her favor, Percy found herself in the midst of this strange arrangement quite innocently.

The therapist assigned to Bud's in-home therapy and Bud had a difference of opinion regarding his treatment. The therapist insisted he cooperate the best he could with all of her exercise routines, including those she wanted him to perform on his own — three times a day — with Bud insisting, he not.

A loud altercation ensued between Bud and the therapist. The end result was the therapist escaping Bud's room with a barrage of shoes and several throw pillows (ironically, living up to their name) whizzing by her head in rapid succession.

The ruckus could be heard all the way down into the restaurant's kitchen, where Percy had become a regular fixture helping Camilla out by taking on most of Bud's responsibilities. The two women had become fast friends, and Percy truly enjoyed the work. Although she had not taken the steps, Percy considered leasing her truck out to, or maybe hiring, someone to take over her route. These were thoughts she had toyed with before but had never found anything more to her liking. By all appearances, at that point, she had.

Camilla seemed to take it all in stride. She asked the therapist, as she ran past her, if she would like to stay for something to eat. The therapist did not reply. Instead, she kept running through the kitchen — making her escape out into the parking lot and to her car. Within a few seconds, the screeching of tires could be heard, and the odor of burning rubber wafted into the kitchen where both women still stood.

Percy ventured, "Do ya think I should go to see how he is?"

"Hmmm — I don't know. Maybe we should give him a minute to cool down." Camilla headed back to the stove.

"No, he doesn't get to do that. He needs to get better, and we gotta stop cuttin' him slack where he doesn't deserve it." Percy sounded assured.

"Well dear, if you think that's best." Camilla turned to a pot on the stove and began to slowly stir its bubbling contents.

Percy took in a deep breath and turned around heading towards the stairs to Bud's apartment above the restaurant. As she made her way up the stairs picking up shoes and pillows along the way, she thought to herself, "He's a grown ass man! It's time he starts actin' like one!"

Camilla looked up to the ceiling; maybe, she was thinking of James, or maybe she was thinking of someone higher up. Either way, she seemed very much at ease, even calm.

If she knew anything, she knew her James, and she knew love when she saw it too. She chuckled quietly to herself, because it tickled her what she and others had come to see as clear as day, her son and Percy worked overtime to hide — from each other and from themselves.

A child-like smile came across Camilla's face as she continued to stir the pot. Calling out over her shoulder and loud enough for Percy to hear, Camilla offered, "You may want to lock the door behind you."

Percy was reaching for the doorknob to Bud's apartment when she heard Camilla's voice, and she was pretty sure she heard what Camilla had said was correct. If she had understood Camilla, Percy questioned, "Why would she suggest such a thing?"

After realizing Bud's door was slightly ajar, Percy gently pushed it open and found herself having to duck in her attempt to avoid being hit by the airborne, rolled-up newspaper which flew past her head.

"Whoa! Hey — whadda ya think you're doin'?"

"Sorry, didn't know it was you. Thought it might be that KGB agent. She's tryin' to kill me, ya know!" Bud looked relieved to see it was Percy and not the physical therapist he had abruptly forced into exile only minutes earlier.

Percy, standing with a shoe and two pillows in her arms, took a long look at Bud's face and finally said, "James, your expression looks like you're a man baby that's tryin' to poop."

"Hey what's that supposed to mean?" Bud sounded wounded.

"Your face," Percy continued while she put the pillows back on the couch and picked up a few other items she believed he had used, or was planning to use, as projectiles in his warfare against his unsuspecting therapist.

"Your face, it's all scrunched up. It makes you look like a baby trying to poop. And, what is your deal with the poor PT anyway?"

"She's not poor! She's horrible. She bends me this way and that and isn't happy until I'm in agony." Percy could not help but notice Bud started to look more pathetic by the second.

"How bad could it be, James? I know ya got bad injuries, but we gotta get ya better so you can get your life back. You want your life back, right?"

Percy picked up the stapled copies of exercise routines the therapist had left on the coffee table — the exercises Bud was supposed to have been doing on his own. Then she gently pushed his feet over a few inches, so she could sit on the edge of the couch where Bud was laying.

Thumbing through the pages she stopped at one exercise and asked, "What about this one? Have ya done this one yet?" Percy held the page up so Bud could better see the picture of a stick figure performing a leg stretch.

"I dunno." Bud looked away from both Percy and the picture. "I don't think I'm gonna get better." Percy's eyes followed Bud's as he looked over at a cane which was hung over a highbacked wooden chair a few feet away.

"I'll be like an old man and have to use that thing forever."

Percy knew what depression looked like. She had seen it many times over the years, on rare occasions, in her own mirror. For Percy, letting Bud disappear into the dark shadows of which depression invited its guests to live within was not an option.

"I'm gonna help you. C'mon, let's do a few of these exercises. We can start on page one and do a few every day. I'll do 'em with you."

"Why do you care? Really — why? Is good ol' Benny out ah the picture now?" Bud's question stung, but Percy pushed past it.

"He was never in the picture." She stood up and reached for both of Bud's hands with hers. "C'mon take my hands."

"Why wouldn't ya want to be with him, he sure wants to be with you." Bud took Percy's hands and started to pull himself up to a partial sitting position.

"Because" was Percy's only response to Bud's inquiry.

"Because why?" Bud continued his taunt. "He's got the use of both of his legs and can't take his eyes off ah yours!"

"Oh Jesus — James! I can't do this anymore. If you have to know why I'm not with him — or any other man — it's because they're not you!"

Percy angrily pulled her hands out of Buds, and she sat down so hard her butt sank into the couch causing her knees to go higher than her head giving her petite frame the appearance, it was being devoured by hungry couch cushions. Promptly, she pulled herself up into a straight-backed sitting position. Shaking her head and rolling her eyes she blurted out, "Damn it, James! Are ya happy now?"

While trying to right himself into a sitting position, he could not hide the wide smile which began to overtake the grimaced expression on his face caused by his uncomfortable sitting position.

"Yeah." Bud swallowed hard at which time he realized he had little if any spit.

"Yeah — I'm happy now."

With her eyes squinted, Percy turned to see Bud had a full smile on his face, but what caught her more by surprise was the glint in his eyes. It made them appear they were smiling, too.

At first, Bud started to move closer to Percy, and then she, without thought or reservation, felt herself lean towards him. Together, they drew closer and closer, until their lips were gingerly and gently touching the other's.

A warm tingling sensation, starting where their lips met, began to radiate throughout their entire bodies. It encompassed them both from the top of their heads to the tips of their toes.

First, there was one gentle kiss. Then, there was a second — and then, another. The silence in the room was only broken by the beating of their pounding hearts. Percy gently placed her hands on the sides of Bud's face and pulled her face away from his.

"Wait, here," she whispered.

She got up from the couch and walked to the front door. Once she was there, she checked to be sure it was closed all the way, and then she turned the lock until she heard it click into place. After making her way back to the couch, she reached down to Bud and helped him up into a standing position.

The only light coming into the room was through a large, partially opened window causing the chiffon shears to lazily flow with the breeze. The window perfectly framed their silhouettes as their lips touched, and their bodies slowly and tenderly swayed in the other's engulfing embrace.

Between kisses, Bud softly asked, "What about exercising?"

Percy took his hand and slowly began to lead Bud to the bedroom. "It's about time we start our own exercise routine."

Bud hobbled slowly and through his broad smile whispered to Percy, "You sound just like a man!"

Percy started laughing softly and tenderly cupped her hand on Bud's wounded butt cheek.

"I'll be gentle," she cooed, as she closed and locked the bedroom door, too, behind them.

CHAPTER TWENTY-TWO

If the circumstances surrounding the group having reached the one-year anniversary their sessions had begun with Dr. Marksdale were normal, they likely would be in a celebratory mood. Unfortunately, their circumstances were nowhere near "normal." Instead, they were faced with marking the occasion with Dr. Marksdale still lying unconscious in his hospital bed, and Bud barely able to walk was haunted by the constant trepidation he may never have proper use of his leg again.

The day was upon them after weeks of everyone pensively waiting. His doctors were hopeful but remained reserved as to what they believed Dr. Marksdale's mental and physical condition, and ultimately how his recovery, may be. Regardless of any of their concerns, it was time for them to bring him out of his medically induced coma.

Bud and Percy had not yet arrived, but they had sent word they were on their way; and, once Dill Bigley had arrived, Mrs. Fins was noticeably calmer. As they all nervously waited in the hall just outside Dr. Marksdale's room to hear what his doctors believed his status to be, a similar thought ran through each of their minds.

There was no mistaking, no one in the group was immune to the trauma the shooting in Judge Glib's courtroom had on them. Some suffered nightmares, while others felt a constant uneasiness they had not experienced prior to the event. There were members of the group who experienced both and, of course, there were the physical injuries both Dr. Marksdale and Bud had incurred. The group did acknowledge their talking to each other provided some comfort, even though they did not have Dr. Marksdale's steady and assured hand guiding them.

They were all in agreement: Even though some members did not believe they needed therapy to start with, Dr. Marksdale had helped each of them in some way to ultimately improve their lives. Being in total agreement Dr. Marksdale had been an exemplary doctor to them was quite a statement, for the members of the group rarely agreed with each other about anything.

Reflecting on the shooting, each member of the group had to ask himself or herself how such an event would affect their life afterwards. One would assume there would have to be a psychological scar of some sort from such an event. Yet, on the outside, no one in the group showed any sign of life-altering trauma other than Dr. Marksdale and Bud. One was left with a bullet in his head, and the other was left with the real life consequences of having been shot in the butt. As for everyone else, the aftermath of the horrendous experience may have been easier for some to compartmentalize than for others. There was always the possibility the effects may lie hidden — perhaps even dormant — awaiting the exact moment to reveal themselves.

Dr. Marksdale would rely upon this theory if he were to be treating a patient with the same set of circumstances in his earlier and more cynical days. Convincing his patient this theory should be considered a real possibility would be a priority for him. Privately, he would consider the possibility, whether real or conjured up, regarding "job security."

Mrs. Fins, although terribly nervous and concerned about both the doctor and Bud's recoveries, had become even closer to Dill. The fact of the matter is their relationship had begun to grow while they were in Park City. Over time, their friendship only grew deeper, and they found themselves spending an exceptional amount of time in each other's company. This was to the absolute delight of Dill Bigley — as one may imagine.

Then there was Emma. She had cast any restrictive confines of accepted or expected protocols aside and went on a wild search to find a man she had only met once. She believed the two of them were star-crossed lovers and meant to be together. While this was taking place, unbeknownst to herself, her daughter, granddaughter and other members of her therapy group followed her. Fortunately for Emma, it worked out just as she had imagined it would — a most rare and unique occurrence.

The likelihood the two people least likely to end up together — which actually happened — was quite an unexpected development. For the better part of the year, the sharp-tongued, barbed insults each directed with such antagonistic precision towards one another had turned into a briefly budding courtship; and then, precipitously, they found themselves engulfed in full blossom *amoré*.

After acknowledging neither one had ever engaged in such a passionate encounter before — while languishing between the sheets and snuggled in each-other's arms — Percy and Bud surmised their relationship had started where most relationships ended. For them, there was no way but up from there.

It just so happens, from the day their loving relationship began to flourish, their open display of kind consideration and affection for one another may have been a bit much for some to observe. However, no one could say it was not a marked improvement over the revulsion induced by their insidious name calling. Indeed, Percy and Bud had not fared so well together as nemeses, but James and Percy were perfectly suited as lovers.

Emma stopped her pacing long enough to address Camilla who, she noticed, was sitting patiently and quietly in her chair.

"Bud seems to be getting better. I guess his therapy is working?"

"Yes, it is coming along. He started improving when Percy took over helping him with it," Camilla answered Emma while keeping her smile hidden. She knew Percy had her son exercising as he should be, and it was helping to heal his physical wounds. Her smile came from knowing James and Percy were helping one another to heal their long overdue, untreated heart wounds, too.

Camilla added, "Love is God's miraculous elixir."

"Oh yes, Percy and Bud — some would think it wouldn't work. I'd have to disagree." Emma said with a light chuckle, "I think they're perfect for each other — such passionate souls."

Emma continued as if in deep thought, "If not for being in this group, I'd probably never have looked for Jack, and we wouldn't be together." A soft smile started to form on Emma's lips.

"But I was — and I did — and now we are," her smile broadening as Emma sat down on the empty chair next to Camilla.

"We've all come so far from that day — a year ago now — I think." Emma tilted her head while calculating the many months of therapy and the several weeks since the group's sessions had ended.

Emma continued putting words to her inner thoughts, "Time's gone by fast and so much has happened, it feels like it should've been longer."

She turned to look at Camilla who remained quiet and still.

"And so very much has happened in your life too — two sons in love — how wonderful."

Camilla's ears perked up.

"Yes, I am pleased, quite pleased." Camilla looked at Emma and then looked at Ally and Donato who were leaning against the hospital's hallway wall.

Camilla looked back at Emma, "It was because the group went looking for you that my Donato met her." Camilla's eyes moved from Emma's to Ally, who was leaning her head against Donato's chest, as he had wrapped his arms around her.

"Funny thing to think, if Bud had not jumped on top of Dill, we would never be where we are right now — none of us." Emma's voice had taken on a serious tenor, "I mean it. We, Jack and me, would never have ended up together and . . . ." Emma's voice trailed off until it was inaudible, as Dr. Marksdale's hospital room door opened.

Mrs. Fins noticed the door opening right after Emma had, and she quickly put her hand over the top of Dill's and squeezed it tightly.

"Oh my, Mr. Bigley." Her eyes met his, and Dill could see clearly the fear in them.

He turned his hand over and firmly engulfed hers, pulling it close to his chest and said in an unassuming voice, doing his level best to assure her everything was going to be alright.

"He's going to be okay. Even if at first it may be difficult, he will prevail."

Mrs. Fins exhaled and noticeably appeared to relax due to Dill's encouragement.

"Oh, Mr. Bigley, thank you. I don't know what I would have done without you for all these weeks. You have been a godsend." Mrs. Fins had no idea how much her words meant to Dill. Nor did she know he would have been completely satisfied if all she had said to him was, "Hey you!"

Indeed, his desires went deeper than what he was willing to reveal, but Dillard Bigley was, as often as has been noted, a gentleman. For him, from the first day he had laid eyes on her, just being in Mrs. Fins' presence was all the satisfaction he would ever require. The time they had spent together — in particular, since their trip to Park City — had been, by far, the happiest days of his life. Now, together, hand in hand, they would face the truth of Dr. Marksdale's diagnosis.

Two doctors came out of Dr. Marksdale's room, and while speaking softly to each other, they headed away from those waiting and towards the nurse's station. All heads turned towards the others as they looked back and forth between each other — everyone hoping someone would say something to relieve all of their building angst and anticipation.

The presence of a pregnant pause spawned by the awkward silence created an oppressive atmosphere. Not until the sound of the rubber tip of a walking cane making contact with the highly polished hospital floor was heard — immediately followed by the distinct sound of shuffling feet — did the tension in the hallway finally break. Bud and Percy were slowly making their way to where everyone else waited, and just as they made it to the group, Stelle came out of the doctor's room — visibly shaken.

Immediately, both Mrs. Fins and Dill went to her side. They each took one of Stelle's arms and helped her to the closest chair.

"Mrs. Marksdale, please sit down." Dill kept a hold of her arm until she was seated.

"Is there anything that I can do for you?" His voice was gentle and sincere, "Please Mrs. Marksdale, let me be of service to you."

"Thank you, Dill," Stelle began, her voice breaking and sounding weak. Every ear in the hallway was tuned into her every word. No one moved a muscle while they stood staring blankly as if they were mannequins — absent of all life.

"I've lost him — my Phillip's gone."

An audible gasp was heard coming from everyone, while at the same time, all of their faces seemed to lose color as though the blood had drained out of them.

Ally shouted out — "No!" While her knees buckled beneath her, Donato grabbed a hold of her preventing her from falling to the floor.

Mrs. Fins turned to Dill and threw her arms around his neck, and as he wrapped her securely in his arms, she broke down into a full-blown sob.

Within moments, there was not one dry eye in the group.

In a quiet voice Stelle said, "He doesn't know who I am."

A deafening momentary silence fell over everything, until Mrs. Fins shrieked, "What?" As she pulled away from the shelter of Dill's embrace.

"What did you say?"

Stelle continued, appearing like she was in a daze.

"He doesn't know me. I looked right at him, and it was like he looked right through me."

Everyone was rapidly blinking their eyes in hoping it would help them better understand what had just transpired. Their teary eyes darted around looking at the others and saw the same shock and confusion on each other's faces. Adding to that mix was the anxiety of whether they should feel relief or not over what they all thought they had just heard.

"You mean he's not dead?" Mrs. Fins seemed to need authentication of some sort from Stelle, before she could adjust her mind from the boomerang effect it had just experienced.

"Yes."

"What? Yes? Yes — he's dead or yes — he's not!" No one had ever heard Mrs. Fins voice so loud or shaky before — not even in the early days of their therapy, when she had to take the group to task on more than a few occasions.

"Yes — he's not dead!" Stelle looked directly at Mrs. Fins, and in an almost child-like voice she said, "But Marlene, he doesn't know who I am!"

"I have to sit down; I think I'm going to be sick." Dill guided Mrs. Fins to the chair next to Stelle who was sitting directly next to Camilla. He then began to rapidly wave his hand in front of Mrs. Fins' face, as though cooling her down would help her to stop feeling ill. Grabbing his wrist with a strength unexpected from such a small hand, Mrs. Fins' intentions were for him to cease what he was doing — Dill had no doubt. He immediately obliged her mute instruction. No one would expect anything less of him when it had anything to do with Mrs. Fins' wishes.

"That's great!" Bud wiped his eyes and blurted out. "That's freakin' great!"

Stelle whipped her head around towards where Bud stood.

"Great? Great that he doesn't remember me?"

Bud's face looked perplexed.

"No, that he's alive! It's great the doc's alive! And he'll figure out who ya are pretty soon. He's been in a comma for ah couple ah months ya know." He looked around at everyone else who still looked like deer caught in headlights and offered, "Sometimes I sleep so deep, it takes me a few minutes to figure out who I am!"

Percy could not hold back her smile, but she instinctively knew it would be best if Bud were to keep his thoughts to himself. So, she stood on her toes and kissed his lips. It was a quick, soft kiss, and for a brief second, it kept him from talking. The temporary quiet was just long enough for his mother, Camilla, to start speaking.

"This is wonderful news. Your husband is awake and trying to get his bearings. What did his doctors have to say?"

"They said that he will need some time. But I, well, I —" Before Stelle could finish, Camilla took her hand and held it warmly in hers.

"If it is time he needs, he shall have it. Seeing you and the rest of his family should help him to come back to you."

Stelle started to smile. "Oh, Camilla, you're so kind —" Stelle looked around at all the faces looking at her and continued, "You've all been kind — so kind to me. I don't think I would have been able to do this without you."

Everyone felt relief they had never felt before, and once they had their wits about them, each offered Stelle some kind words of encouragement. One by one — some in twos — they went into Dr. Marksdale's room for a very brief visit. Stelle thought it would be a good idea, because maybe Bud was right. Her husband may take a while to "wake up," and when she shared her gratefulness with him for suggesting the possibility, Percy thought proudly to herself, "That's my James."

"Oh my — my," as Mrs. Fins was used to saying — how far they had each come from that first meeting in Dr. Marksdale's office on that windy Wednesday just over a year earlier. The group members believed it was Dr. Marksdale who had brought them to the pinnacle they had found themselves at, and all were grateful to a deep degree and felt indebtedness to him.

Stelle was drained and elated at the same time and was happy to have the group with her at that point in time. Unlike her and her husband's supposed friends, the members of the group along with Mrs. Fins, Donato and Camilla waited with her during all those weeks of ups and downs. Stelle felt they each deserved to see him, too. The possibility existed, maybe seeing one or all of them would spark a memory in her husband. Stelle was desperate for something to help bring him back into the light from the dark.

Each one of them spent a short period of time with the doctor, but it was Emma who came out of his room with the biggest smile; she, for some unexplained reason, was the one the doctor remembered first. When she entered his room and slowly approached the side of his bed, Dr. Marksdale looked up at her and immediately said, "Hello, Emma."

There was no rhyme or reason for his memory to be sparked by her face more so than anyone else's, but like the first time he had met her, there was something about her which made him feel comfortable in her presence. The doctor could not explain it then, and he was not in any condition to try at that point in time. It did not matter to anyone, least of all to Stelle, the reason behind it — it had happened — the doctor knew Emma. Stelle was even more eager to get back into her husband's room.

Once there, she realized he had indeed regained some of his memory, but he was far from the man she knew him to be.

"Time," she thought, "Just like his doctors told me." It would take time, too, but at least Stelle knew, she could finally take him home; and, that is what she did. Phillip Marksdale's children and both his and Stelle's parents surrounded him. If he ever doubted he was loved, the outpouring from his family of raw emotion and gratitude — he had survived his treacherous ordeal — would put an end to that.

Dr. Marksdale's recovery would indeed take time. Stelle found herself reflecting often on something Camilla had whispered to her, as she left the Marksdale's estate after one of her many visits.

"Time — will be your friend." Camilla had said, "It won't take more than it needs."

Stelle began to understand what she meant, for she helped her husband to re-learn most of the simple things we all take for granted. The injury to his brain was more severe than what the doctors first presumed it had been. But, Stelle proved to be an exemplary aid in his recovery just as Percy was to her James. Both women's patience and love kept them by the side of the men they loved through both the difficult and more difficult of times.

When it became clear to Stelle what the extent and resulting ramifications the injuries would have on her husband, she gave Mrs. Fins the okay to begin the process of referring both of their patients to other therapists in the area. In addition, she gave Mrs. Fins full rein over settling any financial obligations for each of their practices.

The day eventually came when Mrs. Fins had fulfilled the requirements needed to complete the tasks handed to her. She packed the last of the doctors' personal items, and the movers had just left with the furniture Stelle had decorated the office with. Mrs. Fins stood in front of the expansive windows and observed the extraordinary view she had become so familiar with.

By that time, it had been over a decade she had enjoyed the view, and it never ceased to amaze her. She had watched the sky change along with the seasons and had embraced the view out of those same windows while watching storms developing over the Olympics, as they surged up and over the extraordinary office building she had come to think of as her home away from home.

Mrs. Fins felt a pang she had always believed she would feel, when the time came for her to end her days as the doctor's receptionist; regardless, the pang was more intense than she had expected. Only she understood how close she felt towards the Marksdales.

They were young enough to be her own children, and she had always felt a motherly instinct to protect them both. With all that had happened in the recent past, Mrs. Fins felt a sadness and regret, she was incapable of doing just that.

"Had I only known what an evil man —" She began to say out loud, "A horrible evil man that Dr. Glenn was, I would have . . . ." Her words were cut short, when she saw the reflection of Dill Bigley in the window coming into the room.

"You would have done what?" Dill questioned her after having overheard what she had said in what Mrs. Fins had come to know, and rely on, as his comforting voice.

Mrs. Fins turned to face Dill, and then she turned back around and continued, while looking out of the window, "I'd like to think I would have at least tried to intervene in some way."

Dill stopped and stood next to her. He looked out of the window and said, "I know we all would have liked to have been able to do something." He looked down at the floor in front of him and then back out of the window. Mrs. Fins glanced in his direction and nodded her head slightly in agreement. For a few moments longer, neither of them said a word. They just stood perfectly still, taking in the view together.

"You know," Dill's voice broke the silence, "I remember thinking that this glorious view was only second to one other." Dill swallowed and took in a deep breath.

"I looked forward to seeing both for every one of our sessions."

Mrs. Fins was no one's fool. She knew she was not mistaken in her assumption her Mr. Bigley was as interested in her as she was in him. It was that, in her estimation, she had waited — what was approaching an unbearable length of time — for him to cross the barrier they both had kept in place for far too long. That barrier, in Mrs. Fins mind, had kept their relationship a platonic one.

Mrs. Fins was growing increasingly more desperate the barrier not pose as an obstacle preventing their relationship from growing. In fact, as more time passed and Dill had not made any advances towards her — nor did he even hint at any such behavior — Mrs. Fins found herself contemplating hurling herself over what she had come to scream about in her own mind as "that damned barrier!" But always, reluctantly, she had stopped herself.

"So, Mr. Bigley, what was this other 'glorious' view of which you speak?"

Dill took in another deep breath, and with a shaky voice, he let out, "You, Mrs. Fins. You were — are — the other —"

He turned to look at Mrs. Fins, his face turning crimson, as his palms began to sweat.

"You are the most beautiful and captivating woman I have ever known."

With that, Dill started to stammer slightly when he said, "Please forgive me for being so forward, Mrs. Fins."

"Oh my, Mr. Bigley. I cannot tell you how long I have waited to hear words like that from you!" Mrs. Fins' face was lit up with pure happiness, and her smile and words nearly melted Dill in his shoes.

"Hey! Mrs. Marksdale said we'd find ya here."

The unexpected voice coming from the office doorway caused both Dill and Mrs. Fins to jump and turn around.

Percy and Bud started to come into the furniture bare office.

"We figured with such short notice, it'd be better to just ask in person," Percy started.

Bud interrupted, "Yeah, Donato and Ally wanted to invite ya two, to their weddin'."

"Oh my!" Mrs. Fins' face still lit up only added to her radiant smile.

"How wonderful! Of course we —" She looked at Dill's face and saw his wide smile and continued, "Of course, we would love to attend. How wonderful! When?"

While walking towards the window, Bud and Percy said at the same time, "Saturday."

Dill and Mrs. Fins looked at each other with questioning expressions on their faces.

"Which Saturday?" Dill proceeded. "What is the actual date?"

Neither Bud nor Percy turned around but kept admiring the view. "I sure love this view." Percy spoke first.

While staring at Percy, Bud said, "So do I."

Percy realized he was referring to looking at her which made her eyelashes flutter. She shook her head and continued to address Dill and Mrs. Fins as though she did not hear Bud's comment.

"Yes, it's this Saturday, three days away. Everyone in the group will be there, and the doc too."

"Really? Dr. Marksdale will be there too?" Mrs. Fins asked.

"Yep," Bud replied while walking with a pronounced limp — even with assistance from his cane — up to the window where he pressed his face against it.

"And Mrs. Marksdale — she said it would be his first real outing, and said he was all excited about it," Percy added, also getting closer to the window.

"I sure will miss this view," Percy continued, "I loved this the most about this place."

Bud looked over at her with a frown, and she rolled her eyes. He could not help but chuckle, as he remembered when Percy would get quite upset with Ally for doing the same thing with her eyes.

"Well? Whadda ya say? It'll be at our restaurant in our backyard." Bud turned around towards Dill and Mrs. Fins. "It's really big, it has to be for our family; and of course, the food is there!"

Dill smiled at Mrs. Fins, his eyes never diverting away from hers, and said, "We would be delighted to attend."

Mrs. Fins gasped, "I must get to shopping! Will it be formal attire?"

Bud scoffed, "Nah, it's just a backyard weddin' — nothin' fancy."

Percy added with a laugh, "We're still in our four weeks of summer, so be sure to wear a summer dress."

"Oh my, yes. I know exactly what I'll wear." Mrs. Fins was excited — bordering on giddy — which noticeably tickled Dill.

The four of them made reference to how the "kids" (as they came to refer to Ally and Donato) wanted the day to be filled with friends and family. They were like two little cooing doves nuzzling each other while holding on to a branch together.

Pulling back to see and listen to all four of them (Dill, Mrs. Fins, Bud and Percy) giggling while standing at the window with their backs facing the otherwise empty room — all of them pointing to and talking about what they saw within their view — would give one the impression the "kids" may not be the only love birds in the tree.

CHAPTER TWENTY-THREE

In addition to their lucrative practices, and more so, with their extremely wealthy patients paying their bills, the Marksdale doctors both had been born into very well-to-do families, thus compounding their wealth. By itself, the latter opened opportunities and made possible a lifestyle few will ever know. Their lives may be considered by some to be likened to living a fairy tale of sorts. However, let it be said that even exorbitant privilege does not guarantee total absolution from consequence. And, too, let it be said — fairy tales often have hideous creatures wielding evil wizardry, and not every fairy tale meets with a happy ending.

The bullet lodged in Dr. Marksdale's brain would present life-altering and life-lasting ramifications. The resulting brain injury caused him to lose some of what otherwise would have been his normal faculties. These facts, however, did not expunge him of guilt or responsibility for prior actions or, in his case, a lack of action — when his revelation of the truth was called for — all of those years ago.

The letters Dr. Marksdale had sent to his university's president and to Leon Fisker's parents revealed he was present during, and had complete knowledge of, the events which led up to Leon's death. Although his letter named the responsible parties, he had become complicit in the cover-up, because he had held back the truth and chose the path of silence.

Both the doctor and Leon Fisker were barely past their eighteenth birthdays when the hazing event took place, but they were still of legal age. Most damning for the doctor was his having held back the truth for over two decades. His alarming confession put him in serious jeopardy, as it revealed he had direct knowledge of a crime which could have easily fallen under one of the degrees of manslaughter.

Still in a coma at the time the issues came to bear, Dr. Marksdale was relieved of having to deal with any of the initial repercussions his confessional letter-writing spree had created. One could argue that the direct result of one of those letters he had written had instigated the actions of the deranged Elan Glenn — which resulted in a bullet taking up permanent residence in Dr. Marksdale's brain. Thus, it could be construed the good doctor was not really being relieved of anything. Even so, someone would have to address the resulting aftermath of the truth his letters revealed, and that someone would turn out to be his wife, Stelle. She was the one left to deal with the whole messy calamity; consequently, she did so with staunch dignity, proving she was up to the task.

Being a psychiatrist herself, Stelle was adept at behavioral indicators and knew the investigators were keenly observing her every word and move. She drew upon all that she knew during the investigation to handsomely convince the investigators, at no time was she in any way privy to any of the information surrounding the hazing. After hours of questioning, the investigators reached the same conclusion Stelle had intended them to reach. With the remaining outpouring of legalese presented to her, she called upon her and her husband's personal attorney to handle all of the details.

Within the three letters he had written, Dr. Marksdale had laid out all of which had happened — at least, that was the impression he wanted to make. Truth be told, he had not been totally forthcoming. He omitted his role in changing the other students' grades and introduced only the matter of hazing and Leon Fisker's ultimate death (at the hands of the named individuals in the fraternity).

Whatever Dr. Marksdale had assumed he would face, as a consequence for his involvement in the hazing, would remain a mystery. By all appearances, he was no longer capable of processing the question about his reasoning behind his confession all of those years later — let alone, conjuring up an answer.

Once Dr. Marksdale had regained consciousness and it was revealed he no longer possessed the cognitive reasoning capability which would be required for testifying — to either condemn others or to defend himself — the university board decided not to proceed with any litigation involving him. An expedient out-of-court settlement was reached to pay compensation to Leon Fisker's parents. The university agreed to pay an exceptional price to keep the whole unfortunate episode quiet. A part of the settlement was dependent upon everyone involved never speaking of the whole ordeal — ever again.

As for the Fiskers' position in regards to Dr. Marksdale, they had a completely different take on the doctor's not coming forward when he should have, and they filed a civil suit against him for quite a sizable amount of money. Their attorney argued Dr. Marksdale had revealed the truth prior to Dr. Glenn's scrambling of his brain. The case was made for, due to the timing of his revelation, Dr. Marksdale to be held legally liable regardless of his more recent mental incapacity. The Fiskers' argument was a strong one and brought the truth to bear: The guilty parties would have faced the consequences of their actions two decades earlier instead of having lived free of punishment for that duration. Their argument was a sound one. After all, the Fiskers' son had lost his life.

Dr. Marksdale's attorney used the fact that the medical condition Dr. Marksdale was faced with would no longer allow for his being able to fairly defend himself, and he asked the court to dismiss the case. Any attorney worth his legal fees would have done the same.

The judge hearing the arguments was not dissuaded by Dr. Marksdale's state of mind at the time of the hearing or by his attorney. In fact, he was adamant the Marksdales' estate be appraised for its worth. This was, as one can imagine, a very unnerving order. Stelle was barely holding on, with the situation being as it was, and this little bit of news from their attorney did not bode well for her.

Possessing monetary wealth can be intoxicating to its recipients, and extreme wealth often creates the same sensations an aphrodisiac would. The Marksdales had never known a life where true wanting was a reality — quite the contrary.

Because they had been born into privilege, neither Stelle nor her husband had the slightest concept of how inebriated they were — or of how the love affair they had with their money had affected them and the advantage it had provided them with. Their lavish lifestyle should have left them satisfied, but like alcoholics, their tolerance to "the drink" built up over the years leaving them craving for more. And, for the first time, it looked like their money would provide them with something they never had imagined they would have needed to buy — their freedom.

And so it came to be that Stelle, with a shaky hand, signed all the papers required and witnessed a very large sum of money transferred out of her possession. It was all done with swift precision.

Stelle knew she was capable of spending quite a lot of money in quite a hurry, but this expenditure had left even her breathless and with a sizeable dent in their portfolio. Still, the Marksdales would not starve nor would they end up having to live in one, of any number, of their many cars — regardless of the huge settlement Stelle had to fork out.

As was also true for the university, all of the business of settling with the Fiskers was resolved expeditiously and, for all concerned, kept quite hush-hush. Stelle finally felt a sense of relief knowing no one had anything they could hold over her, or her husband's head, anymore. It gave her a sense of new beginnings, and she decided it was time for just that.

Everyone in her immediate and extended family had begun to see better where to place their priorities, and all it took was for Dr. Marksdale to be shot in the head.

Now, that the process of the dissolution of their estate appeared to be left up to Stelle, she was going to make some major changes in her families' lives — to start with, the selling of their mansion and most everything it housed. They had no need for all the cars they owned, either — nor could she find any reason to stay in the Seattle area. After all that had transpired, it was only a matter of time before their inner circle would be swimming with gossip — gossip spread by people who could not have cared less about her or her husband as far as Stelle could see. She had no need to hear the whispers.

Both Stelle's and Dr. Marksdale's parents would be willing to pick up and move somewhere else too. She was sure of it, whereas the six of them had discussed it over the years after the children were born. And if that plan did not pan out, her in-laws and parents were more than capable of coming for extended visits to be with both of them as well as with their grandchildren.

Stelle remembered Phillip's dad joking that the world was filled with nuts. He half-jokingly assured both Stelle and his son, if that scenario did not change, neither she nor Phillip would ever have to worry about having a career.

"Job security, son!" Phillip's dad belted out, "Damned job security, I say!"

Although Stelle did not see her husband starting another practice as a therapist again, she was excited thinking about the prospect there could very well be a new beginning in store for the Marksdales.

"In fact," Stelle said out loud, "That's exactly what I've always wanted, a store — a women's boutique — high end, of course."

Stelle giggled and felt sheer delight. She had not felt so encouraged for longer than she could remember. Her idea sent chills all over her body.

"I do so want to share my ideas with Phillip, but when? I know, I'll tell him at the wedding. Yes — I'll tell him at the wedding!"

They say that when it is clear in the Seattle area, those who live there are reminded of why they live in western Washington: The crisp clarity and brilliance of the sky; the majestic mountains; the islands; the waterways; and, the wildlife — all breathe new life into the soul. It is likened to waking up over and over again into a new spring after a long winter. The day of Ally and Donato's wedding was one of those days.

Ally's birds were not the only ones singing melodiously in their beautiful and ample aviary Donato had built for them. All species of birds known to the area were joined in a brilliant euphony of song, and while bustling in the kitchen, Camilla joined the singing in her native Italian. Her operatic voice proved to be quite impressive.

Known for her remarkable talent for being able to put together a ten-course meal on a moment's notice, planning and pulling off a backyard wedding in three days for the youngest in her brood was as easy for Camilla as bringing water to a boil. Her youngest son's wedding day was something she had been looking forward to since the day he was born. Since Donato was in his twenties, bringing his wedding to a glorious fruition was something she had plenty of time to plan. What she did not take into account during all those years of planning was her soon to be daughter-in-law, Ally, would turn out to be as engaging, delightful and eager to pitch in as she was.

Ally's friends had lent a hand in the decorating as well, leaving the Jeffries' restaurant courtyard (what the Jeffries referred to as their backyard) looking like something out of a fairy tale in a magical land. Tiny white, lavender, blue and green lights festooned the aviary Donato had built with special attention given to the aviary's front doors, where the young love birds would exchange their vows. Rows of tiny white lights were intertwined within the branches of the budding trees which lined the patio area, and the gargantuan-sized opaque canopy which covered the patio had green, lavender and blue lights elegantly strung and crisscrossed back and forth across the entire width and length of it.

Each table had vases filled with bouquets of fresh cut flowers in a plethora of colors to compliment the different colored tablecloths on which they sat. The odors emitting from the kitchen mixed with those of the flowers could lend to the idea one had awakened into a fragrant heaven.

As the guests began to arrive, Ally, with the help from several of her girlfriends (some exhibiting an array of hair colors, piercings and tattoos), was nervously getting dressed in Bud's apartment above the restaurant.

One of Ally's friends squealed, "God girl, he's plain gorgeous. I can see why you're marryin' him!"

"No kiddin'," another one of her friends added. "Wow, he's like uptown compared to the low-rent guys we hang out with."

Ally's two friends giggled like silly school girls. Ally did not seem to mind their comments, although it was not clear whether or not she was paying them any mind. She and Percy were involved with getting the flower crown she was to wear in her hair situated in the exact, right place until, finally, Ally said, "That's it. It's perfect."

Percy stood back a few feet and looked at Ally. Tilting her head from side-to-side, Percy said wistfully, "Yes, that is perfect, and you — you are the most beautiful bride that . . . ." Her voice trailed off until no sound emanated from her. It took Ally to snap her attention back into the room.

"The most beautiful bride that what?"

Percy's mind had raced back to the beginning when they first met, and her mind flooded with memories spanning the length of time she had known Ally and all of the nonsense she felt she had to deal with in just knowing the girl. But in that moment, she knew her feelings would never go back to what they had been before. She had grown to admire Ally in some strange way.

Percy could not explain the evolution from her disdain for the high-heel wearing, two-eye colored, outlandishly dressed young thing she once knew into the sensitive and caring young woman who stood before her now.

"That I have ever seen," Percy swallowed. "You're the most beautiful bride I have ever seen."

✶✶✶✶✶

Not one member in the group had any inkling their personal path would intersect with the others. Nor, did any of them have the notion one day their appearance in traffic court (over a minor traffic infraction) would lead them to become innocent bystanders caught in the middle of a decades-old twisted plot — a plot which brewed in the mind of a mentally ill and vindictive man — a man who found himself hell-bent to torment an old nemesis.

No — none of the members of the group could have known how their lives would be forever changed due to their chance encounter with the other members on that day, in that courtroom, over a year before. Undoubtedly, no one in the group would hasten to venture a thought the once crass and obnoxious Bud, a.k.a. James Elliot Jeffries, and his ruffian act against Dillard Bigley (the hurling of the poor proper English gentleman over a chair) would lead to the chain of events which ensued — least of all, not James Elliot Jeffries himself. He was probably more surprised at how he had come around to enjoying (to some degree) Dill Bigley's company. More than likely, when it came to what Bud believed to be Dill's obsessive attraction to "Miss Prim," a.k.a. Mrs. Fins, he would not have predicted he would eventually stop taunting "English" but, to a great extent, he had done just that.

Someone had made Ally an offer she was, without hesitation, able to refuse. The drummer and want-to-be lead singer of the group Shamed and Maimed (and Ally's ex) offered to play at her wedding for a discounted price. Her response to this proposal had been a simple and polite, "Thank you — no." Ally, instead, was able to secure a local band, well known in the music circles of Seattleites, with whom she was familiar.

For Ally, her life had begun again. Donato was her present and her future. What was in her past (as well as some of those who had played minor, and not so minor, roles in it) was to remain there. While soft string music played in the background, the guests mingled with one another while waiting for the ceremony to begin.

New beginnings were not to be exclusive to Ally. Everyone involved with the group, including the good doctor himself, were venturing out onto new paths. There may have been some cases of mild trepidation for some stepping out into their futures, but every one of them, while taking those first steps, did so with open hearts' welcoming the adventure with bright enthusiasm.

In the delightful and beautifully decorated courtyard, the chairs had been set up in a horseshoe pattern with an empty space in the middle for Ally to walk through to her birds' aviary — the focal point — where, in front of that, the ceremony would take place. At Bud's instruction, the guests cheerfully began to take their seats; and arm-in-arm, he walked Camilla to hers, and both he and Percy took their seats next to his mother.

Camilla's Italian immigrant parents instilled their deep faith in all of their children, Camilla being no exception, but Camilla's children had their own ideas as to how they chose to live their lives. Camilla would have preferred to have all of her children marry in the church, but she was no fool. Decades older and decades wiser, she knew instinctively her children would be alright — even if it meant she was to pray overtime. When it came to her children, that was something she did often and with gusto.

Emma and Jack sat together in the second row of chairs, and Lizzy sat next to Jack which greatly pleased Emma. She was aware of her bringing a new man into both her daughter's and her granddaughter's lives came with risk, but it was clear to Emma both Monica and Lizzy had warmed to Jack as he had to both of them. For Monica, it took a little longer than it did for Lizzy. For Lizzy, it was immediate. Being a child, she was open to joy and still possessed a free spirit — unlike her adult counterparts who had honed and mastered the acts of hesitancy and caution.

When Monica's wayward ex-husband decided to take his leave of absence from their marriage and cavort with his mistress elsewhere, Monica had to face bigger challenges put before her than at any other time in her life. When Emma witnessed Monica finally meeting those challenges head on, she knew her daughter would be alright.

Perhaps what Emma was not expecting was Monica's finding herself in a very serious relationship so soon afterwards. Not only did the timing of it cause Emma to ponder her daughter's thought process, it was whom she had decided to involve herself with — another woman — that gave her cause to pause.

After delving deep, Emma realized so much of Monica's life had been living up to what others, including Emma herself, had expected of her. It was very possible, Emma had to admit, she had suppressed and avoided acknowledging having seen the signs, her daughter was not living her truth.

When Monica faced that crossroad in her life, she made the decision to live her life honestly, and Emma sincerely welcomed (as most mothers would) her daughter's new love, Rhonda (who chose to go by "Ronnie"), into her life too. Her concern, at first, as to how it would affect Lizzy was easily dashed away once she saw Ronnie and her granddaughter together.

"Who am I to question who someone loves?" Emma asked herself, "I, who searched to find a man I didn't know — but somehow knew — we were meant to be together." Emma's face lit up with a smile as she sat next to Jack. She gently squeezed his arm, and for a brief moment, laid her head against his shoulder knowing all was right within her world.

Indeed, who was Emma? From the beginning, she was the one member of the group who somehow managed to get all the other members (including the good doctor) to work together. It was their feelings towards her which drew them all together in search of her, while she followed her own heart. She was the catalyst of the group. While trying to find her, they found themselves. The myriad of events had taken form — from the group making that one decision — to the culmination of everyone joining together on that beautiful day to celebrate Ally and Donato's wedding.

Emma looked up and saw Monica and Ronnie coming towards them. They both bent down and gave her a kiss and hug before taking their seats next to Lizzy. Although Emma had already seen the three of them together enough times and under enough varied circumstances to know they fit the perfect description of a real family — on that day, surrounded by unmistakable joy — Emma could not have been more grateful.

Stelle and the good doctor had just made their way to their seats which Dill and Mrs. Fins had kept open for them; for by that time, it was standing room only, because so many guests had arrived. The soft string music which played in the background increased in decibels, as Ally began her walk to the aviary where her handsome groom stood. For a young groom, Donato was surprisingly calm and showed no fear of "tying the knot." Perhaps it was because he would be tying that knot with Ally — the only girl he had ever introduced the constellations to or had counted the stars with.

Because Ally and Donato had decided to create and exchange their own vows and wanted all of their family and friends to remember what those vows were, they had them printed out on fine stationary. They had included a thin sprig of fresh lavender before putting them in matching envelopes which were then placed on each of their guests' chairs. The instructions to open them after the couple began to exchange their vows were to be announced by Bud, when he announced it was time for everyone to be seated.

Originally, Ally was to read hers in English and Donato would read his in Italian. That was the original plan. Both Ally and Donato not only surprised their guests, but they surprised each other, when neither needed to read their lines for each had memorized their lines perfectly.

Ally and Donato professed their love to one another and ended by loosely quoting verse from a song entitled "Return to Love" by one of Camilla's favorite Italian singers and composers, Andrea Bocelli.

Before taking Donato's hands in her hands, Ally gently touched the snuggling birds on the necklace that hung around her neck — the same necklace Donato had given her on their way home from Park City. Then she began with, "I stopped hoping — but all of a sudden — you. Awaken in the deep — a fire that lights me up."

Translated from Italian into English, Donato shakily continued with, "Who cares about the past — who knows about tomorrow?"

With Donato's voice breaking now, he continued on, "And maybe this won't last — maybe this moment's all we have. Let's find out."

Ally picked up with, "And though I'm still afraid, you're worth the leap of faith." Her voice getting softer and softer with each word, "I'll return to love and risk it all — to see the world that we make."

Donato, barely able to speak above a whisper, "I'll risk it all — to give you the world." And then, Ally, noticeably shaking, concluded with, "And I'll return to love — and I'll stay — to build a dream."

Some of the guests did not hear everything one or both of them said to each other, and so along with those who did not understand Italian, they read their printed version of the vows. It was then, some of their guests were overtaken by emotion, and the beginning of sniffles could be heard.

The bride held herself together fairly well. On the other hand, the groom having started off in control began showing signs, that holding himself together was becoming more and more difficult.

Percy shed a few tears of her own. "What is it?" She questioned. "What is it about weddings which does this to people? Maybe it's the fear it won't last or, maybe, the fear is that it will!" Percy's self-induced protective shield, camouflaged as cynicism, was always just a breath away.

She had watched helplessly as Bud's brother struggled to get the words out without gasping, and that was when she heard loud sniffling coming from Bud. Sitting next to him, Percy saw the man Donato had told her all about months before in Park City. What she had come to know was even more so confirmed in that moment. The man whom James Elliot Jeffries really was — the man sitting next to her openly showing his heart — was exactly the man she had always wanted.

The young couple had not wanted a church ceremony, but for Camilla's sake, they agreed to have a pastor officiate their ceremony. After Donato and Ally had completed exchanging their personal vows, the final words came from the pastor when he began with, "Do you, Anna Leigh, take Donato Santino . . . ." A wide smile stretched across Donato's face, as he had never heard "Ally" called by any other name.

"Anna Leigh" rang in his head as the most beautiful sound he had ever heard — second only to the sound of his young bride's laughter. From that moment, Donato knew what he wanted to call her.

"Anna Leigh," Donato repeated it aloud, but softly, "Anna Leigh." He looked into his bride's beautiful eyes and said softly, "Anna Leigh," one more time. The look on Ally's face gave him all the assurance he needed. She did, indeed, approve.

As the young couple were pronounced "husband and wife" and turned to face their guests, there was a boisterous cheer followed by a rousing and even louder round of applause, as everyone stood to give the young couple a standing ovation.

Percy shared the last of her tissues with Bud and could not help but take a moment to acknowledge the beautiful young woman standing before her guests had come so far from the three-hair-colored, cat-eyed, high-heel clicking girl she had spent so much energy to antagonize. What she saw when she looked at the young newlyweds was the promise of what life may have in store for anyone willing to give themselves over to love. Her heart was warmed with the realization love could happen to anyone at any age — even to her.

Mrs. Fins was overcome with emotion too, and Dill was as he was expected to be — a complete gentleman offering her his handkerchief. The Marksdales, sitting directly next to Mrs. Fins and Dill, were moved as well. Stelle patted her husband's leg and commented on how beautiful the ceremony was. She was equally impressed with the beautiful way the courtyard had been tastefully decorated. Dr. Marksdale seemed to be at ease although, perhaps, a little distant. No one would have guessed what he was thinking, and after having been shot in the head, no one dared to suggest to what degree his brain may have been affected by it.

One course of food after another was served, and as the wine and champagne flowed, everyone — including all those in the group — was relaxing into what would turn out to be several hours of jovial celebration. The pitch of voices, laughter and music rose as the day blithely joined the night. Even Ally's birds appeared to be enjoying the celebration, for they looked on from their beautiful new home which met perfectly with pride of place in the Jeffries' courtyard.

Engrossed in a deep conversation, the good doctor surprised Stelle when he said, "A year ago, no one in the group would have believed they'd be together in this place now."

Stelle sat back in her chair and looked at her husband. The surprise she felt in response to his lucid comment was written all over her face, and the tenor of her voice revealed she was experiencing inner conflict.

"Phillip, you sound like your old self."

Dr. Marksdale turned to look directly into his wife's eyes and said so only she could hear, "I've never stopped being my old self."

Stelle's face revealed her confusion.

"You mean — do you mean to say —" The color had washed out of Stelle's face. "Do you mean to say that you've been okay since coming out of the coma?"

Dr. Marksdale took Stelle's hand, kissed it and gently rubbed it against his cheek. It was then Stelle saw a familiar glint in her husband's eyes which she had often referred to as his "smiling eyes."

"How many times," Stelle questioned, "have I witnessed that glint in your eyes?" Dr. Marksdale said nothing and then kissed her hand again. Her confusion was fading as the reality of what she believed was happening crept closer to the surface.

Her husband was showing signs he was back. The unsettling issue for her was the fact she may have to acknowledge, he may have never left. All of the time she had spent retraining him to do the simplest of tasks — could it have all been for show? If it were to be proven true, then Stelle should have been furious with him; but instead, she was overtaken by her husband's returning to her from his long absence. It did flash momentarily across her mind: If she should find out he had feigned his mental lack of capacity, she could always pay him back at some later, undisclosed date. In the meantime, the couple sat closer and began to talk.

There was no reason to be concerned with anyone overhearing their conversations, for the audible level of the wedding guests celebrating was high enough to muffle out anything they had to say. They discussed Stelle opening up her own high-end boutique and what the good doctor may want to do now that he knew he had a future. On many occasions, he had toyed with the idea of writing, and found this new start offered him the opportunity to do so.

Dr. Marksdale relayed to his wife he was interested in writing a series of books addressing treatment of the mentally ill, and he planned to use a *nom de plume* to keep his real name private (a high priority for both himself and Stelle). He hinted he wanted to start with two books in particular. Each would delve into the mysteries and intricacies of the "id." According to Freud, the id was one of three components making up one's personality. Stelle and her husband were familiar with Freud's belief the id is the driving force in the subconscious of humans where hidden desires exist. Dr. Marksdale would entitle these two books The Id in You and The Id in Me.

Stelle thought it sounded like her husband had spent a good deal of time and energy mulling over this plan. Normally, her initial reaction would have been to ask why he had not shared these ideas with her sooner, but within the merry atmosphere enveloping her, she was delighted by the possibilities of what lay open for both of them and deliberately chose to let negative thoughts fall away.

"Rather," she said to herself, "I will spend my energies sharing my excitement with Phillip and our plans to move on with our new lives."

The group Ally had chosen to play at their wedding took a short break at Camilla's insistence and proceeded to eat all she offered them along with a glass of wine or champagne — whichever they preferred.

While the musicians took their break, Stelle waved the members of her husband's group over to the table where they were sitting. She wanted to share with all in the group, they would be moving to the Park City area and, once there, would be opening a boutique. They had fallen in love with the area while there, and thought it would be good to get out of the big city — especially under their new set of circumstances. Park City would be a healthy place to raise their children. The good doctor remained relatively quiet and did not mention his future writing plans.

No one could have been happier for the Marksdales than the members of the group. They wanted nothing but the best for both of them. The doctor seemed sincere when he asked everyone what their plans were, now that their required therapy sessions were behind them.

Emma and Jack announced they would split their time between living in the Seattle area and Park City where Jack was from. They told the Marksdales they looked forward to seeing them on occasion when all of them were in Utah.

Although not in the group, Monica and Ronnie offered they too were considering moving to Utah but were still not sure where they wanted to live — only that they would be together. Wherever they ended up staying, they were sure they were going to open a small pastry shop together.

Ally caught a glimpse of the group all gathered together and took Donato by the hand and hurried to join them. Once the commentary on how beautiful the ceremony was and what a stunning bride she made was behind them, Ally knelt down next to Dr. Marksdale and said, "Thank you, doc. If it weren't for you, I'd of never made it to here." She stood up and gave him a gentle kiss on his forehead.

Ally panned the table with her eyes and then looked back at the doctor.

"You made me know there was something better out there for me, and I found him, 'cause ah you." She looked around the table once again, being sure to let her eyes singularly acknowledge each and every person sitting there, and said, "Because of all of you."

Between playing and dancing with the other youngsters (mainly nieces and nephews related to the Jeffries' clan) who attended the wedding, Lizzy stopped by the table where her mother was sitting with Ronnie and breathlessly added she could hardly wait to help make fancy deserts.

Percy offered her plans were up in the air, but she was sure she was done with being a long hauler and was ready to settle in one place. It was evident to everyone sitting at that table where that one place would be. As they looked at Bud, they could see in the way he looked at Percy, wherever that one place would end up being, he would be there with her.

Dill began next and awkwardly said he and Mrs. Fins had considered taking a trip to Europe, now that she was retired. He added he would especially like to take her to a ballet in Paris. Mrs. Fins and his eyes met as he continued in a most uncharacteristic and almost salacious tone, "There are so many things I would like to show her."

Bud whispered under his breath just loud enough for Percy to hear, "I bet there are — you old dog." Percy gently jabbed him in the side with her elbow.

The musicians had finished wolfing down all Camilla offered them, and after emptying their wine glasses and champagne flutes, they headed back to their instruments. They started to play softly at first and then really picked up the beat, until almost everyone was up and dancing.

Mrs. Fins and Dill Bigley, looking very relaxed and in quite good spirits, were on the dance floor too. Perhaps it was the spirits they had consumed, or maybe it was because of something else which had taken place a little while earlier. Either way, it had started with Camilla taking Mrs. Fins aside and whispering something in her ear.

Whatever it was she had said — no one would ever know exactly. But, Mrs. Fins told Dill, Camilla wanted to thank both of them for being so good to her sons on the trip to Park City and, in particular, after Bud's butt met with a bullet. She wanted to show her gratitude for all they did — including all the times they had come to visit him in the hospital and when Bud was back at home. Camilla was impressed with how, after all which had transpired between her son and Dill, he had become one of James' biggest sources of encouragement.

Mrs. Fins relayed to Dill that Camilla had left them a present in the restaurant pantry. She opened her hand to reveal a key Camilla had given her, and she suggested they both go to get their present before too long. As the music level rose along with the voices and laughter of everyone in the courtyard, Dill agreed with Mrs. Fins. It would be a good time to follow up on Camilla's suggestion.

Dill took the key and unlocked the pantry door, and as they entered the room, they saw there was a little table with two chairs in the middle of the room. There were two champagne flutes and a bottle of some of the finest champagne available chilling in a champagne bucket. A greeting card addressed to both of them was leaning against one of the empty flutes.

Mrs. Fins was quite taken by surprise by Camilla's thoughtful gesture, and when she read the card out loud, both she and Dill were equally touched by Camilla's kind words. But more than that, they were touched by her words of encouragement they move forward with their own lives. She wrote that whatever was in store for them, it was time to get on with it. She wrote, "Time is a fleeting mirage."

In her note, Camilla warned further, "Mirages can be gone in a blink, and this is your mirage. Don't blink." Dill and Mrs. Fins looked into each other's eyes for a quick second, and then Mrs. Fins went back to Camilla's note. She had ended it with *"Celebrare la vita* — Celebrate life!"

Dill popped open the bottle of champagne, and Mrs. Fins walked to the window while he poured enough champagne to fill each flute halfway. They tapped their flutes together before toasting, *"celebrare la vita,"* before they each took a sip.

From the pantry window, they could look down onto the courtyard below. It offered a great vantage point from which to see all the celebrants enjoying themselves. A sheer pale green lace curtain covered the window, and as Mrs. Fins held it back so they could see better, Camilla looked up at them with a wide smile.

Mrs. Fins, known to dress in what some would call a relatively modest attire — especially for work — had taken on a more relaxed persona, since she was no longer the good doctor's receptionist. After completing the tasks Stelle requested of her to help close both of the Marksdales' practices, Mrs. Fins decided to tend more to her early retirement which required less of the formal attire than her prior employment had. More notably, since she and Dill had been spending so much of their time together, her overall attitude, in general, had relaxed. That newly found relaxed attitude encompassed her wardrobe choices too.

For Ally and Donato's wedding, Mrs. Fins chose to wear a chiffon skirt splashed with soft pastels which, in a slight breeze, gently fluttered, while still fitting in such a fashion it tenderly embraced and flowed over her sinuous form. Her off-the-shoulder, light-cream colored blouse swept delicately just below her shoulders exposing a slight, but still noticeable, cleavage.

After she and Dill had begun what had, for some time, felt like their eternal courtship, she had cut her hair to just below the bottom of the nape of her neck. It was a flattering and fetching style, and combined with the cut of her blouse she wore that day, the feminine contours of her upper back were revealed.

While she stood at that window in the Jeffries' restaurant pantry, her sun-lit profile took Dill Bigley's breath away. She was always beautiful in his eyes, but on that day, in that hour and in that room, her graceful form was alluring beyond what even the most refined English gentleman could have endured.

Taking both of their emptied flutes back to the table, he turned to look at her once again and began to walk back to where she stood — never diverting his eyes away from hers. As he approached her, Mrs. Fins could no longer hold back her growing attraction to the ever so proper and refined Englishman. The cliché, "It would take wild horses," came to her mind; but for her, at that point, it would take wild horses to stop her. Reaching down, she took his hand in her hand, and it was in that moment all of their propriety for formal manner of being flew right out of that window.

Wildly wrapping their arms around each other, their lips lovingly surrendered into each other's. Then, and with just as much sudden urgency and without need of further enticement, Dill pulled his lips away from hers, freeing them to tremulously explore with his kisses Mrs. Fins' neck, shoulders and bare back. They ran their hands around the gambit of the others' welcoming bodies, thus, releasing the unbridled longing and pent-up passion which had built steadily over the course of their painfully intense and seemingly endless courtship. In a flurry of colors, their clothes were strewn in every direction.

Ally and Donato would not be the only ones celebrating an anniversary on that same date, for it was there, in the Jeffries' restaurant pantry, on top of the three-and-one-half-foot high stack of 75 pound bags of flour — between the shelves of bottled capers on one side and pitted Castelvetrano olives on the other — Mr. Dillard Bigley and Mrs. Marlene Fins met with the long overdue consummation of their love affair.

In those first few moments following the most explosive exhibition of passion either had ever experienced, Mrs. Fins and Dillard Bigley were left spent and breathless. In the aftermath, they shared the same intoxicating euphoria which joining their emotional, and at long last, physical love had created. Dill laid his hand on Mrs. Fins' bare thigh, and with a shaky and weakened voice uttered, "My love — my lovely — Marlene."

Mrs. Fins' head was spinning, because everything had happened so quickly. It would take a bit of time for her to realize one particular undergarment had not been completely removed.

Trying to organize her thoughts was difficult to do. They were like hundreds of pieces of a puzzle randomly floating around in her head. She could not put together who was pulling on, unbuttoning or unzipping, what item of clothing or from whom. All she knew was her right leg had managed to pull its way free of her cumbersome underthings, while her left leg was left with her delicate dainties still dangling around her quivering ankle. After replaying the delightfully rapturous experience in her mind, all she could muster was, *"My — oh my — Mr. Bigley!"*

Had it not been for the light-headed bliss each was experiencing when they retrieved their respective articles of clothing from all areas of the pantry, they may have noticed Mrs. Fins had pulled her skirt on — inside out. As luck would have it, a term not always used in relation to a fortunate event, it was Bud who noticed the wardrobe malfunction upon their return to the courtyard.

By the time the lusty couple had returned from their rendezvous with *amoré*, the music had risen to an almost frenetic level, and everyone was dancing — even the good doctor. Although everyone was dancing like nobody was watching, the good doctor had a good excuse for his spastic and jerky gyrating — he had been shot in the head where the bullet still remained.

As Bud danced his way towards Dill and Mrs. Fins, his whole body was moving like he had some kind of affliction making his limp unnoticeable. That was when he took note English and Miss Prim looked like they had been in the sun a little too long. The glow of their cheeks, along with Mrs. Fins' skirt being on inside-out, was an easy calculation of one-plus-one equals two — something even Bud could tally up. For Bud, it was a dead giveaway what the two had been up to.

Interestingly, he could have — and months earlier surely would have — made any combination of unsolicited and crude comments. But instead of creating an extraordinarily awkward situation, he moved close to Dill; and, under his breath, he politely and discretely suggested Dill escort Mrs. Fins to the ladies' room, so she could adjust her skirt. To a slight degree, James Elliot Jeffries had grown up.

Dill looked down and saw the label of her skirt and took in a sudden short breath. He swiftly turned his head towards Bud, his mouth dropping open. He looked like he had been caught with his pants down, and he was left speechless. Placing his hands on Mrs. Fins' shoulders, he moved closer behind her with his body covering her skirt label. He whispered something in her ear, to which she responded with an audible gasp; and, in tandem, they made their way to the restrooms.

Dancing next to Bud, Percy observed the whole scene unfold. She looked up at him and said, "You're really pretty amazing. That was a kind thing you just did."

Any inhibitions Percy may have had were overtaken by the mood and the moment. She put her arms around Bud's neck and pulled his face close to hers, and while looking directly into his eyes, she said, "How 'bout you and me gettin' married too. I promise, I could make you miserable for the rest of your life."

After that, she ran her hands down his back, stopping at his rounded buttocks. She squeezed both of his cheeks, noticing that one was a little smaller than the other — a direct result of the surgery to remove the bullet which had been embedded in his butt cheek. It was that cheek which she had come to call her favorite.

She teased, "You know you want it, too." In Percy's mind, she was referring to marriage, and for a moment, she entertained the notion that Bud being a man may have thought she was referring to something of a more salacious nature.

Grinning from ear-to-ear, Bud put his arms around Percy and teasingly whispered in her ear, "You're such a man!"

Laughing out loud, Percy pulled Bud so close to her lips he could feel her words, and in her sultriest voice, she purred, "One of us has to be!"

*****

How does one begin to end a story when the end of that story is so deeply intertwined — within the beginning of so many others?

Perhaps somewhat blithesomely like — "Once upon a time, not so long ago . . . ."

ABOUT THE AUTHOR

S. Wilbur shares her island home with her husband in the Puget Sound of Washington State. She looks forward to their vacations to the warmer waters of the Caribbean, and she eagerly awaits their brief respites there.

After completing her second book, she is joyfully immersing herself into what she sees unfolding before her — a planet of possibilities where she knows new adventures await her.

Some of her interests include enjoying music in all genres and observing the myriad of wildlife on the island where she lives. An interest she holds dear is to create and prepare new recipes to share with her family — something that has always and continues to be one of her passions and a favorite way to express love.

She holds onto the hope that everyone will find their own path leading to their passions and, once achieving that, to be able to nurture those passions to fruition and without hesitancy to openly embrace their own brilliance.

www.ingramcontent.com/pod-product-compliance
Lightning Source LLC
Chambersburg PA
CBHW020415010526
44118CB00010B/265

www.ingramcontent.com/pod-product-compliance
Lightning Source LLC
Chambersburg PA
CBHW020415010526
44118CB00010B/265